A Climate of Injustice

Global Environmental Accord: Strategies for Sustainability and Institutional Innovation
Nazli Choucri, series editor

A complete list of books published in the Global Environmental Accord series appears at the back of this book.

A Climate of Injustice

Global Inequality, North-South Politics, and Climate Policy

J. Timmons Roberts and Bradley C. Parks

The MIT Press
Cambridge, Massachusetts
London, England

MIT Press books may be purchased at special quantity discounts for business or sales promotional use. For information, please email special_sales@mitpress.mit .edu or write to Special Sales Department, The MIT Press, 55 Hayward Street, Cambridge, MA 02142.

This book was set in Sabon on 3B2 by Asco Typesetters, Hong Kong and was printed and bound in the United States of America.

Library of Congress Cataloging-in-Publication Data

Roberts, J. Timmons.
A climate of injustice : global inequality, North-South politics, and climate policy / J. Timmons Roberts and Bradley C. Parks.
    p.   cm. — (Global environmental accord: strategies for sustainability and institutional innovation)
Includes bibliographical references and index.
ISBN-13: 978-0-262-18256-0 (alk. paper)
ISBN-10: 0-262-18256-4 (alk. paper)
ISBN-13: 978-0-262-68161-2 (pbk. : alk. paper)
ISBN-10: 0-262-68161-7 (pbk. : alk. paper)
1. Climatic changes. 2. Climatic changes—Government policy. 3. Climatic changes—Economic aspects. I. Parks, Bradley C. II. Title.
QC981.8.C5R59   2007
363.738′74526—dc22   2006048214

Printed on recycled paper

The views expressed in this book are the authors' own and do not necessarily represent the views of the Millennium Challenge Corporation.

10   9   8   7   6   5   4   3   2

Contents

Series Foreword

A new recognition of profound interconnections between social and natural systems is challenging conventional constructs and the policy predispositions informed by them. Our current intellectual challenge is to develop the analytical and theoretical underpinnings of an understanding of the relationship between the social and the natural systems. Our policy challenge is to identify and implement effective decision-making approaches to managing the global environment.

The series Global Environmental Accord: Strategies for Sustainability and Institutional Innovation adopts an integrated perspective on national, international, cross-border, and cross-jurisdictional problems, priorities, and purposes. It examines the sources and the consequences of social transactions as these relate to environmental conditions and concerns. Our goal is to make a contribution to both intellectual and policy endeavors.

Nazli Choucri

Acknowledgments

This daunting and exciting project has a history now reaching back over a dozen years, yet its shape continues to change even as we put the final touches on the book. It has shifted from a sociological analysis of the complex problem of climate change to one that incorporates insights from international relations, development economics, geography, and other fields. Much of the original work, which is here represented by a part of the analysis in chapter 5, was done with our colleague Peter Grimes, and was partly funded by the National Science Foundation's grant titled "Social Roots of Environmental Damage: A World-System Analysis of Global Warming." Grimes and Roberts conceived that project back in 1992, and worked with the help of Jodie Manale from 1993 to 1995. Our original idea was to attempt to explain the emissions of greenhouse gases by nations using concepts from world-systems theory, a sociologically informed branch of political economy that is inspired by scholars from Latin America and Africa and seeks to understand the global economy in a holistic way.

The project sputtered along for years after that, with Roberts attempting to use structuralist theory to explain proenvironment actions by states, specifically which nations tend to sign more environmental treaties. Alexis Vasquez, then completing her master's degree in Latin American studies at Tulane University, where Roberts was teaching, created an updated index of state participation in environmental treaties. That index appears in chapter 6, surrounded by an entirely new theoretical framework and analysis of ratification of these treaties and the Kyoto Protocol in particular.

The project shifted in its approach with the addition of Brad Parks as co-author. His training in international relations, economics, and development studies brought new insights to bear in the areas of theoretical synthesis, the global political economy of development, and international negotiations. He first set out with Roberts and Vasquez to explore theoretical complementarities in international relations that might provide a more complete explanation for patterns in ratification of environmental treaties (chapter 6). This led to a second bridge-building effort (in chapters 3 and 4) to marry the proximate causes and deeper social and historical determinants of vulnerability to climate disasters. Parks then began to wrestle with the causal significance of trust, worldviews, causal beliefs, and principled understandings in North-South politics and their relationship to climate policy. This has now become the central framework for our understanding of why Kyoto and other major global environmental institutions remain embroiled in conflicts between the wealthy and poor nations of the global North and South. His thesis at the College of William and Mary and his master's dissertation at the London School of Economics and Political Science also led to our collaborative work on the Project-Level Aid (PLAID) database and the international environmental aid measure used in this study (which is employed as a proxy for compensatory justice in chapter 6).

Roberts would like to acknowledge the institutional support of the College of William and Mary, especially Kate Slevin, Dee Royster, Dianne Gilbert, P. Geoffrey Feiss, Carl Strikwerda, Joel Schwartz, Linda Luvaas, Sue Peterson, and extraordinary collaborators Mike Tierney and Robert Hicks. The love, patience, understanding, and support of Gann and Jim Roberts, Phoebe and Quinn Roberts, and especially Holly Flood were critical to the completion of this long project. He dedicates his effort on this book to his father, James O. Roberts (1930–2005).

Along the way, Parks also accumulated a number of intellectual debts. He would like to thank Dr. Michael Tierney, Dr. Robert Hicks, and Dr. Arnab Basu of the College of William and Mary; Dr. Robert Hunter Wade and Dr. Kenneth Shadlen of the London School of Economics and Political Science; and Dr. Patrick Noack of UNAIDS and the Blair Commission for Africa. This publication also would not have been possible without the generous financial assistance of the Andrew Mellon Foundation summer student fellowships in Environmental Science and Policy at the College of William and Mary, and the Dean of Arts and Sciences Research Fellowship. Finally, he would like to personally thank

Eric, Susan, and Scott Parks; Ryan King; Sam Pritchard; Randal Ruilova; Christian Lesnett; Whitt Farr; Marty Purks; and his wife Sarah, for her infinite patience and encouragement.

Parts of various chapters were presented in early drafts on which we received useful feedback from Thomas Dietz, Marc Levy, Craig Humphries, David John Frank, Michael Tierney, Robert Hicks, Dennis Taylor, Douglas McNamara, Tom Athanasiou, Paul Baer, Al Bergeson, Dana Fisher, Steven Brechin, Paul Mohai, Stephen Perz, Christopher Chase-Dunn, Craig Harris, Eugene Rosa, Scott Johnson, Deenesh Sohoni, Diana Seales, Hannah Arkin, Maria Carmen Lemos, Misty McPhee, Dan Cristol, John Swaddle, Adil Najam, Dimitris Stevis, Kathryn Hochstetler, Michele Betsill, Alastair Whitson, Tom Boden, Diana Liverman, Bruce Pobodnik, Paul Wapner, Sharon Goad, Elisabeth Corell, Peter Dauvergne, Sal Saporito, Jennifer Bickham-Mendez, Elizabeth Ransom, S. Desai, Matthew Paterson, Chukwumerije Okereke, and several anonymous reviewers. Any errors of course are entirely our own. We sincerely appreciate the patience and encouragement of Clay Morgan at MIT Press through all the time this book was in incubation, and Katherine Almeida's able editorial shepherding.

A Climate of Injustice

1

Introduction: Wet Feet Marching

Blame It on Rio?

Imagine you carefully save money your entire life to buy a beautiful piece of land in the country to farm. The land and equipment cost more than you expect, and you quickly become dependent on a narrow margin of profit to sustain yourself and your family. Soon after you move in, however, someone buys the property bordering your land and immediately opens a landfill, accepting trash and hazardous wastes from the entire region. A mountain of trash rapidly grows; the landfill stinks, the noise of the trucks and bulldozers is deafening, and the waste leaks into your groundwater. Since the land is in an unzoned, unincorporated township, you have no recourse to stop the dumping through zoning limits, and the landowner is best friends with the major political and economic players in the county, state, and even the federal government. The value of your property plummets, and you cannot afford to move. The owner of the dump lives elsewhere and grows rich on its income; you suffer all the costs of his operation and gain none of the benefits.

You seek to make an agreement with the neighbor, asking for some limits on his behavior. He negotiates with you for years, but never agrees to any substantial changes in his dumping. Instead, he says it would be unfair to have to do so unless you also agreed to stop dumping your farm waste, which would prevent you from being able to farm effectively. You turn to your other neighbors, seeking partners who will force the dump owner to clean up or close. Some agree, but these are only the poorest and least powerful of your neighbors—the others are friends of the dump owner, or own businesses that they fear might be hurt by the restrictions you seek.

The dump owner suggests that the impacts of his dumping require more study and promises enormous research projects by scientists of his choosing. Repeatedly and with great fanfare he promises to lend you money on good terms to build a wall as a visual screen, to clean your drinking water, and to help you deal with other effects. Desperate for any progress, you accept his offers, but his promises are quickly forgotten, and the improvements are never completed. He asks you again to sign an agreement that in a few years would make it impossible for you to increase production on your farm to the point where your family could live decently. You and the other less powerful neighbors resist the agreement.

With only slight changes in the details, this is the story of global warming and all the years of discussion and action since the issue was identified in the late 1980s.

Now picture this nonfictional scene: After three years of frustrating negotiations following the drafting of the world's first framework for a treaty on global warming, Atiq Rahman, of the Bangladesh Centre for Advanced Studies, rose to his feet in a huge Berlin conference room. Looking out across a sea of scientists, negotiators, and lobbyists from around the world, Rahman struggled to express the urgency of the injustice of global warming in as plain words as he could find.[1] In the decade leading up to the 1995 conference, Bangladesh had been struck by two devastating floods and two typhoons that left over a hundred thousand people dead and tens of millions of people homeless.[2] With climate change, scientists predicted a rise in sea level and more severe tropical storms. "If climate change makes our country uninhabitable," Rahman warned, "we will march with our wet feet into your living rooms."[3]

Looking back a decade later, Rahman's warning remains as painfully absurd now as it was then. The globe's wealthy and poor nations live in worlds so distant and disparate, and the wealthy are so sealed off from the poor, that Rahman's words might sound farfetched. Yet the plight of the world's poor cannot be ignored. The issue of reconciling social justice with environmental protection has surfaced at every major international meeting since the first environment and development conference at Stockholm in 1972, Nairobi in 1982, Rio in 1992, Rio+5 in New

York, and Johannesburg in 2002. At the Rio Earth Summit, poor nations feared limits on their efforts to grow economically and care for the basic needs of their people, but several powerful industrialized nations refused to curtail their own excesses unless poor nations did the same. President George H. W. Bush's famous statement that "the American lifestyle is not open to negotiation" remains a colorful reminder of this key sticking point.

The most controversial issue at Rio was global climate change. Under intense pressure to do something, 187 nations eventually signed the United Nations Framework Convention on Climate Change (UNFCCC).[4] However, the treaty avoided tough details. It called on nations to "protect the climate system . . . on the basis of equity and in accordance with their *common but differentiated responsibilities and respective capabilities,*" but consensus on these "first principles" masked profound disagreement on the issue of actual obligations. Developing countries interpreted the "common but differentiated" language with great precision: industrialized nations would need to take the lead by cutting their own emissions and transferring large sums of environmental assistance to the South.[5] However, developed countries saw more room for selective interpretation.

Before the ink had even dried on the UNFCCC agreement, rich nations began to backpedal on their promise of massive technology transfer and technical assistance to the developing world.[6] The estimated price tag for sustainable development in the Third World was $625 billion a year, with the North supplying about 20 percent of the total cost in grants or below-market rate loans.[7] However, the rich nations delivered less than one-fifth of that promise.[8] Three years later, the "Berlin Mandate" called for the rich nations to first reduce their emissions, with the poorer nations joining on the second or third round. More rounds of negotiations foundered on the rocks of equity and justice at Kyoto, Buenos Aires, Bonn, The Hague, and Marrakech.[9] President Bill Clinton signed on to the Kyoto Protocol to limit carbon dioxide emissions in 1997, but even before he did, the U.S. Senate voted 95 to 0 to support the Byrd-Hagel Resolution, which would block any "unfair" treaty that did not require the poor nations to also address the problem.[10]

This move by the United States bred great animosity in the developing world because of what was widely perceived to be Americans co-opting and thus undermining the Southern position of "climate injustice." Third World policy makers and activists were quick to point out that the average U.S. citizen dumps as much greenhouse gas into the atmosphere as nine Chinese and eighteen Indians, and that developing countries are immeasurably more vulnerable to rising tides, tropical storms, droughts, and flooding than rich nations. However, as we will argue in this book, social understandings of fairness are highly elastic and subject to political manipulation. The ominous 95 to 0 vote on the Byrd-Hagel Resolution specifically tried to discredit the protocol on the basis of the "*disparity of treatment* between Annex I Parties [essentially the wealthy OECD] and Developing Countries."[11]

Eventually, U.S. Secretary of State Madeline Albright declared a "diplomatic full court press to encourage meaningful developing country participation," but poor nations continued to hold out.[12] Yet interestingly, almost all developing countries refused to accept scheduled commitments for future reductions of emissions in the name of fairness. In fact, the very suggestion that poorer nations should restrict their economic growth by reducing emissions led to an openly hostile negotiating environment. China's lead negotiator said "In the developed world only two people ride in a car, and yet you want us to give up riding on a bus." Facing pressure from President Clinton, Chancellor Luiz Felipe Lampreia of Brazil flatly stated, "We cannot accept limitations that interfere with our economic development."[13]

President Clinton and Vice President Gore never dared to bring Kyoto to the Senate for ratification. Their successors, President George W. Bush and Vice President Cheney, then pulled the United States out of the Kyoto treaty entirely in March 2001 and in February 2002 offered a much weaker policy on reducing U.S. contributions to global warming. The Bush administration continues to oppose Kyoto because it is "an *unfair* and ineffective means of addressing global climate change concerns" and "would cause serious harm to the U.S. economy."[14]

Diametrically opposed perceptions of "climate justice" among rich and poor nations, we argue, pose a serious threat to political resolution and pollute a diplomatic atmosphere already teetering on the edge of disaster. Scientists and environmentalists in the world's wealthier nations are mystified as to why this life-threatening issue has elicited such an anemic policy response, but many of them miss the point: Responses to climate change are wound up with other social and economic issues facing nations and are fundamentally about inequality and injustice. The Kyoto Protocol suffers from a similar short-sightedness. While Russia's ratification of Kyoto has put the treaty into effect, and public concern about climate change seems to be increasing, the foot dragging of the world's largest emitter and the skittishness of developing countries cast a long shadow of uncertainty over the future viability of any post-2012 North-South climate pact. A better understanding of the current policy impasse is therefore urgently needed.

Our Argument in Brief

Over the past twenty years, the theoretical literature in international environmental relations has blossomed. Scholars have argued that international environmental policy outcomes are the result of material self-interest,[15] bargaining power,[16] and the ability to strong-arm weaker states through more coercive forms of power.[17] Others have emphasized the importance of exogenous shocks and crises,[18] salient solutions,[19] a scientific "burden of proof,"[20] environmental nongovernmental organizations (NGOs),[21] postmaterialist values,[22] epistemic communities,[23] transnational activist networks,[24] corporate nonstate actors,[25] intergovernmental organizations,[26] and political leadership.[27] Yet curiously, few scholars speak of the one variable singled out repeatedly by policy makers: global inequality. The small body of theoretical work that does exist on the topic rarely provides clear causal explanations of how inequality matters and under what conditions it affects outcomes in international environmental politics. Most analysts rely selectively on anecdotal evidence and particularize explanations without explicitly addressing the generalizability of their claims.[28] And rather than explaining the origins of global inequality and the forces leading to its persistence, scholars often take it as given. Inequality as it relates to climate change is also rarely measured systematically in its several dimensions, and its roots are poorly understood.

We take a different approach. We develop scientific measures of climate inequality, utilize statistical methods to evaluate its proximate and deeper social and historical determinants, and examine the causal channels through which inequality influences the form, frequency, timing, substance, and depth of international cooperation. Our account of the North-South stalemate on climate policy relies on the integration of three types of arguments: general theories about the behavior of states, intermediate explanations about international environmental politics and North-South politics, and issue-specific insights concerning the "problem structure" of climate change.

In the first group are issues of trust, worldviews, causal beliefs, and principled beliefs—issues we believe are largely attributable to the position of countries in the global division of labor. Inequality, we argue, dampens utility-enhancing cooperative efforts by reinforcing structuralist worldviews and causal beliefs, creating incentives for zero-sum and negative-sum behavior, polarizing preferences, generating divergent and unstable expectations about future behavior, eroding trust and civic norms among different social groups, destabilizing policy coalitions, and making it difficult to coalesce around a socially shared understanding of what is "fair."

At the intermediate level are explanations of the ongoing development crisis and those arising in environmental debates over the definition of sustainable development, foreign assistance for the environment, and global versus local environmental concerns. Climate negotiations do not take place in a vacuum. They are taking place at a time when concerns about Northern callousness and opportunism in matters of international political economy are rising, levels of generalized trust are declining, and calls for fair processes and fair outcomes are being marginalized. The North-South impasse on climate policy is, in other words, linked to larger systemic problems that hinder cooperation between rich and poor nations more generally. Compounding this problem, for more than thirty years the environmental issues of most concern to developing countries have been brushed aside and replaced with First World issues. However, global commons issues, such as ozone depletion, habitat loss, and climate change, are much less pressing to most poor nations than providing safe drinking water, slowing soil erosion, treating sewage, slowing the spread of deserts, and reducing lung- and eye-burning air pollution.[29] This wedge between Northern and Southern interests has put rich donor countries in the difficult business of "persuad[ing] recipient countries...to take the environmental actions of [lowest] priority to them."[30]

Finally, we rely upon a series of explanations that are specific to the "problem structure" of climate change. Part of the reason cooperation on climate change is so difficult to achieve is intrinsic to the problem itself: the number of parties needed to resolve the problem, the complexity of the problem, the time sensitivity of the solution, the quantity and quality of information, the high levels of uncertainty surrounding the issue, the stability and intensity of actor preferences, the "observability" of climate-related behavior, and the asymmetry of externalities. We argue that to understand why countries are willing or unwilling to cooperate and make sacrifices for the protection of what may be their way of life, we must first identify which nations are most responsible for global climate change, which nations will most suffer the effects of climate change most profoundly, and which nations will most likely bear the largest costs of cleaning up the mess. This "triple inequality" of responsibility, vulnerability, and mitigation, which is also intrinsic to the problem, offers a powerful and parsimonious explanation for the negotiation positions adopted by rich and poor nations.

To test the observable implications of these theories, we rely on the new cross-national indicators of climate responsibility, vulnerability, and action, as well as the statistical tools of multiple regression and path analysis. Rather than proposing that one factor outweighs all others, we synthesize complementary theoretical insights and attempt to empirically discriminate between competing explanations. While recognizing that there are often aspects of truth in multiple explanations, we studiously avoid the "indeterminate 'everything matters' approach" adopted by many international relations scholars.[31] Some of the factors emphasized in the extant literature hold up in this large-N empirical analysis; many do not.[32]

In taking this synthetic approach, we hope to demonstrate a need for theoretical bridge building in international environmental politics. Theoretical synthesis has figured prominently in the study of security,[33] human rights,[34] public health,[35] and development finance,[36] yet self-conscious attempts at bridge building in international environmental politics are surprisingly rare. There are, of course, important battles to be fought in international relations—for example, realism versus institutionalism, rationalism versus constructivism, and structure versus agency—but we must remember that "[t]heory and method are ... means not ends; they exist to promote our understanding of empirical causes by encouraging theoretical breadth, logical coherence, and empirical objectivity."[37] Many of us are guilty of retreating to our preferred "islands of theory" and ignoring theoretical complementarities, but pursuing this strategy comes at a high scientific price.[38] Failing to thoughtfully consider bridge building prospects often means overlooking interconnected causal processes and thus creating caricatures of a complex social world.[39]

Rising Tides in an Unequal World

How does inequality drive so much of the noncooperative behavior observed between the global North and South? We argue that it does so by two paths. First, there is the direct path, which we discuss briefly in this chapter. The extreme poverty of dozens of nations and the relative powerlessness of a larger number leaves them without the capacity to negotiate effectively with the North and unable to meaningfully address their emissions of greenhouse gases because of their extremely undeveloped economies and government agencies. The second path driving noncooperation on climate change has been almost universally overlooked, but we argue it is potentially more important than the shortage of technical capacity. The experience of poorer nations in the world economy and their interaction with rich nations across multiple issue areas has reinforced a worldview and a set of causal beliefs that are at odds with those of the wealthy nations; this has bred generalized mistrust and polarized expectations about how to proceed on climate issues. Mistrust and divergent and unstable expectations have also led to defensive negotiating strategies by poorer nations and reduced the likelihood of reaching a mutually acceptable agreement.

In the remainder of this chapter we discuss the broad contours of global inequality in wealth, relative power, knowledge, negotiating skills, vulnerability to hydrometeorological disasters, responsibility for climate change, and in who has made efforts to clean up the atmosphere.[40] As mentioned earlier, to understand the non-cooperative postures of developing nations, we first need to understand the defining features of climate change as a political issue: the unavoidably global nature of the problem, the enormous divide in responsibility for the problem, the highly asymmetric distribution of burdens and benefits associated with the warming of the earth's climate, and inequality in who is expected to deal with its causes and consequences.

Globalization and the Unequal Costs of Climate Change

The existing body of scientific evidence on global climate change strongly suggests that the emissions coming out of our exhaust pipes contribute to a layer of heat-trapping carbon dioxide that will create—and perhaps has already created—a warmer and wetter atmosphere, and, in turn, terrible outcomes like more flooding in Bangladesh, devastating hurricanes in the Caribbean, and droughts in the Sudano-Sahel region of Africa.[41] Climatologists have observed a sharp upswing in the frequency, magnitude, intensity, and duration of hydrometeorological disasters over the past two decades:

• The five warmest years on historical record were 2005, 1998, 2002, 2003, and 2004, and hydrometeorological disasters have more than doubled since 1996.[42]
• The number of major natural catastrophes was four times larger, and cost the world's economies eight times more during the 1990s than in the decade of the 1960s.[43]
• Ninety percent of natural disaster fatalities during the 1990s were the result of hydrometerological events (e.g., droughts, floods, hurricanes, and windstorms).[44]

These shifting hydrometeorological patterns are not lost on global opinion leaders. In 2004, British Prime Minister Tony Blair characterized climate change as "a challenge so far-reaching in its impact and irreversible in its destructive power, that it alters radically human existence," and stated his intention to use the G-8 presidency as a bully pulpit for reform.[45] Former chair of the Intergovernmental Panel on Climate Change (IPCC), John Houghton, has described climate change as a weapon of mass destruction.[46] And *The Economist* calls global warming "a potential time bomb capable of wreaking global havoc."[47]

It therefore appears that with the expansion of international contact and scientific understanding of global environmental issues such as depletion of the ozone layer and climate change, there is a growing understanding about the "commonality of problems," a new global consciousness that we are all together on this "Spaceship Earth."[48] Yet curiously, this new global consciousness about environmental issues often occludes important differences in blame. With only 4 percent of the world's population, the United States is responsible for over 20 percent of all global emissions (see chapter 5 for more detailed comparisons). That can be compared with 136 developing countries that together are responsible for only 24 percent of global emissions. Clearly, poor nations remain far behind wealthy nations in terms of emissions per person. The average American citizen dumps many times more greenhouse gases into the atmosphere than the majority of humans who live on Earth—four or five times the global average. Overall, the richest 20 percent of the world's population is responsible for over 60 percent of its current emissions of greenhouse gases. That figure exceeds 80 percent if past contributions to the problem are considered, and they probably should be considered, since carbon dioxide, the main contributor to the greenhouse effect, remains in the atmosphere for more than a hundred years.

Those who emphasize that climate change is everybody's problem, or a "global public bad," also obscure the ways in which its impacts are socially distributed across human populations. Some populations suffer worst and first, and they are often not those who caused the problem. Rapidly expanding populations in Africa, Asia, and Latin America are facing more frequent and more dangerous droughts, floods, and storms, and have suffered immeasurably more loss of life and livelihood from hydrometeorological disasters than those in rich nations.[49] According to the World Bank, "[b]etween 1990 and 1998, 94% of the world's disasters and 97% of all natural-disaster-related deaths occurred in developing countries."[50] Many of these regions are of course already afflicted by chronic underdevelopment, water scarcity and pollution, land degradation, food insecurity, civil conflict, infectious disease, and feeble domestic institutions. Large informal squatter settlements in overcrowded coastal cities find themselves just meters away from eroding shorelines and riverbanks.[51] Small island states, already at risk because of their highly climate-dependent exports, struggle to overcome high transport costs, weak coastal defense systems, and fragile ecosystems.[52] Groups of "climate refugees" are on the move because of resource scarcity, growing insecurity, and violent conflict.[53] Yet, somewhat ironically, many of the largest contributors to global warming could gain from the effects of climate change in the short to medium term. Experts predict that North America and parts of northern Europe may enjoy economic gains from longer growing seasons, less frost, and thus increased agricultural output.[54]

There will also likely be inequality in who will be most responsible for reducing emissions. Since the low marginal costs of reducing emissions in developing countries make near-term reductions in the industrialized world relatively inefficient, many Western policy makers and scientists believe that countries like China and India—where average annual incomes are less than $1,000—should cut their greenhouse gases before or at the same time as rich countries. Congressman David M. McIntosh, the chairman of the U.S. House of Representatives Subcommittee on National Economic Growth, Natural Resources, and Regulatory Affairs, stated in 1998 that "[the Kyoto Protocol]... is patently unfair because it exempts 77 percent of all countries from any obligations. China, India, Mexico, and Brazil, just to name a few, are completely unfettered by the Treaty—these countries already have the competitive advantages of cheap labor, lower production costs, and lower environmental, health, and safety standards. If President Clinton has his way, now these countries will be free to develop and pollute all they want, while the U.S. economy goes into a deep freeze."[55] In fairness, many Western policy makers have come to accept the idea that poorer countries should be assisted in this transition, but the onus is in some measure being placed on developing countries, and this raises extremely difficult issues of actual and perceived unfairness.

These inequalities in climate vulnerability, responsibility, and mitigation also exist in a wider context of "asymmetric globalization."[56] In the interest of space, we will not review the highly contentious literature on whether inequality in global income is increasing or decreasing.[57] More important for this discussion is the scale of global inequality. World Bank data suggest that the average per capita income of the richest twenty countries exceeds the average for the poorest twenty countries by thirty-seven times.[58] Measuring individual incomes rather than national incomes, the United Nations Development Programme (UNDP) estimates that the richest 20 percent of the world's population controls 80 percent of the world's income. By comparison, the poorest 20 percent controls just 2 percent of the world's income, and the middle 60 percent controls 6 percent of global income.[59] Branko Milanovic reports that roughly the same share of global income accrues to the richest 1 percent of the world's population as to the poorest 57 percent.[60]

A few nations are seeing median household incomes rise, but most are not, and the cavernous divide between the world's rich and poor nations is not disappearing. In fact, one of the defining characteristics of the global distribution of income is its so-called "missing middle." Most of the world's population earns an average annual income either below $1,500 or above $11,500, while an astonishingly small fraction of the global population makes up the so-called global middle class (between $5,000 and $11,500; see figure 1.1).[61] This apparent lack of mobility in the global division of labor has reinforced the popular perception that the world is divided into "haves" and "have-nothing-at-alls."[62] G-77 scholar Adil Najam puts it clearly indeed: "[t]he self-definition of the

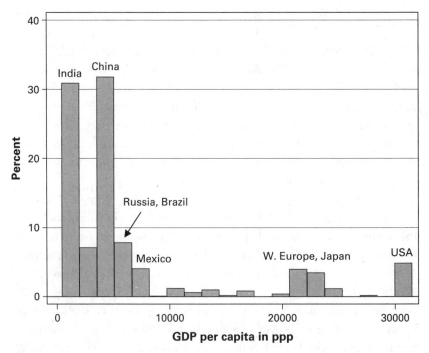

Figure 1.1
The "missing middle": distribution of people according to per capita income of the country where they live (year 2000). x-axis, per capita GDP in 1995 international prices; y-axis, share of world population. (From Milanovic 2005b)

South . . . is a definition of exclusion: these countries believe that they have been bypassed and view themselves as existing on the periphery."[63]

Further reinforcing these structuralist ideas are the callous—and at times opportunistic—actions taken by Western governments as well as the contemporary forces in the global economy that make upward mobility in the international division of labor extremely difficult. In a 2005 *Foreign Affairs* article, Nancy Birdsall, president of the Center for Global Development, Harvard economist Dani Rodrik, and International Monetary Fund (IMF) division chief Arvind Subramanian provide one such example: "In the context of international trade agreements in particular, developing countries have been asked to take on obligations that have been clearly inimical to their development interests. Perhaps the most egregious example of this in recent times has been the WTO's intellectual property agreement, TRIPs [The Agreement on Trade-Related Aspects of Intellectual Property Rights]. TRIPs will have the effect on poor countries of increasing the costs of and reducing access to essential medicines and this at a time when one of the worst health epidemics ever known by man—AIDS—ravages the developing world. The flip side of the costs to these countries is the profits that will be transferred from consumers and taxpayers in poor countries to pharmaceutical companies in the rich world. In other words, TRIPs will entail a pure transfer of rents from poor to rich."[64]

Another example of callous and opportunistic behavior is the Western crusade to limit the use of industrial policy instruments by developing countries. Through international financial institution (IFI) conditionality, bilateral reprisals, tariff escalation policies, restrictive multilateral and bilateral trade and investment agreements, and "expert advice," poor nations have been strongly encouraged to develop in line with their comparative advantage.[65] Yet, many of these very same comparative advantages have left developing countries at the bottom of the global income pyramid after generations of working in mining, agriculture, and low-wage labor. Their economies and government revenues continue to ride the rollercoaster of price volatility as their bread-winning exports rise and fall on the global market. World Bank economist Paul Collier likens the impact of a typical commodity price shock in a developing country to an event more familiar to Western audiences: "[T]he sort of shocks that are hitting those developing countries which are dependent upon a narrow range of primary commodities are *analogous only to the great depression of the 1930s*. In the case of the typical large negative export shock, directly costing 7 percent of GDP [gross domestic product], the shock then triggers a cumulative contraction in the economy over the next two or three years, leading to an additional loss of output of around 14 percent of initial GDP."[66] As we document in the coming chapters, by punishing resource-dependent nations that make efforts to upgrade their industrial capacity, increase local value-added, and encourage employment, rich nations effectively seal their own fate in global environmental negotiations.

This is, of course, only the tip of the proverbial iceberg. A whole range of Western policies that fail to acknowledge, or deliberately overlook, the structural dilemma of developing countries are also fatefully unhelpful to North-South climate negotiations. These include austere bilateral and multilateral conditionalities that limit national autonomy in setting policy, tariff escalation, agricultural protectionism, bilateral investment treaties and other "deep integration" agreements, commodity support funds that offer loans rather than grants, and IFI governance structures that prevent the institution's main clients from having any significant voting power. Our thesis is simple: When powerful states disregard weaker states' position in the international division of labor in areas where they possess structural power, they run a high risk of weaker states "reciprocating" in policy areas where they possess more bargaining leverage. The issue of global climate change—which itself is characterized by tremendous inequality in vulnerability, responsibility, and mitigation—can therefore not be viewed, analyzed, or responded to in isolation from the larger crisis of global inequality.

One Man Against an Army: Negotiating Climate Treaties for Poor Nations

Vast differences in absolute and relative income have a tremendous impact on the ability of countries to attend international conferences, participate in international organizations, and hire skilled negotiators.[67] This is what we call the direct route through which inequality reduces the likelihood of cooperation on climate change. It determines whether nations can pay for salaries and accommodations, draft proposals with proper legal argumentation and nomenclature, attend the many formal and informal meetings at conferences, and respond to the demands of powerful nations with well-thought-out counterproposals. It also determines whether a nation can provide reliable information about its intentions, abilities, and past behavior, and whether it can evaluate other nations' intentions, abilities, and behavior.[68] "The reason why many poor small countries are hardly represented in negotiations that concern them directly," writes Robert Wade, "is that they cannot afford the cost of hotels, offices, and salaries in places like Washington DC and Geneva, which must be paid not in PPP [purchasing power parity] dollars but in hard currency bought with their own currency at market exchange rates."[69] Furthermore, to avoid being eaten alive in negotiations, the governments of less developed countries (LDCs) must hire lawyers, economists, scientists, and consultants to assist them in negotiations. This requires hard currency, generally U.S. dollars. More often than not, they go without this help.

Michael Richards of the Overseas Development Institute has studied the average number of delegates sent to climate change negotiations and found that numbers vary greatly between developed and developing countries.[70] To give an idea of the disparity, he describes the situation at COP-6, where the United States brought ninety-nine formal delegates and the European Commission brought seventy-six, while many small island and African states were lucky if they could assemble a delegation of one, two, or three persons. These numbers gloss over even greater disparities. Wealthy nations typically show up at international conferences with a convoy of lawyers, legal experts, scientists, economists, skilled diplomats, and observers, allowing them to read every document, attend every committee meeting, and painstakingly weigh the pros and cons of proposals. Our experience at COP-10 in 2004 and an examination of the list of its 6,200 approved participants confirmed these trends. By contrast, developing country delegations often struggle to stay abreast of even the most important meetings and proposals, and negotiating drafts often pass through their hands faster than they can read, process, or respond to them.[71]

Decision costs are also especially high for poorer nations because of the specific type of human capital that they draw upon during climate treaty negotiations. "Developing country teams tend to be composed of scientists, especially meteorological specialists, who are less adept at negotiating with lawyers and economists, and diplomats or politicians."[72] Developing country governments also have fewer negotiators skilled in the ways of Western diplomacy and brinkmanship. "Even if the negotiator has a position," writes Gupta, "it is not enough. He or she needs techniques to influence the process of negotiation. These include influencing the agenda, the process, drafting text, circulating it informally among colleagues, submitting it formally to the Secretariat, responding to other's queries, negotiating the text and suggesting alternative formulations, checking the consensus view against the reserve position and, if not happy, bracketing the text or using the words 'can accept,' 'maybe' and/or 'too early to make a commitment'."[73] Chasek and Rajamani also make this point: "If the delegate is a technical expert, her usefulness in the negotiations could be limited. Unless she had prior multilateral negotiating experience, her interventions could be ignored simply because they are not couched in the proper lingo, even if what she is saying makes eminent sense. Technical experts may miss the political or procedural fine points of the debate or the larger international context within which a particular negotiation takes place."[74]

The importance of the number of attendees that developed and developing governments send to negotiations can also not be overstated. In principle, most decisions in international environmental negotiations require formal consensus—that is, "everyone has the power of veto"—but reality bears little resemblance to the ideal.[75] In practice, many different issues are often being negotiated in different meetings simultaneously, placing smaller delegations at a sharp disadvantage. Mike Moore, former director-general of the World Trade Organization (WTO), celebrates the fact that the WTO has "144 handbrakes and one accelerator, which can only be used by consensus,"[76] but deals are routinely struck in the absence of understaffed and overstretched LDC governments.[77]

Starting at the sixth Conference of the Parties to the UNFCCC and the Kyoto Protocol (COP-6) in 2001 in The Hague, the chairs insisted that negotiations be divided among groups, subgroups, and subsubgroups in order to cover the wide range of issues raised by climate change, such as national action plans, monitoring, emissions trading, compliance, technology transfer, and technical assistance.[78] Rather than "leveling the playing field," which many students of international negotiations see as a necessary precondition for achieving a mutually acceptable agreement, this decision strengthened the relative bargaining power of larger delegations.[79] Since the consensus rule, in practice, requires that dissatisfied parties actively voice their opposition, large delegations that have the ability to be many places at once wield tremendous agenda-setting power and are often able to push through policies that skew benefits strongly in their favor.[80] There are also social pressures—well known to students and teachers—that prevent uncertain participants from speaking up.

It is also not uncommon for developing country delegates to be "buried" with paper, brought to the point of extreme fatigue, and then presented with a *fait accompli* in the eleventh hour of negotiations and asked to accept or reject the proposal in an unrealistically short period of time. At the COP-6 Hague meeting, Ashton and Wang claim that "commitments were imposed by muscular chairmanship, or gaveled through without reaction from negotiators exhausted to the point of sleep."[81] These types of tactics often work to the advantage of rich nations, but they can also backfire. The North's "Green Room" meetings and take-it-or-leave-it proposal at the 2003 Cancun trade negotiations led to a walkout by G-77 delegates. Climate negotiations at COP-6 were equally unsuccessful, partly because the G-77 (a group of 132 developing nations) and China felt completely marginalized.[82] In cases where poor nations go along with railroaded agreements, the resentment created in securing victory in the battle can make winning the larger war impossible.

Because of their general lack of information and insufficient ability to process large quantities of legal and scientific information, Joyeeta Gupta argues that developing country negotiators tend to fall back on rhetorical statements, rather than making concrete problem-solving proposals.[83] Lynn Wagner has carefully studied the statements made by different coalitions—the Umbrella Group (Canada, Japan, Australia, New Zealand, Iceland, Norway, Russia and Ukraine), the Alliance of Small Island States (AOSIS), OPEC oil-producing countries, and the G-77—during the 1994, 1996, 1997, and 1998 sessions of the UN Commission on Sustainable Development (CSD). She found that the G-77 is less likely than any other negotiating bloc to make problem-solving statements.[84] In climate negotiations, G-77 countries instead have relied on three broad arguments: that the West is most responsible for the problem; that binding commitments jeopardize their economic development; and that global climate change is inextricably linked to larger problems in the global economy.[85]

Defensive strategies may prevent the outcomes poor nations most immediately fear, but they also significantly weaken their ability to get what they want. Anil Agarwal, Sunita Narain, and Anju Sharma—three well-known Southern intellectuals from the Centre for Science and Environment in New Delhi, India—argue that "[t]he weakness of [the South] lies in the failure of its political leadership to articulate and develop a coherent vision of a greener and [equitable] world. While it is true that the U.S. and various other Northern nations have been resistant to Southern concerns, the Southern leadership, too, has had no agenda of its own."[86]

Knowledge is also instrumental in developing a strong bargaining position, and here again global inequality has significant effects. Gupta refers to a "structural imbalance of knowledge"[87] between rich and poor nations, and Miland Kandlikar and Ambuj Sagar offer strong support for this assertion by examining the cross-national distribution of authors in IPCC Working Groups (WG) I, II, and III in 1990 and 1995.[88] They report that out of 512 WGI authors in 1995, 212 were from the United States, 61 were from the United Kingdom, and only 12 authors came from India and China combined.[89] The impact of this imbalance is both underresearched and underappreciated. Policy makers rely heavily on climate scientists for both the "facts" and their understanding of the policy implications.[90]

Finally, global inequality affects the ability of developing countries to provide reliable data and comply with negotiated agreements. The UNFCCC and Kyoto treaties both rely heavily on "national reporting" to ensure compliance, but poor nations have far fewer scientists and engineers per capita,[91] less NGO support, less private sector involvement, and the "[m]onitoring and data collection infrastructure of most developing countries is severely handicapped or non-existent."[92] Therefore, many LDC governments must hire outside consultants, scientists, and legal experts to help them put together their national communications, national climate change programs and national adaptation programs of action (NAPAs), greenhouse gas inventories, and vulnerability and adaptation assessments.[93] While noncompliance is often characterized as deliberate defection, the reality is that, in relative terms, it is much more expensive for developing countries to fulfill their obligations since foreign environmental technologies can only be bought and foreign experts can only be paid for with hard cash.[94]

Still, the most potent determinants of the North-South climate policy impasse are probably not transmitted through the direct route of global inequality: the shortage of technical, financial, and administrative capacity in poorer nations. The current stalemate in climate negotiations, we argue, has less to do with the seen than the unseen. Financial resources, technical expertise, and negotiating prowess matter, but the indirect impact of global inequality on conditions of generalized mistrust and diffuse reciprocity, structuralist worldviews and causal beliefs, risk aversion, perceived unfairness, and zero-sum and negative-sum behavior is probably even greater on the frequency, form, substance, depth, and timing of cooperation.

Charting a New Course: A Roadmap and Some Caveats

The goal of this introductory chapter is to tie global inequality to the stalemate in North-South climate negotiations through its direct impact on the ability of absurdly outgunned poor nations to negotiate effectively. Chapter 2 outlines a series of explanations about how global inequality more indirectly retards international cooperation. It describes a series of steps from actual and perceived inequality and its roots, through the disparate worldviews and causal beliefs of nations, to feelings of generalized mistrust between the two sides. This mistrust leads to divergent expectations and dysfunctional negotiations as poorer nations become risk averse, resist bearing such a large share of mitigation costs, and contemplate "getting even" with Northern nations for earlier injustices. These negative strategies prevent negotiators from reaching a shared social understanding of fairness from which to build the ambitious cooperative agreement needed to address climate change effectively.

Readers who are not interested in the theoretical intricacies of international relations may wish to move directly to chapters 3 and 4, where they can find concrete information on climate-related disasters and their causes. There we develop three cross-national indicators of suffering from such disasters over the twenty-three years from 1980 to 2002. The indicators rank nations by the cumulative number of people killed, made homeless, or otherwise affected by more than 4,000 hydrometeorological disasters: floods, windstorms, droughts, and heat waves. We then closely examine three major climate disasters: Hurricane Mitch in Honduras; a trio of hurricanes that hit Mozambique in early 2000; and rising sea levels, which are threatening Tuvalu and other low-lying Pacific islands. We use these case studies to explore how disasters unfold and what happened before the disasters that caused these nations to be so vulnerable. These cases have helped us to identify factors we might prioritize in cross-national testing and a theoretical approach that might explain more than the proximate causes of vulnerability.

Chapter 4 discusses a number of important insights from the extant literature on vulnerability, risk, and disaster and tests five causal factors that might explain national patterns of suffering: geographical vulnerability (populations near coastlines and urbanization rates), social vulnerability (high inequality and weak civil societies), institutional vulnerability (limited press freedom and restricted property rights), economic vulnerability (low per capita national income), and environmental vulnerability (a broad indicator of ecological damage). We then test the value of these different explanations of who is suffering worst from climate-related disasters. Using multivariate ordinary least-squares (OLS) regression and path analysis, we test their ability to predict the national patterns in death, homelessness, and the number of people affected by climate disasters that we observed in chapter 3.

Our last step in this effort is to go beyond proximate causes to test the deeper social and historical determinants of national vulnerability to climate disasters. Structuralist theories suggest that lying beneath the proximate factors is a nation's position in the global hierarchy of wealth and power. Our proxy for a nation's colonial legacy of extraction and its position in the world system is the narrowness of its export base—how dependent it is upon the ups and downs in prices and production of a few products it sells on the world market. Our findings suggest that a narrow export base is associated with lower national income, higher inequality, less secure property rights, fewer press freedoms, weaker civil society, lower levels of urbanization, and higher levels of environmental degradation. Path analysis helps us establish that this factor is indeed strongly predictive of national patterns of suffering from climate disasters. That is, in spite of the substantial randomness of hurricanes, drought, and other extreme weather events, a narrow economy predicts from one-eighth to nearly half of how many people have died, been made homeless, or otherwise affected by climate-related disasters over the past two decades.

In chapter 5, we examine who is causing the problem of climate change and how responsibility can be fairly measured and addressed. We investigate the four main ways that have been proposed for measuring responsibility for climate change and who is seen as most responsible. Each represents different positions on what is "just" held by different nations and different interest groups within nations. The stakes can be seen in the conflict between the approach taken in the Kyoto treaty, which took the politically expedient approach of granting rights to pollute based on 1990 levels of emissions, and the per capita approach proposed by poor nations, in which each person on Earth is given an equal share of emissions. Again, using the tools of multiple regression, we take a look at the factors driving global variation in responsibility for production of carbon dioxide (as differently conceived): national wealth, population, geography, industrial structure, urbanization, trade openness, civil society strength, and democracy. What we find is striking; there is strong evidence that the historical legacy of a country's incorporation into the global economy has a critical impact on its available avenues of development and its carbon future. We also find strong support for theories of ecologically unequal exchange. The so-called ecological debt perspective espoused by many developing country policy makers— that emissions are skyrocketing with growing trade and industrialization in poorer nations because wealthy nations are "offshoring" the production of their resource-intensive products—can therefore not be dismissed as an erroneous mental model.

This leads us to the questions of who is participating in environmental treaties and efforts to address climate change, so chapter 6 examines which countries are joining global efforts to address the problem. We describe patterns in which countries sign and ratify the Kyoto Protocol. And since the terms of LDC participation have not been completely negotiated, we also develop an index of twenty-two international environmental agreements and attempt to explain the generalizable patterns of participation among 192 countries. Though critics rightly point out the lack of enforcement in the Kyoto Protocol, we argue that the act of ratification represents costly signal and is an important measure of a state's willingness and ability to implement specific policy commitments. As Charles Lipson once put it, treaty ratifications "are a conventional way of raising the credibility of promises by staking national reputation on adherence."[95] While new institutionalism and other rationalist approaches have done an admirable job of identifying the domestic sources of credibility, we argue that they are theoretically crippled without an explanation of how states acquire that credibility in the first place. Hence, we develop a theoretically sequenced model that exploits complementarities between rational choice institutionalism and structuralism. We recognize that credibility—or the willingness and ability to honor one's international environmental commitments—matters, but we also argue that state credibility is strongly influenced by a legacy of colonial incorporation into the world economy.[96] Our results indicate that dependence on one or a few exported products directly and indirectly explains nearly 60 percent of the treaty ratification rates overall and one-third of the variation in Kyoto ratification. These structural constraints on countries' willingness and ability to cooperate suggest that the spread of institutions and values may not necessarily create a world with more adherents to environmental treaties.

A new measure of vulnerability to hydrometerological disasters (developed in chapter 4) also allows us to subject to empirical scrutiny the claim that poor countries—unjustly suffering the effects of a problem to which they contributed virtually nothing—craft negotiating tactics and environmental policies on the basis of their principled beliefs. Also, with a new systematic tally of environmental assistance from wealthy nations to the South over the period 1970 to 2002, which we have compiled for 80 bilateral and multilateral donors and 190 recipient nations, we are able to evaluate the alleged empirical significance of "compensatory justice," a principle embedded in many international environmental regimes.

A key feature of this book is our attempt to synthesize theories whenever possible, examining both the proximate political causes and the deeper social and historical determinants of vulnerability to hydrometeorological disasters, responsibility for carbon dioxide emissions, and participation in environmental treaties. We do so because much of the existing literature has relied on single cases and small-n datasets and have failed to test competing theories side by side. The case study literature is crucial, but we can only know if the cases examined are bizarre coincidences or bellwethers if we understand the broad patterns.

Our findings suggest that any effective post-Kyoto climate treaty will have to address credibility, compensatory justice, the strategic leverage of major global environmental actors, and national development profiles, which bear heavily on nations' willingness and ability to ratify these treaties. By way of conclusion, we return to the core questions that drove our interest in this analysis: Does North-South inequality hinder cooperation on climate change? As a December 20, 2004 newspaper article called "Is Kyoto Kaput?" suggested, the Kyoto Protocol is ultimately more symbolic than it is substantive.[97] The truth is that we are far from a consensus on the post-2012 climate regime, and a gaping chasm still divides North and South on crucial questions: Who should have to reduce emissions? How much? When? Who should pay for adaptation to the impacts of climate change and how much should they pay?

In the remainder of this book we argue that even the best-designed institutions—treaties with funding for poor nations, staggered deadlines for reductions in greenhouse gas emissions, differing ways of counting emissions, etc.—will not resolve the underlying causes of the North-South stalemate on climate policy. Climate change is fundamentally an issue of inequality and its resolution will most likely require unconventional, perhaps even heterodox, policy interventions. Climate negotiations, we must remember, take place in the context of an ongoing development crisis and what the global South perceives as a pattern of Northern callousness and opportunism in matters of international political economy. They take place at a time when levels of generalized trust are declining. And they take place at a time when the concerns of poor nations regarding fair processes and fair outcomes have frequently been marginalized.

Negotiators must therefore redouble their efforts to address conditions of generalized mistrust, structuralist causal beliefs and worldviews, risk aversion, and the perceived need to retaliate. They can do this by promoting policies that explicitly signal concern for the structural obstacles facing developing countries. Such policies include transferring meaningful sums of environmental assistance to developing countries; funding "brown" aid and adaptation aid as well as green aid; providing greater "policy space" and "environmental space" to late developers; abandoning international economic regimes, like TRIPs, that threaten the long-term interests of developing countries; helping nations diversify their exports and create strong, resilient economies with internally articulated markets; creating a commodity support fund to insulate countries that rely on natural resources from exogenous shocks; giving developing countries a greater stake in the governance structures of international financial institutions; and reducing Western agricultural subsidies and tariff escalation policies. Committing to the so-called Hippocratic principle and promoting predictability and generalized norms in trade, debt, aid, and investment issues may also pay handsome dividends in eliciting LDC cooperation.[98]

However, all the best climate policy interventions may be undermined by the structural shift of manufacturing and extraction of resources going on in the globalizing world economy. The globalization of economic production and trade is causing many industrializing nations to become heavily reliant upon earnings from carbon-intensive export products, including oil and mineral extraction, petroleum-based input-intensive agriculture, and manufactures whose components require energy-intensive transport and processing. This important structural point is often lost in discussions of climate policy and attempts to include developing nations in the crafting of a post-2012 climate regime.[99] Many of our best climate policy tools—including emissions trading, public-private partnerships, and technology transfer to increase the efficiency of power plants and factories—may have only marginal effects on this looming structural shift. This point is profoundly political and in avoiding it, the policy recommendations of the *Special Report on Emissions Scenarios* (SRES) and other IPCC reports have remained fatefully unhelpful to policy makers. We suggest that aiding nations in making the difficult transition to more equitable and economically sustainable and lower-carbon pathways of development may be the only way to resolve the issue of climate change. But this transition needs to be built on generalized reciprocity, a climate of trust, shared principles of justice, and a common worldview of environment and development.

2

A Model of North-South (Non-)Cooperation

A Right to Social and Economic Development?

On the last official day of the Rio Earth Summit, inside the RioCentro's vast exhibition hall in the office of India's delegation, Environment Minister Kamal Nath broke for coffee with two visiting ministers from Kenya. The delegates had worked all night to craft the wording of the "Rio Declaration" whose Principle 3 states that "The right to development must be fulfilled so as to equitably meet developmental and environmental needs of present and future generations."[1]

Nath was livid: "At 6 o'clock in the morning, the United States told us they want to remove the phrase 'right to social and economic development'.... [W]e must not budge from 'the right to social and economic development'." A reporter from the *New York Times* described how the visiting Kenyans "quietly whistled in amazement." Nath went on: "I have talked to the Chinese, they are with us. The Swedes also. Finland seems to be on the fence.... We are seeking that the developed world plow a little of their prosperity back into the earth."[2]

Before the Rio Declaration was adopted at the nineteenth plenary on June 14, 1992, the U.S. delegation submitted an "interpretative statement expressing reservations"[3] on this article and others: "The U.S. does not, by joining the consensus on the Rio Declaration, change its long-standing opposition to the so-called 'right to development.' Development is not a right. On the contrary, development is a goal we all hold.... The U.S. cannot agree to, and would disassociate itself from, any interpretation of Principle 3 that accepts 'a right to development' or otherwise goes beyond that understanding.... The United States does not accept any interpretation... that would imply a recognition or acceptance by the United States of any international obligations or liabilities, or any diminution in the responsibilities of developing countries."[4]

This exchange, twenty years after similar debates at the Stockholm summit, illustrates how issues of development persistently spill over into environmental ones. Despite the strenuous efforts of rich nations to separate climate issues and development issues, the development concerns of poor nations are not going away. Now, a decade and a half after Rio we are still fighting the same battle, which by now we should understand: environment and development are inextricably linked, and developing countries will never meaningfully participate in a global climate agreement that flouts their development needs.

In chapter 1, we explained the more obvious ways in which the poverty of the world's poor nations makes it difficult for them to meaningfully participate in international environmental treaties. Frequently summarized under the all-encompassing phrase "lack of capacity," the weak technical, administrative, negotiating, and financial abilities of developing countries are generally thought to have a negative impact on cooperation. The path-breaking volume, *Institutions for the Earth: Sources of Effective International Environmental Protection*, opened this line of inquiry in 1993, and since then a series of authors have made important contributions to this field.[5] This has led to suggestions that poorer nations should be given technical assistance to improve their environmental agencies, clean up corruption, and train and support treaty negotiators.[6] However, caution must be exercised when basing policy recommendations on proximate explanations.

Is lack of capacity the primary channel through which global inequality weakens the likelihood, form, frequency, timing, substance, and depth of international environmental cooperation? A priori, it would seem equally plausible that even with improved capacity, the gaping divide in global wealth and power could affect the worldviews, causal beliefs, expectations, material self-interests, principled beliefs, and emotions of both rich and poor nations. Therefore, we believe that a critical appraisal of the received wisdom is overdue. Perhaps the persistence and deepening of global inequality promotes a "structuralist" mentality among developing country policy makers and breeds a generalized mistrust of developed countries. Perhaps the North-South trust deficit makes tit-for-tat reciprocity difficult and diffuse reciprocity seemingly impossible. Perhaps conditions of institutionalized suspicion lead to totally divergent and unstable expectations of future outcomes. Policy makers overcome with anger, resentment, suspicion, pride, envy, spite, and embarrassment, as well as those who come to the negotiating table with a victim mentality, may also be more concerned with self-protection or revenge than contributing to the collective good. These are all serious empirical questions without satisfactory answers.

In this chapter, we introduce a new causal narrative about the role of global inequality in international environmental politics. We postulate that global inequality makes it more difficult for rich and poor nations to identify socially shared understandings of "fair" solutions, and even when rich and poor countries can agree on general fairness principles, the preference heterogeneity generated by global inequality aggravates disagreements about how to make those principles operational. Global inequality also contributes to conditions of generalized mistrust and weak reciprocity, which in turn makes developing countries—countries that possess strong preferences for "cheap" economic development and weak preferences for stringent environmental policies—more inclined to take self-damaging actions for their emotional satisfaction (e.g., spite or retribution). Southern nations' suspicion of Northern behavior and their inability to constrain Northern opportunism also promotes risk-averse behavior and defensive negotiating strategies. While we are only beginning to unravel a complex causal web, we believe these factors have particularly negative effects on global efforts to preserve the planet's environment.

Some of the causal linkages described in this chapter have been explored elsewhere. However, to our knowledge no one has yet attempted to pull these disparate arguments together into an integrated, multistep model. Rationalist authors, for example, have hypothesized that ethical norms and principles reduce the costs of negotiating, monitoring, and enforcing an international agreement (see Phase V of figure 2.1) by providing tacit or constructed "focal points" that prevent endless haggling, by cementing cooperative solutions that increase the willingness of domestic audiences to support agreements negotiated internationally, by weakening nations' incentives to hide information and

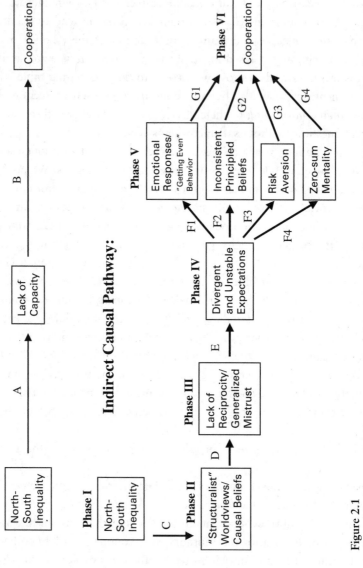

Figure 2.1

A model of international noncooperation: Direct causal pathway (A–B) and indirect causal pathway (C–D–E–F–G).

misrepresent behavior, and by reducing the risk-averse and self-damaging emotional behavior of would-be cooperators.[7] Conversely, the absence of socially shared understandings of fairness and justice can reinforce zero-sum worldviews and causal beliefs, erode conditions of mutual trust, promote risk aversion, and foster retaliatory attitudes.

However, the new institutional solutions that rationalists propose are often "institutional bandage[s] applied to a structural hemorrhage."[8] That is, their case-by-case, problem-solving approach to global environmental problems rarely focuses on why highly asymmetric distributions arise in the first place and thus seldom addresses the root causes of North-South conflict. Inequality, in effect, is taken as given.[9]

Some rationalists, for example, have emphasized the proximate need to address divergent social understandings of fairness without explaining the social production and reproduction of highly asymmetric distributions; others have emphasized the importance of worldviews and causal beliefs without explaining the origin of those ideas.[10] We take a different approach by measuring whether Southern worldviews and causal beliefs are based on observable empirical regularities. The extant literature suggests that material and ideational preferences exert an influence on a nation's negotiating position; however, without understanding the origin of those preferences, it is hard to say how stable they are or under what conditions they might shift.

For example, many climate policy analysts dismiss the claims of "environmental imperialism," "ecological debt," "ecologically unequal exchange," and "climate injustice" made by developing country negotiators as empty and distracting rhetoric used as a negotiating tactic. But however irrational and uncooperative these claims may seem, we argue that these are real perceptions and these perceptions shape the way governments view their interests. And importantly, a growing body of empirical evidence suggests that Southern worldviews and causal beliefs in some cases cannot be dismissed as false constructs or erroneous mental models used to justify poor performance. By almost any measure, for example, we can say with confidence that ecologically unequal exchange is not just a perception; it is a social reality (see chapter 5). Structuralist mental models—understandings of world events based primarily on perceptions of inequality in global economic and political matters—will therefore likely persist unless Western governments make efforts to reverse this inequality.

Much of the quantitative work in this book focuses on causal linkage C in figure 2.1: the determinants of Southern worldviews and causal beliefs. Regression analysis is also used to test the significance and strength of causal explanations G1, G2, G3, and G4, but evaluating the strength of the model as an integrated whole requires mixing methods (case study research, process tracing, etc.). These methods are complementary and mutually reinforcing, and we utilize all of them in the following chapters. However, we acknowledge that there are both observable and unobservable processes and outcomes, and that the evidence in this book supports some causal mechanisms more than others. The research supporting causal linkages D, E, and F, for example, is admittedly weaker than other parts of the model. Since these are areas of perennial concern for international relations scholars where significant accumulation of knowledge has already occurred, we aim to break new ground on the front end and the back end of this theoretically sequenced model, rather than focusing excessively on the intermediate causal linkages.

We are also keenly aware that our model omits plausible alternative explanations. However, our goal is to focus on the root causes of North-South noncooperation; in other words, we are most interested in general causal explanations that are, broadly speaking, transferable to other issue areas in international environmental politics.

A Hierarchy of Explanations

As a theoretical point of departure, we start with global inequality.[11] Nations can move up and down the international division of labor, but we argue that the inherently unequal structure of the world system remains intact largely because of structural barriers: unstable commodity prices, declining terms of trade, domestic political unrest, high levels of social inequality, and feeble postcolonial political institutions. Persistent global inequality is useful as a starting point because it directs our attention to the root causes of political conflict in international environmental relations. Global inequality promotes a social distribution of economic benefits and environmental burdens that advantages rich countries and disadvantages poor countries and thus creates political conflicts of an intrinsically structural nature.[12]

In taking this approach, we draw on two separate literatures. One can loosely associate the first with structuralism, world-systems theory, and other theories of colonial development and unequal exchange.[13] The second is less identifiable by a common theoretical perspective and more by its substantive focus on the role that the current international political economy of development plays in reinforcing existing patterns and creating new patterns of global inequality.[14] We hope to show that insights from these literatures can be fruitfully integrated with more mainstream theories of international relations. Such an integrative approach, we believe, helps paint a more complete picture of complex social reality.

We also rely on a series of mid-range causal explanations in this book, which address a narrower set of empirical phenomena and are less abstract than "grand theory." Here mid-range explanations refer to those that can be generalized across multiple issues of global environmental politics. For example, the unraveling of the "Rio bargain," the North-South divide over "green" environmental issues of global concern and "brown" environmental issues of local concern, and the vigorously-contested effort to define sustainable development have all contributed to a toxic North-South political environment and "shallow" international environmental agreements.

Finally, we articulate a number of issue-specific causal explanations. Previous "problem structure" explanations of climate policy have emphasized the large number of (relevant) actors, the complexity and uncertainty of the issues, the stability of actor preferences, and the difficulty of monitoring government behavior. These are all important factors; however, an understudied aspect of climate change's "problem structure" is the inherently asymmetric nature of climate benefits and burdens. Global inequality plays a determining role in who suffers most immediately and profoundly from the impacts of climate change, who is most responsible for climate change, and who is most willing and able to seriously address the problem. These compounding inequalities, we argue, overlie an already polarized North-South debate and make cooperation exceedingly difficult.

Having introduced this hierarchy of grand, mid-range, and issue-specific explanations, we will now briefly map out the causal argument that ties each of the chapters in this book together. The logic of this argument is also presented schematically in figure 2.1. First, we should point out that it is not our intention to resolve any metatheoretical debates. The more modest objective of this book is to specify and empirically evaluate different causal explanations of the existing North-South impasse on climate policy. This requires theoretically sequencing a series of arguments.

The causal chain in figure 2.1 begins with persistent North-South inequality, which is multifaceted and owes its origin to a variety of general, mid-range, and climate-specific factors that we will soon discuss. Its persistence, we argue, promotes distinctly structuralist mental models and causal beliefs, which attribute inequality to external forces. Even after twenty years of neoliberalism; the failure of the New International Economic Order project (NIEO); the end of the Cold War; and global convergence in literacy, infant mortality, caloric intake, and life expectancy rates,[15] structuralist presuppositions remain salient in the minds of many policy makers in less developed countries.[16] And since worldviews and causal beliefs precede expectations, and expectations shape preferences (material or otherwise), we argue that structuralist ideas are an important determinant of the negotiating behavior of poor nations, including the way Southern leaders measure responsibility for climate change and gauge progress toward resolving the problem. One commentator explains it this way: "The self-definition of the South...is a definition of exclusion: these countries believe that they have been bypassed and view themselves as existing on the periphery."[17]

Through the lens of a structualist, the international system is characterized by a division of labor. There is a global stratification system that places nations on the top, in the middle, or on the bottom (the core, semiperiphery, and periphery in world-systems terminology), and only a few manage to move up (figure 2.2).[18] This global division of labor not only shapes the social distribution of environmental burdens, but also the willingness and ability of countries to participate in global environmental solutions. In the words of one Malaysian ambassador, "You cannot address environmental issues unless you address questions of

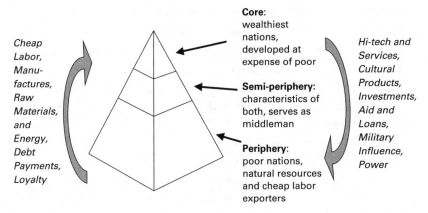

Figure 2.2
Structural perspectives on global inequality and the flows of materials, energy, and power that maintain it.

structural inequity. It is the entry point to sustainability."[19] Waste flows downhill in the social structural sense, while benefits flow up.

These sorts of structuralist ideas, we argue, bear profoundly on North-South interactions at subsequent links in our hypothesized causal chain.[20] The structuralist way of making sense of the world promotes generalized mistrust among rich and poor nations, which in turn suppresses conditions of diffuse reciprocity, and leads to divergent and unstable expectations going into future negotiating rounds. Structuralist ideas also can promote particularistic notions of fairness, a victim mentality, and zero-sum, or even negative-sum, behavior. This confluence of forces has conspired to undermine North-South environmental cooperation and will likely affect the prospects for meaningful, long-term environmental cooperation far into the future.

Global Inequality, Viewing the World from Below, and Climate Treaty Deadlock

In the late 1980s and early 1990s, international relations theorists engaged in an "either-or" debate over the role that self-interest and ideas play in international politics.[21] Most scholars now agree that this was a false dichotomy. Ideas *and* interests are important determinants of negotiating behavior and cooperation outcomes. However, scholars only recently have begun to address the more interesting and important questions of how ideas matter, how much they matter, and under what conditions they matter.[22]

Judith Goldstein and Robert Keohane distinguish among three types of beliefs that influence policies and outcomes: worldviews, principled beliefs, and causal beliefs.[23] We find this conceptual framework useful and will make similar distinctions in this book.[24] "At the most fundamental level," write the authors, "ideas define the universe of possibilities for action." Culture, religion, rationality, emotion, ethnicity, race, class, gender, and identity all shape the way humans perceive the world in which they operate. Almost by definition, then, having a world view implies "[limited] choice because it logically excludes other interpretations of reality, or at least suggests that such interpretations are not worthy of sustained exploration."[25] By limiting one's menu of available options, ideas have an instrumental impact on how cost-benefit calculations are carried out. Ideas also influence the very way in which actors come up with their policy agendas. For example, depending on one's position in the international system, states may seek to maximize absolute gains, relative gains, fairness preferences, or emotional utility. Highly risk-averse governments may want to freeze the status quo.[26] Leaders who feel cheated by others may seek to punish their enemies or strengthen their relative power, regardless of the efficiency implications.[27] Those who see themselves as marginalized by social structures may seek to overturn regimes rather than making changes within them.[28] Weak states that look down the decision tree and anticipate being exploited at the discretion of powerful states may even take self-damaging steps to promote their principled beliefs.[29] Whatever the particular course of action, ideas about how the world works "put blinders on people" and "[reduce] the number of conceivable alternatives" that they choose from.[30] Worldviews and causal beliefs, in this sense, influence issue definition, expectations, perceived interests, principled beliefs, and ultimately the prospects for mutually beneficial cooperation.

In the developing world, we argue that structuralist ideas about the origins and persistence of global inequality still form the central worldview of most policy makers, including how they have viewed the issue of climate change.[31] The vast majority of goals that Third World leaders have sought since the end of World War II have remained elusive, and this, we believe, has shaped developing countries' perception of the world as fundamentally unequal and unjust. Twenty years ago, Steven Krasner argued in *Structural Conflict: The Third World Against Global Liberalism* that ideas about "dependency" affected how many LDC decision makers viewed the world, their identity in relation to other states, their goals, and how they believed such goals would be most effectively realized.[32] "The [dependency perspective] embraced by developing countries," Krasner argued, "[is] not merely a rationalization. It [is] the subjective complement to the objective condition of domestic and international weakness."[33] Sadly, since the release of *Structural Conflict*, the objective condition of many developing countries and the perceptions of their policy makers have remained largely unchanged.[34]

To the surprise of many observers, the economies of many Latin American nations grew and became more diverse during their relative isolation during the global depression in the 1930s and World War II. A group of economists working in Santiago, Chile, under the leadership of Raul Prebisch in the Economic Commission for Latin America (ECLA) developed a theory to account for these changes. They argued that during the years before the Great Depression, the influx of investors and cheap goods from Europe and the United States had driven out smaller local producers, and created dependent economies that could grow only to a certain point, without creating the jobs or revenues needed to become a dynamic system. Being isolated during the Depression and World War II created new opportunities for local industries to flourish, and the end of the war brought a rush of outside firms to recapture the markets and production facilities. Thus, these observers saw their national development hindered by forces larger than their national society—by the "structure" of the world economy and its politics. The structuralists' views developed in response to strong pressures from the White House, international financial institutions, and Western academics who believed that to overcome their poverty, poor nations needed to import ideas, technology, and capital from the wealthy nations.[35]

Prebisch, the ECLA authors, and those who followed them believed that there were "core" and "peripheral" areas of the world economy. Power and high-value goods flowed out of the core nations, while low-value goods flowed from the periphery up to these "centers." Figure 2.2

attempts to depict this theory in simple terms. From the beginning, these theorists were of two types: the "structuralists" and the "dependency theorists." The former group argued that the global economy created opportunities and limitations on their growth, and that strategic decisions would be required to navigate a path toward national development. The latter group basically saw no way for their development to occur without their nearly complete withdrawal from global markets.[36]

During a period of attention to poor nations brought on by the Cuban Revolution, the Vietnam War, and their aftermaths, the main ideas of structuralism were incorporated into the U.S.-based world-systems theory. Sociologist Immanuel Wallerstein added a third category of nations between the core and the periphery that had features of both, which he called the semiperiphery. These nations also did the work of exploiting their local peripheries, serving as global "middlemen" or more aptly, "foremen." Critics charged that the theory did not account for the upward mobility of some nations, but world-systems theorists always argued that some mobility is possible and indeed expected, but that the overall structure of global inequality remains intact over time.[37]

While we would not argue that world-systems theory comes close to explaining complex social reality by itself, it does offer important insights that have not yet been explored in the context of global environmental politics. Therefore, we seek in this book to wed its structuralist insights to more mainstream theories of international relations—that might better explain the agency and perhaps the psychology driving strategic choices.

There are at least three widely held perceptions that we believe obstruct North-South efforts to protect the climate: that climate change is primarily an issue of profligate Northern consumption; that a nation's ability to implement meaningful environmental reform depends upon its position in the international division of labor; and that the North is using environmental issues as a ruse to thwart the economic development of poor nations.

Adil Najam has argued that "[w]hat galvanized the North-South polarization at [the 1972 Stockholm conference and the 1992 Rio Earth Summit] was the totally different perceptions that industrialized and developing nations hold about what the 'real' environmental issues exactly are."[38] During the 1970s, there was intense debate about the relative environmental significance of Southern population growth and patterns of profligate resource consumption in the North. In the more recent case of negotiations on global climate change, rich and poor nations have staked out diametrically opposite positions (underpinned by perceptional differences) concerning the "real costs" of climate change. As we will see in chapters 3 and 4, the threat of rising sea levels, stronger storms, and longer droughts is a question of basic survival for many poor nations—and importantly, many countries are experiencing these disasters now, not in the distant future. By comparison, many rich nations see the threat of climate change as a long-term environmental problem that may put beachfront properties, sectors of the economy, and certain crops at risk. One might therefore say that rich nations pay for climate change with dollars and poor nations pay with their lives.[39]

Nations also perceive responsibility for climate change from markedly different vantage points.[40] The president of Kiribati likens island states to "little ants making a home of a leaf floating on a pond" and industrialized countries to "elephants [that] go to drink and roughhouse in the water." "The problem," he argues "isn't the ants' behavior. It's a problem of how to convince the elephants to be more gentle."[41] Brazilian Ambassador Paulo Nogueira Batista similarly pins the blame directly on Northern consumption: "We are more concerned with the threat that is coming from the North—the patterns of production and consumption of the overdeveloped countries—rather than the threat that may come from the developing countries themselves."[42] Yet, some Western countries and citizens argue that the Kyoto Protocol is unfair because it exempts developing nations from making meaningful policy commitments.

Gareth Porter and Janet Brown also write that "[t]he tone and substance of North-South bargaining on environmental issues are influenced by the structure of the global economic system, which exerts indirect pressure on the policies of developing countries toward their natural resources and thus constrains the quest for global cooperation to save those resources."[43] This observation is consistent with many of the public declarations made by Southern policy makers at environmental conferences. At the Rio Earth Summit in 1992, for example, Malaysian Prime Minister Mahathir Mohamad laid emphasis on what he called the North's "environmental colonialism": "When the rich chopped down our forests, built their poison-belching factories and scoured the world for cheap resources, the poor said nothing. Indeed, they paid for the development of the rich. Now the rich claim a right to regulate the development of the poor countries. And yet any suggestion that the rich compensate the poor adequately is regarded as outrageous. As colonies we were exploited. Now as independent nations we are to be equally exploited."[44]

According to Porter and Brown, "developing states' *perceptions* of the global economic structure as inequitable have [also] long been a factor in their policy responses to global environmental issues."[45] Southern policy makers, in other words, view their ability to implement meaningful environmental reform as conditioned by their position in the international division of labor. After Rio, one G-77 adviser wrote that "the South...saw poverty, underdevelopment, and unequal global economic relations as the principal causes of its environmental problems and it still mistrusted the North's environmental agenda as a guise to perpetuate this plight. It was this perception of causality of its environmental problems that informed the South's interests and strategy at both [the 1972 Stockholm and 1992 Rio] conferences."[46] Notice that it is a structuralist perspective that seems to inform the decision making of developing country policy makers.[47] The same analyst suggests that the South's "principal fear...[is] that the North is using environmental issues as an excuse to pull up the development ladder behind it—[a suspicion which] has remained unallayed through two decades of environmental diplomacy."[48] Although the North may perceive these mental models and cause-and-effect presuppositions "as a distraction, as extortion, and as exploitation,"[49] they still exist and affect the behavior of developing country policy makers. This sense of injustice is further compounded when wealthy nations flaunt environmental treaties by failing to achieve their goals, resist limits on their conspicuous consumption, fail to transfer technology and environmental assistance, and seemingly undermine the poor country's own right to development in the short and longer terms.

To be clear, this is much more than a general sense of frustration with development. It is also a perception that the rules are continually being rewritten unilaterally by the rich, industrialized countries in order to enrich themselves at the expense of the South, and that the structure of the world system is largely to blame for their grinding poverty and chronic vulnerability. Many LDC policy makers, for example, believe that TRIPS, TRIMS, and GATS (trade-related agreements on intellectual property rights, investment, and services) were imposed upon them to give an advantage to special interests in Western countries. Incidentally, this view is also supported by the scholarly literature.[50] Dani Rodrik writes that "WTO rules on anti-dumping, subsidies and countervailing measures, agriculture, textiles, TRIMs, and TRIPs are utterly devoid of any economic rationale beyond the mercantilist interests of a narrow set of powerful groups in the advanced industrial countries."[51] In the run-up to the TRIPS negotiations, UNCTAD Secretary General Rubens Ricupero noted that developing countries were "not aware of the real intentions of the developed countries."[52] Resistance has also mounted against the ever-expanding WTO "deep integration" agenda.[53] Ugandan Nathan Irumba, who represents the least developed countries at the WTO, summarizes the Southern perspective on the deep integration issue: "We are simply asking for fair and equitable rules that would take into account our development needs and allow us to participate fully in the trade system. *But instead we risk being pressured once again into accepting rules we don't need and can't afford.*"[54]

Further reinforcing beliefs about Northern callousness and opportunism is the perceived disingenuousness of neoliberal arguments about liberalization of capital markets. Before, during, and (to a lesser extent) after the Asian financial crisis, the U.S. Treasury, the International Monetary Fund, and Wall Street all argued that open capital markets would allow LDCs to tap into global resources that would not otherwise be available in a "closed" economy. They claimed that when capital was allowed to enter and exit markets freely, it would allocate itself efficiently and enhance global welfare.[55] Today, however, it is widely understood that this interpretation of the crisis corresponds rather awkwardly with the facts.[56] Capital markets are highly imperfect and prone to irrational exuberance and skittishness, and many developing countries now possess an intimate understanding of such capital market imperfections after experiencing them firsthand. And importantly, many Southern policy makers have come to perceive the West's crusade for liberalization of capital markets, not as an honest mistake, but as an attempt to pay off parochial interests on Wall Street at the expense of the global collective good.[57]

During the Asian financial crisis, the U.S. Treasury stood aside as the South Korean economy went into a complete meltdown. At a time when the United States could have intervened with a bailout package, it instead conspicuously sidelined itself and watched investors repatriate tremendous sums of capital back to Wall Street.[58] Former U.S. Secretary of State Henry Kissinger put his finger on an important perception in Asia at that time: "Even friends I respect for their moderate views argue that Asia is confronting an American campaign to stifle Asian competition. *It is critical that at the end of this crisis, when Asia will reemerge as a dynamic part of the world, America be perceived as a friend that gave constructive advice and assistance in the common interest, not as a bully determined to impose bitter social and economic medicine to serve largely American interests.*"[59] Kissinger's point is an important one: powerful nations have a strong interest in not reinforcing Southern assumptions about Northern malfeasance.

We will document more cases like this one in the coming chapters but our central point is that a series of events can lead to a cumulative picture of how the world works and other states' underlying interests, and if poor nations see rich nations as kicking the "development ladder" from beneath their feet, they will be less likely to participate in global environmental institutions. Strategic interactions between rational actors do not take place in a vacuum. Interactions across issue areas profoundly affect the likelihood that weaker states will believe they are being dealt a fair—or at least a predictable—hand in global environmental negotiations.

A Climate of Mistrust

Among the many causal pathways through which global inequality influences international environmental cooperation, perhaps the most important and understudied factor is the level of trust among developed and developing nations. Despite an extensive literature in economics, sociology, and political science on the causal link between trust and cooperation,[60] efforts to apply such insights to international environmental politics are virtually nonexistent. The irony is that commentators and policy makers have repeatedly emphasized that the "climate of mistrust" surrounding international negotiations has become a tremendous obstacle to cooperation.[61]

One of the first great social thinkers to identify the "noncontractual elements of contract" underpinning economic exchange was Emile Durkheim.[62] He emphasized the importance of a social commitment to honest behavior, reciprocity, and mutual trust. By fostering norms of reciprocity, it is thought that trust increases communication and information, reduces uncertainty and transaction costs, enhances the credibility of commitments, makes defection more costly, creates stable expectations, and ultimately promotes cooperative solutions.[63] Trust, in effect, allows would-be cooperators to bank on promises to honor policy commitments.

There is some disagreement, however, about how individuals, societies, and nation-states can best promote conditions of mutual trust. In most cases, reciprocity seems to work best. If I treat you well today, you will be more likely to do me a favor tomorrow. Cicero wrote, "There is no duty more indispensable than that of returning a kindness. All men distrust one forgetful of a benefit."[64] However, as societies become more complex and information asymmetries widen, opportunities to shirk, cheat, or otherwise commit malfeasance grow, and conditions of reciprocity slowly erode.[65] The solution to this problem in a domestic setting is simple. The creation of a state as an overarching coercive authority eliminates many perverse incentives "by enabl[ing] its subjects to do what they cannot do on their own—trust each other."[66] With its "monopoly of violence," the state enforces contracts and "coerces trust" on behalf of its citizens.[67] However, internationally, where contracting takes place under conditions of anarchy, states do not have the luxury of third-party enforcement.[68] They must "decide whom to make agreements with, and on what terms, largely on the basis of their expectations about their partners' willingness and ability to keep their commitments."[69] In the absence of a world government, rational states seeking stable and effective solutions to problems of international public good provision must develop self-enforcing agreements.[70]

So, one of the central questions of international relations is how governments can convince potential partners that they will honor their commitments. John Mearsheimer, a structural realist, sees "little room for trust among states" because verifying others' promises is nearly impossible and conditions of anarchy breed constant fear.[71] Arthur Stein has challenged this view. He argues that governments can achieve deep cooperation if they "specify strict patterns of behavior and ensure no one cheats."[72] As other institutionalist authors have pointed out, Mearsheimer would be hard pressed to explain why states spend such an extraordinary amount of time and money drafting and negotiating international agreements, monitoring and enforcing obligations, setting up side payments regimes, and recruiting new participants. Mearsheimer's view of the world is also difficult to reconcile with the unprecedented growth in intergovernmental and multilateral treaties signed and ratified over the past fifty years.[73]

On this issue we side with the institutionalists. States, in our view, are capable of fostering conditions of trust, but doing so is neither easy nor inexpensive. We highlight four ways in which states may seek to enhance relations of trust among themselves: specific reciprocity, diffuse reciprocity, costly signals, and ex ante evaluations of others' beliefs and expectations. These all merit attention since they are crucial to understanding the obstacles to meaningful North and South environmental cooperation.

Specific reciprocity takes place when nations "exchange items of equivalent value in a strictly delimited sequence."[74] OPEC and non-OPEC nations, for example, have agreed on occasion to cut oil production in tandem. Norway's oil minister Einar Steensnæs said in 2001 that "if OPEC and non-OPEC countries carry out cuts, then I have the mandate to carry out cuts of 100,000 to 200,000 barrels a day."[75] However, this type of strategy has tremendous disadvantages. Unequal partners often find it difficult to reciprocate equally; contingencies may unexpectedly affect an actor's ability to reciprocate; and different interpretations and measurements can degenerate into situations of mutual recrimination. Much more valuable to states is an accumulated stock of "diffuse reciprocity." In situations where "the definition of [equivalent value] is less precise, one's partners may be viewed as a group rather than as particular actors, and the sequence of events as less narrowly bounded,"[76] diffuse reciprocity does not require that all aspects of a contract be specified ex ante. What it does require is that states make deposits at the "favor bank" when they can.[77] Over time, it is thought that this will allow states to accumulate trust and build stable expectations for future cooperative efforts.[78]

The need for diffuse reciprocity has been singled out by climate policy makers. Atiq Rahman argues that "The only way developing countries would feel comfortable getting into the system is through trust.... Once this happens I think the ice will break."[79] Former advisor to the Indonesian delegation, Agus Sari, has also argued that the U.S. decision to withdraw from Kyoto makes "rebuilding the climate of trust... imperative."[80]

However, some policy domains and interstate relationships are characterized by conditions of mutual suspicion and deep distrust, and under these circumstances, there is a real risk that even tit-for-tat reciprocity will never occur. To overcome this obstacle, states actively seeking the trust of others must send a costly signal of reassurance to disinterested or resistant parties.[81] Such signals "serve to separate the trustworthy types from the untrustworthy types; trustworthy types will send them, untrustworthy types will find them too risky to send."[82] This has special relevance for international environmental politics since states vary dramatically in terms of the stock of accumulated trust underpinning their cooperative efforts. Western states have a long history of cooperating across a wide range of policy arenas, so arriving at new self-enforcing contracts is relatively inexpensive. However, in a negotiating environment characterized by high levels of mistrust and power asymmetries, as is the case in North-South environmental relations, demandeurs must strategically manipulate the payoff structures of their would-be cooperators such that voluntary participation becomes economically rational.[83] In some cases, they must send special signals of reassurance (i.e., their trustworthiness) to skeptical parties that are discernible, irrevocable, noncontingent, and costly.[84] Rich nations, for example, may devise compensation schemes or promote issue linkage to account for LDCs' competing policy priorities and high discount rates.[85] In the case of the Montreal Protocol, developing countries refused to participate in "deep cooperation" with rich nations until the threat to trade sanctions was offset by positive incentives.[86]

Fourth and finally, states may seek to enhance conditions of mutual trust by evaluating other actors' expectations (and preferred strategies) ex ante and readjusting their own strategies in line with those expectations. This type of trust building tends to occur when there is a great deal of disparity between the goals of actors for a stable and effective solution.[87] This is relevant to North-South environmental politics because inequality leads to preference heterogeneity, and as Knack and Keefer explain, "in polarized societies, individuals are less likely to share common backgrounds and mutual expectations about behavior, so it is more difficult to make self-enforcing agreements."[88] Yet, having experienced the world from different vantage points, states in a highly polarized global community are likely to perceive morality, justice, progressive reform, and the costs and benefits of cooperation very differently.

Take for example the way in which countries experience and calculate the "costs" of climate change. As we mentioned earlier, rich nations tend to assess the cost of climate change in terms of dollars, while poor nations tend to view the costs through the prism of lives lost and livelihoods destroyed. Given these vast perceptional differences, one way for states seeking to enhance conditions of trust and prospects for cooperation with more reluctant parties is to voluntarily put themselves in the shoes of their potential cooperators to better understand the pros and cons of cooperation from their point of view. There are some initial indications that Western nations may be moving in this direction. Since the COP-6 in Bonn, Canada, Denmark, Finland, the Netherlands, Norway, Sweden, Germany, the United Kingdom, New Zealand, Switzerland, Portugal, and Iceland have set up three climate funds specifically for developing countries: one that seeks to cover the costs of adaptation, technology transfer, and greenhouse gas mitigation for all developing countries; a second that rewards countries that intend to ratify the Kyoto Protocol; and another that targets the least developed countries.[89]

It is also important that we not treat trust strictly in issue-specific terms. Ignoring the wider North-South trust deficit can lead to a remarkably thin empirical understanding of the relations governing interstate environmental negotiations. One of the more interesting points made by Gupta is that "[LDC] negotiators tend to see issues holistically and link the issue to all other international issues. Thus linkages are made to international debt, trade and other environmental issues such as desertification."[90] Students of global environmental politics have surely known this to be the case for quite some time, yet to our knowledge no one has sought to explain why we see this lack of generalized reciprocity and how this climate of mistrust influences negotiating strategies and cooperation outcomes. One possible explanation for this gap in the literature is that institutionalists have selected on the value of the dependent variable; that is, they have chosen to focus on those cases where meaningful, long-term cooperation has occurred, rather than concentrating on cases where cooperation was seriously encumbered by a lack of generalized trust (or some other factor).[91] Others may simply dismiss the lack of generalized trust as residual variance, something that matters only at the margin.

We do not find either of these arguments convincing. The standard narrative about trust and cooperation among rational-choice scholars is that rational individuals value trust for its instrumental worth. Therefore, people choose to trust only under certain conditions. However, this "strategic trust" narrative underestimates the importance of "moralistic trust." As Uslaner explains, "Trust in other people is based upon a fundamental *ethical* assumption: that other people share your fundamental values. They don't necessarily agree with you politically or religiously. But at some fundamental level, people accept the argument that they have common bonds that make cooperation vital. And these common bonds rest upon assumptions about human nature."[92] It is therefore imperative that we understand the broad contours of North-South environmental relations, changing patterns in contemporary global political economy, and the wider conditions of (mis)trust governing interactions between rich and poor nations.

At the first international conference on the global environment in 1972, it became clear very quickly that no consensus would emerge between developed and developing countries on issues of global environmental protection. Late developers feared restrictions on their economic growth, emphasized the West's profligate use of planetary resources, and pushed for a redistributive program that would help them make the transition toward growth and development.[93] Developed countries wanted Western consumption off the negotiating table, Southern population growth on the agenda, and nonbinding language on issues of financial assistance and technology transfer. From the outset, global environmental negotiations were characterized by high levels of preference heterogeneity and deep discord.[94] Neither group was willing to budge, and deeply held feelings of marginality and injustice among poor nations made for an adversarial negotiating atmosphere.

The South's confrontational attitude built to a crescendo in the late 1970s under the banner of the New International Economic Order. During this period, developing countries put forth a "series of proposals...which included significant wealth redistribution, greater LDC participation in the world economy, and greater Third World control over global institutions and resources."[95] While notable successes were achieved,[96] many of the hardest-fought victories were rolled back during the years of Thatcherism, Reaganism, and neoliberalism. In the NIEO's heyday, late developers also became strident in their criticism of Northern environmentalism, an environmentalism they perceived as "pull[ing] up the development ladder."[97] The North for the most part ignored these calls until the conflict came to a head during negotiations over the ozone layer in the late 1980s.

The Montreal Protocol was a landmark event in global environmental politics because it set a precedent of compensatory justice, which before then had existed only on the pages of lofty conference declarations.[98] It is important to note that it did not spontaneously emerge from a socially shared understanding of "appropriate" principles among nations, as the logic of social constructivism would suggest. Rather, developing nations bargained hard for the side payments—environmental aid, technical assistance, and technology transfer—that would help them comply with their negotiated obligations. China and India, in particular, sent clear and credible signals that they would not participate in an ozone regime without financial compensation.[99] One Chinese environmental protection agency spokesperson warned that "the call for modernization is so irresistible that China will continue to produce these ozone depleting chemicals."[100] Even more explicitly, he later went on the record as saying "[W]ithout the help of developed countries, China will continue to quickly expand the use of harmful chemicals."[101] India's environment minister, Maneka Gandhi, was equally clear about her country's position: "We didn't destroy the layer. You did. I'm saying that you [the West] have the capability and the money to restore what you have destroyed."[102] While the West eventually did cave in and sign onto a more redistributive Montreal Protocol, President George H. W. Bush made his support contingent upon the protocol not being used as a template for future environmental negotiations.[103] He used as plain words as possible to get the message across: "We do not have an open pocket-book."[104] In this regard, the United States clearly signaled its opposition to any recognition of compensatory justice as a generalized principle for future use.

However, in subsequent biodiversity, desertification, and climate change negotiations, calls for financial compensation and more equitable representation grew louder and more frequent.[105] Debate over the voting structure of the Global Environmental Facility (GEF), which distributes hundreds of millions of dollars of environmental aid each year, became especially conflict ridden. Poor and middle-income countries protested "donor dominance" and the lack of transparency in decision making, while rich, industrialized countries insisted that only the "incremental costs" of global environmental projects be financed.[106] Relations of trust deteriorated even further during the 1992 Rio Earth Summit.[107] As noted earlier, the South took a hard line, insisting that their coopera-tion be made contingent upon a "Rio bargain." The North initially seemed sympathetic, agreeing that a financial package of $100 billion a year in new and additional concessionary funds for "sustainable de-velopment" and $15 billion for global environmental issues would be necessary,[108] but ultimately failed to follow through on their policy commitments.[109]

The 1990s did not see an improvement in conditions of mutual trust. In fact, relations between North and South became more polarized, and the South's "bruised optimism" after Rio matured into a profound suspi-cion of the industrialized North.[110] At the COP-6, developing country delegations expressed outrage after the (Western) chairs allegedly deleted text that had been agreed upon earlier.[111] The G-77 and China also charged that many of the important decisions affecting developing coun-tries at The Hague (COP-6) were being made in nontransparent Green Room meetings, attended only by powerful nations. This set the stage for the 2002 World Summit on Sustainable Development (WSSD), where one reporter observed that "[T]he reservoir of mistrust and cynicism be-tween prosperous Northern nations and poor Southern ones has wid-ened since the last Earth Summit in Rio de Janeiro a decade ago."[112] Najam also commented that "effective governance is [im]possible under the prevailing conditions of deep distrust."[113]

The Washington Consensus, the Development Crisis, and Declining Trust

Returning to Gupta's point that poor nation "negotiators tend to see issues holistically and link the [climate] issue to all other international issues,"[114] we believe it is important to understand the wider context of mistrust plaguing North-South relations. The 1970s, 1980s, and 1990s were punctuated by seismic shifts in the rules governing the global political economy, and these changes in the external environment have made "late development" considerably more difficult than under the earlier Bretton Woods regime. The result of these changes has been characterized as "the decline of the development contract,"[115] the shift from a "development project" to a "globalization project,"[116] "the shrinking of development space,"[117] and "the new agenda of global integration."[118] However you label these changes, we believe they have had a nontrivial impact on levels of generalized trust between rich and poor nations and reduced the likelihood of "deep" North-South cooperation in matters of global environmental protection.[119]

Our argument is simple. When powerful states consistently treat weaker states like second-class citizens in areas where they possess structural power, they run the risk of weaker states "reciprocating" in policy domains where they possess more bargaining leverage. Since climate change is a problem that requires near-universal participation to solve, North-South negotiations have suffered this fate.

Explaining this erosion of trust requires a brief review of LDC goals and the degree to which they have been realized. This is critical to addressing climate change, but will take a few pages to explain. Briefly, the top Southern development policy objectives have been economic advancement and insulation from Northern opportunism. After World War II, relations between the global North and South were governed by a "development contract."[120] The main architects of the Bretton Woods institutions sought to balance the need for multilateralism, financial discipline, and social well-being. This is reflected in the IMF's original charter, which stated that the Fund would "facilitate the expansion and balanced growth of international trade and...contribute in this way to the promotion of a high level of employment and real income."[121] Such norms of "embedded liberalism" disallowed the IMF from "[opposing] any exchange rate change on the grounds that the social and political policies of the country led to the disequilibrium."[122] Another distinctive characteristic of this period was the widespread recognition that "late development" required infant industry protection and domestic resource mobilization. For nations to "upgrade" their comparative advantage, it was believed that states would have to serve as "surrogate entrepreneurs" by creating large, concentrated, and competitive firms; coordinating investment; and drumming up finance through savings, taxes, and tariffs.[123] For much of the 1950s, 1960s, and 1970s, this "development contract" seemed to be a huge success. Though we do not have reliable cross-national data on economic growth during the 1950s, we do know that from 1960 to 1979, developing countries registered annual median per capita income growth of 2.5 percent.[124]

The 1980s ushered in a period of sudden and spectacular changes in the global political economy of development. Following OPEC's decision to quadruple the price of oil in 1973, oil-rich nations with huge trade surpluses began investing their rents in Western commercial banks, forcing Wall Street bankers to scour the globe for new lending outlets. Neither developed nor developing countries could absorb such large sums of money in such a short period of time, so private financial institutions began lending recycled petrodollars with adjustable-rate loans that were given without proper consideration to borrower creditworthiness.[125] This followed President Nixon's 1971 decision to suspend the dollar's convertibility to gold, which sent global liquidity skyrocketing even further (since the United States could only finance their current account deficit with U.S. government debt securities, or IOUs).[126] Leaders in the South, suddenly flush with hard currency, made massive investments in development megaprojects and their militaries, paid off their enormous import bills (caused by the rise in oil prices), and indulged in a number of infamous personal expenditures.[127]

Then in 1979, OPEC again boosted oil prices and the United States contracted their money supply. This had the devastating effect of driving up international interest rates and leaving a large part of the developing world, which was holding variable interest rate loans, saddled with an oppressive debt burden. Needing new debts just to service their old debts, LDCs quickly found themselves begging at the doorsteps of international financial institutions. Fearing an entire collapse of the international banking system, rich nations provided funds through bilateral and multilateral channels, but conditioned disbursement on painful belt-tightening measures. In the early 1980s, most public lenders saw the debt crisis as a crisis of liquidity; therefore debtors were urged to pursue fiscal and monetary retrenchment. However, many countries, even those that avoided default, were unable to attract new capital flows and remained deeply mired in economic recession. Creditors soon began to think that what debtors faced was not a "crisis of liquidity," but a "crisis of solvency" requiring an overhaul or "restructuring" of the local economy. In response, U.S. Treasury Secretary James Baker spearheaded an effort to force "growth-oriented adjustment" on debtor countries, which meant that loans would be conditioned, not only on belt-tightening, but also on devaluation of the exchange rate, the privatization of state-owned enterprises, revisions to the tax code, liberalization of trade and financial markets, deregulation of foreign investment, and tighter monetary policies.[128]

The list of conditions attached to World Bank, IMF, Paris Club, and U.S. Treasury funds also came to represent a certain intellectual convergence in development economics and the wider development community, a convergence dubbed by one IFI economist as "The Washington Consensus."[129] According to this view, if countries could "get the prices right"—that is, if they allowed markets to freely express themselves by removing all "distortions" like government support for consumer goods and services and subsidies to "infant" industries—economic growth and development would naturally and spontaneously follow.

The Washington Consensus was a disastrous failure. Creditors neither paced nor sequenced reforms and largely ignored local conditions and institutions.[130] Austerity measures tore at the very social contract binding governor and governed and led to unprecedented social upheaval.[131] In some cases structural adjustment programs made countries poorer.[132] In Russia and Poland, "shock therapy" taught us that liberalization in the absence of strong financial institutions leads to massive unemployment, and that privatization without sound legal institutions is a perfect recipe for asset stripping, corruption, imperfect competition, and higher prices.[133] In East Asia, where countries have consistently performed well on the

World Bank's measures of sound macroeconomic policy, crushing financial blows were experienced as a result of liberalization of capital markets —a reform tirelessly promoted by IFIs and the West, more generally, during the 1990s. During this period (1980–1999), the developing world registered annual median per capita income growth of 0.0 percent.[134]

More telling still, countries that achieved consistently high, or even moderate, levels of economic growth throughout the 1980s and 1990s are now widely regarded as those that flouted the Washington Consensus. High-growth nations, such as China, India, South Korea, Taiwan, Mauritius, Botswana, Poland, Malaysia, and Vietnam, have all experimented with local institutional arrangements and pursued a mix of orthodox and heterodox economic policy reforms.[135] "[T]he set of policies which underlay the Washington Consensus," concludes Joseph Stiglitz, "are neither necessary nor sufficient, either for macro-stability or longer-term development."[136]

Stiglitz also points out that this empirical observation influences the causal and principled beliefs of developing countries and conditions of North-South trust. "[A]round the world," he explains, "anger at the traditional [Washington Consensus] policies is growing. The developing countries are saying to the industrialized nations: 'When you face a slowdown, you follow the precepts that we are all taught in our economic courses: You adopt expansionary monetary and fiscal policies. But when we face a slowdown, you insist on contractionary policies. For you, deficits are okay; for us, they are impermissible'.... A heightened sense of inequity prevails, partly because the consequences of maintaining contractionary policies are so great."[137]

The main goals of developing nations—economic growth, poverty reduction, and industrial transformation—have also proved elusive due to unfavorable changes in the global rules for multilateral trade, investment, and intellectual property rights. Poor nations have adamantly opposed these changes, but in matters of international political economy, there are "makers, breakers, and takers,"[138] to borrow a phrase from Stephen Krasner, and in all of these issue areas, most developing countries are takers. In a sense, the best that they can hope for is a rule-based system that reduces uncertainty and insulates them from the discretionary actions of the North.[139] However, their risk aversion presents a paradox because they actually "may become protagonists of institutions that disfavor them substantively."[140] "[T]he 'price' of multilateral rules," one author argues, "is that [LDCs] must accept rules written by—and usually for—the more developed countries."[141] Lloyd Gruber argues that powerful states, particularly those with large markets, possess "go-it-alone power" in that they can unilaterally eliminate the previous status quo and proceed gainfully with or without the participation of weaker parties. "Faced with a choice between joining the winners' new cooperative system or being completely shut out," writes Gruber, "the losers enthusiastically submit their applications for membership. They do so, however, only because the winners' actions have had the effect of removing the status quo from their choice sets, leaving them with what they view as a bad option (cooperating with the winners) and an even worse alternative (incurring the costs of exclusion)."[142]

The notion of go-it-alone power has many applications in North-South political economy, but perhaps the most fitting example comes from the so-called "Grand Bargain" at the end of the Uruguay Round trade negotiations in 1994.[143] From the outset, poor nations knew they were getting a bad deal, but it was a deal nonetheless, and as British economist Joan Robinson once said, "The only thing worse than being exploited . . . is to be exploited by no one at all."[144] In what came to be known as the Single Undertaking, rich nations agreed to provide poor nations with unprecedented market access (for mostly primary and low value-added products) and technical assistance, in exchange for lower tariffs and compliance with three new trade-related agreements: TRIMS, GATS, and TRIPS.[145] There is still an important debate over how voluntary this agreement actually was, but there is a general consensus that rich countries rewrote the rules of the game to their advantage.[146]

Under TRIMS, developing countries lost their ability to control many requirements they placed on multinational corporations: prohibiting the use of domestic content requirements, trade balancing, foreign exchange restrictions, and local procurement requirements for public agencies.[147] Previously, these had all served as tools for creating jobs and income, building local industrial capacity, encouraging export diversification, and moving up the value chain in the international division of labor.[148] East Asian countries, for example, required foreign investors to employ local labor and use local inputs as way to promote forward and backward linkages, build a trained workforce, and create a more resilient, internally articulated economy.[149]

The introduction of GATS further weakened the ability of states to protect their service sectors. The agreement was drafted to include private goods such as tourism and financial services, but also public goods such as health care, education, and water and sanitation. Countries were required to provide a "positive list" of sectors they were willing to protect—as opposed to a "negative list" that left any sector not specified as "protected"—and allow foreign firms to compete with every other service sector. Again, this agreement represents a significant encroachment into the "domestic policy space" of countries.[150]

Finally, the TRIPS agreement placed restrictions on the ability of states to refuse patents for certain products, standardized the period of patent coverage at twenty years, limited third-party access to patented products, clamped down on the use of compulsory licensing, and made non-compliance punishable through the WTO's dispute resolution mechanism (DSM).[151] The strategic use of patents has historically played an instrumental role in late development.[152] East Asian countries, such as Korea and Taiwan, successfully upgraded their industrial capacity by allowing local entrepreneurs to reverse engineer and imitate foreign technologies under patent protection in order to encourage domestic innovation, knowledge diffusion, and technology transfer. It is also important to note that almost every other Western country also did the same during the early stages of their own development.[153]

Notwithstanding their dubious effect on development, TRIMS, TRIPS, and GATS are extremely costly for poor countries to implement. It is estimated that it "costs a typical developing country $150 million to implement requirements under just three of the WTO agreements (those on customs valuation, sanitary and phytosanitary measures [SPS], and intellectual property rights [TRIPs]),... which is a sum equal to a year's development budget for many of the least-developed countries."[154] Yet, "[f]or the advanced countries whose systems are [already] compatible with international conventions (or vice versa) the WTO brings no more than an obligation to apply their *domestic regulations*... at the border."[155]

Deteriorating conditions of mutual trust are also attributable to the unraveling of the "Grand Bargain." After years of crusading for a comprehensive North-South trade regime that would cover investment, services, and intellectual property rights, rich nations ultimately failed to hold up their end of the bargain. They reneged on their commitment to expand market access for developing country goods and services and failed to keep earlier promises to scale up technical assistance.[156] Making matters worse, developing countries find themselves at a comparative disadvantage under the WTO's new dispute settlement mechanism. The DSM represents a move toward a more rule-based trading system, which just about everyone assumes is a good thing, but as Busch and Reinhardt point out, "the new premium on legal capacity...[makes litigation] less burdensome for most of the advanced industrial states, which generally maintain large, dedicated, permanent legal and economic staffs tasked with WTO and trade law matters....But for poorer countries, such a move simply substitutes (or compounds) the traditional source of weakness—namely, the lack of market size and thus retaliatory power—with a new one: legal capacity."[157]

Finally, a series of events in international monetary relations has also contributed to the growing trust deficit between rich and poor nations. Here again, the rules seem to have been written to the advantage of rich nations (especially the United States) and to the detriment of poor countries. Much like the "development contract" of the 1950s and 1960s, international monetary relations prior to the mid-1970s were governed by a set of norms that leveled the playing field between rich and poor nations. From the late nineteenth century onward, gold served as the anchor of the international monetary system. By providing a store of value and a medium of exchange that no one nation could manipulate to its own advantage, it functioned as a self-adjusting mechanism from which every nation could benefit. Countries running trade deficits—importing more than exporting and therefore paying out gold reserves—would eventually induce a contraction in domestic credit, which would in turn push prices down and trade competitiveness up. Lower export prices would then pull gold reserves back into the central bank's coffers as national exporters deposited their earnings, restoring balance to the current account. Countries running trade surpluses would experience the opposite process. The "Gold Standard" had certain weaknesses, in particular the inability to prevent devaluation of competitive currencies, but its underlying logic of self-correction remained intact even through the Bretton Woods era. Fixed exchange rates were again established during the post-World War II monetary regime to keep countries out of perpetual external imbalance, but the U.S. dollar became the anchor currency. The idea was that countries would hold dollars and the U.S. Federal Reserve would stand ready to change those reserve dollars into gold.

However, during the late 1960s and early 1970s, the United States began to consume much more than it was selling internationally; U.S. multinationals began investing significant amounts of money abroad; and the government was financing an expensive war in Vietnam. In so doing, the United States accumulated a tremendous external deficit, and countries holding dollar surpluses began to request gold. As the flow of gold hemorrhaged out of the Federal Reserve, the dollar experienced a rapid decline in confidence, which in turn encouraged further withdrawals. Fearing a massive recession in the United States or even a collapse in the international monetary system, in 1971 President Nixon suspended the dollar's convertibility to gold. This ushered in a new monetary system—what has been called the "Dollar Standard."[158] Under this new regime, the logic of self-adjustment ceased to exist for the United States. Freed from the "gold restraint," the United States began to finance its current account deficit by issuing debt denominated in its own currency; in other words, by printing U.S. Treasury bills (or IOUs). This exemption from the "debtor's curse" essentially freed the U.S. government from the balance-of-payment constraints faced by other countries.[159]

The shift to the Dollar Standard after 1971 also had far-reaching implications for developing countries. The creation of excessive liquidity has generated unprecedented levels of domestic financial fragility in the South and led to more frequent and more dangerous financial crises. During the 1990s, the composition of financial flows to the developing world shifted away from commercial bank loans and toward portfolio investments.[160] The rise of bonds and equity instruments, which both have deep secondary markets, push and pull capital flows in and out of emerging markets much faster and in much larger amounts than ever before, and can leave LDCs in financial ruin literally overnight when investor sentiment shifts.[161] "Hot money" wreaks tremendous havoc when states lack the capital controls necessary to dampen euphoric expectations and prevent investor herding behavior. In the case of the Asian financial crisis, "countries which had largely kept their capital controls were protected from the...attacks which followed: China, Taiwan, Vietnam and India. Those that had liberalized in the key areas found their macroeconomic management failures exploited by devastating speculative attacks. And even Hong Kong, which could not have been said to have had serious macroeconomic problems but did have a liberalized capital account, was to be subjected to sustained, repeated hedge fund assaults for more than a year."[162] Yet throughout the 1990s, and even during financial crises, the U.S. Treasury, IMF, and Wall Street crusaded single-mindedly for liberalization of capital markets in the developing world.[163] When the World Bank and IMF's recommendations to reduce government influence on the economy did not work, rich countries turned to "the threat of sanctions or . . . [withheld] needed assistance in a time of crisis."[164]

The Spillover: How the Development Crisis Breeds Mistrust in Climate Negotiations

To summarize, when one looks at North-South relations holistically, it becomes much clearer why conditions of trust are declining. The "development contract" governing North-South interactions prior to 1980 has all but disappeared;[165] the Washington Consensus has proven a spectacular failure; the Grand Bargain has unraveled; the Dollar Standard has shifted the burden of adjusting to the creation of excessive liquidity onto the developing world; and on many occasions powerful regime makers have imposed their will on weaker, regime-taking, developing countries to achieve short-term economic gains.

Yet interestingly, while developing countries have little influence over the substance of these development issues, they do possess unprecedented leverage in global environmental politics, and thirty years of environmental negotiations show that they will use this leverage when they can. We therefore must not rule out the possibility that coercive or "go-it-alone" power in certain (highly valued) issue areas will have negative spillovers in other policy areas. In fact, our reading of the evidence is that Northern callousness and opportunism has for three precious decades eroded conditions of generalized trust and dampened the South's enthusiasm for participating in global environmental solutions.

Casual observation supports this link between generalized mistrust and unwillingness to participate in global environmental institutions. At the World Summit on Sustainable Development in Johannesburg in 2002, LDC leaders repeatedly linked issues of political economy to their willingness to cooperate on environmental matters. Tewolde Berhan Gebre Egziabher, head of the Ethiopian Environmental Protection Authority, for example, noted that "There is a greater distance between the North and the South now.... Rio actually brought us together.... [But] now we've seen the creation of institutions like the [World Trade Organization], and we've had international trade talks, and the trends clearly show it is the rich who have benefited from them, not the poor."[166] In the run-up to the WSSD, the European Union's (EU) environment minister, Margot Wallstrom, also acknowledged that Northern agricultural protectionism was breeding a considerable amount of mistrust among poor nations. "A lot of the tensions in Johannesburg," she explained, "will be about the lack of trust from the developing countries in our ability to actually implement what we are saying and to be serious about our own objectives and targets."[167]

There are those who remain cynical about negotiating multiple issues simultaneously and tying development issues to environmental cooperation. Former U.S. environmental treaty negotiator Richard Benedick sees all of this talk about a North-South trust deficit as distracting and unhelpful—nothing more than the bluff and bluster of politicians. Revealingly, he describes himself in a 2001 article as being mystified as to why rich nations would ever include developing countries in the Kyoto Protocol's monitoring and compliance system. "A major and dubious concession to the South," he writes, "was an agreement to grant developing nations, who have no commitments, a decisive role in the protocol's compliance system, assessing and enforcing the commitments of industrialized countries."[168] His comments in many ways resonate with the rational-choice models that assume away issue spillover, generalized mistrust, and weak conditions of diffuse reciprocity. We would argue that Benedick, like many rational-choice theorists, focuses so much of his attention on individual trees that he loses sight of the larger forest.[169] It does not occur to him that rich nations may need to rebuild conditions of trust with poor nations before asking them to make costly policy commitments.[170]

Trust, sincerity, and diffuse reciprocity, we argue, can only be sustained by principled, consistent behavior. By contrast, current North-South relations are characterized by mutual suspicion, zero- and negative-sum attitudes, and what Robert Wade calls "a-bit-better-than-the-jungle-morality."[171] Many poor nations, convinced that they have been bamboozled in global environmental negotiations and a series of issues related to trade, debt, investment, intellectual property rights, and finance, are in our judgment guarding themselves against what they see as further Northern opportunism.[172]

As a result of this growing trust deficit, North-South expectations have failed to converge around a stable set of mutually acceptable principles, norms, rules, and decision-making procedures. Instead, what we see are informal, ad hoc, extra-legal rules that leave plenty of room for selective interpretation, shirking, and opportunism. This aversion toward legalization poses a number of serious problems that impede cooperation.[173] First, informal rules tend to increase the costs of transacting because they force parties to constantly renegotiate standards of behavior "according to new, untested criteria."[174] Second, informal rules decrease the credibility of state commitments and make enforcement more costly since they create space for states to interpret the law in self-serving, opportunistic ways.[175] Hard law "allows allegations and defenses to be tested under accepted standards and procedures." Soft law, by comparison, puts implementation failure and defection in the eye of the beholder.[176] Ambiguous and unstable rules also promote mutual suspicion because they make it more difficult for parties to determine who can and cannot be trusted. Recent work in domestic politics suggests that "[t]he more universal, uncorrupted and impartial the government institutions responsible for the implementation of laws and policies are, the more social capital you will get."[177] The same is probably true in international politics.[178] In short, conditions of generalized reciprocity and trust require stable expectations, and informal rules do less to advance this cause than formal rules.

Having examined the larger external environment in which North-South environmental negotiations are enmeshed, we now return to the issue of climate change, which threatens to reinforce, if not exacerbate, current patterns of global inequality. As we document in the coming chapters, some LDCs will suffer the effects of climate change worst and first, enjoy fewer economic benefits because of the disproportionate amount of environmental space expropriated by rich nations, be asked to forgo significant amounts of "cheap" economic growth, and shoulder relatively larger implementation costs. In light of these compounding inequalities, we argue that developing countries are highly averse toward cooperative equilibria that will mothball existing asymmetries and are unlikely to seriously consider proposals that offer absolute gains but ignore distributional concerns. Global inequality no doubt has strong direct effects on the prospects for cooperation, but we argue that the indirect effect of inequality on trust is considerably more potent.[179] This basic insight reinforces the need for long-term, incremental trust-building efforts.

Thinking Post-2012: Inequality, Fairness, and Getting to Full Participation in a Climate Treaty

The ratification of the Kyoto Protocol by the Russian Duma in November 2004 led to its going into effect in February 2005, less than three years before the beginning of the deadline by which nations would have to meet their reduction goals from the 1990 baseline year. This is a daunting prospect; growing economies now face double-digit reductions in emissions in just a few years. As the five-year (2008 to 2012) averaging period ends, nations such as China (soon to be the world's largest emitter) that have no commitments to reduce their emissions, will still have no binding limits on their carbon-dioxide emissions. Kyoto's limited scope has prompted much thinking about ways to bring developing nations on board, although many nations are extremely hesitant to even discuss post-2012 cooperation. One proposal under consideration is that policy makers should explicitly address the principled beliefs of developing countries.[180]

Cynical analysts suggest that "[e]quity is merely a word that hypocritical people use to cloak self-interest."[181] David Victor writes that "for most states most of the time, the decision-making process is mainly a selfish one. Consequently, there exists very little evidence that fairness exerts a strong influence on international policy decisions."[182] This position cannot not be dismissed out of hand. Members of the Alliance of Small Island States, which probably are feeling the effects of climate change earliest and most profoundly, have pushed forcefully for early action on climate change.[183] OPEC countries, by contrast, stand to lose considerably in the short term (and perhaps the medium term) from reductions in fossil fuel use and have demonstrated high levels of resistance to carbon reduction commitments. Australia and the United States, both of which have strong fossil fuel lobbies, have also opposed Kyoto. Then there are the "emissions entrepreneurs," states in which mitigation projects are already under way to gain some of the potential investments from trading carbon permits or technology transfer.[184] These nations have been very savvy about turning emissions trading programs and reforestation and preservation projects into opportunities for financial redistribution. Students of environmental treaty signing and ratification have described these broad patterns as groupings of "leaders and laggards,"[185] or in the case of the Kyoto, "greenhouse skeptics and greenhouse entrepreneurs."[186] At a descriptive level, such patterns suggest that states base their behavior on material self-interest.[187]

However, theories that assume rational, egoistic actors are unable to account for an important empirical anomaly: Almost all developing countries, including those with intense and weak preferences for climate stability, have resisted scheduled commitments for future emission reductions in the name of fairness.[188] It is of course possible that much of this is rhetoric and fairness is in fact a codeword for self-interest, as some have suggested.[189] However, we argue that under certain circumstances principled beliefs do indeed affect the form, frequency, timing, substance, and depth of international environmental cooperation.

The idea that "fairness matters" has gained currency among some policy makers and scholars familiar with climate negotiations; however, we still lack a solid understanding of how fairness can matter and under what conditions. For this, it is worth assessing models of game theory, whose assumptions may not capture the complexity of decision making in the real world, but can be useful because of their parsimony. Game-theoretic models simplify the complex social world by paying attention to the most important elements of cooperation games—namely, strategic interactions among rational, self-interested unitary actors with fixed, transitive preferences. Economists and political scientists have developed a number of metaphors that claim to explain the underprovision of public goods. Garrett Hardin's "Tragedy of the Commons," Mancur Olson's *Logic of Collective Action*, and Robert Axelrod's "Prisoner's Dilemma" all yield the same basic prediction: Actors lacking the ability to make a credible commitment to a particular policy adjustment face strong incentives to free ride.[190] Knowing this, each actor anticipates the defection of every other actor. According to the standard noncooperative game-theoretic storyline, rather than accepting a "sucker's payoff," rational actors, conscious of their partners' payoff structures, will choose not to cooperate. Hence, in the absence of a Leviathan that enforces contracts and coerces trust, international agreements must be self-enforcing. Stated differently, contracts must be structured so that no sufficiently important country stands to lose by participating, and no country stands to gain by not participating.[191]

This is no easy task. Global public goods require the participation of many players as well as costly information about the players' past behavior and future intentions. As the number of players increases, the intensity of preferences for environmental protection often declines, pushing international agreements toward a least common denominator.[192] Potential cooperators must also be assured that other players are abiding by the negotiated rules; without reliable information, this is almost impossible.[193] Finally, since states must make decisions in the presence of uncertainty, it is important that they make institutions robust enough to withstand unforeseen, exogenous shocks.[194]

These issues, as well as a number of others, make fairness considerations especially important when crafting self-enforcing international agreements. Climate negotiations illustrate this better than almost any other environmental issue. Since no state can force another to sign or ratify an agreement, and the large number of parties necessary for an effective climate treaty are highly heterogeneous in terms of both preferences and capabilities, states that are eager to stabilize the global climate have virtually no other option, short of economic and military warfare, than to strategically manipulate the incentives facing more reluctant parties. As we saw with the case of the Montreal Protocol, this often means paying special attention to the long-term interests of poor nations.[195] However, here's the problem: Poor nations may possess strong fairness preferences. Here we briefly explore three ways in which Southern utility functions may be at variance with the standard assumptions of economic theory. We integrate these insights with more conventional arguments about principled beliefs that do not require relaxed assumptions.

First, poor nations may forfeit absolute gains for the sake of maximizing their power relative to rich, industrialized nations. The ongoing development crisis, the decline of the development contract, the failure of the Washington Consensus, and the perceived disingenuousness of Northern intentions have shaped poor nations' worldviews, causal beliefs, and self-perceptions; reinforced enduring assumptions about Northern opportunism and callousness; and contributed to an erosion of generalized reciprocity and mutual trust.

Second, poor nations may hold certain fairness preferences that can only be explained by socially shared norms of what is "right," "fair," or "legitimate." For example, one of the founding principles of international relations, outlined in the Charter of the United Nations (Article 2.1), is the right of sovereign states to be free from outside interference. Every developed country publicly advocates this principle, yet as we will see in chapters 3 and 4, poor nations appear to be suffering from the increased frequency and intensity of climate change-related disasters due to profligate use of natural resources in the industrialized world. Some say that the threat to nations and cultures has become an ethnicide that approaches genocide.[196] The Universal Declaration of Human Rights, a document championed by Western nations, also states that "everyone has the right to a nationality," and "no one shall be arbitrarily deprived of his [sic] property."[197] What motivates Southern preferences for fair outcomes may therefore be nothing more than a desire for a stable and predictable rule-based system that treats all nations equally.[198]

Third, poor nations may base their behavior on what they perceive to be fair because of emotions. The role of emotion in decision making has gotten little attention theoretically, but the empirical reality is that poor nations have a lot to be angry, envious, and spiteful about. They feel snubbed in matters of trade, investment, debt, aid, finance, and intellectual property rights. Many of the environmental problems of most concern to them have been ignored by rich nations, and they are routinely marginalized in global environmental negotiations.[199] It is therefore not surprising that they often thumb their noses at the West when they are asked to limit their development in order to promote First World global environmental issues.

Our argument, to summarize, is that the global economic system, the history of global environmental politics, and the three central issues of climate change—vulnerability, responsibility, and mitigation—have a profound impact on how developing countries perceive the fairness of proposed solutions and the prospects for meaningful North-South cooperation. At the same time, fairness does not always matter, and developing countries hardly have a monopoly on what constitutes a fair deal. Definitions of fairness are highly elastic, and countries frequently manipulate definitions for their own narrow advantage. Furthermore, there are strong constraints on where, when, and how "fairness" may affect international bargaining, monitoring, and enforcement outcomes.[200] We attempt to identify some of these conditions. National perceptions of fairness, we argue, affect state behavior and international policy outputs and outcomes by either increasing or decreasing the costs of negotiating, monitoring, and enforcing agreements.

First, norms and principles of fairness, embodied in institutions, can reduce the costs of negotiating international agreements. It is now widely held that institutions are more than the epiphenomena suggested by realist and neo-Marxian scholars.[201] By providing information and lowering transaction costs, mutually acceptable "rules of the game" are said to reduce uncertainty, stabilize expectations, constrain opportunism, increase the credibility of state commitments, and promote collective action.[202] For example, in coordination dilemmas, where multiple equilibria exist along the Pareto frontier, establishing shared principles, norms, rules, and decision-making procedures can enable states to zero in on a limited range of possible equilibria and enhance their prospects for cooperation.[203] Shared understandings of fairness therefore provide what game theorists call "focal points." By isolating one point along the contract curve that every party would prefer over a noncooperative outcome, states can stabilize expectations for future behavior and reduce the costs of arriving at a mutually acceptable agreement.[204] However, there are often huge differences in perceptions of what is fair, so for cooperation to occur, states often need to be explicit in identifying potential focal points. Mutually acceptable focal points are most likely to emerge when states are willing to reconsider and negotiate their own beliefs about what is fair.[205]

In collaboration games, where states have mixed motives for cooperation and face powerful free-rider incentives, fairness principles may also affect the costs of monitoring and enforcing agreements.[206] Every state faces a strong temptation to free ride on others' climate stabilization efforts in collaboration dilemmas because asymmetric information reduces the observability of deviant behavior, and the benefits of a stable climate are nonexcludable and nonrival. Thus, it is in every state's self-interest to disguise their preferences and misrepresent their level of contribution to the collective good. For these reasons, demandeurs may address concerns about fairness by making compliance economically rational for more reluctant nations through financial compensation schemes, issue linkage, and other forms of incentive restructuring.[207] This can significantly weaken incentives for cheating and defection. Argentine Ambassador Raúl Estrada-Oyuela has said that "equity is the fundamental condition to ensure compliance of any international agreement."[208]

In addition, norms and principles of fairness can help cement a collaborative equilibrium and reduce monitoring and enforcement costs through their impact on the domestic ratification process. Benito Müller lays much emphasis on this point: "[A skeptic] might...concede that equity has a role to play in the selection of *initial* allocation proposals. But surely, he is bound to interject, the *outcome* of the negotiations will be determined by good old-fashioned strategic bargaining, reflecting only the bargaining powers of the parties and the bargaining skills of the negotiators. [What the skeptic has overlooked is that] an agreement has to be implemented. This, in turn, requires political ratification which normally is beyond the power of mere negotiating agents." He bluntly states that "It would be foolish to assume...that bodies such as the U.S. Congress or the Indian Lok Sabha could be...bullied into *ratifying* an agreement [because] parties may refuse to ratify an agreement if they feel it deviates unacceptably from what *they* perceive to be the just solution."[209] After the Kyoto Protocol negotiations came to a close, former IPCC chair Robert Watson pointed out that "the ultimate success [of Kyoto] depends on whether national governments can sell it back home to the parliaments and lawmakers."[210] At the same time, an internationally agreeable fairness principle may be flatly rejected by domestic audiences. This point is explored in chapter 5.

Institutions do not only have efficiency implications; they also have distributional consequences. Norms and principles of fairness therefore also influence the costs of bargaining.[211] Developing countries are particularly sensitive to distributional concerns because of their structural vulnerability to changes in the international system.[212] As one author explains, the South, "as a self-professed collective of the weak...is inherently risk-averse and seeks to minimize its losses rather than to maximize its gains;...its unity is based on a sense of shared vulnerability and a shared distrust of the prevailing world order . . . [and] because of its self-perception of weakness [it] has very low expectations."[213] Stated differently, to prevent power asymmetries from widening and to insulate themselves from Northern opportunism, developing countries may seek relative gains, rather than absolute gains.[214] A number of international relations scholars therefore suggest that efforts to close the distributional gap can induce a Pareto improvement by reducing the costs of bargaining.[215]

In the study of international environmental politics, "social" preferences, the nonmaterial components of players' incentive structures, are rarely recognized as important causal variables affecting state behavior and cooperative outcomes.[216] However, economists have recently cast their theoretical and empirical spotlights on the idea that "if somebody is nice to you, fairness dictates that you be nice to him. If somebody is being mean to you, fairness allows—and vindictiveness dictates—that you be mean to him."[217] Fehr and Gachter, for example, find from experimental evidence that sanctioners continue to punish defectors even when this entails a personal utility loss.[218] Scott Barrett, an environmental economist at Johns Hopkins University, suggests that fairness is no less important in international relations.[219] He argues that states possess social, or fairness, preferences, which dictate that "all countries should play their part—that the equilibrium for symmetric players should itself be symmetric."[220]

Do these claims survive serious scrutiny? Can we assume that states behave the same way ordinary people do? The extant literature has not seriously wrestled with this question; however, a small number of scholars have suggested that emotions play a nontrivial role in institutional bargaining.[221] Take for example a passage from Oran Young's 1994 publication, *International Governance*: "Some [N]ortherners may doubt the credibility of [threats from Southern nations to damage the global climate] and advocate a bargaining strategy that offers few concessions to the developing countries. But such a strategy is exceedingly risky. Many of those located in developing countries are increasingly *angry* and *desperate*. . . . Faced with this prospect, [N]ortherners will ignore the demands of the South regarding climate change at their peril."[222] The implication here is that some nations sometimes act out of envy, spite, or some other emotion, rather than material self-interest.[223] Adil

Najam also explores how feelings of marginalization, frustration, anger, bitterness, and hopelessness have affected bargaining positions held by developing countries, and explains that retaliatory—or "getting even"—attitudes frequently lead to zero-sum outcomes.[224]

In this chapter we have tried to explain the various ways in which trust between the global North and South has reached a low ebb, and how this has made arriving at a meaningful climate treaty only a dim possibility. Even as we complete this book, the Kyoto Protocol is in effect, but its future is uncertain beyond 2012. Our point is this: Without addressing the economic and social needs of developing countries, Kyoto is going nowhere. The next two chapters examine the impacts that Southern nations are already facing from climate-related disasters, using both qualitative and quantitative approaches. Below the proximate causes cited by scholars and journalists, we again argue, lies an ongoing development crisis. This suggests that efforts to provide "relief" and "adaptation assistance" will only address short-term problems. Rather, aid to address climate change needs to be reoriented and combined with much more favorable trade, debt, investment, finance, and intellectual property rights policies that promote transformational development.

3

Not the Day after Tomorrow: Learning from Recent Climate Disasters

Same Hurricanes, Different Outcomes

For the first time in anyone's memory, in August and September 2004, four major hurricanes ripped through the Caribbean and threatened its island nations and the coastal areas of Florida in the United States. Charley, Frances, Ivan, and Jeanne each took a devastating toll, inflicting billions of dollars in damage to property and killing scores. Hurricane Charley was the worst in the United States, killing more than a dozen Americans. When Jeanne came ashore in the United States on September 25, its category 3 winds made many homeless but killed only a few.

By contrast, the same storm killed more than 1,500 people in Haiti a week earlier. Hurricane Jeanne dropped rain for thirty hours on a nation that is 98 percent deforested, where deep ravines cut to the bedrock on mountainsides once green with rain forests.[1] The water ran down unprotected mountainsides into four rivers, which innundated the city of Goncaives with mud, sewage, and carcasses. Rice and fruit harvests were destroyed, and diseases began to spread. To make a more cautious comparison than Haiti with Florida, the other half of Haiti's island is occupied by the Dominican Republic, less poor and not nearly as deforested. There, Jeanne killed only about twenty-five people.[2]

The lessons are instructive. We can plant 60 million trees, as the U.S. Agency for International Development (USAID) has done in Haiti over the past twenty years, but when poor people remove them at a rate of 10–20 million trees a year to make charcoal, the effort can be for naught.[3] The roots of the desperation that lead the poor to deforest must therefore be addressed. As Haitian ecologist Jean-Andre Victor said immediately after Jeanne's devastating impact, "The situation will continue, and other catastrophes are foreseeable."[4] We therefore focus on the fundamental causes of suffering from climate-related disasters in this chapter because they point us to the roots of problems that must be addressed before the problems will go away.

A growing number of geographers, economists, political scientists, and sociologists are pioneering a new literature on disaster, risk, and vulnerability to better understand who is most vulnerable to natural disasters and why.[5] Piers Blaikie and his colleagues define vulnerability as "the characteristics of a person or group in terms of their capacity to anticipate, cope with, resist, and recover from the impact of a natural hazard."[6] They argue that vulnerability is tied to a complex web of geographic, economic, social, institutional, political, and environmental factors.

In this chapter, we take two very different approaches that seek to explain why some have suffered so much more than others from climate disasters. In the first half of the chapter, we examine broad patterns in climate disasters over the last two decades and develop three cross-national indicators of impact on human populations. In the second half, we describe three climate disasters in detail and trace their proximate and deeper social and historical determinants: Hurricane Mitch in Honduras, a succession of floods in Mozambique in early 2000, and sea level rise and flooding in the Pacific atoll island of Tuvalu. We could have chosen any number of disasters and made the same points, such as drought in Brazil's Northeast, Bangladesh's lowland flooding, and so on. The case of Hurricane Mitch in Honduras bears some similarities to the Haiti disaster of 2004, with more than 10,000 people dying and 2.5 million needing disaster relief. Terrible flooding in Mozambique in early 2000 led to the deaths of 700 people, but preparation and international assistance helped rescue 45,000 people and prevented malnutrition and epidemics. In the case of Tuvalu, the impending destruction of a whole nation and people by flooding from a rising sea opens a series of lines for discussion in future chapters. While we mean these examples to be suggestive and brief, we believe that the patterns that emerge paint a coherent, nuanced, and tragic picture.

Finding Patterns in Climate-Related Disasters: Counting the People Lost, Homeless, and Affected

Natural disasters may seem to have an underlying random origin, but their impacts are anything but random. As will become plain by the end of this section, the same nations again and again are among those who suffer the most from climate-related disasters. We begin with totals of the number of people killed by major hydrometeorological disasters: windstorms, droughts, floods, and heat waves.

To examine more systematically who stands to lose most from global climate change, we have catalogued all climate-related natural disasters between 1980 and 2002. Using raw disaster data compiled by the U.S. Office of Foreign Disaster Assistance (OFDA) and the Centre for Research on the Epidemiology of Disasters (CRED) in the Emergency Events database (available at http://www.cred.be/emdat/), we have developed three separate cross-national measures of climate risk.[7]

Previous disaster research has emphasized the economic costs associated with climate change. However, using estimates of monetary damage as a proxy for climate-related risk is highly misleading because it systematically underestimates the real economic costs borne by developing countries. Income-dependent measures make poor people and poor nations —whose wealth is often not captured in measures of income—appear as though they are suffering smaller economic losses than they actually are.[8]

By contrast, in this chapter we focus on real human suffering: the number of people killed, made homeless, or otherwise affected by climate-related disasters. Economic costs no doubt figure prominently in the decision-making calculus of some countries as they weigh the pros and the cons of taking action to protect the climate. However, in our view, a more appropriate way of measuring climate-related losses (and the "costs" of climate change as perceived by many nations) is to tally the number of people killed, made homeless, or otherwise affected by climate-related disasters in individual countries.[9] This method levels the playing field by focusing on those who will endure the greatest hardship—such as those who die or become homeless (two of the most costly outcomes one can imagine)—rather than those who will simply forfeit luxury consumption (e.g., beachfront property).

Our measures certainly have flaws,[10] but we believe they are reasonably accurate indicators of the short- and medium-term risks associated with climate change. Perhaps more important, they provide a unique opportunity to systematically evaluate many of the nagging questions that continue to plague the extant literature on climate vulnerability, risk, and disaster: Are the human effects of hydrometeorological hazards largely driven by preexisting vulnerabilities or by the natural strength of "acts of God"? If vulnerability does matter, what matters most— geographic, economic, social, environmental, or institutional vulnerability? Is vulnerability to climate change highly context specific, or can empirical regularities be identified in the cross-national data? Are certain regions of the world predisposed toward higher levels of climate risk than others? More to the point, who has already suffered from climate disasters worst and first, and which human populations are likely to suffer most in the future? Virtually none of these questions can be addressed without reliable cross-national measures of hydrometeorological risk.

To construct our dependent variable, we rely exclusively on what we call climate-related disasters. Global climate change has arguably contributed to the sharp increase in hydrometeorological disasters since 1980, but it would be impossible to attribute any direct causality between global warming and individual hydrometeorological events. Still, by isolating all disasters between 1980 and 2002 related to the climate, we can create reliable measures of those countries already suffering repeated and severe human disasters that are due to hydrometeorological events. Since the Emergency Events Database encompasses a wide variety of human disasters between 1900 and 2002 (12,800 in all), the first step was to separate out all of the technological disasters, geophysical disasters, epidemics, forest and scrub fires, and famines.[11] Technological disasters include such events as chemical spills, building collapses, explosions, radiation and gas leaks, industrial fires, poisonings, and industrial transportation accidents. Geophysical disasters include earthquakes, volcanic eruptions, avalanches, and landslides. In almost all of these cases, the trigger for disaster was unrelated to the climate and therefore eliminated. Epidemics, forest fires, scrub fires, and famines are more problematic since the weather may influence any one of these events.[12] However, since the causal role of climate is either distant or absent in the majority of these cases, we decided to filter these types of natural disasters out of the dataset.

Having pared down our population of cases to 6,024 extreme weather events over the period 1900–2002, we then assessed the longitudinal reliability of the data. Coverage on the number of people killed, made homeless, or otherwise affected seemed to be much more systematically reported after 1970. However, we chose to limit our sample to hydrometeorological disasters between 1980 and 2002 because of the period's special significance in the "anthropocene," and because the data are more reliable.[13]

This final procedure left us with more than 4,000 cyclones, droughts, floods, heat waves, hurricanes, tidal waves, tornadoes, tropical storms, typhoons, winter storms, hailstorms, dust storms, rainstorms, thunderstorms, and cold waves. Using this set of cases, we created three separate cross-national tallies of the number of people killed, made homeless, or otherwise affected by climate-related disasters during the period 1980–2002. To smooth out the "lumpiness" in the data, we created a single total for each nation for each indicator covering the entire time series. Rather than explaining individual weather events, our goal is to understand why some countries (and human populations) suffer chronically and profoundly from extreme weather, while others are persistently resilient to human disaster.[14] This "smoothing" procedure is important because it eliminates much of the year-to-year randomness associated with the weather and allows us to identify those countries that repeatedly experience weather-related human disasters.[15] Each of these indicators was then adjusted by the size of each nation's population to reflect the relative significance of the final fatality, homeless, and affected tallies. These dependent variables were also logarithmically transformed to render their distributions less skewed.

Finally, we created a second version of each indicator that included only non-zero values in order to determine whether there are issues of selection bias. Why might some countries be missing data in nonrandom ways? Why do we observe underreporting? There are several possible reasons, and we cannot correct for them without introducing potentially new sources of bias into the data. They include repression, lack of press freedom, and the invisibility of rural disasters to an urban-based media and political machinery.[16] We take up these issues in chapter 4.

The Toll of Two Decades of Climate-Related Disasters

Table 3.1 shows that the global South—poor nations in Asia, Africa, and Central America—repeatedly tops the list of the nations with the most deaths from these disasters. The worst human disaster in the last two decades of the twentieth century was East Africa's 1984 drought, which killed nearly half a million people in Ethiopia, Sudan, Chad, and other nations. The case of Ethiopia gained worldwide attention as desperation and death took an estimated 300,000 people. Political control, warfare, and the manipulation of aid worsened a severe drought in the Wollo, Tigray, Eritrea, Shoa, Gonder, Harerge, and Sidamo provinces. The U.S. government's Office of U.S. Foreign Disaster Assistance, which coordinates U.S. foreign humanitarian assistance, reported that there was "no reliable figure for number of killed, [but] estimates ranged between 250,000 and 1 million."[17] Ethiopian Prime Minister Meles Zenawi has said that the disaster killed nearly 1 million people, but the CRED-OFDA database uses the 300,000 number.

Hurricanes may strike wealthy nations, but they do not kill many people when they do. Honduras' Hurricane Mitch in 1998 was outdone by tenfold when Typhoon Brendan hit Bangladesh's Cox's Bazar, Chittagong, Patuakhali, Noakhali, Bhola, and Barguna regions on April 30, 1991, killing 138,866 people. The UN's Office for the Coordination of Humanitarian Affairs (OCHA) reported that nearly a million acres of crops were either destroyed or damaged, and three-quarters of a million houses were destroyed.[18]

Hundreds of floods a year occur in wealthy nations,[19] but the only ones with large numbers of deaths lately have been in China, Bangladesh, India, and a huge flood in Venezuela in 1999. The Venezuela flood is instructive: the UN's Pan American Health Organization reported 120 dead; the U.S. National Oceanic and Atmospheric Administration (NOAA) estimated between 20,000 and 50,000 dead; the International Federation of Red Cross and Red Crescent Societies (IFRC) reported intense rain causing flooding and landslides with an "unofficial" estimate of 30,000 dead and 5,944 persons registered missing. In the press, estimates ranged from 20,000 to 50,000 deaths (Agence-France Presse), 50,000 dead (LCW), and "at least" 20,000 dead (Swiss

Re Insurance).[20] The CRED-OFDA database team settled on 30,052 as their estimate.

The only type of climate-related disasters whose "top ten" list includes wealthy nations are heat waves. India saw four of the top ten most deadly hot years during the period studied, but Greece, the United States, and Russia also made this list. Clearly, something different is going on to cause a deadly inability to prepare and respond to heat waves in rich nations, as shown by the 2003 heat wave in France which the National Institute of Health and Medical Research reported killed as many as 14,802 people.[21] Eric Klinenberg's book *Heat Wave: A Social Autopsy of Disaster in Chicago* suggests that the urban heat island effect, fear of crime, social isolation of older African-American men, and political denial combined to create the deadliest heat wave in U.S. history in Chicago in 1995.[22] Similar forces conspired with 104-degree heat in France in 2003; poor elderly care, a complex health system, and government agency failures hastened the death of thousands.[23]

Far exceeding the number of those who die from climate-related disasters are those who suffer in other ways but do not die. There are two available numbers: how many persons are reported to have been affected by the event, and how many are made homeless. We use the "affected" category cautiously here, but the vagueness of the term suggests that it could include people who merely had to replace flooring or appliances as well as those who lost everything or were severely injured. We therefore report both, but favor the number made homeless. Both numbers are estimates and are less reliable than numbers of deaths, which are more carefully tallied, and many terrible disasters in fact lacked data altogether for these categories. To simplify, we show only the two worst categories of climate disasters in terms of making people homeless: windstorms and floods.

This time the list seems even less random. Again, a few poor nations top the lists, with the lists dominated by Bangladesh, China, the Philippines, and Pakistan. The July 1988 cyclonic storms that created tidal surges and the worst flooding in a century in Bangladesh caused an estimated 28 million people to be forced from their homes, according to USAID's OFDA. Other estimates are very different: "hundreds of thousands" homeless were reported by one United Nations regional conference.[24]

Table 3.1
Top Five Climate Disasters by Type and Human Impact, 1980–2002, as Measured by Number of People Killed, Made Homeless, or Reported as Affected

Top Five Windstorms by Number of Human Deaths

Country	Year	Number Killed
Bangladesh	1991	138,866
Honduras	1998	14,600
Bangladesh	1995	10,000
India	1999	9,843
Phillipines	1991	5,956

Top Five Droughts by Number of Human Deaths

Country	Year	Number Killed
Ethiopia	1984	300,000
Sudan	1984	150,000
Mozambique	1985	100,000
Chad	1984	3,000
China	1988	1,400

Top Five Windstorms by Number of People Homeless

Nation	Year	Number Homeless
China	1998	11,000,000
Bangladesh	1988	2,000,000
Philippines	1994	1,170,875
Philippines	1990	1,110,020
Philippines	1991	1,048,024

Top Five Floods by Number of Human Deaths

Nation	Year	Number Killed
Venezuela	1999	30,000
China	1980	6,200
China	1998	3,656
China	1996	2,775
Bangladesh	1987	2,379

Top Five Heat Waves by Number of Human Deaths

Nation	Year	Number Killed
India	1998	2,541
India	2002	1,030
Greece	1987	1,000
United States	1995	670
India	1995	558

Top Five Floods in Number of People Homeless

Nation	Year	Number Homeless
Bangladesh	1987	28,000,000
Bangladesh	1988	28,000,000
China	1998	15,850,000
China	1994	5,600,000
Pakistan	1992	4,698,670

Top Five Floods in Number of People Affected		
Nation	Year	Number Affected
China	1998	223,000,000
China	1991	206,000,000
China	1996	150,000,000
India	1993	128,000,000
China	1995	114,400,000

Top Ten Windstorms in Number of People Affected		
Nation	Year	Number Affected
China	2002	100,000,000
China	1989	30,000,000
Bangladesh	1991	15,000,000
China	1996	15,000,000
China	2001	14,990,000

Top Five Droughts in Number of People Affected		
Nation	Year	Number Affected
India	2002	300,000,000
India	1987	300,000,000
India	1982	100,000,000
India	1983	100,000,000
India	2000	90,000,000

Top Five Heat Waves in Number of People Affected		
Nation	Year	Number Affected
Australia	1993	3,000,000
Australia	1994	1,000,000
Australia	1995	500,000
Australia	1994	100,000
Peru	1983	2,700

Note: Rankings are authors' calculations based on reported figures as assembled by OFDA CRED/EM DAT 2004.

In China's 1998 flood it was reported that 3.5 million houses had collapsed and 3.5 million others were damaged in torrential rains.

The index of the number of people affected contains hundreds of millions of people each year, especially in China, India, and Bangladesh (table 3.1). The smallest numbers, again, are in heat waves, and again a wealthier nation (Australia) tops the list. In India, during the well-documented 2002 drought it was reported that 300 million people were affected, with substantial damage to maize, pulse, oilseeds, and paddy crops. In India's 1983 drought, the UN Office for the Coordination of Humanitarian Affairs reported that 100 million were threatened with dehydration and disease.[25]

A closer examination of these figures reveals some problems of uneven documentation, but they do provide general figures from which strong overall patterns emerge. As we said, rather than looking at individual events, we summed twenty-three years of climate-related disasters; these are shown in table 3.2. The totals are sobering, with 62 million Bangladeshis and nearly 50 million Chinese made homeless over the two decades. More than 1 million were made homeless in Laos, Sudan, India, Sri Lanka, Vietnam, the Philippines, and Pakistan. In the total cumulative number of people affected by such disasters, 1.7 billion Chinese and nearly 1.5 billion Indians were counted over the twenty-three years. For Bangladesh, more than 330 million were described as affected in media and NGO reports of climate-related disasters during the period.

However, many of these countries are very large in population size, which makes it extremely difficult to judge the severity of impact for a nation. Therefore, we adjusted these totals by national populations in 2000, near the end of the period. Doing so, we arrived at the following three hydrometeorological risk indicators, as shown in table 3.2. We have also included the United States to allow comparison.

The findings are startling. In some nations, substantial proportions of the national populations have been made homeless over the two decades. Numbers killed are per thousand population, but comparing U.S. rates with the leaders shows four nations with a rate 100 times our own. These comparisons starkly show how much more suffering from climate-related disasters is already going on in these nations than in our own. Tens of times more, and in the case of some nations, hundreds of times more people are dying in some nations, in relative terms.

Table 3.2
Top 20 Countries by Climate Disaster Vulnerability Indicators, 1980–2002
A. Cumulative Number of People Killed, Made Homeless, or Affected

Rank	Country	Cumulative Number
Killled		
1	Ethiopia	300,964
2	Bangladesh	168,584
3	Sudan	150,362
4	Mozambique	101,473
5	India	59,883
6	China, Peoples' Republic	43,707
7	Philippines	20,353
8	Honduras	15,423
9	Viet Nam	. 12,639
10	United States	7,617
11	Pakistan	7,254
12	Mexico	4,409
13	Nepal	4,344
14	Indonesia	4,341
15	Nicaragua	3,683
16	Iran, Islam Republic	3,549
17	Venezuela	3,519
18	Chad	3,195
19	Somalia	3,121
20	Korea, Republic	2,857
	United States	7,617
Homeless		
1	Bangladesh	62,553,000
2	China, Peoples' Republic	48,989,940
3	Pakistan	8,679,282
4	Philippines	7,823,102
5	Viet Nam	3,716,879
6	Sri Lanka	2,647,601
7	India	2,464,730
8	Sudan	1,254,700
9	Laos, Peoples' Democratic Republic	1,000,000
10	Brazil	805,144
11	Korea, Democratic Peoples' Republic	728,542
12	Mexico	685,240
13	Nigeria	635,002

Table 3.2
(continued)

Rank	Country	Cumulative Number
14	Korea, Republic	605,969
15	Mozambique	505,550
16	Somalia	480,000
17	Argentina	468,304
18	Yemen	444,650
19	United States	405,637
20	Madagascar	367,000
Affected		
1	China, Peoples' Republic	1,693,034,285
2	India	1,471,348,437
3	Bangladesh	331,710,931
4	Ethiopia	69,459,751
5	Iran, Islam Republic	65,560,495
6	Viet Nam	65,320,432
7	Philippines	63,951,017
8	Brazil	41,439,426
9	Thailand	37,999,019
10	Sudan	31,544,906
11	Mozambique	28,305,247
12	Pakistan	27,713,409
13	Zimbabwe	27,351,000
14	Malawi	23,163,825
15	Kenya	15,963,808
16	Australia	15,679,457
17	Sri Lanka	15,672,381
18	Argentina	13,022,808
19	Tanzania	11,316,146
20	Korea, Democratic Peoples' Republic	10,454,486
	United States	4,190,583

B. Rates Adjusted by Population

Rank	Country	Rate
Killed per Thousand Population		
1	Mozambique	5.55
2	Sudan	4.84
3	Ethiopia	4.78
4	Honduras	2.40

Table 3.2
(continued)

Rank	Country	Rate
5	Bangladesh	1.23
6	Nicaragua	0.73
7	Swaziland	0.60
8	Papua New Guinea	0.49
9	Vanuatu	0.49
10	Micronesia, Fed.	0.42
11	Chad	0.41
12	St. Lucia	0.39
13	American Samoa	0.37
14	Somalia	0.36
15	Djibouti	0.28
16	Philippines	0.27
17	Haiti	0.25
18	Tajikistan	0.24
19	Solomon Islands	0.23
20	Belize	0.19
	United States	0.03
Made Homeless, % of Population		
1	Tonga	50.51
2	Bangladesh	45.51
3	Laos, Peoples' Democratic Republic	18.94
4	Samoa	17.61
5	Sri Lanka	13.99
6	Solomon Islands	13.67
7	Marshall Islands	11.76
8	Antigua & Barbados	11.55
9	Philippines	10.34
10	Guam	10.07
11	Virgin Islands (U.S.)	9.92
12	Maldives	8.20
13	Comoros	7.08
14	St. Lucia	6.99
15	Pakistan	6.14
16	Vanuatu	5.53
17	Somalia	5.47
18	Viet Nam	4.76
19	Benin	4.56
20	Sudan	4.04
	United States	0.14

Table 3.2
(continued)

Rank	Country	Rate
Affected, % of Population		
1	Botswana	279.8
2	Antigua & Barbados	245.7
3	Bangladesh	241.4
4	Zimbabwe	216.6
5	Malawi	204.8
6	Samoa	178.6
7	Tonga	174.4
8	Djibouti	173.0
9	Mozambique	154.7
10	Swaziland	154.5
11	Mauritania	147.1
12	India	145.8
13	China, Peoples' Republic	135.1
14	Fiji	130.5
15	Albania	110.4
16	Ethiopia	110.4
17	Sudan	101.4
18	Kiribati	101.2
19	Mongolia	97.3
20	Vanuatu	97.2
	United States	1.5

The case of homelessness is even more alarming. Adding the number of people made homeless over the twenty-three-year period led to rates of half the population of Tonga and nearly half of Bangladesh having to evacuate their damaged homes after climate-related disasters sometime in the 1980s or 1990s. Of course, included in these sums are people who had to evacuate repeatedly. The rate for the United States was less than one-seventh of 1 percent of its population. Dozens of nations were more than ten times more likely to experience high rates of homelessness from climate disasters than the United States.

Finally, summing the number of people affected showed that in eighteen nations the number of people affected by climate disasters over the study period equals or exceeds the national population. In the United States, only 1.5 percent of the population has been affected any time over the past twenty-three years. Again, we are cautious about this indicator, but still the numbers give an overall idea of the disparity between nations in human suffering. To limit ourselves to looking only at deaths would be to miss many of the other important impacts that storms have on people's lives and livelihoods.

This effort to capture broad trends in who is suffering from climate-related disasters appears to show clear patterns of devastating impacts from tragedies over the 1980 to 2002 period. Again, we can take an agnostic approach about whether climate change caused this suffering. However, if the consensus predictions of the future impacts of climate change come to pass, the worst impacts will likely fall upon the same nations. The storms will be similar and perhaps much worse.

Understanding Trends in Suffering: The Role of Poverty and Three Revealing Climate-Related Disasters

Our goal is to understand why these patterns in human vulnerability to climate-related disasters are emerging. What created these patterns? Is it merely random, or just national poverty, as often portrayed in the media? A first step we took was to compare the three indicators of vulnerability against gross domestic product (GDP) per capita. Figure 3.1 shows that some relationship does exist, most clearly in the steep drop in the number of people killed by these disasters in the wealthiest thirty or so nations, when considering GDP per capita.[26] There was a slight downward trend in the number of homeless people as a proportion of the population (figure 3.1B). The number affected appears to drop more consistently as one moves to wealthier nations (figure 3.1C).

Two further things were immediately noteworthy. First, there is a tremendous amount of scatter in all three relationships, and the number least well explained by GDP per capita appears to be the cumulative number of people made homeless. This number barely decreases with national wealth. An additional point is methodologically important. We have included the zeros in these graphs, showing the nations where no significant storms or droughts occurred, and so no deaths or destruction of homes occurred at all over the twenty-three years we summed. This procedure shows the significant randomness with which nations get hit

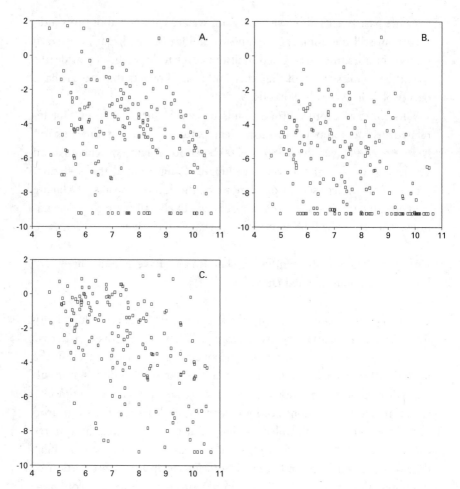

Figure 3.1
Is vulnerability simply the result of a lack of wealth? (A) Number of people killed, (B) made homeless, and (C) affected by climate disasters in all nations, 1980–2002, compared with national wealth (per capita GDP). Both measures are natural logged. Zeros appear along the bottom.

by hurricanes or droughts, heat waves or floods. It also shows why explaining a major proportion of the variance in these indicators may be difficult. The weather is still somewhat unpredictable, and major weather events are even more capricious in where they come ashore.

We now examine three case studies as part of our attempt to understand the causal mechanisms that have driven some of the world's worst climate-related disasters. In these studies we attempt to briefly describe the economic, political, and social history and current state of these nations before explaining the disaster they faced. We first turn to Hurricane Mitch's devastating trip through Honduras, urban flooding in Mozambique in early 2000 after three hurricanes, and the case of rising sea levels swamping the tiny Pacific nation of Tuvalu. The choice of these three cases is somewhat arbitrary; there are many, many more out there. However, we believe these three cases are illuminating since they reveal how colonial histories leave poorer nations in difficult positions when it comes to caring for the current needs of their people and disaster preparation and remediation. The consequences of this inequality and inability to respond are deadly.

The Perfect Storm in Honduras

The fact that the poorest and most vulnerable countries suffer worst from climate change is illustrated dramatically by the case of Honduras. Though it would be impossible to say that any single hurricane was caused by global warming, the increase in air and water temperatures has undoubtedly increased the evaporation and energy in the climate system. In this regard, the story of Hurricane Mitch in Honduras serves as a parable about uneven vulnerability to global climate change, whether present or likely for the future.[27] The effects of Mitch were devastating in Nicaragua, El Salvador, and Guatemala, but Honduras is a particularly extreme case of economic, social, and environmental vulnerability in the region.[28]

After the conquest of the 1500s, Spanish nobles were granted land in huge *latifundias*, on which they used the forced labor of Indians in exchange for a plot to till (minifundia).[29] The economy generated some wealth for a few and a meager subsistence for the rest. After gaining independence from Spain, a narrow oligarchy that was closely allied with the country's military took over, supported by multinational

corporations and the U.S. government.[30] Like other postcolonial plantation economies in Central America, there is a regional core in Honduras
that drains surpluses and resources away from the surrounding peripheral areas. Large coffee *fincas* prosper while paying a pittance to
workers, and vast banana plantations lining the coast contract with
Chiquita and Dole to supply the huge U.S. market.[31] Even today, most
export-oriented production of bananas, coffee, beef, cotton, and shrimp
is controlled by a small number of landholders and large multinational
firms.[32] This inequality is reinforced by the fact that real land reform
has never taken place.[33] In 1998, three-quarters of all land was held by
just 228 landholders.[34] And since the most fertile lands were granted to
large U.S. multinationals in the early 1900s, the majority of Hondurans
live alongside riverbanks and steep hillsides outside Tegucigalpa,
Comayaguela, San Pedro Sula, Choloma, La Ceiba, El Progreso, and
Choluteca, where they can afford to live while having access to work.
Lacking formal title to any land, most peasants migrate to already overcrowded cities or squat illegally on less fertile lands surrounding the city
and adopt survival techniques—such as slash-and-burn agriculture—
that render the land more vulnerable to erosion and landslides during
periods of heavy precipitation.[35]

The opulent wealth of the few who fly to Miami for shopping, vaca-
tions, and hospitals stands in striking contrast to the fate of the rest.
Forty-four percent of the population lives on less than $2 a day; 53
percent of Hondurans remain below the national poverty line; and the
country ranks among the four worst-performing countries in Latin
America and the Caribbean on the Human Development Index.[36] The
government faces an uphill battle because of its unreliable revenue
streams, poor institutions, and susceptibility to exogenous economic
shocks. According to the Economist Intelligence Unit, "[t]raditionally,
economic performance has been related closely to fluctuations in international prices for the country's main exports, bananas and coffee."[37] Take
for example the coffee industry. Between 1997 and 2002, Honduras'
main foreign exchange earner—Arabica coffee—saw its price plunge
from $1.89 a pound to 61 cents a pound.[38] Despite some diversification
into agricultural processing and the light assembly *maquila* sector, Honduras still remains highly reliant on low-value and highly volatile primary product exports.[39]

In addition, Honduras is plagued by extremely weak and distorted political institutions. Corruption remains endemic in the judicial system, the procurement system, and the police force. Press freedom is limited and the rule of law remains fragile; the military intervenes in government affairs; and basic public services are often unavailable.[40] "While in theory all property rights are guaranteed by the constitution," writes one observer, "the reality is that the economically advantaged have firmer property rights than do the poor. Title is allegedly held to lands in excess of 100 percent of the total national territory, the result of a lack of cadastres and enforceable property rights. Indeed, personal property rights are tenuous due to elite manipulation of the law, including contracts."[41] The insecurity and narrowness of property rights is a direct result of extractive Spanish colonial institutions, which granted exclusive privileges to a narrow group of elites and actively discriminated against most Hondurans. As we show in chapter 4, the rents associated with these property rights create enormous barriers to institutional development in many countries like Honduras, thereby significantly enhancing their vulnerability to hydrometeorological disasters.

Much like a bomb detonated in a highly volatile environment, Hurricane Mitch dumped six feet, or one normal year's worth, of rain in two days in the fall of 1998 amid highly explosive social, economic, environmental, and institutional conditions. To be fair, the strength of the storm was unprecedented. However, socioeconomic vulnerability, institutional fragility, and poor natural resource management practices seriously magnified the effects of the disaster.[42] Owing to extraordinarily high levels of deforestation, when the rains came down, so did the topsoil from the denuded uplands, leading to more than one million landslips and mudslides and monstrous flooding that engulfed entire towns and wiped out much of the region's infrastructure.[43] As torrential rains poured down the mountains and hillsides, rivers swelled uncontrollably, in some cases as much as 30 feet higher and 1,500 feet wider. The River Choluteca burst its banks near one of the nation's larger cities, "creating...an eerie lagoon of untreated sewage and chemical effluents in which corpses flowed by."[44] With only four helicopters at its disposal, the Honduran government faced a country where 60 percent of the land was engulfed in mud and water. The Food and Agricultural Organization (FAO) estimated economic losses on the order of 80 percent of annual GDP.[45] Half of the country's agricultural production was destroyed; ninety-four bridges were destroyed; sewerage and electricity systems were knocked out; and hospitals, schools, railways, and telecommunication networks were rendered inoperable. As President Carlos Flores Facussé put it, "In 72 hours, we lost what we had built, little by little, in 50 years."[46]

Early estimates indicated that $5 billion would be necessary for reconstruction, which meant that even with millions of aid dollars pouring in, much of the reconstruction burden would have to be borne by local communities.[47] Furthermore, the country's main economic sector, in terms of foreign exchange, took a heavy hit from the storm and slid into rapid economic decline. In the northern Sula valley, flooding wiped out nearly three-quarters of the banana plantations and production plummeted to roughly one-fifth of pre-Mitch levels, forcing Dole and Chiquita to lay off 25,000 workers.[48] Yet what distinguished Hurricane Mitch from other natural disasters were the almost unimaginable human costs: 7,000 deaths, 8,000 "missing," 1.5 million made homeless, and many more left without access to basic public services.[49] As time wore on, Mitch also exposed underlying vulnerabilities in the country's soft infrastructure. Overcrowded schools functioned as shelters and medical stations, but were unable to stem a massive outbreak of deadly disease. Days after the rains ended, a "silent" disaster of disease quickly consumed the nation. Swollen and surging floodwaters carried excess waste and corpses through the country's water supplies, and cracked pipes and latrines seeped sewage into the floodwaters, creating an ideal breeding ground for epidemics. Diarrhea, a result of dehydration and contaminated water (and the leading cause of death in children worldwide), was commonplace. Leptospirosis, a bacterial infection spread by rodents and exposure to water contaminated with animal urine, also affected large numbers of people. Mosquitoes began to proliferate in stagnant pools of water, boosting the transmission of vector-borne dengue fever and malaria. Ultimately, health officials believe 20,000 people contracted cholera, 31,000 became infected with malaria, and diarrhea affected an additional 208,000.

The case of Honduras clearly illustrates why poorer nations are at a structural disadvantage in preparing for, coping with, and responding to hydrometeorological disasters. Countries with colonial legacies of resource extraction are structurally predisposed toward higher levels of social, economic, and institutional vulnerability because they suffer chronically from declining terms of trade, commodity price volatility, low levels of internal integration, degraded natural environments, weak civil societies, feeble domestic institutions, high domestic inequality, and large informal sectors.

Three Hurricanes and Heroic Assistance in Mozambique

Two years after Hurricane Mitch, increasingly erratic weather slammed into Maputo, the coastal capital of Mozambique. With a large and vulnerable population lying within fifty kilometers of the coast, the southeastern African nation suffered huge social, economic, and environmental losses during back-to-back-to-back cyclones.[50] Mozambique, to be sure, is geographically predisposed toward heavy cyclonic activity because of its location on the coast of the Southwest Indian Ocean, but these storms were exceptional.

During the fall of 1999 and the first two months of 2000, a series of low pressure systems and tropical depressions brought record levels of rain and extensive flooding to central and southern Mozambique. These precipitation events were followed by three cyclones: Connie, Eline, and Gloria. Torrential rains caused rivers and dams to brim over in Mozambique and in Zimbabwe, Botswana, South Africa, and Swaziland. Because of the severity of the flooding, a number of neighboring states decided to open their floodgates, sending "walls of water" into Mozambique.[51] The result: 700 people dead, 1 million displaced persons, 450,000 homes destroyed, 30,000 drowned cattle, 180,000 drowned chickens, 140,000 hectares of farmland (or 10 percent of the country's cultivated land) lost, severely damaged infrastructure, and a $700 million reconstruction bill for the government.[52]

A series of explanations are necessary to understand the human effects of this disaster. First, the rainy season was wetter than usual and Connie, Eline, and Gloria were stronger and longer lasting than previous storms. These patterns are consistent with recent meteorological findings that show less predictability in the seasonal shifts of the intertropical convergence zone—a pattern that many scientists attribute to global warming.[53] Second, upstream waters released by bordering states caused much greater flooding than there would have been otherwise. Finally, and perhaps most important, decades of accumulated vulnerabilities made Mozambique a "disaster waiting to happen."

Until 1975, the Portuguese controlled Mozambique. This part of Africa served as source of cheap labor, with well-positioned ports and good beaches for Europeans. Under colonial rule, "there had been a ban on trade by Africans and restrictions on the jobs they could hold, which insured that at independence most existing companies of any size were reliant on foreign management and technicians."[54] As a result, "the country had no significant indigenous business class, and most companies of any substantial size were in the hands of Portuguese owners or other foreigners, such as the British and South Africans."[55] Most of these firms were in the business of extracting and exporting raw agricultural materials, and this legacy remains firmly intact. Due to extremely low levels of human capital accumulation and global economic constraints, efforts to diversify out of primary products have largely fallen flat, and attempts to move toward higher value-added activities in the global commodity chain—for example, processing, flavoring, packaging, and branding—have proven equally unsuccessful. In 2002, primary products still represented 91 percent of all merchandise exports.[56] And between 1980 and 2002, Mozambique experienced a 50 percent decline in its terms of trade.[57] Not surprisingly, 78.4 percent of the population still lives on less than $2 a day.[58]

During a period of socialist administration, Portugal abandoned many of its colonies, including Mozambique. Their Lusophone colonial imprint, however, remains deeply embedded in virtually all aspect of social, economic, and political life. Take, for example, the absence of an indigenous bourgeoisie, private land ownership, Weberian (meritocratic and effective) bureaucratic structures, human capital accumulation, basic infrastructural services, a competitive manufacturing sector, and backward and forward linkages between economic sectors. Tarp et al. argue that "even by the standards of colonial administration in Africa, little investment was made in social infrastructure in Mozambique, especially in the rural areas.... [T]he accumulation of human capital was [also] extremely limited during the colonial period, and black Mozambican literacy remained at less than 10 percent."[59] As of 1998, approximately 3,000 people in Mozambique had a university education, and almost all of them were part of the government's extremely narrow ruling elite.[60]

Mozambique is also plagued by weak institutions that are in large measure "carryovers" from its colonial past. Since the Portugese failed to establish control over large expanses outside of Maputo, the government remains highly decentralized today and provincial officials are subject to remarkably little oversight.[61] Emboldened by this lack of control, such officials exercise high levels of discretionary power and often promote their own self-enrichment.[62] Mozambique scores 170th out of 195 countries on Kaufmann et al.'s much-celebrated index of corruption, and on-the-ground experience suggests that venal behavior pervades all aspects of government life: political finances, the budgetary process, the judiciary, the civil service, procurement, privatization, customs and taxes, auditing, regulation of the financial sector, and law enforcement.[63] By the attorney general's own admission, the entire judicial system remains hobbled by corruption, and in a recent World Economic Forum survey of undocumented extra payments or bribes connected with getting favorable judicial decisions, Mozambique scored 98th out of 104 countries.[64] Making matters worse, the state continues to control almost all media outlets, and many reporters have admitted self-censorship.[65] Low public sector wages—in no small measure a product of austerity programs imposed by international lenders and aid agencies—also ensure that the corrupt political system reproduces itself. Civil servants are forced to either moonlight or supplement their income by seeking illicit payments,[66] and donors exacerbate this problem by offering substantially higher wages to the limited pool of university-educated professionals, thereby draining local bureaucracies of their best and brightest.

The Portuguese also left behind a whole slew of foreign laws, policies, procedures, and regulations that have practically no modern applicability and reflect narrow parochial interests from hundreds of years ago. The 1888 Commercial Code, for example, remains in effect and imposes an extraordinary number of cumbersome regulations on indigenous and foreign businesses.[67] In 2004, it took "34 procedures, 625 days, and $11,045, or about 50 times the income per capita, to fulfill all requirements for entry of a new manufacturing firm," and investors report that Mozambique is one of the most difficult countries in the world to do business in.[68] Acemoglu et al. argue that in many "extractive colonies," like Mozambique, the ruling elite benefited from highly inefficient economic policies and institutions because of the rents they generated.[69] Unfortunately, many of these policies and institutions have persisted for centuries for the simple reason that the rents create vested interests and thus patterns of rent seeking.

Highly unequal patterns of land distribution and tenure also remain problematic. The Portuguese imposed a European land titling system on top of preexisting land tenure systems and effectively expropriated the best lands for themselves.[70] Despite the fact that a 1997 land law in Mozambique recognized occupancy rights as registered land rights, neither private ownership of land nor the use of land leases as collateral for bank loans is currently allowed. Moreover, significant redistributive changes have not been achieved in the structure of land ownership.[71] It is therefore not surprising that interest rates remain extremely high—between 24 and 28 percent per year. This is reflected in a 2004–2005 World Economic Forum survey of 104 countries, which scores Mozambique last on their ease of access to loans indicator.[72] As we argue in chapter 4, access to loans can be critical for people who have lost everything in the wake of a natural disaster.

Land policy has a long and complicated history in Mozambique.[73] As a backlash against colonial rule, all land was nationalized by President Samora Machel in 1975. This led to a mass exodus from the surrounding *cidade de canico* (cane city) to the traditionally Portuguese-dominated central *cidade de cimento* (cement city), which overwhelmed local administrative authorities and led to a rapid deterioration in urban housing conditions.[74] Even after moving to "cement city," many Mozambicans still found themselves in marginal settlements made of the same "cane" (or corrugated iron) that they had in the *cidade de canico*. Sidaway and Power report that in 1985, ten years after independence, "it was estimated that only about 8% of the Mozambican population lived in permanent houses made of brick or cement."[75] By 2000, not much had improved: UN-HABITAT estimated that 94 percent of the urban population lived in a slum dwelling.[76] That means that close to all urban Mozambicans lack a permanent housing structure that complies with local regulations, provides an electricity and sewer connection, and has access to water within 200 meters. According to the most recent figures from the Global Urban Indicators database, only 5 percent of waste-water is treated in Maputo, building codes are not integrated with hazard and vulnerability assessments, and the environmental plan drawn up for the city has not yet been implemented.[77] The absence of these basic protections created ideal conditions for a human disaster when cyclones Connie, Eline, and Gloria arrived in early 2000.[78]

Four floods hit Mozambique in the terrible time of January–March of 2000. The first was from heavy and early rains brought by climatic shifts under the La Niña pattern; then Cyclones Connie, Eline, and Gloria hit one after another.[79] In the city of Xai-Xai, the Limpopo River waters were twelve feet deep for nearly a month, making it the worst flood in 150 years. The Maputo and Umbelúzi Rivers reached serious flood levels, as did the Incomáti, Save, Buzi and Púngoè. On most of these rivers, the flood levels were two or four times higher than what had ever been recorded.

It could have been much worse. Because of the changing La Niña weather patterns, heavy rains were predicted in Mozambique from September 1999 to January 2000.[80] Some substantial planning was done to prepare for the floods, and weather forecasters worked to warn residents quite early on. After the early rains, soils became saturated and were unable to absorb more water. Dams were unable to contain the rivers and may have made the damage worse since smaller floods would have had the beneficial effect of scouring out sediments that clogged the river bottoms.[81] Road and railway embankments funneled the water downstream more quickly during the floods and kept waters trapped behind them. Some experts pointed out that wetland losses and farming left the land less able to absorb large rainfalls.

The floodwaters swept through neighborhoods "like a monster," entirely engulfing homes, schools, and train stations.[82] Seven hundred people are believed to have died. Some people survived by moving up into trees and tying themselves up there; some were stuck there for days or even weeks. They drank the contaminated waters that flowed by, grabbing crops or anything else they could eat. South African helicopters saved thousands of victims as television cameras transmitted the dramatic rescues around the world.

In their detailed account of the floods, journalists Frances Christie and Joseph Hanlon argue that the massive outpouring of foreign support during the aftermath of the floods was due to those televised images.[83]

They also describe a coordinated effort by the Mozambiquan navy, ten air forces, the Red Cross, and hundreds of other groups who worked together to rescue 45,000 people. Half a million people were supported in hastily constructed accommodation centers. Diseases and malnutrition were almost entirely averted.[84] The Mozambiquan national emergency response agency (INGC) was remarkably prepared and coordinated the rescue efforts with the help of foreign aid and emergency workers. The United Nations' World Food Program and the foreign assistance groups and air forces drew on lessons learned from coordination failures during Hurricane Mitch and in Albania. Christie and Hanlon report that the response to the floods in Mozambique in 2000 was the largest air rescue operation ever mounted and "will be a model for future cooperation between humanitarian agencies and military forces."[85]

Rising Sea Level and the Likely Evacuation of Tuvalu
This brings us to the case of Tuvalu, a small Pacific island state whose existence is mortally threatened by climate change. Tuvalu is one of five countries in the world that consist solely of atolls, islands built by coral reefs on the rims of ancient volcanoes. Atolls, as well as many other small island states, are small, isolated, fragmented, and extremely susceptible to rises in sea level. The average land elevation on the island of Tuvalu is about 1 meter. While some parts are higher, many are lower. Experts therefore believe that the 20- to 90-centimeter rise in sea level predicted by the Intergovernmental Panel on Climate Change could literally put much, if not all, of the country permanently under water. In anticipation of imminent and catastrophic impacts, Tuvalu's prime minister, Koloa Talake, has lobbied Western governments to grant his citizens permanent asylum.

Patrick Barkham, a reporter from the London-based *Guardian* newspaper, paints a picture of life in Tuvalu: "Daily life ... revolves around the ocean. It is the islands' garden, washroom, swimming pool and slaughterhouse. As dawn quickly rises on the island, men and women stand neck-deep in the sea, eating fish and bits of coconut, or periodically raising pans they are silently scrubbing beneath the surface of the water. At midday, a father and son heave four pigs into the lagoon for slicing up; the pigs' slashed-open bellies turn the water red and their entrails drift off on the ocean. At dusk, islanders gather on motorbikes to watch the sunset from the low concrete jetties jutting out into the lagoon. Children slide down algae-covered boat ramps into the water and a man clutches a fish the size of a dog to his chest."[86]

The island was missed by the Spanish explorers of the area, and remained isolated more than a hundred years longer than many of its neighbors.[87] However, as part of what was formerly the Gilbert and Ellice Islands, Tuvalu became a British colony at the beginning of the twentieth century. It was granted independence in 1978. Regional experts attribute its structural vulnerability to bad geography (small size and remoteness), unpredictable global markets, and dependence on a single export crop (copra). It is also chronically vulnerable to trade deficits because of its heavy reliance on imported goods, with imports outnumbering exports twenty to one in a normal year. Among the fifty least developed countries in the world, Tuvalu scores last on the UN's 2003 economic vulnerability index, which measures "structural economic vulnerability" by averaging measures of merchandise export concentration, export earnings instability, agricultural production instability, manufacturing and modern services as a share of GDP, and population size.[88]

Tuvalu is representative of the problems of a category of nations: as a group, small island states are some of the most economically vulnerable countries in the world.[89] Their high degree of economic openness as measured by imports plus exports over GDP makes them extraordinarily vulnerable to shifts in the global economy, and their size sharply narrows the range of possibilities for economies of scale in production. Small size also lends itself to natural monopolies and oligopolies. Furthermore, their dependence on an extraordinary number of imports reduces their ability to self-protect, and their remoteness exposes them to the "uncertainties, delays and cost indivisibilities in foreign trade."[90] Perhaps most important, many small island states rely on an extraordinarily narrow export base made up of weather-dependent primary products, which weakens their ability to insulate themselves from external shocks.[91] "One of the defining characteristics of [small islands]," according to the UNDP, "is the limited natural resources endowment. The dominant form of land use for the production of agricultural commodities for export (coffee, spices, sugar, cocoa, copra) has its foundation in colonial history, where the land resources were cultivated primarily to provide reliable sources of supply of tropical crops to the consumers in the mother countries."[92] According to Neil Adger, this point cannot be overemphasized since "the impacts of climate change are likely to be greater on those countries more dependent on primary sector economic activities [mostly farming], primarily because of the increase in uncertainty on productivity in the primary sectors."[93]

Tuvalu's economy is largely a subsistence one, with the cash that arrives coming from farming and fishing, government work, foreign aid, and remittances from those working in Nauru's phosphate mining industry, on merchant ships, or in Australia. Funafuti, the capital, is overcrowded and lacks potable water. Its population and infrastructure are located perilously close to a constantly eroding shoreline, and its soil is weak and degraded. Because of the pressing need for fuel and limited natural resources, Tuvalu is also highly deforested. Together, these factors have cumulatively and synergistically weakened Tuvalu's ability to respond and adapt to flooding, tropical storms, and sea-level rise.

On this point, Tuvalu is also not alone. According to the World Meteorological Organization (WMO), "sea-level rise would increase the impact of tropical cyclones and other storms that drive storm surges" and these "effects [will] be disastrous on small island states and other low-lying developing countries, such as the Maldives, Tuvalu, Kiribati and Vanuatu where 90 percent of the population lives along the coasts."[94] More broadly, Anthony Bigio of the World Bank notes that "[w]ith a 40 centimeter rise in sea level, the midpoint of the projection ranges from the Intergovernmental Panel on Climate Change for the end of the century, the world population at risk from annual flooding is expected to increase from the current 10 million to 22–29 million by the 2020s, to 50–80 million by the 2050s, and to 88–241 million by the 2080s."[95] Some experts predict that the vulnerability to flood risk of Pacific islands could increase by as much as two hundred-fold by 2080.[96]

However, the 2002 *World Disasters Report* suggests that many of the worst effects of climate change are already occurring in the South Pacific. The number of people whose lives are affected by hydrometeorological disasters has risen exponentially over the past thirty years, from 275,000 to 18 million. Stated differently, sixty-five times more people are affected by inclement weather today than during the 1970s. Tuvalu, a country that typically sees very few tropical storms, has also faced an unusual number of cyclones over the past fifteen years.[97] In 1993, Cyclone Nina destroyed thirty homes, submerged much of Funafuti, and left 150 people homeless.[98] Four years later, Tuvalu was struck three consecutive times by different cyclones.[99] In 2000, storms and flooding relentlessly pounded the island nation for five months.[100]

However, rising seas, increased hydrometeorological activity, and economic vulnerability provide only a partial explanation for why Tuvaluans continue to suffer the effects of climate change disproportionately. High levels of environmental degradation also interact with Tuvalu's uniquely hazardous geographical position.[101] Coral bleaching has adversely affected marine life and led to a decline in the fish catch. Coastal flooding,[102] which saturates fertile land with salt water, has forced many islanders to rely on imported foodstuffs, and greater saltwater intrusion into groundwater and estuaries has made fresh water increasingly scarce.[103] High levels of deforestation have also reduced the number of trees that can absorb excess water during storms and floods.[104]

To conclude, Tuvalu's extreme vulnerability to sea level rise makes it one of the coastal and island warning signals of global warming. The prime minister of this country of 11,000 has been attempting to locate a nation willing to resettle the entire population of the island in case water should flood it. They first sought refuge in Australia, whose government reportedly refused to discuss the issue. New Zealand later approved their resettlement, at a rate of seventy Tuvaluans per year, starting in 2002.[105] Some residents are also considering moving to the neighboring country of Niue, whose population largely abandoned the island when Cyclone Heta struck in January 2004.[106]

Conclusions: Vulnerability to Climate-Related Disasters

The three cases and some of the trends in suffering quantified in the first half of this chapter leave us with a rather grim picture of how the vulnerability of our species to climate change has been made critically worse by the extra-local demands of colonialism and the current global division of labor. In Honduras and Mozambique, unusually slow-moving hurricanes dumped extreme amounts of rain on altered landscapes, literally washing decades of development away. These might seem to be unusual cases, but the level of death and suffering they experienced reflects wider patterns of vulnerability in the developing world. The histories of these nations suggest that vulnerability to climate disasters is in large measure tied to economic and political weakness. There are more than enough directions in which to point fingers: a colonial legacy of dependence on the export of a few low-value tropical crops, low levels of internal economic integration, bad geography, weak and underfinanced government, environmental degradation, and sprawling informal settlements. All of these factors made Honduras and Mozambique perfect recipes for human disaster. Tuvalu awaits its disaster from the rising sea.

We certainly could have chosen another set of cases that would have made the same points: Hurricane Jeanne, which in 2004 killed 1,500 in Haiti; the flooding and mudslides in Venezuela in 1999 that killed 30,000; Typhoon Brendan, which led to 138,866 fatalities in Bangladesh; or the 1999 floods in China that killed almost 1,000 and seriously injured 24,000 more. In almost all of these cases, governments were unable to effectively prepare for and respond to climate-related disasters. The socioeconomic roots of these disasters are twofold. First, the world's poorer nations have been affected by foreign actors wielding overwhelming political, economic, and military power. Part of the story is explained by the actions of foreign governments. Another part of the story is the expansion by and operation of transnational corporations that dwarf the governments of poor nations. Sometimes both are related, as when the U.S. government removed the democratically elected president of Guatemala in 1954 to protect U.S.-based banana companies operating there. The ineptitude and dispreparation of poor states is also attributable to decades and centuries of extracting natural resources, which left political institutions and social structures weak and deformed.

What differed between the Honduras case and Mozambique was that many more people were rescued in Mozambique and cared for effectively with international assistance. The experience of Hurricane Mitch in Honduras and Nicaragua in 1998 led to better planning in Mozambique for the floods of 2000 and much better coordination of responders. However in both cases, hundreds of millions of dollars and heroic efforts were expended to begin to put things back together. In both cases, national development and the lives of millions of people have been set back by years. Certainly all that disaster relief money would have been better spent on development assistance to create economic opportunities as well as prepare for disasters. Deeper changes are needed to prevent and ameliorate the suffering associated with climate-related disasters. This discussion has finally reached global climate change negotiations in the past few years, but progress on adaptation funding has been slow.

Finally, we return to the North-South deadlock with which we began in chapter 1. Many climate experts argue that negotiators should continue with the same kind of self-interested bargaining tactics that have characterized the first fifteen years of climate negotiations. In their view, expanding the scope of climate negotiations to include issues like inequality, trust, and fairness will severely limit any effort to stabilize the climate. Instead, it is thought that Western governments should invest in clean technologies, decouple economic growth from carbon dioxide emissions, strengthen compliance mechanisms, and proceed with or without the participation of a majority of developing countries. One might call this the pragmatic justice approach: an approach that says a perfectly fair agreement existing only in the minds of negotiators is ultimately unfair to all parties.[107]

However, as we have shown in this chapter and will show in the following chapters, the issue of global climate change is fundamentally about injustice and inequality—in vulnerability, responsibility, and mitigation, as well as participation in the global economy. In chapter 6, we examine who has already taken action to address the problem of climate change and employ one measure of vulnerability to hydrometerological disasters from this chapter to subject to empirical scrutiny the claim that poor countries, who are unjustly suffering the effects of a problem to which they contributed virtually nothing, craft their negotiating tactics and environmental policies on the basis of their principled beliefs. Vulnerability may affect pro-climate action in ways that seriously challenge the conventional wisdom in international politics. Rationalists predict that vulnerable countries have a stronger incentive to participate in a global climate agreement than nonvulnerable countries. However, poor nations suffering from rising sea levels, devastating droughts and storms, declining agricultural yields, increased disease burdens, and murderous flooding are also unlikely to be enthusiastic about cleaning up an environmental problem that the industrialized world created in the first place. Therefore we explore the role that social, distributive, normative, and emotional preferences play in shaping international negotiations in subsequent chapters.

Our next step is to combine the insights from the three case studies in this chapter with additional theoretical insights from the literature on vulnerability, environment, and development. We pick up this issue in the next chapter by systematically examining the complex web of causal forces producing and reproducing human vulnerability to hydrometeorological disasters, shown so dramatically by the indices on death and homelessness we developed in the first half of this chapter. This quantitative multivariate analysis is exploratory, but we believe it can help us understand which factors are, broadly speaking, the most important in explaining inequality in vulnerability to climate-related events.

Postscript: Hurricane Katrina and Vulnerability in the Global North

The scene was extremely shocking to TV viewers around the world: Americans waving from rooftops and huddling in the Superdome, on highway overpasses, and screaming for rescue from the floodwaters brought by Hurricane Katrina in late August, 2005. More than a thousand died from the flood, and at this writing over 4,000 are still listed as missing. The horrors were seen especially in New Orleans, Roberts' hometown for ten years from 1991 to 2001. Many viewers wondered how the seemingly impervious United States could suddenly appear so vulnerable to a climate disaster and how so many Americans could have been left without assistance for days and days after the levees broke. This short postscript seeks to make sense of what happened in the light of our framework and three cases we just described: Honduras, Mozambique, and Tuvalu.

Who died in New Orleans and why? We don't claim that global warming created or stoked Hurricane Katrina, but it is possible, especially since Gulf of Mexico waters were unusually warm. Hurricane Katrina was mighty, but was not a "worst case" direct hit of a storm of the magnitude feared most: the storm weakened a bit and wobbled to the east just before hitting land, and the winds largely spared the city. Still, the hurricane sent a surge of water across damaged wetlands and up barge canals and over levees into the poor Ninth Ward neighborhood (majority black) and St. Bernard Parish (nearly all white). And the 17th

Street Canal famously broke its levee into the middle- to upper-class white neighborhood known as Lakeview. Yet morgue listings of the dead released at this writing in November, 2005 show that the majority of those who died were elderly: nearly two-thirds were over sixty-one years old.[108]

Katrina was somewhat surprising in that it affected people even in a wealthy nation. However, the 1995 Chicago and 2004 Paris heat waves also hit isolated and poor people in wealthy capitals; even considering these disasters, these wealthy nations are many times safer than poor nations who have suffered climate disasters, as we will see in the next chapter. People are now saying that Hurricane Katrina was the worst disaster in America since the 1906 Earthquake in San Francisco, perhaps worse.

Many people were shocked by the looting reported in the streets of New Orleans. To understand the reactions of the poor in New Orleans, one has to understand the current violence there and the history of inequality and racism in that city. Africans were brought there and sold right in the French Quarter into some of the most violent oppression in the nation's history, to build those very levees and work on sugar plantations along the river. After the North retreated from the project of Reconstruction in the 1880s, votes were taken from ex-slaves by manipulated laws and what we would today call terrorism—more than 330 blacks were lynched in Louisiana from 1880 to 1950 as part of a very calculated campaign of intimidation and repression by some very powerful people.[109] Blacks were excluded from almost all decent jobs into the 1960s, and savage inequalities in the education system to this day continue to create generations of hopeless young people. Words can hardly describe how criminal the state of the public schools in Orleans Parish was in 2005, before Katrina hit. And the inequality is stunning between the beautiful huge mansions of St. Charles Avenue and the Garden District and the poor Central City ghettos or St. Thomas housing projects just a block or two away.

It now seems that the reports of widespread mayhem in New Orleans were largely fabrications—important fabrications, but not reflective of the majority of cases. Ten thousand people were locked a bit like slaves in the Superdome with dwindling food, water, and air and with the roof flying off. The conditions worsened as they waited and waited to be rescued. Apparently only one was killed in violence. Similar exaggerations were made of violence at the Convention Center, where there were even less provisions and control. In fact thousands of people did behave decently in spite of being confronted with horrifying conditions created by their needs being ignored in the wealthiest nation on Earth.

In Roberts' previous book on environmental justice in Louisiana, we described the terrible condition of Nature and poor enforcement of environmental regulations there. Louisiana is among the poorest and most unequal in the union, and so to be poor and black there is a triple curse. As U.S. District Judge Tucker Melancon remarked to the state's lead environmental enforcement officer, "I used to get upset when big newspapers referred to Louisiana as a banana republic or Third World country. Regrettably...[Louisiana's environmental enforcement] resembles more closely what one would find in a Third World country, rather than in the richest..."[110] Racism, inequality, and political exclusion left the poor there without means to evacuate and without an organized structure to mobilize their rescue.

In this regard, the fragmented and uncoordinated aid effort in Louisiana after Katrina was more like the aftermath of Hurricane Mitch in Honduras than the surprisingly coordinated and effective effort after the 2000 floods in Mozambique. It would appear that the lessons of Mitch were learned in the international community, but not in the United States.

There is even greater value in moving to the deeper causes of vulnerability to climate disasters we sought to explore in the other three cases. Louisiana's weak economy, based almost entirely on extraction and processing of oil, tourism, and a port, lends itself to comparisons with many Third World nations. Indeed, its economy is the result of its colonial past—as the site of huge sugar and cotton plantations which "mined the soil" using repressed slave labor. This left the legacy of desperate poverty and stark inequality described above—a recipe for violence, and for weak public institutions and frail civil society institutions. Why? Tourism provides mostly nonunion, low-wage "service sector" jobs. Petroleum extraction and refining has among the lowest rates of employment to capital investments of any industry. A $2 billion refinery, for example, might employ fewer than 400 workers. Furthermore, in its desperation to attract industries—and since these same industries wielded mighty lobbying prowess in the legislature—the state of Louisiana extended massive tax exemptions to oil processing firms.[111] These tax breaks were estimated in the late 1990s to cost public schools in the state over $100 million a year.

So among the U.S. states, Louisiana is in some ways less like the rest of the nation than it is like poorer nations. New Orleans and the river parishes around it struggle with some of the most damaging "legacies of colonialism" among the U.S. states.

4

An Analysis of Cross-National Patterns of Risk

Proximate and Root Causes

Photos of swirling hurricanes, windswept trees, volcanoes, and earthquake damage framed an October 2004 piece in the *Washington Post* reporting on the scientists who believe that natural disasters are increasing in frequency and sceptics who do not.[1] The piece was an improvement upon many journalistic reports that begin and end their description of the causes of damage and human injury by saying it was an "act of God" or "Nature's wrath." Trying to make sense of the unusually high death toll resulting from tragic Haitian flooding after Hurricane Jeanne the month before, the article's author emphasized what he saw as the underlying cause: poverty.

International organizations, think tanks, and insurance companies have popularized a similar interpretation of vulnerability to natural disasters. One perennially cited statistic is that losses from natural disasters in *developing countries*, as a percent of gross national product, are twenty times higher than those in developed countries.[2] The World Bank, UNDP, and the International Federation of Red Cross and Red Crescent Societies report that 90 percent of disaster victims live in *developing* countries, and 97 percent of all disaster-related deaths occur in the *developing* world.[3] Both casual and expert observers therefore imply that poverty is the primary determinant of human vulnerability to natural disasters.

In this chapter we apply the insights from chapter 3's case studies of Hurricane Mitch in Honduras, the floods in Mozambique in 2000, and sea-level rise in Tuvalu. We use the indices of climate risk developed there, and advance the argument that poverty is only part of a much more complex and nuanced causal picture. Using the tools of OLS regression and path analysis, we control for a number of variables emphasized in the extant literature and empirically evaluate a series of novel, structuralist-inspired hypotheses. We find that journalistic accounts and expert case studies rarely do justice to the complexity of the forces producing and reproducing vulnerability. The most powerful predictors of fatalities, homelessness, and disruptions of livelihood related to hydrometeorological disasters are a country's level of urbanization, the security of its property rights regime, its coastal exposure, the freedom of its media, and the scale of income inequality among its citizens. These stories are almost never told, and the need for social science research on their causation is critically needed.

As indicated in chapter 3, our core hypothesis is that the way a country is "inserted" into the world economy bears heavily upon its ability to cope with climate-related disasters.[4] We focus on countries with a legacy of extraction of raw materials, which goes back to how they were treated in colonial times, and which is reflected currently in how narrowly a country relies on one or a few main exports. These same nations, we argue, are structurally predisposed toward higher levels of social, economic, environmental, and institutional vulnerability. We will explain how, because of their being set up to maximize the extraction of unprocessed, low-priced goods, they continue to suffer today from declining terms of trade, commodity price volatility, low levels of internal integration, crumbling infrastructure, degraded natural environments, intimidated civil societies, weak and disfigured political institutions, high levels of inequality in incomes and assets, food insecurity, large informal sectors, and low levels of urbanization. The findings of our analysis strongly support these hypotheses. Structural disadvantages indeed limit the ability of many countries to address poverty and environmental degradation and therefore to prepare themselves for, cope with, and respond to climate-related disasters. By way of conclusion, we discuss a series of reasons why disaster prevention and relief efforts that treat only symptoms and not the social, political, and economic structures are doomed to longer-term failure.

In chapter 3 we described the work of sorting, coding, and analyzing the universe of more than 4,000 climate-related disasters over the past two decades to create three new cross-national measures of climate-related risk. These reflected the total impact of all such disasters from 1980 to 2002: the number of people killed, made homeless, and affected by climate disasters. They reflect who is already suffering the most from the types of disasters that are expected to increase with climate change.[5]

In this chapter we build on past research and existing social science theories to develop causal models and expose competing and complementary explanations of climate-related risk to empirical disconfirmation. While this is the bread and butter of positivist social science, the relatively underdeveloped literature on vulnerability, risk, and disaster is still based on many generalizations from an N of three or fewer cases. In fact, the very scholars who pioneered this literature lament the fact that their literature reviews, typologies, conceptual frameworks, analytical definitions, and schematic diagrams have yielded little cumulative and generalizable knowledge.[6] In 1993, Watts and Bohle pointed out that "vulnerability as a concept does not rest on a well developed theory; neither is it associated with widely accepted indicators or methods of measurement."[7] Seven years later, Clark et al. reported that vulnerability, risk, and disaster research remained "highly fragmentary in nature, with competing paradigms, conflicting theory, empirical results often idiosyncratic and tied to particular approaches, and a lack of comparative analyses and findings."[8] This chapter is an attempt to move beyond this indeterminate "everything matters" approach and begin discriminating among competing explanations of cross-national climate risk in a large-N quantitative context.[9]

We then develop a theoretically sequenced model of hydrometeorological risk that integrates insights from multiple disciplines. While the mainstream literature satisfies itself with explanations divorced from history, we argue that many of the most important causal forces driving hydrometeorological risk—from declining terms of trade and deteriorating infrastructure to degraded natural environments and weak and corrupted political institutions—are a direct consequence of extractive colonial legacies. It is therefore not poverty per se, but a highly correlated suite of variables that can be traced back to a common causal origin: dependence on a narrow range of low-value exports. In this regard, we hope to shed light on the root causes of vulnerability that place many developing countries at a structural disadvantage. Building a social theory of vulnerability requires deductive and empirical work.

Without this, billions of dollars of disaster assistance may end up treating symptoms rather than the underlying sources.

Existing Theories of Climate-Related Risk

The earliest explanations of hydrometeorological risk were "unapologetically naturalist (sometimes termed physicalist), in which all blame is apportioned to 'violent forces of nature' or 'nature on the rampage'."[10] For quite some time, this biophysical approach was thought to explain most of the variation in patterns of human vulnerability to natural disasters.[11] Its central contribution was to explain how "environmental variability—including its timing, duration, frequency and magnitude ... [determined] the extent and patterning of human vulnerability."[12]

Despite the obvious importance of this literature, there is a growing awareness among scholars and policy makers that many "natural" disasters are not at all natural.[13] So-called "acts of God" often affect the same countries and social groups repeatedly for reasons that are completely unrelated to weather patterns and bad geography. As Wisner et al. put it, "for many people, a disaster is not a single, discrete event. All over the world, but especially in LDCs, vulnerable people ... suffer repeated, multiple, mutually reinforcing, and sometimes simultaneous shocks to their families, their settlements and their livelihoods."[14] In Central America, for example, a series of hurricanes and human disasters during the 1970s, 1980s, and 1990s (Irene, Fifi, Joan, Cesar, and Mitch) point to a common set of root causes: severe deforestation, fragile political institutions, extraordinary inequality in assets and incomes, and reliance on a narrow range of export crops with highly volatile prices (see chapter 3).[15]

One of the central events leading to the development of the social vulnerability literature was a 1976 earthquake in Guatemala, which earned the name "classquake" because its effects were experienced disproportionately by poor families living in landslide-prone ravines and gorges.[16] The dead, injured, and homeless tolls were difficult to ignore: 23,000, 77,000, and 1.1 million, respectively. Experts argued that poor people living in the rural highlands and urban slums of Guatemala City bore the brunt of the quake's impact because of their inability to afford safe housing. Similar conclusions have been drawn from studies of the 1985 earthquake in Mexico City (9,500 dead), the 1999 Venezuelan floods and landslides (30,000 dead), the 2001 landslides in Las Colinas, El Salvador (700 dead, 2,000 missing), and the 2004 quake in Bam, Iran (24,000 dead).

Amartya Sen's work on the political economy of famine also breathed life into the theoretical literature by drawing attention to the causal significance of domestic political institutions. Sen inductively theorizes from two basic observations: democratic regimes rarely experience famines and famines rarely occur as a result of a collapse in the food supply. From this departure point, he develops and subjects to serious empirical scrutiny the hypothesis that famine is directly related to the responsiveness and accountability of governments. "Famines are easy to prevent if there is a serious effort to do so, and a democratic government, facing elections and criticisms from opposition parties and independent newspapers, cannot help but make such an effort. Not surprisingly, while India continued to have famines under British rule right up to independence...they disappeared suddenly with the establishment of a multiparty democracy and a free press."[17] In war-torn Sudan, Keen suggests that the Khartoum government deliberately funded ethnic militia groups in 1988 to "create famine" in parts of the country to win what would have otherwise been an expensive civil war on the cheap.[18] Therefore climate disasters are often at their base social, political, and economic disasters.[19]

We share this view and advance a structuralist perspective of human vulnerability to climate disasters. Critics will charge that we ignore the literature on rational human agency and coping mechanisms to mitigate the effects of climate change,[20] and we agree with McLaughlin and Dietz that "more simplistic and reductionistic applications of political economy can under emphasize the role of human agency and culture, particularly the capacity of marginalized populations to adapt and resist."[21] At the same time, the fact that many citizens of developing countries live in places where political institutions are fragile and unresponsive, natural environments are degraded, property rights are insecure, civil society groups are unorganized and repressed, and government revenues are depleted and unpredictable, is not a reflection of individual adaptation failures. Rather, poor nations—and the individuals in those nations—are often beleaguered by a whole host of problems that are beyond their control. While each case of climate-related disaster is different and includes human agents and a series of conjunctures that led to its particular outcome, a study of broader trends might uncover some of the generalizable causal forces producing and reproducing some nations' extreme vulnerability to these terrible disasters.

The broad patterns where poorer nations suffer repeatedly and more severely from climate-related disasters—at rates 10 to 100 times those of wealthier nations—raise a more fundamental question. Why are the citizens of developing countries chronically vulnerable to climate-related disasters and those of wealthier countries relatively immune to the most life-threatening effects of climate change? Besides poverty, journalists often attribute these differences to bad geography, government ineptitude, and corruption. Here we blaze a trail in a new direction by attempting to explain the death rates, homelessness rates, and affected rates associated with climate disasters over the past two decades with a series of structuralist-inspired hypotheses.

When we systematically measure who suffers worst from climate disasters, and control for factors like poverty, government effectiveness, and geography in a worldwide analysis of more than a hundred nations, we uncover hidden patterns that are rarely discussed in journalistic accounts and case studies. We also go behind these proximate explanations of climate vulnerability and examine the root causes—for example, long-term declines in the prices of export commodities, commodity price volatility, and low levels of internal integration—driving these proximate causes of human vulnerability to weather-related risk. These explanations may be hard to accept for many scholars, policy makers, and citizen activists since structuralism has been out of style in many academic and policy circles for quite some time now. Nevertheless, we believe the evidence argues for itself. By almost any measure, states that are heavily reliant on the extraction and export of natural resources face a unique set of constraints, and we argue that these are largely due to their incorporation into the world economy as extractive colonies.[22] These findings seem to indicate that a change is needed in efforts to address human vulnerability to hydrometeorological risk and the broader global inequalities that created it. If we treat only the superficial symptoms of vulnerability, we run the risk of recreating the same problems we seek to eliminate.

In the next section we present a series of hypotheses that have received much attention in the extant literature and empirically evaluate these propositions. Most proximate explanatory variables, we argue, have a common structural origin. We discuss eight proximate predictors of climate risk and the structural roots of each of these variables: national wealth, the size of the coastal population, urbanization rates, environmental vulnerability, press freedom, civil society, informal economy, and domestic inequality.

Understanding Trends in Climate-Related Suffering: Modeling Disasters

As we move to predictive models for vulnerability to climate disasters, we need to clarify three points about what exactly we are predicting. First, unlike other authors, we do not conceive of vulnerability as an outcome variable. Instead, we take vulnerability to represent the susceptibility of human populations to climatic hazards. Vulnerability has been theorized as a relative condition, a social phenomenon, and a dynamic process; a relative condition because it "is not the same for different populations living under different environmental conditions or faced with complex interactions of social norms, political institutions and resource endowments, technologies and inequalities";[23] a social phenomenon, because "without people, there is no disaster";[24] and a dynamic process because different combinations of causal factors may interact synergistically and compound each other at different points in time.[25] Broadly speaking, then, by vulnerability we mean the probability that citizens of a nation-state will die, experience severe loss of livelihood (such as homelessness), suffer an injury, or otherwise require emergency assistance.[26]

Climate-related hazards, in this book, refer to extreme weather events. Recall that such events include droughts, floods, heat waves, hurricanes, tidal waves, tornadoes, tropical storms, typhoons, winter storms, hailstorms, dust storms, rainstorms, thunderstorms, and cold waves. They do not include earthquakes, volcanic eruptions, landslides, epidemics, droughts, biodiversity loss, coastal erosion, or industrial hazards, although similar patterns may exist for these. Hazards vary in terms of their frequency, magnitude, intensity, and extent. They display a significant amount of randomness, and are unobservable variables in our models. In spite of their randomness, there are patterns in who suffers from these events. The randomness of weather, however, explains in part why in what follows we are able to account for only 20 to 40 percent of the variation in cross-national patterns of climate risk. The opposite could also be said; it is fairly remarkable that a first effort at modeling social factors explains a third of what has been described as Nature's wrath or an act of God.

Natural hazards themselves are therefore conceptualized as trigger events that have different consequences in different contexts. Essentially, we are trying to identify those countries that are human disasters "waiting to happen." Finally, the term "disaster," as used here, denotes the realization of risk, which captures both human vulnerability to climate-related hazards and the independent effect of the hydrometeorological hazard itself (including its strength, size, and duration). As Alexander puts it, "vulnerability refers to the potential for casualty, destruction, damage, disruption or other form of loss in a particular element: risk combines this with the probable level of loss to be expected from a predictable magnitude of hazard."[27] Some social geographers express this relationship as risk = hazard × vulnerability.[28]

A Theoretically Sequenced Model of Human Vulnerability to Weather-Related Risk

We developed a multivariate path analysis to predict the 1980–2002 population-adjusted rates of vulnerability to climate-related disasters. What follows is our attempt to explain our predictions for the relationships between this series of variables. We discuss each link in turn, moving from proximate explanations of climate risk to deeper structural roots (from right to left in this diagram; see figure 4.1). Some links have been extensively discussed in the literature on vulnerability, risk, and disaster; for others, we are developing explanations based on far less information and theorization.[29]

Wealth, Inequality, and Vulnerability to Climate-Related Disasters
One of the most basic indicators of a nation's vulnerability to climate change is its wealth. Climate-related disasters impose direct and indirect costs upon countries, in some cases wreaking complete economic devas-

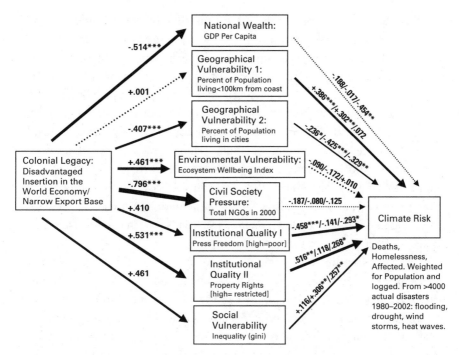

Figure 4.1
Summary figure for path models predicting the proportion of the national population killed, made homeless, or affected by climate-related disasters, 1980–2002. See text for explanation. Values on arrows are standardized regression coefficients (betas), called path coefficients.

tation and in others barely affecting the local economy. Rich nations are better able to protect themselves from climate-related disasters for the simple reason that they have more resources at their disposal. They can support early warning systems and large-scale evacuations; provide disaster insurance; pay for reforestation, soil conservation, mangrove replantation, and other natural defenses; strengthen docks, harbor facilities, and telecommunication and satellite systems; build protective barriers for sea surges and water diversion channels; fortify drainage, irrigation, water supply, and sanitation infrastructure; organize relocation efforts and "managed retreats"; smooth recovery for firms and sectors suffering serious losses; enforce efficient zoning regulations; administer public health and educational services; and offer emergency treatment for victims.[30]

We measure national wealth with the old standby, per capita gross domestic product in market terms.[31] This is hardly a perfect indicator, but for this analysis it has some substantial benefits over the alternatives. A nation's wealth adjusted by the size of the population broadly reflects how much income the average citizen commands. While per capita GDP in purchasing power parity terms corrects for nominal exchange rate values, PPP-adjusted measures of GDP do not reflect what a nation can afford on the world market (including climate modeling and disaster mitigation consultants, technology, and supplies). Nor do PPP-adjusted measures of per capita GDP reflect a nation's relative power in the global economy as well as per capita GDP in market terms. We also use the natural log in order to keep from seeing false trends that may come from the huge differences in per capita GDP.

A nation's wealth is conditioned by its position in the world system. Here we use the shorthand term "extractive state" to describe nations that are heavily dependent upon exports of raw and barely processed materials (mining and lumbering resources as well as ranching and plantation agriculture). Extractive colonial relationships placed host economies at a sharp disadvantage because they were routinely forced to specialize in low-value commodities and trade only with and on the terms of their colonial powers. Even in later years when they mounted drives to develop their national industries, poorer nations did so in a world where there were already powerful economic players with developed industrial bases and relatively overwhelming military and economic might. A nation's mix of leading products has been called by some scholars its national path of development. Several political scientists and sociologists have made the case that the dominant sectors in an economy largely determine the development trajectory of the country and the ability of the state to improve its lot in the global hierarchy of nations.[32] Extractive states are also notorious for their feeble domestic institutions, and institutional quality, according to many economists, is the single most important determinant of long-term national wealth.[33]

There are many elements of export dependence, and our approach is a necessary simplification. Our proxy for a colonial legacy of extraction is a nation's reliance on a small number of exports for its total earnings of foreign exchange.[34] The Export Diversification Index from UNCTAD measures the number of exported products worth over $100,000 (or greater than 0.3 percent of total national exports) in a country. The index itself is derived from the "absolute deviation of the country share from world structure." Higher scores indicate concentrated export structures.[35]

A nation's wealth may be less of an asset in mitigating weather-related disasters if its distribution is highly skewed. High inequality in national income typically means that a disproportionate share of the population is poor and therefore especially vulnerable to climate-related disasters.[36] Even assuming a redistributive state that provides essential protections for its weakest citizens, countries with more poor people are more likely to suffer fatalities, homelessness, internal displacement, serious injuries, and other emergencies.[37] Low-income families tend to rely heavily on land, water, and forests—all weather-dependent forms of natural capital—and especially so in times of crisis.[38] Disasters also exact a heavy toll on the poor through their effect on labor—the greatest asset of the poor. If the breadwinner of a household becomes less productive, earns less income, or is unemployed as a result of an injury, a disability, homelessness, or in the worst case, death, her or his entire family will be affected much more than families with diversified sources of wealth. In addition, poor people tend to possess less information and live in more marginal areas, rendering them more vulnerable to unexpected disaster and less of a priority to government-directed relief efforts.[39] Critically, they often lack access to health care, education, employment, and insurance—goods and services that are essential before, during, and after a climate-related disaster. Finally, there is the sad fact that highly heterogeneous societies—in terms of race, ethnicity, religion, age, or *income*— tend to possess less social capital,[40] place less trust in formal, state institutions,[41] and provide fewer public goods.[42] Inequality in income is one measure of that heterogeneity.

Others have argued that the relationship between social inequality and vulnerability is less certain. Adger reports that "[u]nder certain circumstances inequality facilitates provision of services for the good of communities by those with cumulated assets. An example here is where a set of wealthier actors can provide and maintain irrigation and water management services in agricultural communities which given absolute equality would not exist."[43] Authoritarian states are also thought to sometimes be more effective in providing disaster mitigation and relief.[44] We remain skeptical of these arguments, and the case of the sinking of the *Titanic*, in which the poor were locked in steerage as the wealthy were lowered in the lifeboats, might be cited as a grim object lesson. At any rate, we set out to test the strength of this relationship between inequality and our indicators of climate risk. The link could be positive or negative or too weak to stand up when other variables are considered. Our measure of inequality is another standard, the Gini coefficient. The Gini coefficient measures the average income difference between every possible pair of households in an economy. Its scale ranges from zero to one, with zero representing total equality among households and one representing a situation in which one household controls 100 percent of national income.[45]

High levels of income and asset inequality are a hallmark of extractive states. Since many of these economies were built by a narrow group of political elites who benefited from plundering natural resources and exploiting cheap (or forced) labor, and since many of these elites have an interest in reinforcing existing inequalities,[46] what we observe today is in many ways a reflection of the legacy of the past.[47] Though they bear on two other causal pathways we discuss later, two key features of extractive institutions are related and deserve special attention: limited access to property rights and political power. In countries where a narrow ruling elite with a comparative advantage in extraction is guaranteed secure property rights, chances are these elites will not stand to gain from dismantling the current property rights regime and extending new economic opportunities to the wider population.[48] Furthermore, extractive elites often have a strong interest in repressing civil society and suppressing political democracy, since a reconfiguration of the political status quo could encourage broader investment in the local economy and thus undermine their comparative advantage(s). Under these circumstances, elites are seldom interested in a robust, internally articulated economy with backward and forward linkages because they can purchase luxuries overseas and their low-wage workers cannot afford the products that would be generated.[49] Together, we hypothesize two causal relationships:

H1a: A colonial legacy of extraction tends to lead to lower levels of national wealth.

H1b: National wealth is associated with lower levels of climate-related risk.

H2a: A colonial legacy of extraction leads to higher income inequality.

H2b: Higher income inequality is associated with higher levels of climate-related risk.

Competing Pictures of Urbanization and Informality

Social geographers offer two competing explanations of the relationship between a nation's level of urbanization and climate disaster risk. The first explanation is that many urban areas are already overburdened and incapable of coping with the added stress of climate change. According to this view, Third World cities are densely populated conduits of disease transmission, lacking adequate drainage, sanitation, and potable water, and suffering from unstable and poor housing conditions, high levels of air pollution, heat stress, population growth, crime, unemployment, malnutrition, and social exclusion.[50] High levels of urbanization no doubt pose serious social and environmental problems, but we must be careful not prematurely jump on this theoretical bandwagon based on casual observation. Rural vulnerability to climate-related disasters may be as bad, if not worse, than urban vulnerability. Oftentimes rural populations are too isolated, too dispersed, too uneducated, and too poor to cope with weather-related disasters. Rural areas often lack reliable means of communication and transportation and suffer from government neglect, owing to their social invisibility.[51] Emergency services also tend to be more dependable in urban areas; recovery tends to be quicker; information is more abundant; and it is easier for the media to attract international attention to urban areas. As important, concentrated urban populations help governments and international agencies deliver essential services more efficiently to a large number of people in a limited geographic area. Simply put, population-dense areas often enjoy better roads, schools, hospitals, job opportunities, and water and electricity services. Our prediction may therefore seem somewhat counterintuitive. We expect population-adjusted rates of climate risk to correlate negatively with levels of urbanization. We measure urbanization as the percent of a nation's population residing in "cities" in 2001.[52] This seemingly obvious measure turns out to be quite differently defined in different nations. Still, the measure is broadly reflective of the vast differences by world regions and nations in their ratio of urban and rural habitation.

The extent to which a nation's population is concentrated in urban centers varies greatly across regions of the colonized world, and some of these differences are attributable to precolonial settlement patterns. Latin America has long been much more urbanized than Asia or Africa, based in part on its preexisting cities and on differences in the goals and strategies of their colonial occupiers. However, looking globally across the set of nations, there are a number of reasons why countries with a colonial legacy of extraction tend to be more rural. Here again, we follow the line of reasoning laid out in Acemoglu et al., which distinguishes between European settler colonies and colonies of extraction.[53] Where European colonists settled, they had a vested interest in seeing the country develop a vibrant and resilient internal market. Hence they diversified the economies; set up sound institutions of private property, rule of law, democracy, and Weberian bureaucracy; made large investments in human capital; and created dense interfirm and intersectoral networks that would promote the nation's internal economic integration. Colonists concerned with extraction, by contrast, had incentives to invest only in the infrastructure, institutions, and labor that would facilitate the export of raw materials.[54]

When private property rights are not available to the majority of the population, people are considerably more vulnerable to climate-related disasters for two reasons. First, they are unable to rent, own, or build high-quality, storm-resistant housing in safe places because the government treats property rights as a privilege reserved for the wealthy and well connected, rather than a basic right. Second, they are unable to access the capital, credit, and insurance they need, which could insulate them from the worst effects of extreme weather events.[55] Not surprisingly, where property rights are insecure and unavailable to ordinary people, informal economies and squatter settlements crop up in response.[56] When the good locations are occupied by formal residences and businesses, shantytowns often develop along river embankments, on steep and unstable hill slopes, on floodplains, and near coastal marshes.[57] Such settlements typically consist of flimsy, overcrowded housing facilities with unreliable access to water, electricity, sanitation, and health services.

Our indicator of property rights/informality is an index that measures "the degree to which private property rights are protected and the degree to which the government enforces laws that protect private property." According to O'Driscoll et al., it "also accounts for the possibility that private property will be expropriated,... the independence of the judiciary, the existence of corruption within the judiciary, and the ability of individuals and businesses to enforce contracts."[58] This is a suite of factors that is probably far broader than most readers' initial view of the term "property rights," but it suggests the value of including this index in our study. We postulate that the absence or fragility of private property rights is probably the single most important factor driving people out of the formal sector where they can access credit markets and public services like water, sanitation, telephones, and electricity.

What explains the narrowness and insecurity of property rights as well as the spread of squatter settlements in the developing world? At the risk of oversimplification and repetition of the argument by Acemoglu et al., in places where colonists were interested in settling, they "tried to replicate European institutions, with strong emphasis on private property and checks against government power."[59] Conversely, in extractive colonies, the ruling elite benefited from highly inefficient economic policies and institutions, and many of these policies and institutions have persisted for centuries. The Spanish, for example, granted monopolies and closely regulated economic exchange to facilitate the plunder of local resources as expeditiously as possible. We therefore postulate the following hypotheses:

H3a: A colonial legacy of extraction leads to lower levels of urbanization.

H3b: More urbanized populations face lower levels of climate-related risk.

H4a: A colonial legacy of extraction is associated with weaker property rights and a greater informal economy.

H4b: Weak property rights and higher informality lead to higher levels of climate-related risk.

Climate-Related Risk, Environmental Damage, and Coastal Populations
Preexisting environmental vulnerabilities often exacerbate already bad
situations and lead to higher than usual levels of climate-related risk. In
Bangladesh, for example, upstream deforestation and overgrazing have
reduced the absorption of water and worsened downstream flooding.
In Honduras, Nicaragua, and Haiti, poor farmers trying to eke out
an existence on steep, denuded mountainsides are mortally threatened
by the weak and eroded soil upon which their homes and lives are
built. Preexisting environmental vulnerability can therefore transform
an extreme weather event into a human disaster. This seemingly obvious
link creates some difficulty since omnibus measures of environmental
vulnerability mix a variety of factors, from deforestation to urban
air pollution. Choosing individual measures, such as deforestation rates
or percent of soil degraded, is also problematic because each nation's
physical endowment calls for a different measure of environmental vulnerability. We settled on the Ecosystem Wellbeing Index (EWI) developed by Robert Prescott-Allen and published with the support of the
International Development Research Centre, the World Conservation
Union, the International Institute for Environment and Development,
the Food and Agriculture Organization of the United Nations, and
the UN Environment Programme's World Conservation Monitoring
Centre.[60] The index combines six indicators on preservation of biodiversity; seventeen indicators of water quality; nine indicators of city air
quality; nine indicators of the demands of agriculture, fishing, and tim-
bering on resources; and several others. The risk with such an index,
however, is that the very issue we wish to measure may wash out with
countervailing forces captured in the measure.

Colonial mining, lumbering, and plantation histories savagely
damaged forests and waters. For example, many African economies
were supported by colonists for the express purpose of extracting and
exporting minerals, fuels, and cash crops. Lappé et al. explain that "[in]
West Africa, colonial administrations imposed on local farmers mono-
cultures of annual crops for export, notably peanuts for cooking oil and
livestock feed and cotton for French and British textile mills. But growing the same crops year after year on the same land, without any mixing
of or rotation of crops, trees and livestock, rapidly ruined the soils. Rapidly depleting soils drove farmers to push export crops onto even more

vulnerable lands.... Furthermore, the spread of export crops, by crowding livestock herders into even smaller areas, has contributed to overgrazing."[61] Having lost "first-mover" advantages to the advanced, industrialized countries in more dynamic economic sectors, many developing countries are similarly stuck in specializing in resource harvesting and extraction, which means that they experience higher levels of price volatility and less favorable terms of trade in relation to higher value-added products. Lacking a reliable source of foreign exchange, these governments are often forced to saddle themselves with unsustainable levels of debt, which in turn is "a driving force leading to overexploitation of soil and subsoil resources."[62] The vicious circle feeds itself.

A nation's geography is also a key determinant of its vulnerability to climate-related risk. The world's highest-risk coastal areas include the Nile delta region, eastern China, small island states, southern Bangladesh, much of Africa and South America, and seventeen of the twenty-five largest cities in the world.[63] There are many reasons why coastal areas are at a greater risk of suffering climate disasters. Coastal populations must deal with hurricanes, storm surges, coastal erosion, subsidence, and the intrusion of salt water into drinking water and estuarian systems that produce food and protect shorelines from storms. What's more, extreme weather events and more subtle climatic stresses affect tourism, local agriculture and aquaculture, fisheries, port facilities, roads, communications, housing, waste facilities, septic systems, and the availability of fresh water.[64]

Our indicator for this variable is very much less than ideal: the percent of the population living within 100 kilometers of the coast.[65] Many coastal settlements are well above sea level and will not face severe impacts for a much longer period than low-lying settlements. This number can also hide the fact that some people far inland live just inches above sea level. Altitude above sea level was another variable we considered, but this number is an average of a much broader national population.

Cities are like a circulatory system for the global economy. They network vast and disparate peoples and places, facilitate the import and export of goods and services, and serve as command-and-control points for global capitalism.[66] Many of these global cities are situated along a coastline. Usually lying at strategic economic and geopolitical locations near mouths of rivers, on protected bays and other low-lying areas, coastal cities connect the interior regions of agriculture, mining, logging, and industry to the rest of the world.

Coastal cities offer important economic advantages, which in part explains their existence. However, to attribute their existence, as well as their size, scope, and number, to free and spontaneous market forces is to do serious violence to history.[67] Many coastal cities were developed as colonial outposts and designed to transfer extracted resources from the tropics to western Europe. Large urban coastal populations and squatter settlements therefore bear the imprint of extractive colonialism.[68] Acemoglu et al. suggest that most colonists carefully weighed the pros and cons of creating a settler or an extractive colony based on the size and concentration of the labor force and local disease rates, but they overlook an important geographic aspect of this decision-making calculus: that coastal locations best facilitated the extraction and export of the colony's resources.[69] These points suggest these hypotheses:

H5a: A colonial legacy of extraction leads to higher environmental vulnerability.

H5b: Environmental vulnerability leads to higher levels of climate-related risk.

H6a: A colonial legacy of extraction is associated with a higher percentage of the population living near the coast.

H6b: The percent of a nation's population living near the coast correlates positively with levels of climate-related risk.

Press Freedom, Civil Society Strength, and Climate-Related Risk

Students of political science and political economy have long argued that when information flows freely, rulers—motivated by their desire to stay in power—have a strong incentive to protect their citizens from external shocks.[70] "No issue creates a groundswell of public opinion like that of natural disasters and the plight of victims," writes one author.[71] "Mass suffering due to disaster," according to Wisner et al., "may contribute to the overthrow of elites and lead to dramatic realignments of power."[72] Amartya Sen posited that countries with a free media are better able to cope with famines than those where information is suppressed by the government.

Our measure is the Freedom House index of press freedom. It captures "[t]he degree to which each country permits the free flow of information.... Scores are created by adding three different measures: legal environment, political influences, and economic pressures." "The legal environment," for example, "encompasses an examination of the laws and regulations that could influence media content as well as the government's inclination to use these laws to restrict the ability of media to operate."[73] It is important to note for our analysis that our dependent variables—the numbers killed, made homeless, and affected by climate-related disasters—are based on press and NGO reports of disasters, which may artificially strengthen the (negative) relationship between press freedom scores and the risk indicators.

Following a long line of theorization in economics, sociology, and political science, we hypothesize that extractive colonial legacies have had a negative impact on institutional development in low- and middle-income countries.[74] Since many former colonies began their development under circumstances of high social inequality, the institutions that were put in place largely reflected those inequalities. In short, high levels of initial inequality left political institutions weak and deformed and society less democratic.[75]

However, we are not trying to explain seventeenth-, eighteenth-, and nineteenth-century institutions. We want to explain current institutions: in particular, the democratic institutions that provide for a free media. Yet, the best evidence suggests that institutions are extraordinarily persistent, or path-dependent. Acemoglu et al. and others argue that extractive colonial elites feared that institutional development would jeopardize their political and economic position in society and thus stifled democracy and press freedom for decades, and in some cases, centuries.[76]

Another important factor that scholars suggest bears upon a nation's vulnerability to climate-related disasters is the strength of its civil society. Civil society, as Reuschemeyer et al. define it, "is the totality of social institutions and associations, both formal and informal, that are not strictly production-related nor governmental or familial in character."[77] Here we focus narrowly on the number of non-governmental organizations (NGOs). With respect to natural disasters, NGOs are said to perform a number of important functions. They can raise aid, either domestically or overseas, for disaster victims and attune relief and reconstruction programs to local needs. They can provide useful information before, during, and after extreme weather events to both citizens and governments. They can monitor and evaluate the actions of aid agencies and governments and put pressure on these actors when they fail to deliver adequate services. Or, as one author puts it, they can act as "voice surrogates" that mobilize public opinion.[78] NGOs may also fill gaps in providing services where the public and private sector has failed. Our admittedly imperfect index of civil society strength is the total number of NGOs in a nation, as counted in the Objective Indicators of Governance dataset from the United Nations Development Programme.[79] The raw number of NGOs should provide an indicator of the total number of agents in positions to lobby the state for reform, or to organize disaster relief.

Extractive states are not only infamous for their feeble domestic institutions, but also their weak and unorganized civil societies.[80] A number of explanations have been advanced to account for this phenomenon. Some authors argue that large resource rents provide government officials with enough money to allow them to suppress civil society's desire for democracy.[81] Some have suggested that windfall profits (seen especially from oil) promote patronage and edge out ordinary citizens from public participation.[82] A final group emphasizes how resource booms relieve government officials of their usual need to raise taxes and thus their dependence on public support.[83] Participation in official NGOs, which would be counted by international agencies, was often missing from the histories of colonies, and their rise has been very recent in historical terms. The poverty of their potential members keeps many from collecting dues and becoming formalized. Finally, as Herrera points out for Latin America, because of the history of large land grants to a few rich individuals, and because the land of peasants was expropriated in the mid-1800s, there was never any small and medium class of rural capitalist producers. Furthermore, there was never a middle class of urban intellectuals, who have made up the bulk of (at least early) environmental activists in the wealthier countries.[84] We therefore predict that countries that are highly dependent on a few exports will have an exporting sector elite that depends on the state and its rents,[85] and these elites will suppress civil society.

H7a: A colonial legacy of extraction should correlate negatively with levels of press freedom.

H7b: Press freedom lowers levels of climate-related risk.

H8a: Nations with a colonial legacy of extraction have weaker civil societies.

H8b: Nations with stronger civil society organizations have lower levels of climate-related risk.

Findings: Predictors of Suffering from Climate-Related Disasters

Table 4.2 and figure 4.1 provide some surprises and some expected outcomes in our effort to understand what causes certain numbers of people to be killed, made homeless, or otherwise affected by the climate disasters of the 1980s and 1990s. These models examining the effects of institutions of democracy, national wealth, civil society pressure, inequality, urbanization, environmental vulnerability, and coastal populations managed to explain from 15 to 42 percent of human suffering from those disasters. Since so much randomness is involved in the intensity of a small number of killer storms, the percent of the population killed was much more difficult to explain than our population-adjusted measures of homelessness and affected populations. Leaving out zeros—countries where no major climate disasters occurred during the twenty-three-year period—substantially improved our ability to explain deaths and homelessness from climate disasters.[86]

Our best models overall in terms of their ability to predict vulnerability were those on the percent of the population affected by climate-related disasters. That was largely the case because of the strength of the negative relationship between national wealth (as measured by per capita GDP) and the number of people affected by climate disasters over the period.[87] However, in the cases of homelessness and death from climate-related disasters, per capita GDP explained surprisingly little of the variation across nations. This pattern can also be seen in the first-order correlations (table 4.1), where wealth demonstrated a negative association with climate vulnerability whether measured by deaths,

Table 4.1
Correlations of Dependent Variables: Vulnerability Indicators for Climate Disasters, Year 2000

	No. Killed per Million Population (ln)	No. Killed per Million Population (ln) Zeros Excluded	No. Homeless per Population (ln)	No. Homeless per Population (ln) Zeros Excluded	No. Affected per Population (ln)	No. Affected per Population (ln) Zeros Excluded
No. killed per million population (ln) zeros excluded	1.000** 169					
No. homeless per population (ln)	0.494** 206	0.507** 169				
No. homeless per population (ln) zeros excluded	0.335** 143	0.517** 134	0.988** 143			
No. affected per population (ln)	0.436** 195	0.476** 169	0.622** 195	0.609** 143		
No. affected per population (ln) zeros excluded	0.406** 187	0.493** 165	0.593** 187	0.609** 143	0.999** 187	
GDP per capita in 2000 (ln)	−0.262** 178	−0.212** 153	−0.371** 178	−0.191* 129	−0.529** 170	−0.479** 165

Notes: ** Correlation is significant at the 0.01 level two-tailed.
* Correlation is significant at the 0.05 level two-tailed.
Values are Pearson's correlations and number of cases. Correlation is significant at the 0.05 level two-tailed.
All variables were natural log transformed. Zeros were removed from each vulnerability variable to create a second set of variables.

homelessness, or number of people affected. However, these correlations are all relatively low (explaining only 7 and 13 percent of the variance of the number killed and made homeless, respectively), and the number of people reported affected was far more closely related to wealth ($r = -0.529$; r-squared $= 0.28$). Together these findings suggest that tying climate deaths and homelessness to national wealth alone may be an incorrect reading of the real forces driving climate-caused human tragedies. We consider this a major finding.

There were five predictors of homelessness and death related to climate disasters that were more consistently significant than national wealth in our models (table 4.2). As the literature on vulnerability suggests, geography does matter, but often not in the way expected. The most powerful and consistent predictor—most potent in six of the nine models and statistically significant in all nine—is the percent of a nation's people living in cities. However, this relationship is negative, contrary to the conventional wisdom. People living in more urbanized nations are less likely to be killed, made homeless, or affected by climate-related disasters than people living in more rural nations.

The percentage of a nation's population that lives within 100 kilometers of the coast, a consistently cited indicator of geographic vulnerability, predicted the proportion of that country's people suffering from climate-related disasters in five of the nine models and was positively related to vulnerability in all nine models. This finding confirms what until now had been largely speculation, and a better measure of the population living in very low-lying coastal areas may be able to predict significantly more of this relationship.

What has been called social vulnerability is also crucial; domestic inequality of income was consistently strongly and positively related to all three climate disaster indices. This variable was statistically significant in eight of nine models, losing its significance only when zeros were removed from the homelessness index. The index increased slightly in predictive strength when zeros were removed on the number killed by climate disasters, and saw only a modest shift downward when cases that had no people reported as affected by climate disasters in the two decades were removed. The pattern was clear, however; countries with higher levels of income inequality experience the effects of climate disasters more profoundly than more equal societies.

So domestic inequality kills, and this could be for a number of reasons. First, countries with a high Gini coefficient have a large number of poor people living at the bottom of a very unequal income distribution. These poor are almost certainly less able to prepare for and recover from dangerous climate-related disasters. Second, nations with highly polarized societies tend to possess low levels of social capital. Third, in highly unequal societies, the wealthy may have weak incentives to invest in public goods like health facilities, schools, and security, since they pay for their own and see little connection between their welfare and the welfare of the poor. Future research that can distinguish between these competing explanations would be extremely useful and give policy makers clearer directions on where their efforts will be best directed if they wish to avert widespread death and homelessness from climate-related disasters.

Overall, the press freedom index was significant in predicting homelessness and the number of people affected by climate-related disasters. It is interesting that press restrictions were not correlated directly with disaster outcomes when taken alone, but they had significant predictive ability when they were included in models that controlled for other factors, such as urbanization. At first glance, press freedom seems to exert a *positive* effect on levels of risk. However, we need to interpret these results carefully. Although we did predict that higher levels of press freedom would dampen the impact of climate disasters (following Sen), we must take into account issues of selection bias. Many disasters in rural areas go completely unnoticed in the urban-headquartered media and aid community, and under authoritarian regimes that suppress the free flow of reliable information. We suspect this explains the apparent positive relationship. There are no good reasons, after all, to think that countries with greater press freedom should experience higher levels of climate disaster. It also bears repeating that "[t]he [EM-DAT] database is compiled from various sources, including UN agencies, nongovernmental organisations, insurance companies, research institutes and *press agencies*."[88]

This relationship bears directly upon on the next variable—civil society strength as measured by the total number of NGOs in a nation in 2000. This variable was somewhat perplexing and frankly worrisome. Its effect on climate risk was negative but not significant in three models out of six, near zero in two, but significant and positive in one model.

This single model (model 9) for the number of people killed per million people in a nation's population, including nations reporting zero deaths from climate disasters, leads us to cautiously suggest one possible explanation. As just indicated, our data from CRED-OFDA are compiled from NGOs, and so nations with few NGOs may underreport climate-related disasters, or word of them may never reach the Brussels-based data compilers at all. Clearly, huge disasters in these areas will tend to get reported, but the hundreds of modest ones may not be reported.

Highly restricted property rights—our admittedly crude proxy for the extent of informal activity in the economy—seem to exert a consistently positive effect on the severity of climate-related disasters. It was especially effective at predicting the proportion of the national population that had been made homeless from climate disasters over the twenty-three-year period. Higher scores indicate weaker property rights, so countries with larger informal sectors tend to experience higher levels of climate-related risk.[89] This is a strong relationship in the direction predicted, and this broad indicator of informality in the economy is suggestive on several counts.

Nonsignificant findings are as important as significant ones, and to our surprise there was one variable that in spite of consistently positive and significant zero-order correlations with the three climate risk indicators was a significant predictor in none of the nine multivariate models: the Ecosystem Wellbeing Index. We expected environmental vulnerability and previous damage to the ecosystem to be reflected in this indicator, but the EWI was never significant and in fact registered an effect in the opposite direction from that predicted in eight of the nine models. A high EWI means worse environmental conditions, so the negative co-efficient reflects how lower scores (better environmental status) were associated with slightly more deaths and homelessness in these models. These findings may be explained by the fact that EWI was negatively correlated with the percentage of a nation's population residing in cities ($r = -0.559$), so that variable may be better at explaining climate vulnerability and therefore taking the variance from EWI.

Our second task was to evaluate the extent to which our proxy for a colonial legacy—a narrow export base—explained each of these intervening variables. Turning to the second part of table 4.2 and the path analysis in figure 4.1 (the left side), we can state that a narrow export

Table 4.2
Standardized Regression Coefficients (and *t*-ratios) of Three Measures of Vulnerability to Climate Change: Proportion of the National Population Killed, Made Homeless, or Affected by Climate Disasters, 1980–2002

A. Effects of Intervening Variables on Indicators of Vulnerability to Climate Disasters

Independent Variables	9 No. Killed per Million Population (ln)	10 No. Killed per Million Population (ln)	11 No. Killed per Million Population (ln) Zeros Excluded	12 No. Homeless per Population (ln)	13 No. Homeless per Population (ln)	14 No. Homeless per Population (ln) Zeros Excluded	15 No. Affected per Population (ln)	16 No. Affected per Population (ln)	17 No. Affected per Population (ln) Zeros Excluded
GDP per capita (logged)	—	-0.017 (-0.093)	—	—	-0.188 (-1.138)	—	—	-0.454** (-3.097)	—
Press freedom	-0.126 (-0.994)	-0.110 (-1.012)	-0.141 (-1.176)	-0.310** (-2.709)	-0.110 (-1.084)	-0.458*** (-3.693)	-0.215† (-1.965)	-0.221* (-2.465)	-0.293* (-2.561)
Civil society pressure (NGOs in 2000)	0.253* (2.022)	—	-0.080 (-0.680)	0.004 (0.038)	—	-0.187 (-1.526)	-0.160 (-1.472)	·	-0.125 (-1.108)
Environmental vulnerability (EWI)	-0.034 (-0.316)	-0.041 (-0.364)	-0.172 (-1.625)	-0.098 (-0.970)	-0.043 (-0.414)	-0.090 (-0.824)	-0.001 (-0.012)	-0.018 (-0.194)	0.010 (0.098)
Property rights	0.221 (1.503)	—	0.118 (0.849)	0.463** (3.483)	—	0.516** (3.588)	0.123 (0.968)	—	0.268* (2.023)

Domestic inequality (Gini)	0.303** (3.165)	0.247** (2.606)	0.306** (3.392)	0.227* (2.620)	0.196* (2.233)	0.116 (1.238)	0.311*** (3.754)	0.292*** (3.733)	0.257** (2.972)
Urban population (percent)	−0.390** (−3.287)	−0.371* (−2.595)	−0.425*** (−3.793)	−0.381** (−3.549)	−0.406** (−3.060)	−0.236* (−2.035)	−0.397*** (−3.866)	−0.242* (−2.053)	−0.329** (−3.073)
Coastal population (percent)	0.148 (1.522)	0.086 (0.886)	0.302** (3.299)	0.244** (2.778)	0.245** (2.728)	0.386*** (4.070)	0.069 (0.820)	0.163* (2.039)	0.072 (0.825)
Adjusted R^2	0.177***	0.146**	0.274***	0.328***	0.264***	0.364***	0.384***	0.418***	0.331***
Minimum pairwise N of cases	115	118	114	115	118	93	115	118	115

B. Effects of Narrow Export Base on Intervening Variables Dependent Variables

	1	2	3	4	5	6	7	8
	Urban Population	Coastal Population	Gini	EWI	Press Freedom	Civil Society Pressure	GDP per Capita (logged)	Property Rights
Narrow export base	−0.407*** (−4.67)	0.001 (0.009)	0.461*** (4.90)	0.461*** (5.50)	0.410*** (4.62)	−0.796*** (−13.16)	−0.514*** (−6.43)	0.531*** (6.63)
Adjusted R^2	0.158***	−0.009	0.204***	0.206***	0.160***	0.630***	0.258***	0.275***
Min. pairwise N of cases	112	117	91	114	108	102	117	105

Note: †$p < 0.1$; *$p < .05$; **$p < .01$; ***$p < .001$
Cases selected pairwise; see text.

base is a strong predictor of seven of the eight intervening variables. A narrow export base has a series of negative impacts on nations, being associated with a low number of nongovernmental organizations (r-squared = 0.630), weak property rights and high levels of informality (r-squared = 0.275), low national wealth (r-squared = 0.258), poor environmental health (r-squared = 0.206), higher income inequality (r-squared = 0.204), less press freedom (r-squared = 0.160) and more of the population in rural areas (r-squared = 0.158). Contrary to our prediction based on the literature, nations with narrower export profiles have no difference in the percentage of the population living within 100 kilometers of the coast than the rest of the world. Clearly, having a narrow export base leaves nations more likely to possess the characteristics that we have just seen leave them more vulnerable, as reflected in deaths, homelessness, and the number reported to be affected by climate-related disasters.

It is no simple matter to calculate the total indirect effects of having a narrow export base since we have nine possible models for which to calculate them. Rather than present nine path diagrams, in figure 4.1, we report path coefficients for three models, one for each dependent variable (models 11, 14, and 17), each constructed by excluding nations reporting zero disasters. The GDP path includes coefficients from models 10, 13, and 16, but due to extremely high collinearity these were run as separate models. The total effects of a narrow export base on the three vulnerability indicators as reflected in these nine models varied from 15 to 40 percent.[90] The overall picture is that having a narrow export base explains about a third of homelessness, from one-seventh to a third of deaths, and about 40 percent of national patterns in who is affected by climate-related disasters. Given the randomness of such disasters, this is a remarkable finding: that one characteristic of (mostly poor) nations explains so much of a nation's likelihood to suffer from climate-related disasters.

Conclusion: Suffering from Climate-Related Disasters as an Injustice

In this chapter we have reviewed a diverse set of hypotheses about why some nations suffer much more than others from disasters brought on by climate: floods, windstorms, heat waves, and droughts. These hypotheses were derived from human geographic, political science, and sociological explanations of what makes societies vulnerable to disasters. Our indicators based on more than 4,000 disasters reflect the proportion of a nation's population that was killed, made homeless, or substantially affected by these climate forces between 1980 and 2002 (tables 3.1 and 3.2). We found strong empirical support for many of these hypotheses, but there were also several surprising revelations.

First, when examined alone, national wealth as measured by per capita GDP explains only 7 percent of climate-related deaths, and only 13 percent of homelessness (table 4.2). It explained significantly more of the number of people reported by the press and NGOs to have been affected by climate disasters: between 23 and 27 percent. In all cases the more money a nation has, the lower the proportion of its national population that was killed, made homeless, or otherwise affected by climate disasters over the 1980 to 2002 period. In analyses that hold other factors constant, however, national poverty explained virtually none of the trends in death and homelessness. This result suggests that tying climate deaths and homelessness to wealth is not only a gross oversimplification, but a misrepresentation of the real forces driving climate-related human tragedy. Five other variables were far stronger and more consistent predictors of death and homelessness than was per capita GDP: income inequality, urban and coastal populations, press freedom, and property rights.

Our argument that structural constraints on nations attributable to their colonial past drive national patterns of vulnerability to climate-related disasters was strongly supported. Based on decades of scholarship in the political economy of development, our proxy measure of "colonial legacy," or more cautiously, "insertion in the world economy," was the narrowness of a nation's export base. The analysis of indirect effects showed that this single variable could explain between 15 and 40 percent of national rates of injury and damage from climate-related disasters. The finding bears further exploration. The narrowness of a nation's export base was weakest at predicting the number killed, but this predictive power doubled when "zeros" were excluded—the nations who had entirely avoided "killer storms" over the twenty-three-year period. Storms have a strong random element, and this could be the explanation for this improvement in how our set of variables predicted these national rates. Still, resting so much of our argument on one variable is somewhat worrisome. Future research will examine other variables that might also predict the wide variety of intervening variables we test. We are also concerned about causal priority (sequencing), but given the state of cross-national datasets on this range of variables, we chose to conduct exploratory cross-sectional tests. We believe that a narrow export base is a reasonable proxy for a colonial legacy of extraction, but casual observation of the list of countries ranking "worst" on this index reveals important anomalies. (See appendix B.) Given this, the strength of our proxy for how a nation is inserted in the global economy in explaining death and destruction from storms is remarkable.

To conclude, we believe that the policy community must recognize that disaster prevention and relief efforts that treat only symptoms and not political and economic structures are doomed to longer-term failure. The root causes of suffering lie in colonial histories and current relations with the global economy that keep nations vulnerable in many senses of the word. Dealing with these chronic problems is cost-effective in the sense that assisting nations in building resilience against future disasters is immeasurably less expensive than pouring billions of dollars into emergency relief after disasters happen. A preventive approach has the added advantage of being more easily integrated into national development plans and easing conditions of generalized mistrust over climate change (as we discuss in chapter 7). Ideally, resilience-building projects can serve several goals at once.

As we mentioned in chapter 3, disaster relief money would be better spent on development assistance that creates economic opportunities and prepares governments and citizens for disasters. The finding that national wealth is less important than press freedom, property rights, and income inequality is striking, because the latter are issues that states and their development partners can address with more focused interventions than general efforts to grow the economy. These are elements of a nation's colonial legacy that must be addressed as part of efforts to reduce the massive human suffering from climate-related disasters.

5

Fueling Injustice: Emissions, Development Paths, and Responsibility

Pollution by the Poor and by the Rich

On October 28, 2002, thousands of activists marched for "climate justice" in the streets of New Delhi, India, during COP-8, the Eighth Conference of the Parties of the UN Framework Convention on Climate Change. The coalition in the streets of Delhi consisted of fishers from Kerala and West Bengal representing the National Fishworkers' Forum, farmers from the Agricultural Workers and Marginal Farmers Union, and a delegation of indigenous peoples threatened by the massive Narmada dam and from mining-impacted areas of Orissa. NGO delegates from twenty other countries came to participate. "This is the human face of the rising movement for Climate Justice," the movement declared.[1]

The protestors affirmed that "climate change is a human rights issue" affecting "our livelihoods, our health, our children and our natural resources." They declared that they would "build alliances across states and borders to oppose climate change inducing patterns and advocate for and practice sustainable development. They declared "We reject the market-based principles that guide the current negotiations to solve the climate crisis: Our World is Not for Sale!"[2]

While tempers were flaring out in the streets, inside the conference hall the negotiating situation was going from bad to worse. The European Union and the developing countries, which had been working together since the Berlin meetings as a "Green Group," found themselves increasingly at odds.[3] Fearing that limits on their carbon emissions would lead to economic stagnation, the G-77 group of poorer nations, led by the host nation India, pushed for Kyoto to focus on "sustainable development." The Delhi ministerial declaration on climate change and sustainable development that came from the conference declared that "economic and social development and poverty eradication are the first and overriding priorities" of developing countries, that "climate change and its adverse effects should be addressed while meeting the requirements of sustainable development."[4] At New Delhi, the developing countries signaled that they had effectively taken control of this element of the Kyoto process, chiding wealthy nations that they should "demonstrate that they are taking the lead" in "modifying longer-term trends" in greenhouse gas emissions. They also staked out their own right to development: "Parties have a right to, and should, promote sustainable development. Policies and measures to protect the climate system against human-induced change should be appropriate for the specific conditions of each Party and should be integrated with national development programmes, taking into account that economic development is essential for adopting measures to address climate change."[5]

Friends of the Earth UK declared that the Delhi Declaration was "weak and demonstrate[d] the lack of progress made at COP8 on tackling dangerous climate change."[6] Pushed by many environmentalists who saw their hard-won treaty to address and reverse climate change being transformed into one on Third World development, the European Union negotiators panicked, and attempted to advance in their agenda of preparing for truly global participation in a post-Kyoto treaty that would go into effect after the target year 2012. A Danish delegate was reported to say that "Discussions on what will happen after 2012 has [*sic*] to start, and some developing countries need to start thinking of engaging in measures to mitigate greenhouse gases (GHGs)."[7]

A furious reaction from developing countries called for those most responsible for the problem to take steps to address it. Oil-producing nations, and Saudi Arabia in particular, strongly influenced the G-77 position, which nearly entirely ignored the contingent from the small island states.[8] The Saudis, reportedly with language and strategies from the United States, insisted that the treaty address the "adverse effects of mitigation [reducing emissions] on developing countries." One commentator noted that the United States was able to "bring deliberations on several issues to a complete standstill."[9]

In chapters 3 and 4, we saw through case studies and the systematic analysis of thousands of climate disasters over the past two decades that the world's poorest nations are least able to prepare for, handle, and recover from those disasters. In this chapter we turn to the question of who is putting the world's climate at risk from greenhouse gases. We will see that global warming is all about inequality, not only in who will suffer its effects most, but also in who created the problem in the first place. As we argued in chapters 1 and 2, these compounding inequalities create a toxic political environment within which Northern and Southern governments negotiate. In this regard, we argue that the reluctance of poor nations to commit to scheduled reductions in carbon emissions is not simply a function of high discount rates (a here-and-now orientation) and the weak technical and administrative abilities (e.g., incompetence and corruption). More fundamentally, it is the result of a "host of subtle and cumulative equity problems" rooted in the problem of global inequality: inequality in who is suffering from the problem, who caused it in the first place, who is expected to address the problem, and who currently benefits disproportionately from the goods produced by the global economy.[10]

To a naïve observer, resolving the crisis of global climate change might be a matter of rational measurement of the atmosphere, giving equal shares of its capacity for absorbing greenhouse gases to all humans and assigning responsibility to individuals based on what they have put into it. It is, after all, a basic rule of civil justice, Superfund, and kindergarten ethics that those who created a mess should be responsible for cleaning up their share of the mess. Yet internationally, this simple question of who is to blame for the problem leads to a hornet's nest of contentious issues.

This chapter addresses three questions: Who is responsible for climate change?[11] What are the different ways of accounting for responsibility? Who is making progress toward resolving the problem? Our analysis is built around an examination of four yardsticks that have been proposed for measuring responsibility for carbon dioxide emissions. Each method reflects a different set of principled beliefs and focuses on a different set of nations as most responsible. Politicians have used these yardsticks to defend their positions on what they believe to be "fair" and "just." Not surprisingly, these measures have also led to a series of scientific uncertainties and rancorous debates.[12]

A recurring theme throughout this book is that resolving the climate change crisis will depend fundamentally upon achieving a mutually acceptable understanding of what is fair. Fairness principles, we have argued, can provide focal points that reduce the costs of negotiating and bargaining agreements, induce stable equilibria, make agreements more palatable to domestic audiences (who effectively possess a veto over ratification and implementation), and realign the incentives of rich and poor nations to create fewer opportunities for shirking, defection, and other types of opportunistic behavior.

At the same time, saying that fairness matters is a far cry from specifying how and under what conditions it matters. Norms of fairness are extremely elastic and subject to political manipulation, and explicit or tacit focal points rarely emerge spontaneously. In many cases, countries hold genuinely different perceptions of fairness because of their highly disparate positions in the international system.[13] Poor nations, for instance, believe that they are unjustly suffering the consequences of the North's profligate consumption. They also believe that they are entitled to pursue "cheap" economic growth using fossil fuels and other natural resources at hand, since now-wealthy countries did the same at their early stages of development. Some rich nations, by contrast, argue that a climate agreement that excludes developing countries is unfair and meaningless since non-Annex I emissions will increase exponentially over the next few decades. Some rich nations have also suggested that if they continue to bear the weight of sustaining global economic growth and international financial stability, it would be both unfair and unrealistic to expect them to make sharp and immediate reductions in their carbon emissions.

Making matters more complicated, oil exporters argue that in the absence of a legal text that provides for their compensation and diversification into less carbon-intensive sectors, they cannot reasonably be expected to participate in any agreement. Small island states take an entirely different view. They believe a fair agreement would immediately stabilize the climate, forestall the complete destruction of island nations and cultures, and address their basic economic needs and extraordinary vulnerability to climate-related stress and hydrometeorological disasters.[14] Some nations in cold locations, with higher heating bills, and countries with large land areas have also argued that their special "national circumstances"—which predispose them toward higher emissions levels from transportation of goods and people—must be taken into consideration in crafting a "fair" deal for all nations. Still others argue that a distinction must be drawn between "survival" and "luxury" emissions.

In short, we live in a morally ambiguous world where social understandings of fairness are "configurational," depending on countries' position in the global hierarchy of economic and political power.[15] It should therefore come as no surprise that there are almost as many fairness arguments as there are negotiating blocs.[16]

In the first section of this chapter, we describe the range of principles that have been proposed to assign responsibility for carbon emissions, explain why none of these principles (by themselves) will likely produce a consensus on fairness, and discuss some of the more promising hybrid proposals currently being considered. While recognizing the need to move away from particularistic notions of justice, we argue that the literature on "negotiated justice" obscures the more central question of whether and to what extent an international agreement must favor rich or poor nations.[17]

In the second section, we use the tools of multiple regression to examine the role of different national attributes in explaining global variation in responsibility for carbon emissions: national wealth, population, geography, industrial structure, urbanization, trade openness, civil society, and democracy. Our goal is to shed some light on what drives responsibility for climate change, as differently conceived. This may clarify what would need to change to reduce emissions.

In the third section, we take a closer look at one of the central findings from these regression results: Emissions are skyrocketing with growing trade and industrialization in poorer nations as wealthy nations "offshore" the production of energy-intensive products to such places. We review the theory and the evidence behind claims of "environmental load displacement," "declining environmental terms of trade," "ecologically unequal exchange," and the so-called "ecological debt," and examine their economic and environmental implications.

In the fourth section, we tease out the implications of different sectoral pathways of development for carbon emissions. Our empirical results suggest that the historical legacy of a country's incorporation into the global economy has a critical impact on its available avenues of development. They also suggest that scholars and policy makers stand to gain from a better understanding of the "polluting elites" who direct leading sectors of their economies and exercise disproportionate control over national and foreign environmental policies.[18]

By way of conclusion, we offer some reflections on the types of development pathways that might lead nations to a more sustainable state. Diversification into sectors producing less carbon, we argue, is an intensely political process that requires country-specific knowledge concerning state–society relations and local institutions. In countries where domestic elites have risen to economic and political power using old and inefficient technologies that exploit local natural and labor resources, policy makers should expect these elites to vigorously oppose the shifting of incentives away from their industries toward the introduction of new, more efficient, and environmentally friendly technologies. This leads to a discussion of the need for compensatory mechanisms and conflict management strategies. It also demonstrates that there is a sound logic for linking issues of economic development and environmental protection. Before we get to these points, however, we need to cover a good bit of theoretical and empirical ground.

Cutting the Carbon Cake: Four Ways to Share the Burden

Four central and radically different methods of differentiation have been proposed during the dozen or so years of climate negotiations, each with crucial assumptions and implications for climate stabilization, justice, political expediency, and who will bear the greatest burden of change if it is accepted as the basis for a climate treaty. These are grandfathering, carbon intensity, historical responsibility, and contraction and convergence to a global per capita norm. The Kyoto Protocol, as it was negotiated in 1997, was based on grandfathering—that nations should reduce their emissions incrementally from a baseline year, in this case, 1990. Large emitters, therefore, had their high discharges of greenhouse gases "grandfathered" in, with relatively minor adjustments averaging 5.2 percent, for the foreseeable future. The carbon intensity approach, introduced by the World Resources Institute and favored by the second Bush administration starting in 2002, calls for voluntary changes in efficiency to drive reduction of emissions. In this approach, the goal is to have strong economic growth with as few carbon dioxide emissions as possible. Both of these proposals have the effect of departing from the current status quo without radical demands on powerful nations.

On the other side of the spectrum are two proposals that strongly favor developing countries: historical responsibility and per capita contraction and convergence. India, China, and much of the developing world favor a per capita approach in which each person on Earth is given an equal right to the ability of the atmosphere to absorb carbon. Under this proposal, nations whose per capita consumption of fossil fuels is significantly lower than the world average would be given significant room to grow and emit. Most per capita plans would allow them to trade their extra carbon emission credits for the capital they need for development. By comparison, nations with energy-intensive economies would face sharp requirements to cut their consumption of fuels.

Brazil also introduced a proposal in 1997 that would take into account the amount of damage done by nations in the past to the atmosphere's ability to absorb more greenhouse gases. This historical responsibility approach puts the onus on nations that put greenhouse gases in the atmosphere in past decades to reduce their emissions quickly, most notably Britain and the United States. Some developing countries have supported this approach and demanded that some indemnification be paid for the so-called "carbon debt." We take up each alternative approach here, examining its roots and implications, the principles upon which it is based, and how each has been approached or ignored in global climate negotiations over the past dozen years.

Grandfathering

The treaty that emerged from the backroom bargaining at Kyoto in 1997 was based on the concept of grandfathering—that the world's wealthier nations would make efforts to reduce their carbon emissions relative to a baseline year, in this case, 1990.[19] After a series of drawn-out negotiations, individual reduction targets were agreed upon among rich nations, mostly 6–7 percent below the 1990 baseline by 2010.[20] The approach was decided upon for Kyoto because of its political expediency.

For more than a decade of climate negotiations, similar arguments have been made in response to calls for sharp and immediate cuts in emission levels. Many countries contend that "national circumstances" and economic hardships affect their ability to make deep and immediate reductions. At Kyoto and the many meetings since, the United States, Russia, and several other high-emissions nations bargained hard for minor changes to the status quo. The U.S. Senate and the current U.S. administration have emphasized that even a Kyoto-type treaty would unfairly damage the nation's economy and send jobs overseas. On the Senate floor in November 2003, dozens of senators argued that the McCain-Lieberman Climate Stewardship Act would place painful limits on U.S. economic growth and create terrible suffering among different groups of Americans.

The principle of grandfathering has not been applied to developing countries. However, were it to resurface (as focal points often do),[21] most experts agree it would have the effect of punishing late developers. As Aslam explains, "current emissions of developing countries...are very low compared with those of industrialized countries, but are rising rapidly. This places developing countries at a severe disadvantage when it comes to negotiating emission control targets that are based on a grandfathering system."[22]

Figure 5.1 illustrates the startling extent of inequality in total annual emissions.[23] With the latest figures at this writing, the United States emitted the largest proportion of carbon of any nation—nearly twice that of the next highest nation, China, and nearly four times that of Russia (figure 5.1A). Since the 1990 baselines, emissions have in fact increased in most nations, and in some nations substantially. Besides the ex-Soviet Union republics, whose economies collapsed after the transition to capitalism, virtually no countries in the developed world are on track to meet even their modest Kyoto goals. Wealthier nations who accepted Kyoto targets were listed in Annex I of the treaty, and the rest, who were expected to take up limits only in future rounds of the treaty, were classified as non-Annex I.

While many argue that the grandfathering approach is amoral and baldly based on political power in the international system, it does represent at least three understandings of justice. Entitlement theories of justice, both in their libertarian and Marxist forms, hold that individuals are entitled to what they have produced.[24] In the context of climate change, grandfathering embodies this principle. Every nation possesses a common law (inherent) right to emit carbon dioxide. Grandfathering also exemplifies the justice principle of proportional equality—that na-

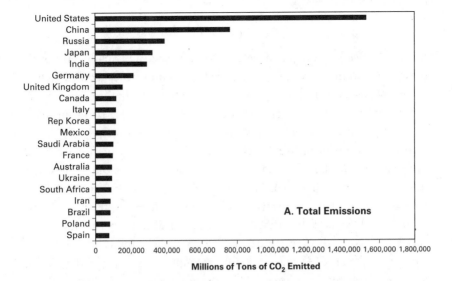

A. Total Emissions

Millions of Tons of CO$_2$ Emitted

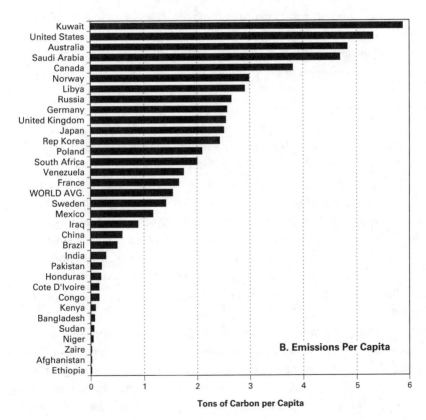

B. Emissions Per Capita

Tons of Carbon per Capita

Figure 5.1
Emissions inequality. (A) Top 20 nations, total carbon dioxide emissions from fossil fuel use, 2000. (B) Per capita carbon dioxide emissions, 2000, selected nations. (From Boden et al. 2003)

tions are unequal and therefore should be treated unequally. Although developing countries were not required to commit to scheduled reductions of emissions in the first round of negotiations, the decision to use 1990 as a baseline year is an implicit recognition of these two principles.

Finally, grandfathering represents the pragmatic principle that if we can solve the problem, we are closer to a just solution than if we insist upon a utopian plan that makes no progress. Cecilia Albin argues that in spite of the fact that international environmental agreements regularly institutionalize fairness norms—for example, the "polluter pays," "no harm," and "shared, but differentiated responsibility" principles—their success is first and foremost dependent upon their ability to yield joint gains for all parties.[25] She offers the example of Sweden and Finland, who despite being victimized by the air pollution of neighboring Baltic countries, did not insist that the polluter pays principle be strictly enforced. Quite the opposite. They financed a large foreign aid initiative to help the less developed countries responsible for the air pollution adopt more environmentally friendly technologies.[26]

Carbon Intensity

Faced with pressure to sign the Kyoto treaty, President George W. Bush promised during his 2000 campaign to do so. However, after entering office, his position shifted and he withdrew the United States from the treaty entirely. U.S. National Security Advisor Condoleezza Rice told EU members in spring 2001 that the Kyoto treaty to address climate change was "dead" without U.S. participation, since the treaty requires that countries responsible for 55 percent of the total amount of emissions from the world's wealthy nations ratify it. A firestorm of reaction from Europe and environmentalists in the United States eventually forced the Bush administration to provide an alternative plan to address the problem.

At the science center of the National Oceanic and Atmospheric Administration in Maryland, on February 14, 2002 President Bush flatly stated that "As president of the United States, charged with safeguarding the welfare of the American people and American workers, I will not commit our nation to an unsound international treaty that will throw millions of our citizens out of work." Rather, he proposed a "New Approach on Global Climate Change" in response to the treaty, and provided a new benchmark by which the U.S. government would measure its own progress on the issue. He "committed America to an aggressive new strategy to cut greenhouse gas intensity by 18% over the next 10 years."[27] The simple measure they proposed was emissions per dollar of GDP. The White House press release argued that: "The President's Yardstick—Greenhouse Gas Intensity—is a Better Way to Measure Progress Without Hurting Growth." It continued, "A goal expressed in terms of declining greenhouse gas intensity, measuring greenhouse gas emissions relative to economic activity, quantifies our effort to reduce emissions through conservation, adoption of cleaner, more efficient, and emission-reducing technologies, and sequestration. At the same time, an intensity goal accommodates economic growth."[28]

The carbon intensity approach is an outgrowth of Bentham's utilitarian theory of justice, which states that mutually advantageous and cost-effective solutions are also just solutions. Since everyone is worse off in the absence of aggregate net benefits, utilitarians argue that inefficient solutions are also unjust.[29] The fair solution, with respect to reductions of greenhouse gas emissions, would therefore be to stabilize the climate as cost-effectively as possible while maximizing global economic growth. Since developing nations currently offer the most cost-effective opportunities to reduce greenhouse gas emissions, the international effort to stabilize greenhouse gas emissions would predominantly focus on the developing world.[30]

On the positive side, the carbon intensity approach forces us to think about designing solutions that will allow growth to occur while minimizing impact on the global climate. A number of analysts have also suggested that the carbon intensity approach creates greater opportunities for developing country buy-in, since it does not impose a "hard cap" on their total emissions (hard caps are often viewed as "caps on development").[31] An added advantage to this approach is that industrialized nations tend to do better in intensity terms since their infrastructure is typically much better than that of poorer nations.[32] So, a carbon intensity approach could promote "early action," which, according to Baumert et al., is important because "many developing countries believe that the industrialized countries lack credibility on the issue of international cooperation to curb greenhouse gas emissions, having done little to address a problem largely of their own making."[33]

On the downside, the proposals made by the Bush administration place no real restrictions on the future emissions of the United States (since most analysts see the nation's efficiency as improving on its own by at least 18 percent) and are widely perceived as a repudiation of earlier commitments. The Bush administration's plan also does nothing about the existing stock of emissions and makes no effort to include include "exported emissions" caused by moving U.S. industries to poorer nations (what is currently called "offshoring"). In addition, the carbon intensity approach has become a tool of political manipulation. The United States used this approach very strategically at COP-8 and COP-9 in an effort to torpedo the Kyoto Protocol and delay post-2012 talks. U.S. negotiator Harlan Watson urged Western nations at the New Delhi negotiations to "recognize that it would be unfair—indeed, counterproductive—to condemn developing nations to slow growth or no growth by insisting that they take on impractical and unrealistic greenhouse gas targets."[34] The following year at the Milan negotiations, U.S. Undersecretary of State Paula Dobriansky tried to forge an unusual coalition with China and the G-77 by rejecting the need for developing countries to undertake scheduled commitments to reduce emissions.[35]

Per Capita

India, China, and the Group of 77 (actually a group of about 133 nations) have developed and advocated a series of proposals that account for carbon dioxide and other greenhouse gases on the basis of a simple, egalitarian principle. As suggested above, the idea is that every human on Earth has equal rights to the global atmosphere, and therefore allocations of how much each can pollute should be done on a per capita basis.[36] France, Switzerland, and the European Union have all endorsed this proposal.[37] Cambridge University economist Michael Grubb calls it "the most politically prominent contender for any specific global formula for long-term allocations with increasing numbers of adherents in both developed and developing countries."[38]

Per capita proposals place rich nations at a sharp disadvantage, since most of them already far exceed the stabilization target (roughly one metric ton of carbon equivalent per capita). Poor nations, by comparison, stand to gain considerably from a per capita allocation of carbon entitlements because their existing levels of income and industrialization place them well below the one metric ton threshold.

Environmentally sustainable per capita proposals typically require that a global "emissions budget" first be specified. The emerging scientific consensus is that to avoid the worst effects of climate change, we need to stabilize the concentrations of carbon dioxide around or below 450 parts per million (ppm). Others have suggested that 350 and 550 parts per million are more appropriate targets. Either way, these proposals suggest drastic reductions for the world's richest nations, and commitments very soon for the poorer ones to slow their increases in emissions and eventually stop and reverse them.

Under most per capita proposals, including the contraction and convergence model proposed by the Global Commons Institute, once the size of the emissions budget is specified, every global citizen will be allocated an equal entitlement to the atmosphere. Rich countries, whose relatively small populations have already used a disproportionate amount of their atmospheric space, must "contract" their annual carbon budget to a level of roughly one metric ton of carbon equivalent per person over the next century. Poor nations, whose citizens have thus far occupied very little atmospheric space, are allowed to increase their emissions for some time and eventually "converge" with rich nations. Developing countries willing to keep their emissions growth below their allowance have the opportunity to trade those allowances in exchange for funding or technical assistance through the Clean Development Mechanism (CDM), Joint Implementation, and other emissions trading mechanisms.

The key question surrounding the per capita approach is its political feasibility. Egalitarian principles played a prominent role in the UN Convention on Law of the Sea negotiations.[39] However, many analysts consider the application of egalitarian principles to climate policy to be politically explosive and economically inefficient. Grubb and his colleagues describe one telling interaction between rich and poor nations at the Kyoto negotiations that lasted late into the night. At 3 o'clock in the morning, amidst heated debate over global emissions trading, China, India, and the Africa Group of Nations expressed their strong support for a per capita allocation of global atmospheric property rights. Chairman Raul Estrada and a representative of the U.S. delegation responded that the contraction and convergence proposal was a political nonstarter, and negotiations were immediately brought to a close.[40]

It is important for the reader to understand just how far apart the people of the world are in per capita terms. Twenty percent of the world's population in the high-income countries is responsible for 63 percent of global emissions, while the bottom 20 percent of the world's people releases only 3 percent (figure 5.2).[41] According to our calculations, the average U.S. citizen dumps as much greenhouse gas into the atmosphere as nine Chinese citizens, eighteen citizens of India, and ninety Bangladeshis. But even more startling is that each U.S. citizen on average pollutes as much as over five hundred citizens of Ethiopia, Chad, Zaire, Afghanistan, Mali, Cambodia, and Burundi (table 5.1).[42] In 183 nations, people emit on average less than half the emissions Americans do. In 130 nations, it would take at least five citizens to generate as much carbon dioxide from burning fossil fuels as one U.S. citizen does. In 90 nations it would take more than ten citizens to generate as much as one American. And in 30 of those nations, it would take more than a hundred.[43]

Historical Responsibility

The polluter pays principle has been central to domestic and international environmental law for more than thirty years.[44] Brazilian scientists and government experts have developed a sophisticated proposal to address climate change based on this principle. They argue that a country's greenhouse gas reductions should depend on its relative contribution to the global temperature rise.[45] The reasoning behind the historical responsibility proposal is that carbon dioxide stays in the atmosphere for 100–120 years. (Methane, by contrast, remains only 12 years.)[46] Therefore it is important to account, not only for future emissions, but all of the damage done from emissions of earlier years.[47] The political implications are obvious: Since virtually all the carbon dioxide emitted since 1945 is still in the atmosphere, and "early industrializers" are almost exclusively responsible for those emissions, rich nations would be required to make deep and immediate cuts.[48] Early estimates suggest that by 2010 Britain would have to reduce its emissions by 66 percent, the United States by 23 percent, and Japan by 8 percent.[49]

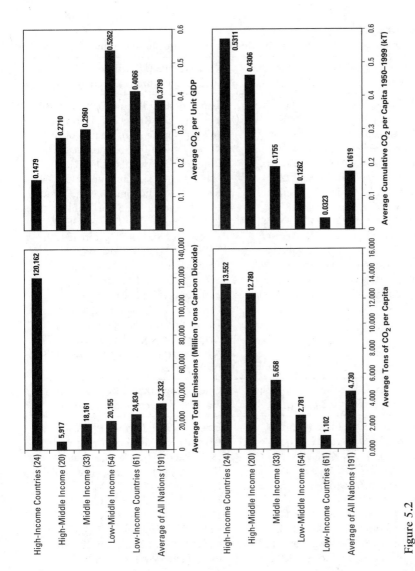

Figure 5.2
Average carbon dioxide emissions by income groups of nations, as measured by four primary approaches, 2000. (Calculated with figures from Boden et al. 2003)

Table 5.1
Comparisons of CO_2 Emissions by U.S. Citizens with Those in Other Countries

One average U.S. citizen = more than 100 average citizens) (30 countries)	One average U.S. citizen = more than 20 average citizens (37 countries)
Ethiopia (>540 citizens = one American), Chad (>540), Zaire (540), Afghanistan (540), Mali (540), Cambodia (540), Burundi (540), Uganda (270), Mozambique (270), Burkina Faso (270), Malawi (270), Rwanda (270), Lao (270), Central Afr. Rep. (270), Tanzania (180), Niger (180), Comoros (180), Nepal (135), Madagascar (135), Guinea (135), Sierra Leone (135), Liberia (135), Myanmar (108), Sudan (108), Zambia (108), Haiti (108), Eritrea (108), Bhutan (108), Gambia (108)	Bangladesh (90), Guinea Bissau (90), Benin (77.1), Kenya (67.5), Kiribati (67.5), Nigeria (60), Ghana (60), Cape Verde (60), Solomon Is. (54), Togo (49.1), Swaziland (49.1), Vanuatu (49.1), Cameroon (45), Senegal (45), Eq Guinea (45), Yemen (41.5), Angola (41.5), Sri Lanka (38.6), Papua New Guinea (38.6), Congo (33.8), Cote D'ivoire (31.8), Djibouti (31.8), Tajikistan (30), Paraguay (30), Sao Tome and Principe (30), Viet Nam (27), Honduras (27), Nicaragua (27), Pakistan (25.7), Samoa (24.5), Guatemala (22.5), Fiji (22.5), Armenia (21.6), Albania (21.6), Kyrgyzstan (20.8), W. Sahara (20.8), Namibia (20)
One average U.S. citizen = more than 10 average citizens (22 countries)	One average U.S. citizen = more than 5 average citizens (36 countries)
Philippines (19.3), India (18.6), El Salvador (18.6), Peru (17.4), Mauritania (17.4), Zimbabwe (16.9), Georgia (16.875), Tonga (16.4), Indonesia (15.4), Morocco (15.4), Bolivia (15), Colombia (14.2), Dominica (14.2), Costa Rica (13.8), St. Vincent and Grenada (13.2), Cook Is. (12.85714286), Niue (12.9), Uruguay (12.3), Moldova (11.0), Brazil (10.8), Maldives (10.8), Tunisia (10.2)	Ecuador (9.8), Guyana (9.5), Grenada (9.5), China (9), Egypt (8.8), Puerto Rico (8.9), Panama (8.9), St. Lucia (8.7), Botswana (8.4), Fr. Polynesia (8.4), Br. Virg. Is. (8.2), Latvia (8.1), Mauritius (8.1), St Helena (8.1), St. Kitts-Nevis (7.8), Cuba (7.2), Seychelles (7.1), Gabon (6.8), Algeria (6.8), Dom. Republic (6.7), Belize (6.4), Jordan (6.3), Mongolia (6.3), Thailand (6.2), Lithuania (6.2), Iraq (5.9), Syria (5.9), Reunion (5.9), Turkey (5.8), Azerbaijan (5.5), Argentina (5.3), Macau (5.3), Romania (5.1), Guadeloupe (5.1), Chile (5.0), Yugoslavia (5.0)

Table 5.1
(continued)

One average U.S. citizen = more than 3 average citizens (25 countries)	One average U.S. citizen = more than 2 average citizens (30 countries)
Jamaica (4.8), Am. Samoa (4.7), Lebanon (4.6), Mexico (4.5), Barbados (4.5), Croatia (4.4), Uzbekistan (4.1), Bosnia-Herzegovinia (4.1), Iran (4.1), Hong Kong (4.1), Suriname (4.1), Sweden (3.75), Bulgaria (3.7), Switzerland (3.7), Hungary (3.7), Martinique (3.7), Antigua and Barbuda (3.6), Macedonia (3.6), French Guiana (3.6), Belarus (3.4), Bahamas (3.3), Portugal (3.3), France (3.2), Malaysia (3.2), Venezuela (3.0), Slovakia (3.0)	Ukraine (2.9), Spain (2.8), Malta (2.8), Turkmenistan (2.7), Slovenia (2.7), Bermuda (2.7), Italy (2.7), South Africa (2.6), Austria (2.6), Cayman (2.6), Iceland (2.6), Poland (2.5), St. Pierre and Miq (2.5), New Caledonia (2.5), Gibraltar (2.5), Kazakhstan (2.4), Oman (2.4), Denmark (2.4), New Zealand (2.4), North Korea (2.4), Cyprus (2.3), Netherlands (2.3), Greece (2.2), Rep. Korea (2.2), Japan (2.1), United Kingdom (2.1), Germany (2.1), Taiwan (2.0), Montserrat (2.0), Russia (2.0)

Source: Calculated from Boden et al. 2003.
Note: Includes carbon dioxide from fossil fuel use only.

Given their tiny contribution to the existing stock of carbon dioxide, it is not surprising that developing countries have been strong advocates of this approach. At their 2000 South Summit in Havana, the G-77 submitted the following statement as part of a larger manifesto: "We believe that the prevailing modes of production and consumption in the industrialized world are unsustainable and should be changed for they threaten the very survival of the planet. . . . We advocate a solution for the serious global, regional, and local environmental problems facing humanity, *based on the recognition of the North's ecological debt* and the principle of common but differentiated responsibilities of the developed and developing countries."[50]

However, the historical responsibility proposal has failed to gain much traction in the policy community. To be broadly acceptable to people around the world, proposals for addressing climate change need to be relatively easy to understand, and making the historical responsibility principle operational requires fairly complex methods of calculation.[51] Nonetheless, the 2000 Special Report on Emissions Scenarios of the IPCC found that summed emissions "supply a reasonable 'proxy' for the relative contribution to global warming" of different nations, if "limited to a few decades."[52] To compare different approaches to "climate justice," we take a similar approach, summing all industrial emissions of carbon dioxide from 1950 to 1999 for each nation to create indicators of a nation's total historical responsibility and another such value of cumulative emissions per capita (figure 5.2).[53]

Figure 5.2 indicates that when emissions since 1950 are summed, the gap between rich and poor nations is much higher and is not narrowing or going away any time soon. The summed emissions from the high-income nations amount to nearly twice the tons of carbon dioxide of the middle income nations, and four times the cumulative emissions of the majority of the world who live in the poorest nations. This is a highly contentious issue, but one we believe must be considered if we are to address inequality and climate change. The "polluter pays" argument is that high-emitting nations, even if they did not know the danger of their behavior, still benefited from it and should be held responsible for its impacts.

Moving toward "Hybrid Justice"

To recap, then, we have four different approaches for measuring climate injustice: the Kyoto grandfathering approach, the carbon intensity approach, the historical responsibility approach, and the egalitarian per capita approach. Climate justice discussions taking place within the Brazilian government, among influential Indian NGOs, between developing country negotiators at environmental conferences, in the U.S. Congress and European Parliament, and at G-77 summits could therefore be placed along a hypothetical principled beliefs spectrum. What our analysis shows is that poor nations and rich nations hold almost diametrically opposed views of climate justice, largely for configurational reasons having to do with their position in the global hierarchy of economic and political power. It is therefore (unfortunately) unlikely that a North-South fairness consensus will spontaneously emerge in the immediate future on the basis of one of these four approaches. Rather, what is needed is moral compromise, or a negotiated "justice settlement." Strict adherence to particularistic notions of justice, by comparison, is a perfect recipe for a stalemate.[54] Therefore it will likely be an optimal mix of principles that will enable rich and poor nations to overcome barriers to cooperation.[55]

However, there are no hard and fast distinctions between "efficient" and "equitable" proposals in the burden-sharing debate. If an "equitable" policy principle lacks implementability—that is, if it fails to yield joint gains—it is in effect inefficient.[56] Moral ambiguity has also complicated this efficiency–equity distinction. Should burden-sharing proposals substantively favor those with the greatest need, the least responsibility, or the greatest ability to pay?

A number of proposals that represent a moral compromise have emerged in recent years. Bartsch and Müller propose a "preference score" method, which combines the grandfathering and per capita approach through a voting system. Their proposal allows each nation, weighted by its population, to choose the methodology that it prefers. Each global citizen's "vote" is then used to calculate national carbon emission allowances. According to their preliminary model, under this proposal, roughly three-quarters of the global emissions budget would be based on the per capita approach and one quarter on grandfathering.[57] Others have focused on more politically feasible per capita proposals that provide for "national circumstances," or allowance factors, such as geography, climate, energy supply, and domestic economic structure, as well as "soft-landing scenarios."[58]

The Pew Center for Global Climate Change has developed a hybrid proposal that assigns responsibility based on past and present emissions, carbon intensity, and a country's ability to pay (i.e., its per capita GDP).[59] They separate the world into three groups: those that "must act now," those that "could act now," and those that "should act now, but differently."[60]

The "triptych" proposal, designed by scholars at the University of Utrecht in the Netherlands (and already used to differentiate commitments among EU countries), "accounts for differences in national circumstances such as population size and growth, standard of living, economic structure and fuel mix in power generation."[61] Its novel contribution is that it divides each country's economy into three sectors: energy-intensive industry, power generation, and the so-called domestic sector (transport, light industry, agriculture, and commercial sector).[62] It applies the carbon intensity approach to the energy-intensive sector, "decarbonization targets" to the power-generation sector, and a per capita approach to the domestic sectors. Similarly, the multisector convergence approach, developed by two research institutes in northern Europe (Netherlands Energy Research Foundation and Center for International Climate and Environmental Research), treats sectors differentially and integrates per capita, carbon intensity, and ability to pay (per capita GDP) approaches.[63]

We believe these hybrid proposals are among the most promising solutions to break the North-South stalemate. However, simply asserting that a negotiated justice settlement is necessary avoids the more central question of whether and to what extent an agreement must favor rich or poor nations.[64] Our reading of the evidence is that the greatest barriers to meaningful, lasting North-South cooperation are not differences in principled understandings of what is fair. Rather, divergent principled beliefs are a consequence of more fundamental root causes; in particular, incongruent worldviews and causal beliefs, persistent global inequality, and an enduring deficit in North-South trust.

Again, it is important that we not focus so much on the individual trees that we lose sight of the large forest. Eric Neumayer reminds us that "[t]he biggest bargaining power of developing countries—especially of big ones like China, India, Brazil and Indonesia—is their ability to obstruct.... As their current emissions and populations grow faster than the ones in developed countries, any comprehensive treaty in the early next century will be futile without the cooperation of these countries."[65] The ability of developing countries to credibly threaten nonparticipation, or even defection, is further strengthened by the fact that they possess worldviews and causal beliefs that predispose them toward inaction and, in some cases, subversion of this treaty.

More important than the adoption of a "hybrid justice" proposal, therefore, is that policy makers redouble their efforts to allay the fears and suspicions of developing countries; rebuild conditions of generalized trust; forge long-term, constructive partnerships with developing countries across multiple issue areas; and create greater "policy space" for governments to pursue their own development strategies.

Our next step is to attempt to get behind this extreme inequality in responsibility for emissions, and attempt to explain why it developed. Our hope is that this approach will allow us to better understand how feasible it will be to move different types of nations to lower levels of emissions.

Understanding Why Some Countries Emit More

In this section we empirically examine the factors that drive inequality in national responsibility for climate change, as it is variously defined. This kind of analysis can help us answer a number of important questions: Does the size of a national economy closely determine emissions rates? Are countries that emphasize their special "national circumstances"—such as land area, climate, or urbanization—actually predisposed toward higher emissions? Which of these national circumstances are most responsible for higher emissions? Are trade and certain types of industries associated with higher carbon dioxide emissions? Answers to these kinds of questions may help negotiators understand the worldviews, causal beliefs, and normative principles of other nations.

First we examined the extent to which national responsibility for climate change was simply the result of national wealth (as measured by per capita GDP) or the size of a nation's economy (as measured by total GDP). A number of economic studies have examined that relationship, focusing especially on explaining carbon dioxide emissions per capita or the carbon intensity measure, CO_2/GDP.[66] Studies on carbon intensity have found a recently developed curvilinear relationship in which intensity first rises as one moves from the poorest to the wealthier nations, but then declines among the very wealthiest.

We found that wealthier nations emit substantially more on average, and this relationship of national wealth and carbon dioxide emissions is a good part of the story, as can be seen in the simple scatterplot of the two variables (figure 5.3). However, this relationship includes substantial variation,[67] and there are some notable cases of nations reducing their emissions substantially while their economies increased in size. (The most obvious case is Germany in the 1990s.) We believe there are important insights to be learned from a close examination of this variation since it shows plainly the extent to which another world is possible, even among current societies.

We now can turn to the impact of a wider series of factors that influence responsibility for climate change. We examine their effects on our four dependent variables: total carbon dioxide emissions, carbon dioxide emissions per unit of GDP (carbon intensity), per capita carbon dioxide emissions, and cumulative emissions over the fifty years starting in 1950.

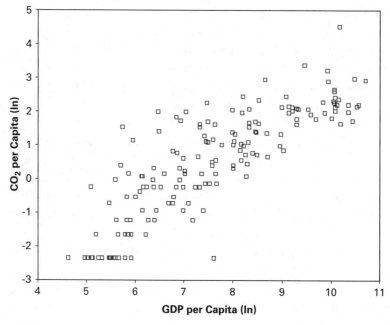

Figure 5.3
Relationship of per capita carbon dioxide emissions to national wealth, per capita CO_2 versus per capita GDP, 2000. Both are natural logged. (From Boden 2003; World Bank 2002)

These are different types of indicators, and as we mentioned earlier, each measure represents one view of "climate justice." They are, however, strongly correlated, as table 5.2 suggests.[68] Specifically, total emissions in 1999 are nearly identical in their distribution to the summed emissions of nations from the fifty-year period 1950–1999 (our measure of total historical responsibility for carbon dioxide emissions, $r = 0.965$). Similarly, the per capita carbon dioxide emissions of a nation in 1999 are also nearly identical to historical responsibility per capita, a measure of the summed emissions of a nation divided by that nation's population in 1999 ($r = 0.934$). The other measures are correlated at the $r = 0.6$ or 0.7 levels, except carbon intensity, which is only correlated between 0.32 and 0.4 with the other measures. Carbon intensity is clearly measuring something quite different than even the simple Kyoto measure of total carbon dioxide emissions during a single year.

Table 5.2
Correlations among Four Measures of Carbon Responsibility

| | Efficiency | | Equity | |
| | Kyoto: Total Emissions ln(total emissions of carbon dioxide) | Carbon Intensity ln(CO_2 emissions per unit GDP) | Per Capita ln(carbon dioxide emissions per population) | Historical Responsibility ln(cumulative carbon emissions 1950–1999) |
Pearson Correlations				
Carbon intensity ln(CO_2 emissions per unit GDP)	0.398** N = 170			
Per capita ln(carbon dioxide emissions per population)	0.616** N = 171	0.324** N = 162		
Historical responsibility ln(cumulative carbon dioxide emissions 1950–1999)	0.965** N = 149	0.325** N = 139	0.735** N = 147	
Historical responsibility per capita ln(cumulative carbon dioxide emissions 1950–1999 divided by population)	0.705** N = 149	0.363** N = 139	0.934** N = 146	0.794** N = 153

Note: ** Correlation is significant at the 0.01 level (two-tailed).

Our goal is to move the literature toward a more nuanced understanding of this complex problem, and so we turn now to our multivariate analysis, which attempts to predict these four measures of responsibility for climate change. We believe that understanding how much each factor predicts responsibility for climate change may be important for setting "fair targets" for national reductions in emissions. We predicted that a nation's propensity to emit carbon dioxide would be due to a series of factors, roughly clustered into five groupings. First, as mentioned earlier, we predicted a strong relationship between economic growth and the use of fossil fuels, a relationship forged with the rise of fossil energy during the Industrial Revolution. This was a fairly straightforward concept to

test since complete cross-national data exist on sizes of national economies as measured by gross domestic product per capita. We also logged
our measure of national income to deal with the extremely skewed nature of the distribution of cases.[69] Based on the now long-running debate
about whether wealthier nations become more efficient, postindustrial,
or "postmaterialist," and reach a turning point and become less polluting (the environmental Kuznets curve hypothesis), we also include the
quadratic form of the variable per capita GDP.[70] We discuss this issue
at some length later.

Among others, Eric Neumayer has recently argued that "geography
matters" in explaining carbon dioxide emissions per capita because in
some places driving distances are longer, climates are colder, and nations
have differing endowments of renewable energy.[71] Here we tested the
land area and population density of nations, their total populations,
whether their climates are very cold, and whether the bulk of the population lived in cities or rural areas. We predicted that nations with larger
populations would be larger emitters of carbon dioxide, and that cities
are highly fossil-fuel intense and use significant amounts of resources for
the production and transportation of their inputs and wastes. We predicted that "wider" nations—those with larger land areas—would tend
to emit more carbon dioxide by any of the indicators. Neumayer finds
that nations with a high number of frost days emit substantially more,
but a measure of maximum temperatures did not predict higher emissions.[72] For cold climates, we used a simpler proxy, the percentage of national area that is within the boreal (subartic) climate zone. Two of these
geographic variables were logged to deal with extreme skewness in the
distribution of nations in population and area. The percentage of the
nation's area in boreal climate zones is a standardized z-score.

We then set out to test three variables on national export structure,
based on the conceptual framework discussed earlier—that nations with
different exports and economic structures will tend to follow different
paths in their emissions of carbon dioxide. We expected that nations
with large manufacturing and fuels sectors would be higher emitters,
and that those with large service sectors would be significantly lower
emitters. We measured these complex variables with World Bank
dummy variables: nations with more than 50 percent of their exports in
each of these categories.

We also set out to test theories that claim nations will become either worse or better environmentally with their increasing incorporation in the world economy. This is a polarized debate, with many authors (including many World Bank economists) claiming that globalization will lead to better environmental performance.[73] Our own hypothesis was that nations would emit more as they participated more in international trade, even holding constant the size of their national economies. We hypothesized that trade drives the production of energy-intensive products, and the commercialization of those products around the globe means that significant amounts of fossil fuels are consumed in transporting them to market. The energy cost of transportation applies as well to imports, which should overall be half of the total trade in most nations.

Following Heil and Selden, we also tested an interaction term for trade, allowing us to examine whether trade intensity has different impacts on wealthier and poorer nations.[74] This methodological improvement is important since it could help us avoid overgeneralizing about whether trade increases emissions or decreases them, and proposing policies that might exacerbate the problem. Heil and Selden argue that a significant negative relationship between emissions and the tradeXGDP per capita variable indicates that wealthier nations decrease their emissions with more trade, while poorer nations increase emissions. (This is consistent with ecologically unequal exchange and ecological debt arguments, which we will review shortly.) Including this variable allows a more sophisticated analysis than just saying whether economic globalization is good or bad for the environment. Rather, globalization can have different impacts on nations of different types. Our predictions follow Heil and Selden's findings. We expect that poor nations will pollute more with more trade, while wealthier nations will be able to externalize or offshore the most energy-intensive phases of their production chains.

Finally, our last two variables test for the impacts of two proxies for democratic institutions and state environmentalism. To test whether more democratic nations tend to emit less, we used Kaufmann et al.'s indicator of voice and accountability, which "represents an aggregation of numerous political rights, civil liberties and political process indicators from various think tanks, NGOs and risk rating agencies."[75] We could have chosen many other proxies for this concept, but this variable seemed to best capture what we believed—that democratic institutions create an enabling environment for environmental movements, which in turn would drive national policies to emit less carbon dioxide.[76] However, a negative relationship would also be consistent with the hypothesis (examined in chapter 6) that democratic countries are more likely to make credible international policy commitments, environmental or otherwise.

In previous work we developed an index of the number of environmental treaties a nation had signed and ratified by April 1999.[77] This factor score was based on its performance on sixteen major treaties, with higher numbers corresponding to greater participation in the group of treaties. If a nation had ratified a high number of environmental treaties, we reasoned, it should have taken some steps to improve its environmental performance, as reflected in its carbon dioxide emissions. Treaty ratifications, we argue in chapter 6, represent relatively costly signals of a nation's commitment to implementing specific policy commitments. Therefore we predicted that a national commitment to global environmental issues would correlate negatively with all four carbon indicators.

Initial examination of the rather high correlations among the carbon indicators suggested that some of the same variables may help explain all four of them (table 5.2). We frankly did not have reason to expect major differences in relations between independent variables and the per capita and historical responsibility measures. For total carbon dioxide emissions, we expected the total size of a nation's economy to be a more relevant predictor than per capita GDP. We also expected a nation's total population to be a better predictor for total carbon dioxide emissions than it would be for the other dependent variables. For carbon intensity [$\ln(CO_2/GDP)$] we expected the existence of an inverted U-curve for nations of differing levels of wealth (GDP/capita), as we have documented elsewhere.[78]

The overall trends for more than 110 nations, when looking at the total carbon dioxide emissions from burning fossil fuel in 1999, include obvious and predicted relations, and a few unexpected findings (table 5.3). The first observation is that the variables we test here are remarkably consistent in their ability to predict national performance on greenhouse gases, however it is measured. Next, as seems quite obvious,

Table 5.3
Standardized Regression Coefficients (and *t*-ratios) of Four Measures of Responsibility for Climate Change

Variable	Model 1 Total Carbon Dioxide Emissions (ln) (million tons)	Model 2 Carbon Intensity ln(CO_2/ GDP)	Model 3 Carbon Dioxide Emitted per Capita (ln)	Model 4 Cumulative Emissions per Capita (ln) 1950–1999
Size of Economy/Wealth				
ln(GDP)	0.792***	—	—	—
	(8.025)			
ln(GDP/capita)	—	−0.164	0.799***	0.587***
		(−0.889)	(7.703)	(5.306)
Squared(GDP/capita)	—	−0.196	−0.094	−0.052
		(−1.662)	(−1.399)	(−0.739)
Geography/Size of Nation				
Population (ln)	0.219**	0.292**	0.173**	0.142*
	(2.857)	(3.076)	(3.135)	(2.439)
Area (ln)	0.017	−0.034	0.021	−0.009
	(−0.471)	(−0.402)	(0.433)	(−0.172)
Climate boreal (ln)	0.067+	0.189*	0.107*	0.154**
	(1.940)	(2.299)	(2.264)	(3.062)
% Population urban	0.221***	0.465***	0.289***	0.345***
	(4.089)	(3.638)	(4.067)	(4.434)
Industrial Structure				
Manufactures/exports	0.075*	0.179*	0.092*	0.137**
	(2.284)	(2.357)	(2.115)	(2.980)
Services/exports	−0.005	−0.012	0.001	−0.062
	(−0.160)	(−0.168)	(0.016)	(−1.427)
Fuels/exports	−0.001	−0.001	0.001	0.005
	(−0.022)	(−0.019)	(0.034)	(0.103)
Trade Intensity				
Trade/GDP	0.272***	0.578***	0.285***	0.250***
	(6.429)	(5.597)	(4.778)	(4.027)
Trade × GDP	−0.260***	−0.506***	−0.257***	−0.237**
	(−5.309)	(−3.960)	(−3.492)	(−3.120)
Democracy/State Environmentalism				
Voice and accountability	−0.014	−0.037	−0.009	0.031
	(−0.261)	(−0.306)	(−0.134)	(0.432)

Table 5.3
(continued)

Variable	Model 1 Total Carbon Dioxide Emissions (ln) (million tons)	Model 2 Carbon Intensity ln(CO$_2$/ GDP)	Model 3 Carbon Dioxide Emitted per Capita (ln)	Model 4 Cumulative Emissions per Capita (ln) 1950–1999
Number of environmental treaties ratified (factor score)	−0.051 (−1.023)	−0.096 (−0.824)	−0.061 (−0.907)	−0.014 (−0.199)
Adjusted r-squared	0.893	0.430	0.813	0.789
N of cases (listwise)	128	128	127	129

Notes: $*p < .05$; $**p < .01$; $***p < .001$; $+p < .10$; missing cases deleted list-wise.
Coefficients shown are standardized betas.

nations with larger economies and populations emit significantly more carbon dioxide, and the size of the economy and average GDP per person were consistently the strongest predictors of emissions.

Geography also matters because nations with larger populations and more highly urbanized distributions of their settlements emit much more than those with smaller and less urbanized populations. Nations with a large part of their land areas in very cold climates, as measured by our crude index of nations in boreal climates, were more likely to emit more carbon dioxide for all four of our indicators. This is not surprising, but the analysis shows that this effect is a relatively small part of the total picture for three of the four carbon indicators. For the carbon intensity measure, climate was the second strongest predictor, while for the other indicators it ranked much lower.

However, that is not the end of the story. The analysis strongly suggests that while the size of a nation's economy and its geography are important, they do not predetermine its emissions. Contrary to the statements of some authors and policy makers, the land area of a nation does not predict carbon dioxide emissions, no matter how they are measured, at least when other factors are taken into account (see models 2–4). In fact the relationship is slightly negative across all four indicators. In regressions not shown, we examined the density of human populations (population per unit of land area) and found the same nonsignificant relationships with each of the four carbon accounting methods.

Our models showed that some structural features of national economies and their relations to world trade explain significant parts of national emissions of carbon dioxide. Nations that had high shares of their total exports in manufactures were higher emitters in all four measures of responsibility. To our surprise, nations in which services were a greater proportion of their economies were not significantly lower emitters on any of the indicators. Perhaps an even greater surprise was that fuel exporters as a class were not greater emitters, holding everything else constant. We discuss these patterns more later, but our initial explanation is that fuel exporters are of quite varied levels of production and national wealth, which may well explain more of the variation in carbon dioxide emissions. The categories excluded from the regressions were dummies for nations specializing more in agriculture and other raw materials exports. Again we believe these dummy variables are extremely crude measures of export profiles.

The measures of trade intensity allow a broad test of the impacts of economic globalization on the global climate. As Heil and Selden found in simpler models, we found a U-shaped relationship between a nation's intensity of trade and its levels of carbon dioxide emissions.[79] Poorer nations that participate more in international trade emit more carbon dioxide, while wealthier nations that trade more emit less than those who traded less. This relationship held up for all four measures of responsibility. Heil and Selden argue that this shows that the effect of international trade and globalization is to shunt off the greatest ecological impacts of production onto poorer nations. Our findings are consistent with this interpretation. In terms of policy, this suggests that trade is not necessarily good for the environment, and that rich nations should be held accountable for the emissions that they have effectively offshored to poorer countries.

Finally, our measures of democratic institutions and participation in environmental treaties overall had almost no impact on national pollution profiles as measured by any indicator of responsibility. We should note, however, that both of these independent variables had weak negative relationships with indicators of carbon dioxide emissions, suggesting that these relationships could become stronger as time passes and political will (it is hoped) increases. It is also important to keep in mind that carbon dioxide is different from smog and other pollutants in that it is not perceptible, was more recently discovered to be a threat, and has no local negative effects.

The overall patterns across these very different indicators of responsibility for climate change, then, are remarkably consistent (figure 5.4). The most dramatic difference we found was that while national wealth

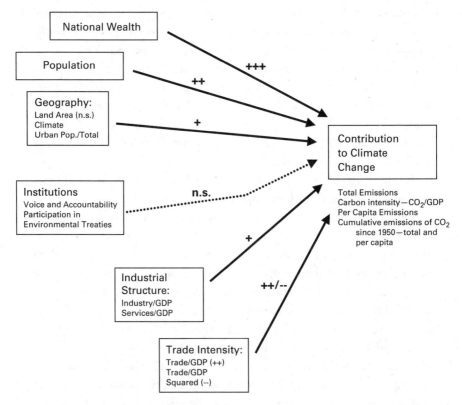

Figure 5.4
Significant predictors of four measures of responsibility for climate change, overall trends. Summary of four models in table 4.2: total carbon dioxide emissions by a nation, carbon intensity/GDP, carbon dioxide emissions per capita, and cumulative emissions since 1950.

increased emissions per capita and historical responsibility for climate change, the opposite was true of carbon intensity. That is, overall, wealthier nations have lower national emissions intensity for carbon, per unit of gross domestic product, than do poorer nations.

By finding that colder and more urban nations tend to emit more than nations who are similar in other respects, we have confirmed that geography does matter.[80] We also suspect that more of the variation in emissions would be explained with more refined measures of geography. However, this finding does strongly suggest that "national circumstances" should be considered in developing targets for national reductions in any future climate treaty. For both wealthy and poor nations, this is one important way that proposals need to be adjusted. Specifically, very cold nations need more flexibility in order to heat living and working spaces.

There is another, and somewhat less discussed, type of need for adjustments and hybrid proposals to gain international acceptance of a climate treaty. That is, leading national economic sectors have proven significant predictors of emissions, and more analysis is needed to understand how dependence on certain types of exports is tied to particularly low, or high, levels of carbon dioxide emissions, a topic we take up shortly. The finding that industry-heavy nations emit more is hardly surprising, but it does reflect the need to consider these economies in future hybrid proposals.

There is a substantial literature showing that carbon intensity drops when incomes are very high, to which we turn after the discussion of asymmetric trade relations between poor and wealthier nations. This point leads us to the issue of who wins and who loses with different indicators of responsibility for emissions. The lower levels of carbon intensity for wealthier nations explain the position of President Bush in proposing intensity as the indicator for measuring future reductions. They frankly make the United States look better, and the U.S. economy is moving in the direction of lower emissions intensity even as its economy grows.

Dematerialization, Environmentally Unequal Trade, and the Ecological Debt

The vast inequality in emissions documented above leads us to three larger issues: the "dematerialization of consumption," "ecologically unequal exchange," and the "ecological debt." This is a lot of ground to cover, and we do not seek to make a definitive contribution on any of them. However, our goal is to treat each initially as an exploratory exercise and show how they are connected to each other and to inequality in emissions. These three issues provide a bridge between our analysis of the causes of inequality and our exploration of the impact of dominant economic sectors on emissions, which follows.

A series of authors and politicians have argued that the world's wealthier nations are "dematerializing" their economies as people become "postconsumerist" or postmodern in their increasing consumption of services and experiences rather than material products.[81] Stated differently, it is thought that beyond a certain income threshold economic growth will decouple from resource consumption. Despite the fact that that a declining material intensity in the GDP does not necessarily translate into lower levels of absolute resource consumption,[82] the dematerialization trend is celebrated as a great environmental victory.[83] This is tied to a second and related claim being made emphatically by World Bank and WTO analysts—that exports from Third World nations are continually being upgraded and are increasing poor countries' prospects for positive economic growth and lasting development.[84]

Both of these arguments have come under attack by a small group of scholars forging a literature on ecologically unequal exchange.[85] They suggest that exports are indeed shifting, but trade relations remain extremely unfair, since poorer nations export large quantities of underpriced products whose value does not include the environmental (and social) costs of their extraction, processing, or shipping.[86] Rich and poor nations are therefore said to possess different "biophysical metabolisms" that shape the global distribution of environmental burdens.[87] This argument has gained force as it has found increasing empirical support and led to the logical but radical claim that the wealthier nations owe some kind of remuneration (the "ecological debt") to the poor nations for all the environmental damage from the energy-extracting and material-rich products from which they benefit.[88]

In late November 2001, a group of scholars and activists from the global South met in the African nation of Benin to articulate a position on the so-called ecological debt (a close cousin of the ecologically unequal exchange idea). The argument, as developed by Spanish economist Joan Martinez-Alier and the Ecuadorean environmental group Acción

Ecológica, is that wealthy nations have been running up a huge debt over centuries of exploiting the raw materials and ecosystems of the poor nations.[89] The debt encompasses both the historical and modern exploitation of non-Western natural resources, as well as the excessive use of "environmental space" for dumping waste (for example, the use of global atmospheric resources). According to the New Economics Foundation, Jubilee Research, Oxfam, the World Wildlife Fund, World Vision, Friends of the Earth, Greenpeace, Christian Aid, Action Aid, the Heinrich Böll Foundation, the International Institute for Environment and Development, Corporate Watch, the Centre for Science and the Environment, and EcoEquity, as well as many other leading NGOs, the ecological debt must either be paid or used as balance to forgive national economic debts.[90] This idea has traveled around the world quickly, and attracted the support of the Chinese government and the G-77 at the 2000 South Summit in Havana, Cuba. Many Southern governments have also articulated this position in climate negotiations.

The intellectual heritage of the literature on ecological debt and ecologically unequal exchange can be traced back to the structuralist school of the 1940s, 1950s, and 1960s. Raul Prebisch and his colleagues at the UN's Economic Commission on Latin America found a striking empirical pattern at that time. The export commodity prices of poor nations tended to consistently fall relative to the prices of items exported by wealthy nations. This was believed to be the result of weak income elasticity of demand for primary products, a massive oversupply of labor, and poor union organization in developing countries. Together these led to stagnant wages, inflation, and lower export prices as opposed to the rising wages and stable prices achieved in core nations. Thus, structuralists argued that the liberal emphasis on global GDP growth was a highly misleading indicator of international well-being. Some nations were growing, some were stagnating, and others were declining or falling into deep depression, and much of this variation could be explained by countries' "natural" comparative advantages—the value of their resource-based exports and labor oversupply.

The intellectual pedigree of the ecological debt and ecologically unequal exchange literature is also rooted in world-systems theory, which postulates that national development cannot be understood in isolation from the global system, where other nations wield greater economic and military power.[91] For world-systems theorists, the global structure of inequality remains a central concern. They argue that nations can move up or down the global hierarchy, but must do so in a world where there are already powerful economic players with developed industrial bases and relatively overwhelming military might that can be used to manipulate political and economic relations. The international division of labor is said to function in the following way: Core wealthy nations import raw materials and export high-value services and industrial manufactures while controlling powerful financial institutions. Poor peripheral nations export their natural resources and some supply cheap labor directly to manufacturers. Semiperipheral middle-income nations lie somewhere in the middle, with some industry, higher-value services, and a partially diversified export structure. In the view of world-systems theorists, then, a few nations move up, but the relations of extraction, production, and consumption between core and (semi-)peripheral nations have changed but not reversed since colonial times (see figure 2.2).

The emphasis of world-systems theory on historicism and structuralism also helps to explain why many peripheral and semiperipheral nations are locked into ecologically unsustainable patterns. For example, the volatility and periodic collapse of prices for their very few exports often lead poor nations to increase the extraction and sale of material goods that they are already selling at near a loss.[92] As Giljum puts it, "low prices for primary commodities allow industrialized countries of the capitalist core to appropriate high amounts of biophysical resources from the peripheral economies in the South, while maintaining external trade relations balanced in monetary terms. . . . [W]hat within the system of prices appears as reciprocal and fair exchange masks a biophysical inequality of exchange in which one of the partners has little choice but to exploit and possibly exhaust his natural resources and utilize his environment as a waste dump, while the other partner may maintain high environmental quality within its own borders."[93] Elsewhere, we have also stressed that a country's colonial incorporation into the world economy shapes its state–society relations, domestic political institutions, civil society strength, and in turn its propensity to participate in international environmental accords.[94] We take up the latter points in the next chapter.

In his path-breaking 1985 book *Underdeveloping the Amazon*, sociologist Stephen Bunker theorized on the issue of ecologically unequal exchange. Based on case study research in Brazil, he argued that every time an economy exports its natural resources, an energy and material loss takes place, "decelerating" the extractive economy and "accelerating" the productive economy. He also suggested that "regions whose economic ties to the world system are based almost exclusively on the exchange of extracted commodities can be characterized as extreme peripheries because of the low proportions of capital and labor incorporated in the total value of their exports and because of the low level of linkages to other economic activities and social organization in the same region."[95] Furthermore, "accelerated energy flow to the world industrial core permits social complexity which generates political and economic power there and permits the rapid technological changes which transform world market demands. It thus creates the conditions of the core's economic and political dominance over the world system to which the dominant classes of peripheral economies respond with their own accumulation strategies."[96] Therefore, in Bunker's model, the core's productive economy consumes commodities directly and indirectly through manufactures, but also effectively consumes the extractive economy, draining it of its energy and matter and damaging the local ecology, social organization, and infrastructure.[97] The core, in other words, relies on the periphery as both a source and a sink (for high entrophic by-products and waste), inevitably degrading it over the longer term.[98]

A number of scholars have exposed Bunker's thesis to empirical testing. One particular hypothesis has attracted much more attention than any other: When nations exchange goods, the market prices of those goods are often undervalued (particularly those from the South), and in the course of extracting, moving, and processing products for export, there is a massive transfer and degradation of materials and energy that goes completely unrecognized. Using a "materials flow" accounting methodology, it is thought that we can use physical numeraires to bring these flows of materials and energy, or "ecological rucksacks," back into the equation. The easiest way to do this is to measure the physical weight of import and export flows. More sophisticated methodologies, however, are being developed to account for indirect flows of materials used in the production process, and the waste and emission flows created during that process.[99]

Empirical work using materials flow analysis has produced a remarkably consistent finding: Developing countries traditionally seen as successful, export-oriented economies are actually suffering huge unrecorded losses, both economic and ecological.[100] Using time series data on consumption of natural resources, Giljum finds that Chile's natural resource exports have increased threefold and their use of material inputs has increased by a factor of six over the period 1973–2000. Giljum identifies a clear link between this pattern and huge export drives in the forestry, fishing, mining, and fruit-growing sectors.[101] In a similar study, Muradian and Martinez-Alier carefully document the responses of developing countries to declining terms of trade.[102] They find that falling prices correlate with large export drives for primary products (raw materials). Of the eighteen natural resource exports from developing countries they examine, all but two had their prices fall between the 1970s and 1990s, yet fourteen of the exports increased dramatically in volume over the same period in physical terms.[103]

Tracking material and energy flows from extraction to production and final disposal is illuminating, not only from an export perspective, but also from an import perspective. The most systematic and comprehensive empirical study employing this latter approach examines the EU-15 region and concludes that the EU runs an enormous trade deficit in physical terms with all other major world regions, while maintaining balanced external trade relations in monetary terms.[104] Primarily owing to the import of fossil fuels, semimanufactured products, and abiotic raw materials, the EU imports, in physical terms, more than four times what it exports. Yet, "EU-15 exports have a *money value* of 4 times that of imports. With regard to trade relations with Southern regions such as Africa and Latin America, one ton of EU exports embodies a money value 10 times higher than one ton of EU imports."[105] Thus, from both an import and export perspective, materials flow analysis suggests that core economies are draining ecological capacity from extractive regions by importing resource-intensive products and have shifted their environmental burdens to the South through the export of waste.[106]

In this regard, materials flow analysis has debunked earlier claims that we have entered an era of falling energy intensities and dematerialization.[107] In fact, what appears to be happening is that some core economies are being relatively dematerialized as they export to poor countries or "peripheralize," the material-intensive stages of the production process. Domestic production has no doubt become more efficient—where efficiency is defined as the material intensity of one's own production—in the core zones of the world economy. However, nations that increasingly import the material-intensive goods required by their lifestyles are clearly no less materialist and no more sustainable than they were when they bore their own environmental burdens.[108]

Development Pathways and the Structural Roots of Carbon Dioxide Emissions: Toward Predictions

We attempt here to incorporate these ideas as we bring together two more emerging literatures on "sectoral analysis" and "paths of development," and unravel the complex picture of responsibility for global warming. By doing so we hope to shed light on three concrete, practical questions: How do national development planners' choices of which economic sectors to support influence their nation's pollution profile? How can countries get the most economic growth with the least pollution?[109] And what is causing national rates of responsibility for carbon dioxide emissions to change over time? This analysis may point to those countries that are more or less likely to participate in a post-2012 global climate accord and suggests the need for sector- and country-specific solutions as we move ahead on this crucial issue.

While acknowledging that production and consumption are the direct or immediate causes of responsibility values, we are searching for their roots in how national economies are linked to the world economy. As we argued earlier, exports often represent the leading sector for nations. In his 1994 book *Winners and Losers: How Sectors Shape the Developmental Prospects of States*, political scientist D. Michael Shafer proposes a renewed "sectoral analysis" in an attempt to nuance dependency and world-systems theories of national development.[110] Shafer argues that "a state's capacity to get ahead depends on the attributes of the leading sector by which it is tied to the international economy: light manufacturing, mineral extraction, peasant cash crop production, or industrial plantation crop production. Particular sectoral attributes result in distinct international market structures, each of which rewards different kinds of actors, presents different opportunities and risks, and demands a different strategy."[111] Using Shafer's core insight on exports as a pivotal sector in national economies, we take the opposite methodological approach; we attempt to categorize all nations of the world to see if their leading export sectors are driving their environmental impact. This allows us to chart total carbon dioxide emitted, carbon intensity (per unit of GDP), carbon dioxide emissions per capita and cumulative emissions over fifty years for countries with different sets of export products.[112]

Many authors have discussed the implications of the demise of the dominant economic system in the post-World War II era, which some have called post-Fordism, flexible specialization, Toyotism, bloody Taylorism, and more recently, simply globalization.[113] Far fewer authors have combined political economy analysis with attention to the environmental implications of the apparent shift of much of the core's productive facilities to semiperipheral nations since the early 1970s. We review two popular hypotheses about those shifts and attempt to use responsibility measures of carbon dioxide emissions to shed some light on their validity.

One popular interpretation has been the "pollution haven hypothesis."[114] This hypothesis proposes that in response to tight environmental regulations in the core, many firms choose areas in the periphery with especially cheap labor and low environmental enforcement as sites for the most polluting portions of their productive operations. One form of the pollution haven hypothesis was utilized in the U.S. Senate with the debate over the Kyoto round of global warming treaties. Senators argued repeatedly that the United States would lose millions of jobs as firms moved overseas, where they could pollute at will, rather than face limits on their emissions under the Kyoto treaty.[115]

As our last empirical exploration for this chapter, we seek here to understand the relationship of leading export sectors and paths of development to concrete climate outcomes, using the World Bank's categorization of nations in their 1995 *World Development Report*. Entitled "Classification of Economies by Major Export Category and Indebtedness, 1995," the table sorts nations by three income and debt levels and by five major export categories. A major export category is defined as "those that account for 50 percent or more of total exports of goods and services from one category, in the period 1988–92.... If no single category accounts for 50 percent or more of total exports, the economy is classified as *diversified*."[116] The validity of the Bank's sorting will be discussed in more detail later, but initially this table is useful as a preliminary test of our inference from Shafer's theory that a nation's predominant export category will largely shape its emissions.

First, we need to examine the distribution of these nations and briefly discuss our predictions of their responsibility for carbon dioxide emissions. First of all, the distribution of nations is highly nonrandom: of the 54 possible categories, 14 were empty sets. Of the 210 "economies" (not societies or countries) in the 1995 World Bank's report, 17 low- and middle-income nations were not classified by indebtedness, and 21 were not classified by export category. Of the 40 cells for classified countries, 6 were empty. Most important, among the export categories, nations often fell into patterns by income and debt levels.

Among the twenty-nine exporters of manufactures (Standard International Trade Classification codes 5–9), only China, Armenia, and Georgia were categorized as low income (a per capita GDP of $695 or less in 1993). Most were Organization of Economic Co-operation and Development (OECD) (core) members or less-indebted middle income nations (with a per capita GDP of more than $695 and less than $8,626 in 1993). Manufacturing involves the transformation of raw materials into intermediate or finished goods, and these processes are highly energy intense. Manufacturers were therefore expected to be high in carbon intensity, and since this the category increasingly includes middle-income countries, it was expected to become more carbon intense in both per capita and per unit of GDP terms.

Among the fifty-one exporters of Nonfuel primary products, such as agricultural commodities and mineral products (SITC 0,1,2,68: food and live animals, beverages and tobacco, etc.), most nations are poor and severely indebted. Very few wealthy nations rely heavily on such exports, and the poor exporters of resources are often cited as examples of both classic dependence by world-systems theory and by the conservation community as nations selling their natural heritage for short-term income. Overall these are weak economies, so we expect low overall emissions in total, per capita, and historical responsibility terms. We expected exporters of raw materials to have highly inefficient economies in carbon dioxide terms, polluting relatively highly with little economic benefit over the longer term, as reflected especially in CO_2/GDP terms.

Of the seventeen exporters of fuels, (SITC 3: fuels, lubricants, and related materials), thirteen were middle-income and most were less indebted. A few nations with oil have reached high levels of GDP per capita, and some others have used these proceeds to diversify into services and finance and so do not appear in this category (e.g., Kuwait, Norway). Oil exporters not only use substantial portions of their fossil endowments in extracting, refining, and transporting the product, but because of high income that is often concentrated in the hands of a few, and because fuel prices tend to be very low in such countries, oil-producing nations have also become known for highly energy-consumptive lifestyles. During the 1960s and 1970s, flaring oil and gas was a common part of oil production and refining (T. Boden, personal communication). This burning of excess fuels improved safety cheaply, but greatly increased many oil-producers' emissions. It is difficult, therefore, for us to imagine any nations with higher emissions profiles than oil exporters, by any of our four measures of responsibility.

Thirty-nine nations were primarily exporters of services, which are defined by the World Bank as "factor and nonfactor service receipts plus workers' remittances."[117] Factor services include investment income, interest, and labor income; nonfactor services cover "transportation, travel, communications, construction, insurance, financial, computer and information services, royalties and license fees, other business services, personal, cultural and recreational services, and government services."[118] Twenty of these were less-indebted middle- or low-income nations. Many are tourist islands, banking, or new processing centers. We expected any of these economic pursuits to be relatively low in energy intensity and therefore carbon dioxide emissions, either per person or per unit of economic growth. To keep it simple, we predict service exporters will rank at the bottom in carbon dioxide per capita and especially in CO_2/GDP terms.

Forty-four nations were classified as diversified exporters, with no category accounting for over half of their exports. This category includes nearly half of the OECD nations, and a wide range of nations throughout the noncore, including a quarter of all middle-income nations. Many of the low-income and middle-income nations have gone into substantial debt, many with the explicit goal of diversifying their export mixes. Perhaps more than the others, this group appears to be a mixed bag, including many so-called "postindustrial" nations that are still largely industrial, and some that export significant quantities of oil (e.g., Norway, Mexico) or other raw materials. Because of its mixed nature, the diversified category is expected to be intermediate in average carbon dioxide emissions per person or per unit of GDP. Among the non-OECD nations, it is expected that many of these nations have taken aggressive state-led development paths, which while leading them into more complex economic output, also led them deeply into debt.[119]

Carbon Dioxide Emissions and Development Pathways: Findings and Implications

Figure 5.5 suggests just how different nations on different development paths are in their national responsibility for climate change, as indicated by our four measures: total emissions, emissions intensity/GDP, average per capita emissions, and average cumulative carbon dioxide per capita (historical responsibility). In total emissions, the basis for the Kyoto Protocol, nations exporting manufactures and diverse categories of exports are by far the nations with the highest total emissions. Exporters of manufactures and nations with diversified export profiles also exceeded world averages on measures of per capita and historical responsibility, and towered over all other types of exporters in terms of emissions intensity (CO_2/GDP). Oil exporters, as expected, performed poorly on per capita, historical responsibility, and emissions intensity measures. Exporters of services, by almost any measure, performed better than all others.

Exporters of Manufactures

Countries that specialize in the production of manufactures are in a precarious position. On one hand, diversification into manufacturing has long been seen as the crowning achievement of successful late developers. Manufacturing promotes backward and forward linkages and leads to higher levels of internal economic integration. Manufactured exports are usually higher priced and more stable.[120] Fiscal volatility is therefore less severe and the phenomenon of declining terms of trade is less

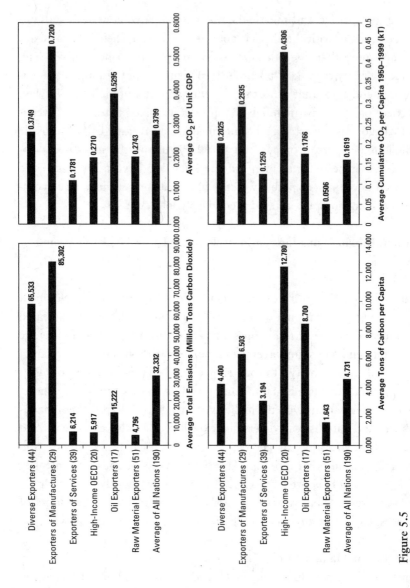

Figure 5.5
Average carbon dioxide responsibility of nations grouped by their leading export sectors.

prevalent.[121] On the other hand, countries with this type of export pro-file are on an extremely high carbon development path. On all four of our responsibility measures, exporters of manufactured goods score worst or next to worst. Recent work by Arrighi et al. suggests that these patterns will not only persist, but worsen.[122] In spite of the developing world's growing share of the global manufacturing market, they find that "each additional increment of manufacturing in developing coun-tries is yielding less income over time."[123] Therefore, just to break even in terms of income, exporters of manufactures will need to export more and more manufacturing units over time. By extension, it is fair to as-sume that many of these exporters will get less income from their carbon use over time. Countries that are specialized in the export of manu-factures therefore may not fit the expected relationship that emissions first rise and then decline as development proceeds, which is consistent with our previous work showing that the relationship between economic growth and environmental impacts is neither necessary nor stage based.[124]

The fact that many poor countries view industrialization and diversifi-cation into manufacturing as the capstone of economic development is thus extremely problematic for resolving the dilemma of post-2012 cli-mate policy.[125] Developing countries will not likely sacrifice their sover-eign right to pursue economic development, as traditionally defined, in the absence of strong financial incentives to do otherwise. It is in this light that we should view the Clean Development Mechanism, Joint Implementation, and other similar initiatives. As one Chinese govern-ment official points out, "whether we will have 20 or 60 CDM projects doesn't really matter."[126] Ultimately, in (larger) developing countries, what matters is trade, direct foreign investment, and access to global financial markets. Decisions concerning global climate change are therefore at risk of being overshadowed by this desire for industrial transformation.[127]

Nonfuel Primary Product Exporters

A number of scholars have suggested that the nations that specialize in the "production" of nonfuel primary products are irrelevant to policy outcomes that matter in international relations. It is true that in mone-tary terms, 130 countries make up no more than 3.6 percent of the global export structure. "That means that two-thirds of all countries in the world are of virtually no significance for the global market. They exert almost no influence on what happens there, but are highly dependent on that market for their imports and exports. Many of the poorest countries have little more to offer than raw materials and agricultural produce, and foreign exchange earnings are often dependent on exporting one, two or three products, which increases dependency to an even greater extent."[128] Baumert et al., for example, argue that 135 countries account for no more than 5 percent of total global carbon emissions: "While theoretically elegant, truly global participation ... is not necessary to achieve the objective of the Climate Convention, nor is it achievable in the foreseeable future. Eighty percent of global carbon emissions are the doing of only 20 countries, which are either rich, highly populated, or both."[129]

Still, there are two important reasons why countries like these matter. The first is carbon leakage. As Harvard economist Robert Stavins explains, "If developing countries are not included in an agreement now, then comparative advantage in the production of carbon-intensive goods and services will shift outside of the coalition of participating countries, making developing country economies more carbon intensive than they otherwise would be (through so-called emissions leakage). Rather than helping developing countries move onto less carbon-intensive paths of economic development, the industrialized world would actually be pushing them onto *more* carbon-intensive growth paths. This would increase their cost of joining the coalition later."[130] The second reason that small, raw material-exporting, developing countries matter is because these countries constitute a much larger part of the global export structure in physical terms than they do in monetary terms.[131] As we discussed earlier, the carbon dioxide emissions caused by Northern consumption habits are increasingly being transferred to resource-rich developing countries. Therefore, the fact that exporters of nonfuel primary products make trivial contributions to global carbon dioxide emissions may be deceiving and not reflective of changing trends over time.

Service Exporters

Service-exporting countries are generally thought to be among the least carbon-intensive exporters. Services include anything from tourism to financial services; research and development; advertising and sales; and transportation, governments, and construction. We expected this category of exporters to fare relatively well in terms of carbon dioxide emissions. Figure 5.5 indicates that service exporters are indeed least responsible for climate change, by three of the four measures, and offer the greatest returns on carbon use. Many of the countries that fall in this category are island nations that are heavily reliant on tourism as a foreign exchange earner. Certainly most tourism is not ecotourism (low-impact, conservation-oriented), and the ability of ecotourism to substantially reduce environmental impacts has itself been questioned. However, the tourism industry has little "industry" in the traditional sense of smokestacks and coal and can bring substantial economic returns.[132]

A second point concerning service exporters is required. The longitudinal trend not captured with sorting nations into one export category in cross-sectional analysis is that most Western countries have recently seen their export compositions move toward services.[133] OECD nations increasingly specialize in high value-added activities, such as research and development, design, distribution, and advertising and sales, which contribute very few direct emissions.[134] This pattern is celebrated as a clear indication that rich nations are become more "postmaterialist," or "postindustrial." However, new research suggests that these service economies still require extraordinary levels of energy and materials. As described in the previous section, studies of ecologically unequal exchange, ecological debt, environmental load displacement, and ecological rucksacks all indicate that production of material goods (and their effluents) has shifted over time to poorer nations. One might therefore say that the material-intensive imports required by rich nations have carbon dioxide emissions "embodied" within them (or a so-called "carbon load").[135] Machado et al. use an input-output model to estimate the amount of energy and carbon embodied in Brazil's exports and imports and find a startling pattern: every export dollar in Brazil embodies 56 percent more carbon and 40 percent more energy than import dollars.[136]

Diversified Exporters

Developing countries with relatively diversified export profiles also pose a special challenge for climate policy makers. On three of our four carbon responsibility measures, they scored second to worst. (Only exporters of manufactures consistently exceeded their emissions.) Though oil exporters register higher levels of carbon intensity, diversified countries emit more than they do by each of the three alternative measures. That said, we must be careful since the World Bank's diversified exporters classification is a catch-all category that includes countries with very different export mixes and carbon profiles.

There are, however, useful policy conclusions to be drawn from this finding. Diversification will remain a top priority for most developing countries in the foreseeable future. They must therefore in some way be compensated for pursuing a less carbon-intensive development path. In a recently published article, Imbs and Wacziarg underline the need (albeit unintentionally) for rich countries to link the issues of climate change and economic development. Using sophisticated econometric techniques, they find that economic diversification does not increase monotonically with economic development. It does up to a certain point—roughly $9,600 annual per capita income[137]—but beyond this threshold countries tend to become more specialized in the production of a few goods and services (especially services). The authors interpret their findings as follows: "The estimated turnaround point occurs quite late in the development process and at a surprisingly robust level of income per capita. Thus, increased sectoral specialization, although a significant development, applies only to high-income economies. *Countries diversify over most of their development path.*"[138]

What are the implications of this finding for climate policy? Only after reaching an extremely high level of per capita national income (approximately that of Ireland's) will countries become more specialized in the service sector. It therefore makes little sense to recommend that poor nations—who have their sights set on further economic growth and development—move into the (allegedly) more climate-friendly service sector anytime soon. The U-shaped curve identified by Imbs and Wacziarg challenges those who ignore the real-world difficulty of diversifying into the service sector at low levels of income.[139]

Fuel Exporters

These types of exporters, not surprisingly, did not fare very well on any of our indicators of carbon responsibility. At first glance, one might think that this third group of exporters performed better than expected (see figure 5.5). However, it is important to remember that many of the Middle Eastern countries that received this World Bank designation did not begin their "development push" until the 1970s.[140] Consequently, these types of exporters are less responsible in aggregate terms for the existing global stock of carbon dioxide emissions. Nonetheless, bringing oil exporters aboard a post-2012 treaty is essential for stabilizing the climate because of their extraordinarily high carbon intensity levels.

During negotiations at Kyoto, OPEC demanded that "the principle of compensation...be built into the protocol."[141] They specifically asked that rich nations help them diversify their economies away from the carbon-intensive oil sector. Their efforts were thwarted on two counts. First, many Western diplomats engaged in two-level games with sovereign governments and their domestic populations. Most thought that the idea of transferring large sums of money to oil magnates in the Middle East would not be viewed favorably by their domestic legislatures. There was also the more technical issue of trying to estimate compensation for lost oil revenues without reliable information on future oil prices. Despite being marginalized in the run-up to Kyoto, this issue has resurfaced at every subsequent Conference of the Parties. OPEC makes their case on the following grounds: "Without a favorable disposition towards the compensation issue among the Parties to the Convention, how can fossil fuel producers be expected to give their wholehearted blessing to measures that could wreak havoc with their economies?"[142] Most recently, at COP-9 in Milan, Italy, Saudi Arabia forcefully argued, with the support of China, for legal text to be included in the convention and the protocol that would compel Western countries to finance the economic diversification of OPEC economies.[143]

The OPEC–OECD standoff is important because it draws attention to the issues of global decarbonization and the profoundly political process of trying to diversify out of carbon-intensive sectors and industries. We argue in chapter 7 that LDCs need to begin "making" new, more economically dynamic and climate-friendly comparative advantages, rather than "taking" the easy path of their natural comparative advantage. This creates an important and controversial window of opportunity for state intervention in the economy. Just as many of the most successful late developers strategically used artificial superprofits to stimulate local investment and innovation, so too will LDC governments committed to climate policy reform need to nudge risk-averse entrepreneurs toward innovation.

Conclusion: Integrating Climate Policy with Development Policy

Any study of responsibility for climate change must state at the outset that the United States is making a disproportionate contribution to the potential destabilization of our global climate. On the three most commonly used approaches to measuring climate responsibility—total emissions, per capita emissions, and historical responsibility for atmospheric carbon—the United States towers above most other nations (figure 5.1; table 5.1). This is stark inequality; table 5.1 lists the 180 nations in which people emit on average less than half the carbon dioxide that Americans do, including the 89 nations where it would take more than ten citizens to generate as much as one American does.[144] A handful of other nations rank near the United States in emissions per capita, and only on carbon dioxide emitted per unit of economic activity (CO_2/GDP) does the United States not rank at the very top. So there are emissions related to poverty and to wealth, and the scale of this "inequality in the air" between the world's wealthy and poor could not be more stark. This is especially the case when it occurs simultaneously with the startlingly unequal suffering from climate disasters documented in chapters 3 and 4.

That is the simple answer to the question of who is responsible for climate change, but it is not the whole answer. We sought also to understand broader patterns of who is emitting more and what might be behind their behavior. We looked at patterns in carbon dioxide emissions as reflected in the four criteria, comparing groups of nations by their national income levels and their "pathways of development." Much of the research in this field has focused on the simple bivariate relationship between GDP and emissions, which is clearly important but is only part of the story. In particular, we find the concept of pathways of development promising but poorly developed in the literature on climate change, and we believe it should be a crucial part of the next round of analysis by the IPCC and other researchers.[145] Building on past social science research and our previous analyses using the tools of structuralist analysis, we focused on the economic sectors that dominated a nation's exports. By this reckoning it is easy to see why Saudi Arabia and other OPEC nations at the COP-8 meetings in New Delhi were so determined to ensure that they would be compensated in the Kyoto and post-Kyoto treaties for losses resulting from any potential limits on burning fossil fuels.

Nations also have a complex series of geographic, economic, and social conditions that have shaped their levels of emissions, as our multivariate analysis showed vividly, no matter how those emissions are measured (table 5.3). We saw that beyond the size of a nation's economy, countries with larger populations, cold climates, and more urban populations tend to emit more. These could be relatively straightforwardly built in as adjustments in national emissions quotas in a post-Kyoto framework.

Attention is beginning to be paid to sectors and pathways of development. Several South Asian authors working on the Fourth Assessment Report of the IPCC that is due out in 2006, for example, argued that "development pathways...societies choose today may be as important, possibly even more important, as the climate measures they take."[146] Initial discussions of the issue began at the COP-10 in Buenos Aires in 2004. The results in this chapter are exploratory, but suggest the importance of this issue. Figure 5.5 shows just how disparate carbon dioxide emissions are for nations with different leading export sectors. After the wealthy OECD nations, it is the oil exporters, exporters of manufactures, and diverse exporters who emitted the most. Our multivariate analysis in table 5.3 showed that nations with more manufacturing are emitting more as a group, even when the size of the economy and geographic conditions are held constant.

Some development pathways (as indicated by their main export products) insulate countries from economic volatility more than others, cause less local environmental damage, and give more options to planners; others are much more difficult to change. Key groups of countries are dependent on the export of a few carbon-intensive products for their national development.[147] These countries will almost certainly push relentlessly for industrialization, even if it comes at the expense of the environment. In those nations, compensation and assistance for them to transition to alternative development pathways will be critical for their participation. As we discuss in the concluding chapter, nations on the high-emitting pathways will require serious attention to their political and class situations in order to manage the conflicts that will almost inevitably arise. However, compensation is an intensely political process, and countries will need "policy space" to pursue strategies tailored to local culture, knowledge, institutions, and politics, while being provided with substantial technical assistance, technology transfer, and aid.

More complex analyses of these factors are needed, but one can imagine a sophisticated hybrid proposal for assigning national carbon-dioxide emission quotas based on this kind of profiling of nations. This would require that a future treaty be developed from the physical science of what the atmosphere can likely handle, principled decisions about which approach is most fair, plus the practical social science of what difficulties nations of different types will face in meeting their allowed emissions. That is to say, brute bargaining strength will never lead us to a workable climate treaty, neither in the sense of atmospheric stability nor the political or social sense.

Since fairness positions are configurational, or based upon a nation's position in the global economy and polity, policy makers will also need to be explicit in identifying fairness focal points and remain open to accommodating multiple principles. Ultimately, for a solution to be possible, there needs to be an understanding that a consensus position must accommodate the circumstances and principled beliefs of many parties. Therefore, no one group can win their fairness argument.

This chapter's analysis also reflects on the larger point glaringly apparent since the 1972 Stockholm Summit on Environment and Development: We need to overcome the false divide between economic and environmental issues. A series of authors and the World Bank have reported on some cases and types of pollutants that seem to first get worse and then get better as nations get wealthier.[148] This idea, called the environmental Kuznets curve, has been repeatedly cited as the reason nations need first to grow economically, after which they will develop the interest and means to address those problems. This curve has been seized upon in the World Bank's influential *World Development Report* and the debate continues in many policy-making circles. However, as figures 5.2 and 5.3 suggest, national carbon dioxide emissions per capita are almost directly related to average income in a nation. Only in carbon intensity were wealthier nations more efficient than their poorer counterparts. Therefore, one can see an environmental Kuznets curve for carbon dioxide only when it is measured this way, and since emissions per capita continue to rise with income, it seems disingenuous and in fact dangerous to say there will be improvement in emissions if nations just grow economically. Global warming will not be resolved by nations passing through some progression of stages where their environmental performance systematically worsens and then later improves as they get wealthier. We have argued in previous work that the "turning points"—the level of income at which the worsening is supposed to halt and reverse—are too high to reasonably expect many nations to ever get there.[149] World history suggests that only a few countries are able to move up through the global stratification system to these levels of wealth.

Improvements in emissions intensity or other measures of carbon responsibility by wealthy nations are not solely the result of improvements in energy efficiency. Rather, much of the apparent improvement comes from their effectively offshoring the most environmentally damaging production stages of the goods they consume. This is in fact the third stage of a longer historical migration. First, starting in the 1960s, oil and mining corporations began to scour the remotest corners of the Third World to uncover reserves of ores and oils to export back to their home nations and around the world. In the 1960s and 1970s, the urgency of this effort was increased by revolutionary movements in Third World nations and the efforts to create exporter cartels. Second, much of the energy-intensive primary processing of those raw materials has shifted to non-core nations, beginning mostly in the 1970s and 1980s. Sometimes this occurred as developing nations sought to capture more of the value of their resources and developed national mills and refineries, or took up joint ventures with foreign firms to do so. Unfortunately the prices of those intermediate goods tended to fluctuate wildly or drop precipitously as demand dropped when synthetic substitutes were developed or other global sources became available. Finally, transnational manufacturing firms and now locally owned contractors or suppliers have quickly shifted production to low-wage havens like China and India. In all three stages, the impacts on carbon dioxide emissions have shifted from wealthy importers of goods to poorer exporters, while relatively few social and economic benefits haved accrued to the poorer partner.

Ecologically unequal exchange is therefore not just a perception by angry and irrational Third World politicians, leftist scholars, and activists marching around the streets of Delhi; it is an observable physical reality. International trade has different effects on rich and on poor nations. Trading more products increases emissions by poorer nations, while lowering them for wealthier nations. This was true in the multivariate analysis (table 5.3) for all four of the carbon indicators, suggesting it is now an extremely robust finding. The literature on ecologically unequal exchange therefore vindicates the Southern claim that Northern consumption is driving much of the problem, taking their resources and leaving them with only their waste and a hole in the ground. Perhaps only the payment of some part of the massive ecological debt the global North owes the South will provide the financing necessary to assist these nations in upgrading from high to lower carbon development paths.

6

Who Is Taking Action?

In the conference hall of the World Bank's modernist Washington, DC, headquarters, a June 2001 panel brought together a group of economists to discuss "Climate Change: A Challenge for the 21st Century."[1] Panelist David Victor, an Adjunct Senior Fellow from the Council on Foreign Relations, strongly advocated a "get the prices right" approach. If the right price signals are sent, he argued, private entrepreneurs will react by investing in climate-friendly technology. When asked to discuss the issues of fairness and justice in the climate regime, Victor avoided the question and quickly moved on to argue that it would probably be better if poor countries did not participate in a global agreement at this point. In his view, "extremely risk-averse" developing countries that have not yet discovered "their marginal costs of abatement" create a big part of Kyoto's problem by increasing preference heterogeneity and driving the pact to a lowest common denominator.

After an hour of similar explanations about the inadequacy of the Kyoto Protocol, Atiq Rahman tried to put the comments of the previous three speakers in perspective: "The Kyoto Protocol had almost nothing to do with developing countries. It was a negotiation between the OECD countries on their agreed allocations, on how to reduce their greenhouse gases. On the last night, the developing countries were brought in to talk about it and to accept it.... I have done an interview of 85 leaders of the negotiations just after the Kyoto Protocol and asked them why they signed this stupid document, which is totally iniquitous. And they said, 'because they will set up an adaptation fund, [and] there could be some money in it'." He paused to let the words settle. "As I said, we are in two different worlds.... Now [developing country negotiators] are saying, 'the Kyoto Protocol, it's so unjust, totally iniquitous, but for the sake of negotiation, let us accept it'."[2]

Rahman's comments get at the crux of the problem: while a strong argument can be made for putting a price on carbon dioxide emissions and creating incentives for technological change in the industrialized world, these kinds of "solutions" do not occur in a political vacuum. Developing countries already feel like second-class citizens in North-South relations and are unlikely to be enthusiastic about being locked out of a global climate regime after fifteen years of repeatedly being promised large environmental aid packages, increased direct foreign investment, and significant technology transfer.

Over the last few chapters, we have seen how inequality in vulnerability to climate-related disasters and responsibility for them can influence North-South negotiations. Here we focus directly on participation in global environmental accords. Since the early 1970s, global environmental problems such as pollution of the oceans, loss of biodiversity, climate change, and depletion of the ozone layer have raised awareness among scholars, activists, and governments throughout the world that issues once considered local now demand unprecedented levels of international cooperation. In seeking solutions to these problems, treaties have proved to be an important mechanism by which states make promises to each other to administer natural resources and manage the global environment.[3] Nation-states are of course the principal political units held responsible for addressing these global environmental problems, but the million-dollar question is, will they? As Hurrell and Kingsbury put it a decade ago, "Can a fragmented and often highly conflictual political system made up of over 170 sovereign states and numerous other actors achieve the high (and historically unprecedented) levels of co-operation and policy coordination needed to manage environmental problems on a global scale?"[4]

Even a casual observer of Earth summits and Kyoto treaties would be struck by the great differences in how states respond to the effort to build environmental treaties. Some nations rush to sign and ratify all of them, some ignore them, and others actively resist participation or undermine them altogether.[5] Analysts of international environmental politics (IEP) have offered a range of competing and complementary explanations to make sense of this variance. Primarily through case studies and small-*n* quantitative research, we have learned a great deal about comparative foreign policy and begun untangling complex causal processes.[6] However, in terms of theoretically self-conscious attempts to systematically produce generalizable findings from a large sample of treaties and participants, it is widely agreed that our collective knowledge in IEP is inadequate.[7] To address the unavoidable issue of overdetermination, we constructed an index of environmental treaty ratification that covers participation by 192 nations in the 22 major international environmental agreements negotiated between 1946 and early 1999.[8] With this index we subjected the predictions that logically follow from constructivism, realism, and rational-choice institutionalism—the mainstream core of the field of international relations—to cross-sectional testing. We thened turn to two indicators of participation in the Kyoto Protocol.

As with vulnerability to and responsibility for climate change, a further limitation hindering the accumulation of knowledge in IEP is the gap between proximate political explanations and theorization on the deeper social roots of state behavior. Along lines similar to those in chapters 4 and 5, we aim here to rectify this shortcoming by offering a theoretically sequenced model of state behavior. Understanding patterns in ratification of environmental treaties, we argue, requires an analysis of both the proximate political factors and the deeper social and historical determinants of state action.[9] Therefore, we attempt to integrate structural insights from world-systems theory with the micro-motives of rational-choice institutionalism. Whereas institutionalists explain why states voluntarily create institutions that facilitate environmental cooperation, world-systems theorists address the underlying factors that condition a state's willingness and ability to participate in such arrangements. Each of these traditions, in effect, speaks to different links in a chain of causation.

We first examine the record of previous international relations theories in explaining the environmental policy behavior of nation-states and go on to expound the underapplied central tenets of world-systems theory. We then describe our cross-national approach to predicting treaty ratification, and our development of an index of participation by states in environmental treaties through April 1999. We operationalize a series of factors suggested by international relations and world-systems theories, and go on to test their ability to predict treaty ratification rates in ordinary least-squares regression and path analysis, as we did in chapters 4 and 5. We conclude with an assessment of the indices, the method, and the relative usefulness of the different IEP traditions. Our results indicate that new theoretical, methodological, and policy approaches are needed to address structural barriers to international cooperation, so our last words suggest some implications of this shift, which leads us to the book's final chapter.

Theorizing State Participation in Environmental Treaties

The rapidly accumulating evidence implicating our species in the creation of environmental crises of global proportions might suggest that states would rapidly and uniformly jump on an environmentalist bandwagon to address these issues before it is too late. Such an expectation, of course, is sadly naïve. Over three decades, efforts to solve global environmental crises have proven to be spotty and contentious. Moments of progress are infrequent, and hopeful signs are often undermined by self-interested players.[10] The central theoretical traditions of international relations scholarship offer different explanations for why some nations accept and others reject environmental treaties. We review their insights briefly, but focus most on rational-choice institutionalism, which has gone the furthest in developing an argument about state behavior in this policy area.

Rational-choice institutionalists have made it their central preoccupation to explain the flowering of voluntary international cooperation. Faced with the spread of international law, institutions, and organizations, scholars from this camp have offered a functional explanation for the creation, maintenance, and implementation of international regimes.[11] Specifically, they posit that under conditions of interdependence, uncertainty, and high transaction costs, states actually need institutions (or regimes—the terms are used interchangeably here) to facilitate cooperation. By increasing transparency and providing reliable information, monitoring and verifying state behavior, assisting implementation, and sanctioning noncompliance, institutions help states move away from pursuing relative gains—where "my gain is your loss"—toward positive-sum outcomes.[12] In short, institutions help states overcome collective action problems and promote their shared interests in a shifting and complex world. International treaties are similarly under-stood as functional solutions to efficiency problems.[13] Lipson explains that when treaties are ratified, "states wish to signal their intentions with special intentions and gravity.... The decision to encode a bargain in treaty form is primarily a decision to highlight the importance of the agreement and, even more, to underscore the durability and significance of the underlying promises.... The effect of treaties...is to raise the po-litical costs of non-compliance. The cost is raised not only for others, but also for oneself. The more formal and public the agreement, the higher the reputational costs of non-compliance."[14]

The prospects for international cooperation, however, fundamentally depend upon the credibility of a state's commitments.[15] If a state's will-ingness or ability to implement an international environmental policy is weak, or even in question, institutitonalists argue that cooperation is un-likely. We would therefore expect a state's propensity to ratify environ-mental treaties to correlate positively with our measures of credibility.[16] Multiple observable implications follow from this hypothesis. Some authors emphasize how international factors—for example, interdepen-dence, the stability of institutional environments, and reciprocity—affect the credibility of state commitments,[17] while others focus on unit-level explanations. Within the latter group, "new institutionalism" has yielded the most consistent predictions and persuasive findings.[18]

We have chosen three variables that affect the ability of a sending state to convince a receiving state that it will indeed implement the policy adjustments required by an environmental agreement. As proxies for willingness, we use measures of environmental vulnerability and civil so-ciety strength. To capture elements of willingness *and* ability, we include an indicator of voice and accountability.[19] Nations experiencing high levels of environmental vulnerability, we predict, will demonstrate a greater willingness to take on international environmental commitments. Unlike theories that causally privilege the spread of global environmental norms or external coercion, a functionalist approach suggests that one's international environmental policy may reflect the degree to which envi-ronmental degradation impinges upon one's welfare. As Sprinz and Vaahtoranta put it, "the worse the state of the environment, the greater the incentives to reduce the ecological vulnerability of the state."[20] However, state preferences are obviously a function of more than just vulnerability. Some states face robust domestic environmentalist pressure, while in many other countries civil society has languished for generations. Following Dalton, we argue that "the existence of an active environmental movement is a sign of the public's interest in environmental issues, as well as a stimulant for politicians and the public to pay even greater attention to environmental concerns."[21] One might think that the number of domestic environmental NGOs would be an ideal proxy, but the definition of "environmental" NGO has become increasingly fuzzy. In the developing world, where the natural environment is often situated in a broader social context, NGO work tends to cut across issue areas and not lend itself to categorization. Therefore, as a next-best measure, we take as a proxy for environmentalist pressure the total number of NGOs as a measure of a nation's civil society.[22]

Our third hypothesis concerning the domestic sources of credibility is a new institutionalist one, drawing on the body of scholarship that addresses regime type. Lake,[23] Fearon,[24] Gaubatz,[25] Leeds,[26] Martin,[27] Mansfield et al.,[28] Schultz and Weingast,[29] Jensen,[30] and Tierney[31] all suggest that states with strong democratic institutions are more likely to make credible international policy commitments.[32] Where such open and responsive domestic political institutions are in place, it is thought that the "domestic audience costs" of defection are higher.[33] With reelection weighing heavily on the minds of elected representatives, "democratic leaders make only the commitments that they can keep, and once made will tenaciously attempt to comply with those commitments."[34] Conversely, where there are no clear lines of political accountability, defection is relatively costless and therefore common.

To be clear, new institutionalism makes no substantive claims about international environmental commitments. The relationship is thought to hold across issue areas. Neumayer has recently put forth an alternative explanation that hinges on the uniqueness of international environmental agreements.[35] He proposes that "in democracies citizens are better informed about environmental problems (due to freedom of the press) and can better express their environmental concerns and demands (freedom of speech), which will facilitate an organization of environmental interests (freedom of association), which will in turn put pressure on policy entrepreneurs operating in a competitive political system to respond positively to these demands (freedom of the vote)."[36] Though data limitations do not permit a satisfactory discriminating test at this time, we suspect that Neumayer's argument will not survive careful scrutiny. There is a well-established theoretical and empirical body of scholarship supporting a general link between democracy and credibility. Democratic leaders are better able to carry out their military, trade, investment, aid, and debt commitments.[37]

International Relations and Theoretical Sequencing: Explaining How Nations Acquire Credibility

Rational-choice institutionalism explains the proximate political reasons for state participation in environmental treaties, but leaves unanswered the deeper questions of how states came to be in their global positions in the first place. Institutionalism, in particular, has provided parsimonious and powerful models of international environmental cooperation, and we recognize its achievements.[38] However, theories are only as useful as what they attempt to explain, and institutionalism sheds light only on interstate managerial problems.[39] The now orthodox notion that solving international environmental problems is a matter of engineering efficient institutions increasing information, reducing transaction costs and uncertainty, facilitating implementation, and limiting the risk of opportunism, is frankly an artifact of the historical era in which institutionalist theory grew up. Institutionalist analysis originally sought to explain puzzles of international political economy; why, for example, states ever cooperated for mutual economic gain under conditions of anarchy.[40] It was therefore hardly surprising that when global and regional environmental issues gained greater policy salience, institutionalists reached for their "off the shelf" textbook models of collective action and applied them to this new issue area.[41] Nevertheless, the managerial approach, while providing "solutions" to particular environmental problems, does not address the role that existing social structures play in producing and reproducing environmental degradation and nonparticipation in international governance.[42]

How is this relevant to our present study? If developing countries are indeed less likely to participate in environmental treaties because of credibility concerns, we must then ask how they acquire credibility. Stated differently, we must bridge the gap between structure and agency by accounting for environmental policy behavior in the world as it exists, where rationality is conditioned by the experience of repeatedly losing in efforts to improve the position of one's nation in the world system.[43] Developing countries face unique structural constraints. These include unpredictability and long-term decline in the prices of their crucial export commodities, internally unarticulated markets, and feeble postcolonial government institutions, all of which limit their ability to implement good environmental policies and participate in treaty drafting conferences. Developing countries also suffer worst and first from deforestation; land degradation; pollution from mining, agriculture, and manufacturing for export; as well as so-called collective bads shared across boundaries.[44]

We need, therefore, to press backward from institutionalist theories that explain treaty participation as a result of domestic political institutions and pressure from civil society (among many other ascriptive factors) to understand the structural roots of national preferences and capabilities. We needn't reinvent the wheel as there are decades of accumulated debate on the topic. Most helpful for our project are political economic ideas loosely associated with world-systems theory.[45] Here we seek to explain how the narrowness of a country's export base can influence its local environment, domestic institutions, and civil society organization.

World-systems theorists and other structuralist thinkers would charge that models of mainstream international relations and economics have done violence to the historical context in which social events occur.[46] Prominent theorists such as Wallerstein, Braudel, Frank, and Chase-Dunn all took "deep historical" approaches to explaining current national relations to the world economy, and a handful of scholars have begun to do the same for understanding environmental degradation and state responses in the world system.[47] Each of these authors has focused on a specific region and/or time period, but the basic story is the same: repressive labor relations were established in colonial nations that were forced to specialize in raw materials exports, usually mining or plantation agriculture commodities. Today, narrow export profiles and chronic underdevelopment provide strong incentives to search for quickly exportable commodities that often harm the environment, perpetuating a vicious cycle.[48] States beholden to narrow groups of "export elites" also tend to have ineffective and corrupt bureaucracies and therefore little capacity to deliver public goods, like environmental protection.[49]

As we mentioned earlier, world-systems theory also draws attention to the role that narrow export profiles play in distorting state–society relations and indirectly impacting environmental regulatory regimes. Extractive states are not only infamous for their feeble domestic institutions, but also their weak and disfigured civil societies. Three reasons are typically cited: large resource rents may provide government officials with enough money to suppress civil society's desire for democracy; windfall profits (seen especially from oil) tend to promote patronage and edge out ordinary citizens from public participation; and, resource booms often relieve government officials of their usual need to raise taxes.[50] Because of the close relationship between taxation and representation, this "insulation effect" may make constituents "less likely to demand accountability from … their government."[51]

Finally, the shape of a country's export profile bears profoundly upon its institutional development. "The distinguishing feature of [extractive] institutions [during the colonial period]," write Acemoglu et al., "was a high concentration of political power in the hands of a few who extracted resources from the rest of the population."[52] And since many former colonies began their "development" under circumstances of high social inequality, the institutions that were put in place often reflected and reinforced those inequalities. As Robert Putnam once observed, "social context and history profoundly condition the effectiveness of institutions."[53] High levels of initial inequality, not surprisingly, left political institutions weak and deformed and society less democratic, and these institutions have persisted for centuries.[54]

From an international relations perspective, then, we believe that the value of world-systems theory is its ability to account for state preferences and capabilities, variables that are typically exogenous to rational-institutionalist models.[55] This chapter therefore takes a historical approach to explain why some nations have particularly vulnerable natural environments, feeble domestic political institutions, and unorganized civil societies in the first place. Following Acemoglu et al., we again argue that in places where colonists focused mostly on extraction—

measured as the narrowness of a state's export profile today—domestic institutions (such as voice and accountability and government effectiveness) will be weakest.[56] Long legacies of resource extraction will also correlate with higher levels of environmental vulnerability. Finally, we expect civil society will be weakest where entrenched export elites are strongest. Of course, sometimes historical legacies are not amenable to quantitative analysis. While it is also faulted for excessive empiricism, world-systems theory often attempts to use current statistics to capture the legacy of historical trends. When historical data cannot be found or utilized, we argue that historical knowledge must inform current analysis. Here we use the lack of a diversified export base as a proxy for a nation's repressive colonial legacy.

Alternative Explanations from Constructivists, Realists, Rationalists, and Ideationalists

Our theoretically sequenced model of ratification of environmental treaties, which exploits complementarities between rational-choice institutionalism and world-systems theory, of course cannot explain complex social reality by itself. Thus we consider a series of alternative explanations from the extant literature that also deserve serious empirical scrutiny.

Constructivists offer a constitutive model of international relations in which global environmental "culture" gradually spreads its tentacles around the world, enveloping more and more states in a world institutional structure. They argue that for over a century the global norm of environmentalism has spread universally and increased steadily. These common global values have in turn created a social system that subsumes the traditional international political world. Thus, treaty ratifications pile up as a growing global network of scientists in international councils for science (ICSUs) and international nongovernmental organizations disseminate their global environmental ideas and values.[57] To gain and keep legitimacy in this evolving cultural "club," states must participate in the major treaties on important issues, including those on the environment. A main hypothesis of theirs is that national memberships in international norm-setting institutions (such as international environmental

NGOs or international scientific unions) will correlate positively with the number of environmental treaties ratified by a country.[58]

Realists, quite differently, consider treaties as barely worth the paper upon which they are printed.[59] They argue that international regime building and treaty making are just so much talk, obscuring the deeper agendas of states to secure power.[60] Treaties, much like international institutions, are written off as a set of epiphenomena that states will contravene when they no longer perceive benefits in continued participation.[61] It should therefore come as no surprise that realist scholarship has paid little attention to the creation, maintenance, and implementation of international environmental treaties.[62] While the sharp increase and growing importance of voluntary international cooperation after World War II has been difficult to deny, realists insist that a power-based explanation still retains the most analytical strength in the study of international environmental politics.[63] Oran Young[64] and Elizabeth DeSombre[65] highlight a number of cases where powerful states have imposed an environmental regime on otherwise disinterested states. To take one example, the Whaling Convention suffered from frequent noncompliance until the United States threatened—and in some cases, actually used—economic sanctions against free riders.[66] The observable implications of realist theory therefore seem relatively straightforward. Given the convergence of Western policy preferences around "green" issues,[67] we would expect powerful states (or coalitions of powerful states) to coerce countries with global environmental significance into cooperative ventures. Countries with high levels of natural capital (e.g., large forested land areas and biodiversity) should therefore be more likely to participate in environmental treaties than those with little global environmental significance.

There are two additional arguments concerning the positive role of fairness in international environmental cooperation that deserve consideration. The first hypothesis follows from the rationalist literature on institutional design, which emphasizes the ways that strategic states with intense preferences for cooperation can craft institutions to promote their long-term goals.[68] The second hypothesis is an ideational one that highlights the role that principled beliefs play in securing stable and deep cooperative agreements. The positivist literature on fairness, to be sure, is thin. However, we believe that its insights are central to North-South environmental relations.

According to scholars working in the emerging field of rational institutional design, demandeurs seeking the cooperation of more reluctant parties must look "down" the decision tree to anticipate the future behavior of their cooperative partners.[69] This often entails restructuring contracts such that disinterested countries stand to gain from participation in the immediate and longer term. However, rational institutional design is not only about making voluntary participation economically rational. It is also about addressing the risk aversion, emotions, social preferences, and bargaining power of would-be cooperators. Poor nations that believe they have been trampled upon in issue areas of most concern to them (especially those with issue-specific bargaining power) may thumb their noses at rich nations that insist on addressing First World issues. In issue areas characterized by generalized mistrust, low density of interaction, and large power asymmetries, risk-averse states may also require discernible, irrevocable, noncontingent, and costly signals. As we discussed in chapter 2, states overcome by feelings of marginalization, frustration, anger, bitterness, and hopelessness may adopt retaliatory attitudes that promote zero-sum outcomes.[70] Finally, weak states that anticipate being exploited at the discretion of powerful states may even take self-damaging steps to promote their principled beliefs.[71]

There are a wide variety of institutional designs that enable demandeurs and recalcitrant parties to overcome such barriers to cooperation, some "hard," others "soft." The role of positive incentives, in particular side payments, has received more attention than perhaps any other institutional innovation. It is said that direct financial transfers can reshape a country's payoff structure, lower its risk aversion, increase levels of trust, and signal shared social understandings. In doing so, side payments make contracting, bargaining, monitoring, and enforcing less difficult, time-consuming, and expensive. Hence, we expect the incorporation of environmental aid transfers within larger international environmental institutions to strengthen the form, frequency, substance, and depth of international environmental cooperation.[72] These considerations lead us to hypothesize that environmental treaty ratifications will correlate positively with the receipt of environmental assistance. We call this the "compensatory justice" hypothesis.

Ideational theorists have also made a series of novel claims about the positive role of fairness in international relations. Here we address just one—that nations base their policies on their principled beliefs, holding all else constant. One group of social constructivists in particular has advanced the idea that states possess principled beliefs that are often at variance with their own material interests, and under certain conditions these beliefs trump narrow self-interest. Kathryn Sikkink, for example, argues that the U.S. government's principled belief in human rights caused it to punish members within its own military alliances and governments pursuing liberal economic policies that benefited the West. The conclusion of her study is that ideas prevailed over interests.[73] Robert Jackson makes a similar argument.[74] He suggests that colonialism, despite economically and militarily advantaging colonial powers, became normatively unjustifiable after World War II, the Non-Aligned movement, and the civil rights movement in the United States.

In the issue area of global environmental politics, the obvious analogue is that highly vulnerable states who are scarcely responsible for the problem of global warming might abstain from participating in an international agreement to stabilize the climate, despite the fact that such a strategy would qualify as self-damaging behavior. This hypothesis stands in contrast to Sprinz and Vaahtoranta's claim that vulnerable countries have a stronger incentive to cooperate than nonvulnerable countries.[75] Stated differently, most rationalist authors would argue that the countries worst affected by climate change are least able to credibly threaten nonparticipation in a regulatory regime. However, poor nations suffering from rising sea levels, devastating droughts and storms, declining agricultural yields, increased disease burdens, and destructive flooding are unlikely to be enthusiastic about addressing an environmental problem that the industrialized world created in the first place. So, while there is some truth to the hard rationalist position, it overlooks the possibility that victim states may possess social, distributive, normative, or emotional preferences that override their narrow material self-interest.

Modeling Ratification of Environmental Treaties

This section links these theories to our measures and hypotheses, and moves on to model building and our predicted empirical results. Beyond institutionalism's focus on how qualities of the state and society determine the treaty performance of nations, world-systems theory provides us with three important insights. First, it offers a theory for why international inequality matters in how states behave. Second, it advances an explanation about how that inequality developed. Third, it has suggested a direction for the type of measure we might seek to show the lingering impacts of colonial history, one of which is the level at which a nation is dependent upon a small number of exports for its foreign exchange.

As we have discussed earlier, the historical legacy of a country's incorporation into the global economy has a critical impact on the avenues of development available to it. This legacy helps to shape the types of products a country makes, the conditions for both capital and labor there, which commodities are traded and with whom, as well as its global power vis-à-vis other nations. In terms of its direct effect, we expect that a colonial insertion into the world economy (reliance on the export of a few, barely processed raw materials) will negatively influence a nation's environmental policy. Our admittedly imperfect measure to test the impacts of a colonial legacy is the index of export diversification developed by the UN Conference on Trade and Development (UNCTAD).

Indirectly, we also expect that a colonial legacy will have strong effects on government policies toward the environment, decisions by firms within countries, and the living conditions of its peoples. In other words, we expect that consistently impoverishing colonial legacies will affect a state's ability to participate in environmental accords. Core nations, for example, will be more likely to have strong civil societies and responsive governments that seriously consider the requests of environmentalists, whereas peripheral nations will be less likely to do so. We also expect that a nation's path of development will have strong indirect effects on its willingness to make international environmental commitments. Elsewhere, Roberts has proposed that behind the dual restraint of workers and environmentalists lay the interests of local ruling classes, transnational corporations, and governments in sustaining both the profitable structures of internal production and the links between these structures and the world economy.[76] Here we test that proposition's value in explaining participation in treaties.

As discussed earlier, nations with high levels of structural vulnerability because of their dependence on a small number of largely unprocessed goods face empty (and/or unreliable) coffers, and substantial pressure from export elites to not implement environmental policies. Therefore our prediction is that a nation's level of participation in environmental treaties will be negatively correlated with a narrow export structure. As discussed earlier, countries that are highly dependent on a few exports typically have a noticeable exporting sector elite that depends on the state and its rents,[77] which in turn suppresses civil society.[78] Not surprisingly, these weak states[79] are also infamous for their feeble domestic political institutions, which is relevant to our study because repressive, unaccountable governments may have a greater ability to ignore the demands of environmentalists. Operationalizing such complex domestic institutional variables for comparative research may be impossible, but here we utilize the index of voice and accountability of Kaufmann et al. because it seems to best capture the concept of government responsiveness.[80]

These arguments led us to propose three possible indirect factors that will lead governments to ratify environmental treaties. First, the narrowness of a nation's export base will be negatively correlated with measures of domestic voice and accountability. These in turn will be positively correlated with the degree of mobilization of domestic civil society, as measured by the total number of nongovernmental organizations in a nation.[81] Less responsive governments resulting from a colonial history will be less concerned with the demands of civil society, including those of environmentalists. Therefore these nations will be less likely to ratify environmental treaties. Unaccountable states, we theorize, will have a direct impact on treaty participation and an indirect impact conditioned by the strength of civil society groups. Controlling for voice and accountability, we expect a strong civil society (and particularly high levels of domestic environmentalist pressure) to induce greater participation in international environmental accords.[82]

We also control for external pressure from "world society" and powerful rich nations. Based on constructivist claims, we predict that international environmentalist pressure on a country will positively affect its ratification of environmental treaties.[83] Here we have chosen data on the number of member organizations in the World Conservation Union in each country per million population. Following realist theory, we also expect rich nations, concerned with their own security and well-being, to employ heavy-handed coercive tools against countries perceived as having global environmental significance (e.g., Brazil, Indonesia, China). For this variable we take a nation's natural capital as a proxy for external pressure by outsiders to deal with environmental problems.[84] Brazil is an obvious example, since it has the huge Amazon forest and faces continuing pressures from outsiders to protect it. Additionally, we have included two variables that test for the impact of fairness: environmental assistance from 1990 to 2000 as a fraction of total global environmental assistance in that same period, and the cumulative number of residents made homeless by climate-related disasters between 1980 and 2000 as a fraction of the total national population (see chapters 3, 4). We expect higher levels of environmental assistance to elicit more ratifications and higher levels of climate-related suffering to correlate negatively with ratifications.

Finally, although it may seem counterintuitive, colonial legacies might actually have a positive effect on participation in environmental treaties if one closely follows the logic of world-systems theory. That is, if having a relatively undiversified export structure does indeed spell environmental disaster,[86] noncore states should theoretically be more open to (potentially mitigating) environmental cooperation and policy reform. That is, countries with poor ecological conditions may be more likely to yield national sovereignty to international environmental institutions in order to promote potentially helpful interstate agreements. Therefore our third prediction is that the narrowness of a nation's export base—which is often associated with raw materials extraction and/or dirty industries—will be correlated with poor ecological well-being. We conceptualized the Ecosystem Wellbeing Index[87] as an indicator of national environmental vulnerability and overall condition of the environment. Note that this index works in a reverse direction, with high scores indicating poor ecosystem well-being.

What Explains Participation in Environmental Treaties Broadly and Kyoto in Particular?

With caveats about the important limitations to cross-national analysis of a complex conjunctural issue,[88] the findings confirm the value of path analysis and the importance of institutional and structural factors in the proximate forces driving treaty ratification in general and participation in the Kyoto treaty in particular (table 6.1, figure 6.1). We first discuss the broad patterns of participation, based on an index of state environmentalism developed by Thomas Dietz and Linda Kalof in 1992. This summed the number of major environmental treaties ratified by nations between 1963 and 1989.[89] We also recently updated and enlarged the index to include participation in twenty-two treaties through April 1999, and created a factor score based on which treaties tended most to move up and down together.[90] Together, Dietz and Kalof's index accounted for more than 1,700 instances of nations deciding whether or not to ratify treaties, and our Environmental Treaty Ratification Index sums more than 4,200 instances.

Columns 1–3 in table 6.1 suggest that about three-quarters of environmental treaty ratifications can be explained by essentially three variables: the voice and accountability of citizens through their domestic institutions, the total number of NGOs in the nation, and the amount of environmental foreign assistance it has received in the recent past. In particular, the number of NGOs in a nation appears virtually synonymous with the likelihood it will participate in environmental treaties. Since this proxy includes many nonenvironmental organizations, it may reflect the strength of civil society more broadly. Such civil society strength may directly influence international cooperation on the environment by lobbying, or indirectly by influencing elections as a counterbalance to business interests.

While all variables correlated at the bivariate level with a nation's propensity to ratify treaties, the other variables—natural capital, international environmental NGOs, and environmental damage—lose all explanatory power when we consider the impacts of domestic civil society, democracy, and environmental aid. This result suggests why international pressure from civil society to encourage nations to participate in environmental treaties is successful only in certain cases. In many cases local groups do not have a voice or, more fundamentally, cannot organize. Another important finding is that narrowness of the export base, which we use as a proxy for peripheral dependence in world-systems terminology, strongly predicts environmental damage as measured by the Ecosystem Wellbeing Index. However, the analysis shows that environmental damage turns out to have very little impact on whether nations actually ratify environmental treaties (which might address those

Table 6.1
Standardized Regression Coefficients and (t-ratios) for Participation in Environmental Treaties and Ratification Status of Kyoto Treaty

Independent Variable	1 1963–1989 Environmental Treaty Ratifications (number)	2 1963–1999 Environmental Treaty Ratifications (number)	3 1963–1999 Environmental Treaty Participation Index (factor score)	4 Ratified Kyoto Treaty by 2003? (dummy, 1 = ratified, 0 = not ratified)	5 Kyoto Treaty Status in 2003: (scale: 2 = ratified, 1 = signed, 0 = not ratified)	6 Kyoto Treaty Status in 2003: (scale: 4 = ratified, 1 = signed, 0 = not ratified)
Civil society presence (NGOs in 2000)	0.603*** (5.082)	0.671*** (6.919)	0.745*** (8.009)	0.130 (0.779)	0.183 (0.987)	0.168 (0.938)
Memberships in scientific conservation organizations, 2001 (IUCN 2001)	0.067 (0.829)	0.024 (0.356)	0.021 (0.325)	−0.100 (−0.876)	−0.038 (−0.299)	−0.056 (−0.454)
Democratic expression: Voice and Accountability Index, 2000	0.150 (1.464)	0.191* (2.280)	0.139† (1.732)	0.425** (2.938)	0.237 (1.480)	0.303† (1.957)
Ln (Cumulative number of residents made homeless by climate disasters 1980–2002)	−0.087 (−1.308)	0.077 (1.408)	0.077 (1.479)	0.092 (0.975)	0.066 (0.631)	0.078 (0.776)
Biological importance of nation: Natural Capital Index, 2000	−0.027 (−0.401)	−0.081 (−1.478)	−0.092† (−1.761)	0.042 (0.448)	−0.127 (−1.212)	−0.093 (−0.923)

Environmental damage: Ecosystem Wellbeing Index, 2000 (high equals poor)	−0.101 (−1.347)	−0.098 (−1.601)	−0.111† (−1.889)	−0.130 (−1.230)	−0.129 (−1.103)	−0.140 (−1.241)
Ln (national population, 2000)	−0.037 (−0.271)	−0.006 (−0.053)	−0.094 (−0.875)	−0.207 (−1.070)	−0.267 (−1.250)	−0.259 (−1.252)
Ln (environmental foreign assistance received as proportion of global total 1990–2000)	0.189† (1.984)	0.256** (3.293)	0.287*** (3.851)	0.318* (2.367)	0.343* (2.312)	0.358* (2.486)
Adjusted R^2	0.646***	0.763***	0.782***	0.293***	0.135**	0.189**
Minimum pairwise N of cases	101	101	101	101	101	101
Total indirect effects of structural vulnerability (narrow export base), through civil society, voice, homelessness, and environmental damage	−0.639	−0.656	−0.692	−0.362	−0.311	−0.335

Note: †$p < 0.1$; *$p < .05$; **$p < .01$; ***$p < .001$
Cases deleted pairwise.

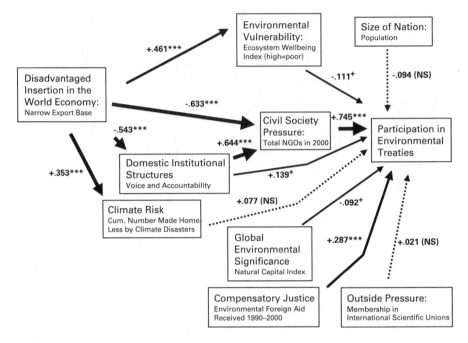

Figure 6.1
Path diagram and standardized regression coefficients explaining Environmental
Treaty Ratification Index.

problems). In fact, nations with more damage (a higher EWI) tend to
sign *fewer* environmental treaties.

Environmental foreign assistance appears to be effective in increasing
participation in environmental treaties. This indicator, as mentioned earlier, sums grants and loans commited in more than 420,000 individual
development projects we coded as strictly and broadly environmental.[91]
In fact, this variable was the most consistently effective at predicting participation in environmental treaties, and was with voice and accountability one of the only two variables that successfully predicted whether a
nation ratified the Kyoto Protocol. These findings suggest that environmental aid is effective in encouraging participation in environmental
treaties overall. We cannot determine, however, whether most of this effect is due to promises of future aid to cover some of the expenses the
treaty might entail, or to positive experience or geopolitical loyalty created with past aid.

In columns 4–6 of table 6.1 we show three different ways to quantify national participation in the Kyoto treaty.[92] Again, national population, environmental damage, and the biological importance of nations were not statistically significant predictors of Kyoto ratification. National memberships in international conservation organizations continued to not be effective at predicting participation, but in the case of Kyoto, the power of domestic civil society organizations appears to have been nearly insignificant. This is a major departure from the broader pattern of participation in environmental treaties and bears substantial further discussion. Democratic accountability had a significant positive influence on treaty participation in two of the three measures of Kyoto participation, an important point to explore further.

The second stage of our path analysis sought to test the ability of structural constraints on nations, specified as the narrowness of a nation's export base, to explain these more proximate factors in participation. As we documented in chapter 4, the narrowness of a nation's export base is a strong predictor of the presence of three variables: the number of NGOs there (path coefficient = −0.633), institutions that provide citizens with voice and government accountability (beta = −0.543), and the environmental damage their ecosystems have sustained (EWI, beta = +0.461). These same effects are utilized here in determining the indirect impacts of a nations' narrow export base on treaty participation and ratification of the Kyoto Protocol. Based on that analysis, we use the total indirect effects of a narrow export base on the cumulative fraction of national populations made homeless by climate disasters over the period 1980–2002 (total beta = +0.353).

In the bottom row of each column in table 6.1 we report the total indirect effect of structural vulnerability in predicting treaty participation rates and Kyoto participation.[93] The results are strong and consistent: Having a narrow export base predicts about two-thirds (from 0.64 to 0.69) of a nation's overall participation in environmental treaties over the period 1963–1999 (columns 1–3) and about one-third (from 0.31 to 0.36) of national ratifications of the Kyoto Protocol (columns 4–6).[94] The greater strength of structural constraints in explaining participation in a broader range of treaties is not surprising, since the 0–1 or even 0–4 scales of participation that we test here (columns 4–6) are far blunter instruments than our more continuous and multifaceted Environmental

Treaty Participation Index. That said, it remains possible that Kyoto is somehow qualitatively different than most other environmental treaties because of its only setting binding limits on about thirty nations, and those nations only agreeing to marginal reductions in carbon dioxide emissions. Paradoxically, it may be different also because of the scale of the changes that will be required if nations are to aggressively pursue reductions in by-products of all fossil-fuel consumption and some other key industrial processes as well (for example, cement production).

The indirect effects on overall treaty participation come mostly through the impact of a narrow export base on the strength of civil society as measured by the total number of NGOs in the nation (columns 1–3). For Kyoto participation, the effect mainly occurs through the effectiveness of the export base in predicting the Voice and Accountability Index of government responsiveness.[95] Homelessness and ecosystem well-being each explain from 2 to 5 percent of the indirect effect of a narrow export base. Based on our earlier analysis, we can rule out some other paths and possible effects on participation in Kyoto and other treaties. For example, the size of a nation's population covaries with export diversification, but the r-squared is very small (0.035, $n = 119$; $p > 0.05$). Total population explains only 2 percent of treaty ratifications ($r^2 = 0.018$; $n = 186$; $p > 0.05$). It is surprising that population explained less than 3 percent of the number of NGOs in a nation ($r^2 = 0.028$; $n = 161$; $p > 0.05$).

So the main findings are four. The strength of civil society positively influences participation in environmental treaties overall, but much less so the ratification or nonratification of the Kyoto Protocol. The measure of openness of government—the Voice and Accountability Index—had the opposite effect, being a better predictor of Kyoto behavior than overall patterns on environmental treaties. Third and significantly, our new index of the share of environmental foreign assistance received by a nation is among the best predictors of participation in the Kyoto Protocol. Finally, the structural dependence of nations on one or a relatively few export products has a major impact on Kyoto participation and an even stronger effect on broader indicators of performance on environmental treaties. In both cases the overall effect of a nation's disadvantaged position in the world economy is negative, if one consider all five of the pathways we theorized here and in figure 6.1. In this regard, we have apparently revealed an important part of the structural roots of the civil society strength and democratic institutions that drive participation in international environmental regimes.

Conclusion: Institutionalism, Structuralism, and Ratification of Environmental Treaties

Although there are limits to international environmental accords, and notable problems associated with their implementation and enforcement, they remain "the centerpiece of international efforts to deal with global environmental problems."[96] While previous studies in the international relations tradition have focused on case studies, the effects of single variables, or subsets of signatories, our large-N cross-national analysis reveals and attempts to explain broad patterns of states' behavior in this important area of global governance. As global environmental issues grow in scope, we believe that it will become increasingly important to understand the diverse factors that motivate countries to cooperate.

We are seeking to fill an important empirical gap in the IEP literature by offering a theoretically sequenced, multistep model that distinguishes between the proximate political causes and deeper social determinants of environmental treaty ratification. Our findings demonstrate that the world-systems tradition and other conventional international relations theories are not necessarily mutually exclusive, and that an additive approach may be quite useful. By placing new institutionalism and world-systems theory in their proper causal order (without any attempt to merge ontologies or epistemologies), we find that a more complete explanation of why environmental treaties are ratified can be offered. Simple correlations between civil society, democracy, and national participation in treaties hide a great deal. Credibility matters, yes, but credibility is strongly determined by a nation's economic structure and vulnerability in the world economy. Thus, we would reiterate the observation of Koremenos et al. that "[m]uch IR research has implicitly endorsed an erroneous presumption that an argument can only be shown to be right by showing that an alternative argument is wrong."[97]

To be fair, institutionalists, constructivists, and realists have emphasized in the qualitative literature the same key variables that we also find to be significant in bivariate analysis. All three of our proxies for willingness and ability correlated with ratification of environmental treaties in the expected direction. And strikingly, our civil society proxy explained more variance than any other single variable.[98] Meyer et al.— who best represent the constructivist camp in IEP—argue that the true agent of change is "world culture."[99] One of their key variables, the number of member organizations in World Conservation Union in each country per million population, also correlated closely with environmental treaty ratifications. Even the realist emphasis on countries of global environmental significance proved statistically and substantively significant in bivariate analysis. However, as we have argued, mainstream IEP theorization is severely lacking in that none of these approaches explain the earliest (and perhaps most important) links in the chain of causation.

As expected, in multivariate models the bulk of explanatory power afforded by these proximate variables is best explained by a nation's disadvantaged insertion in the world economy. Differences in national scores on this variable, which we approximated with an index of export diversification, are rooted in historical legacies of the colonial expansion of the European world system. It also appears that among proximate political variables, the institutionalist emphasis on credibility fits the empirical evidence best. Notably, neither constructivism nor realism held up in the full model. A state's willingness and ability to carry out international environmental commitments is the best proximate predictor of environmental treaty ratification. However, lest the reader rush to an overly optimistic conclusion, we must remember that most of the countries failing to acquire credibility actually failed because of a colonial legacy of extraction. Since extractive states systematically score lower on indicators of democracy and civil society, they also sign fewer environmental treaties. In other words, many countries inherit constrained choice sets that predispose them toward poor environmental policies. Our study, then, offers a substantial shift of focus by clarifying why some states have strong civil societies, healthy environments, and robust domestic political institutions in the first place, while others consistently lack all these.

The lack of participation by economically disadvantaged nations in environmental treaties documented here may of course have several explanations. It could simply be due to their lack of the financial wherewithal and staff to attend the treaty drafting meetings. Alternatively, countries may not sign because they believe it to be unjust to be asked to forgo economic development to resolve environmental problems for which they bear little responsibility.[100] Poorer nations are also growing frustrated at unmet promises by rich nations to provide them with sufficient environmental loans and foreign assistance to comply with obligations under the new treaties. Nevertheless, our cross-sectional OLS regression and path analysis suggests that the single best predictor of treaty ratification is the number of NGOs in a country. Furthermore, we find strong support for our hypothesis that civil society strength and strong domestic institutions (such as democracy) are determined largely by a nation's insertion in the world system.[101] Behind nonratification, therefore, is a fragile, authoritarian, and often corrupt economic structure built on the production and export of a narrow range of products.

Another goal of this work was to develop a much-needed index of environmental treaty ratification. The index presented and tested here goes some way toward producing a satisfactory metric against which we can test our theories, and we hope to see further examination of its potential. However, such an index may suffer the inevitable disadvantages of data reduction—that is, attempting to reduce a number of factors to one. To provide this one index of state behavior concerning international environmental issues, we assumed in this study that the first principal component—the factor that explains the most variance of the seven discovered in our factor analysis—is the best indicator of a nation's propensity to act politically on behalf of the environment. However, future work might examine the remaining six factors or suggest other ways to look at patterns in environmental treaty ratifications. Our study shows that while the contribution of Dietz and Kalof[102] in developing the original index of state environmentalism is significant, it may be more useful to address how countries agree to participate in international environmental agreements in smaller groups of treaties. Treaties might be analyzed in groupings along a series of lines: the process by which they were negotiated; the era in which they were introduced; the distribution of their benefits and costs; and conflicting political, economic, and cultural forces. Still, the strength of the present findings strongly supports the value of looking at the broadest patterns of environmental treaty ratification.

What have we learned about how to improve ratification rates for environmental accords? No matter how important a nation is ecologically (natural capital) or how vulnerable it currently is (ecosystem well-being), other factors tend to lead to adoption of environmental treaties. International environmental NGOs were seen to have little direct impact on treaty participation. When one considers indirect effects, the strongest predictor by far is the narrowness of a nation's export base, which directly and indirectly explained nearly 60 percent of the treaty ratification rates. This suggests that the spread of institutions and values may not create a world with more adherents to environmental treaties. We may, in fact, be approaching an upper limit in the number of countries that will cooperate on international environmental issues since their willingness and ability to participate may be structurally limited. On the other hand, if we include greater development assistance, more favorable trade policies, and wealth redistribution mechanisms in environmental treaties, there may be greater interest from those on the bottom economically.[103]

The strength of the relationship between state behavior on environmental treaty ratification and the rights and position of civil society (voice and accountability and NGO strength) suggests that institutional and grassroots democratization is critical to progress. The powerful predictive strength of our proxy for a colonial legacy—dependence upon a narrow range of exports—suggests that dependency and world-systems theories still have a lot to teach us. National economic development strategies indeed have wide implications for relations between civil society and domestic political institutions. Returning to Raymond Vernon's point, export elites shape state and society relations. Our analysis shows convincingly that these relations in turn have an impact on our ability to build global institutions that protect the environment.

Based on these findings, we conclude that an entirely different tack might need to be taken to improve participation in global environmental treaties. To address the commitment dilemma that lies at the heart of Southern nonparticipation in international agreements, egoistic OECD nations must help poor countries diversify their export profiles, upgrade to more rewarding development paths, strengthen their domestic political institutions, and mobilize home-grown civil society groups. Improvements in these areas will almost certainly bolster credibility, which we believe will ultimately result in better environmental policy positions. Eventually we will have to address the savage inequalities in the global economy and empower those at the bottom. Progress on addressing global environmental issues requires it.

7

Equity, Climate Proposals, and Two Roads to Justice after Kyoto

"Good Winds"?

Outside, the "good winds" of Buenos Aires snap dozens of blue and white flags of the United Nations and Argentina, which alternate atop the old livestock exhibition hall at the front of the massive December 2004 Tenth Conference of the Parties of the UN Framework Convention on Climate Change. Inside, in one low-ceilinged temporary conference room with sagging prefabricated ceiling tiles over flimsy, carpeted prefab walls, a rumbling ventilation system drowns out voices not spoken over the microphones scattered around a long hollow rectangle of tables. Along one of the long sides of the table sit delegates from the European Union, Canada, Norway, Australia, and Japan: the global North. On the other long side, across a massive "development gap" and "color line," sit delegates from Mali, Bangladesh, Mozambique, Bhutan, Tanzania, Samoa, Sierra Leone, and a few others from forty-eight of the world's least developed countries—the neediest of the global South. The former represent delegations consisting of dozens of members. Many of the latter are the sole representatives from their nations at the meeting; the UN subsidized only one traveler from each nation for the trip to Argentina. At one end of the long table sit the co-chairs, one from the Gambia and the other from Portugal. Alone at the far end of the table, separate from the EU and the developing world and rarely speaking to anyone, sits the delegate from the United States.

This is a meeting of the LDC Contact Group, and what is at stake here is money. These poorest of nations are unable to afford the preparation of the assessments, reports, and plans for how they will adapt to climate change that the UNFCCC requires they periodically submit. They fight for full-cost financing of these reports and other projects they need to complete in order to comply with the treaty, and they fight against requirements for co-financing or other diversions of funds from their already meager national budgets that do not cover even basic human needs. Norway's delegate argues for a sliding scale of payment, and Canada's says it wants some co-financing to show some local buy-in.

Sierra Leone's delegate finally bursts out: "Co-financing, I don't understand that phrase! We are the least of the least! If we start attaching strings, we will be unable to do anything! No strings should be attached." The one time he does speak, the U.S. delegate has some blunt words of his own: "The U.S. will not contribute to the LDC Fund, but will donate to LDCs through other mechanisms in the Convention."[1] He is there to make sure that the World Bank-administered Global Environmental Facility, which disburses environmental aid, will keep this fund separate from any to which the United States donates.

One might have expected more celebration at the COP-10 in Buenos Aires with Russia's ratification of the protocol just three weeks earlier sending the treaty into effect (February 16, 2005, seven years after the Kyoto COP). However, as this exchange in the charged room of the LDC Contact Group illustrates, Northern and Southern nations remain sharply divided on even the most trivial of issues. These negotiations are also a parable about how excessive attention to institutional solutions— here the eminently "rational" case is requiring co-financing to ensure ownership and commitment from developing countries—can distract negotiators from the real obstacles to cooperation.

For the forty-eight least developed countries, the total financing necessary for the preparation of national adaptation plans of action (NAPAs) barely amounted to $11 million.[2] If you add in the $22 million that donors have pledged for the implementation of NAPAs, the Least Developed Countries Fund is a $33 million fund. To put things in perspective, an average-sized infrastructure project in one recipient country funded by one donor could cost hundreds of millions of dollars. Yet this $33 million fund, financed by almost a dozen Western countries and divided among fifty desperately poor nations, remains the subject of rancorous debate.[3] This is a pittance compared with the cost of having developing countries believe that the developed countries are indifferent toward their circumstances. Issues like this could provide opportunities to build the social capital that underpins long-term cooperation, but in the hands of short-sighted negotiators following hard-line mandates from their superiors, events like this can just as easily drive a downward spiral of distrust.

Looking Back, Looking Ahead

This book has been an effort to chart a new course in understanding these scenes and the North-South deadlock over climate policy more broadly. We have argued that the greatest problems threatening the viability of a future North-South climate regime are persistent global inequality, an ongoing development crisis in much of the South, and starkly imbalanced suffering from, responsibility for, and action on climate change. Without addressing these, the world moves ever farther away from being able to create a post-Kyoto treaty that slows and ultimately reverses climate change. The root of the problem, we argue, is the spill over of economic development issues into environmental diplomacy; for example, unkept aid promises and the onerous requirements of participating in Western-dominated international economic institutions like the IMF and the WTO.

We have taken a fairly unusual approach. On the one hand, we developed scientific measures of climate inequality (in suffering, responsibility, and action), used statistical methods to evaluate proximate and deeper social and historical determinants, and examined the causal channels through which inequality influences the form, frequency, timing, substance, and depth of international cooperation. On the other hand, we have tried to make sense of those patterns by synthesizing general theoretical arguments about the behavior of states, explanations of international environmental politics and North-South politics, and somewhat idiosyncratic "problem structure" insights about the nature of climate change as a political problem. Even more unusual, perhaps, is our attempt to integrate and sequence theoretical frames that rarely inhabit the same conference rooms—in particular, rational-choice institutionalism and structuralism.

Chapters 1 and 2 took up issues of trust, worldviews, causal beliefs, and principled beliefs—issues we believe are largely attributable to a country's position in the global division of labor. We argued that inequality dampens cooperative efforts by reinforcing structuralist worldviews and causal beliefs, promoting particularistic notions of justice, and creating incentives for zero-sum and negative-sum behavior. At the intermediate level it becomes even clearer that climate negotiations do not take place in a vacuum, but in an atmosphere polluted with mistrust built on decades of unequal experience and treatment in international economic and environmental regimes. To take just one example, the Rio Bargain at the Earth Summit in 1992 called for wealthy nations to provide more than $100 billion a year in aid for local and global environmental issues, yet only a fraction of that promise has materialized.[4]

Climate change is one of the most difficult and critical problems our species has ever faced. Mitigating its effect will require more than a hundred diverse nations to make major changes in their aspirations and economic plans in spite of scientific uncertainty, difficulty in monitoring behavior, and huge disparities in who will suffer worst and first. Therefore, understanding why countries are willing or unwilling to cooperate and make sacrifices to protect their populations and way of life also requires identifying which nations are most responsible for global climate change, which nations are already suffering the effects of climate-related disasters, and which nations are ratifying the Kyoto treaty.

The cases of Hurricane Mitch in Honduras, the three cyclones that flooded Mozambique in early 2000, and the rising sea levels that are threatening Tuvalu and other low-lying Pacific islands examined in chapter 3 suggest the causes and impacts of major climate-related disasters. These case studies showed how disasters unfold and how these nations were left vulnerable by what happened long before the disasters. The economic and political weaknesses of many of these nations can be explained only by understanding the way in which they were brought into the world economy—as extractive colonies. In chapters 3 and 4 we built and tested three indicators of rates of suffering from a complete listing of over four thousand climate disasters over the past two decades: the number killed per million population; the percentage of the population made homeless by climate-related disasters; and the proportion affected in some major way by storms, droughts, or heat waves. In spite of the substantial randomness of hurricanes, droughts, and other weather patterns, levels of export diversification predicts from one-eighth to nearly half of how many people have died, been made homeless, or otherwise affected by climate-related disasters over the past two decades. National wealth, often assumed to be the main explanatory variable, explained only 7 percent of climate-related deaths and only 13 percent of homelessness. When other factors were held constant, it explained virtually none of the variation in death and homelessness. Rather, we found five main significant predictors of suffering: the percent of the population living in cities (safer), the percent of the population living near a coast, high income inequality, a weak civil society, and nations with weak property rights regimes.

Chapter 5 investigated the four main ways that have been proposed for measuring responsibility for climate change and who is seen as most responsible using each of these yardsticks. Each represents different positions on what is "just," held by different nations and different interest groups within nations. The stakes are extremely high, as can be seen in the conflict between the approach taken in the Kyoto treaty—which took the politically expedient approach of granting rights to pollute based on 1990 levels of emissions—and the per capita approach proposed by poor nations, in which each person on Earth is given an equal share of emissions. We found strong evidence to support the claim that the historical legacy of a country's incorporation into the global economy has a critical impact on its available avenues of development and future carbon use. We also find strong support for theories of ecologically unequal exchange and the so-called ecological debt perspective espoused by many developing country policy makers. In particular, it appears that carbon dioxide emissions are skyrocketing with growing trade and industrialization in poorer nations because wealthy nations are shifting the production of their energy-intensive products to poorer countries. This transfer of carbon use was shown to be tremendously important.

Finally, this led us to an investigation in chapter 6 of who is participating in environmental treaties and efforts to address climate change. We described patterns in which countries sign and ratify the Kyoto Protocol. Since the terms of LDC participation have not been completely negotiated, we also developed an index of twenty-two international environmental agreements and attempted to explain the generalizable patterns of participation among 192 countries. Although critics rightly point out the lack of enforcement in the Kyoto treaty and other environmental accords, we argue that treaty ratifications represent important and sometimes "costly" signals, being important measures of a state's willingness and ability to implement specific policy commitments. We then developed a theoretically sequenced model utilizing complementarities between rational-choice institutionalism and structuralism. We recognize that credibility matters, but we also argue state credibility is strongly influenced by a legacy of colonial incorporation into the world economy. Our results suggest that dependence on one or a few export products directly and indirectly explains nearly 60 percent of the treaty ratification rates overall and one-third of the variation in Kyoto ratification behavior. These structural constraints on countries' willingness and ability to cooperate suggest that the spread of institutions and values may not create a world with more adherents to environmental treaties. Our new systematic tally of environmental foreign assistance from wealthy nations to the South also showed the power of compensation in encouraging participation in environmental treaties, especially the Kyoto Protocol.

Some readers will likely appreciate more our attempts to integrate and build theory; others will be more comfortable with our large-N cross-national strategy for testing on those theories. We believe a major shortcoming of the existing literature on climate vulnerability and treaty participation is that researchers have relied mainly on single cases and small-n datasets and have failed to test competing theories side by side. Our goal in doing the latter was to test whether a synthetic approach might be more valuable in explaining the proximate political causes and deeper social and historical determinants of why some nations suffer more from disasters than others, why some are disproportionate polluters, and why some nations rush to sign and ratify—while others actively resist or even undermine—environmental treaties. We are strong believers that case studies are crucial, but that only if we understand the broader patterns can we know if the cases examined are outliers or bellwethers.

As we have attempted to show in as systematic a way as possible, climate change is fundamentally an issue of inequality. To state the obvious, the dire poverty of many nations has a direct impact on the ability of their absurdly outmatched negotiators to do anything more than foot drag or agree to pledges of funding (chapter 1). The actual and perceived inequality between nations also creates starkly disparate worldviews and a poisonous mistrust that makes it impossible to reach the ambitious cooperative agreement needed to address climate change effectively (chapter 2).

This is why a resolution will likely require unconventional—perhaps even heterodox—policy interventions. Climate treaty negotiations, we have sought to remind ourselves and our readers, take place in the context of the ongoing development crisis, so to break through the cycle of mistrust, we would argue that Western nations need to wage a campaign to convince poor nations that they understand and care about their position in the international division of labor and want to help them to escape the scourge of poverty and structural vulnerability.

The North, in our view, needs to offer the South a new global bargain on environment and development issues and signal their commitment to this new "shared thinking" through a series of confidence-building measures. They could do this by providing greater "environmental space" to late developers, supplying meaningful sums of environmental assistance, funding aid for adaptation and dealing with local environmental issues ("brown" aid) as well as global issues like climate change ("green" aid), and by identifying and investing in win-win technologies and sectors that both address local environmental issues and reduce greenhouse gas emissions. On trade and loans, we believe the IMF and other international financial institutions would serve the long-term interests of their rich-country shareholders well by eliminating onerous conditionalities and providing greater flexibility for local experimentation on economic policy. International economic regimes, like TRIPs, which threaten the long-term interests of developing countries, should also be publicly abandoned. Western agricultural subsidies also cannot be maintained while demanding reduction of subsidies in poor nations. By comparison, a commodity support fund that buffers poor nations from exogenous shocks would go a long way toward helping the world's poor and signaling concern for the structural dilemma of developing countries.[5] Giving developing countries a greater stake in the governance structures of international financial institutions would also lend greater credibility to a new North-South environment and global development bargain. More generally, rich nations must exercise greater self-restraint when the short-term payoff of opportunism is high.

The ultimate goal of these strategies, which we discuss next, is to help nations upgrade their development pathways, diversify their exports to create stronger and more resilient economies, transition to lower-carbon futures, and most important, elicit commitment to a new shared world-view of North-South relations.[6] We believe that progress on what may be the thorniest issue confronting humanity—the global climate crisis—requires this broad an approach.[7]

Breaking the Impasse

This final chapter is about building a long-term foundation for meaning-ful North-South environmental cooperation, but before suggesting the need for changes in the "rules of the game" that govern contemporary global political economy, it may be worthwhile to first assess the level of urgency of addressing climate change. In terms of the most basic science, we know that left unattended, greenhouse gas emissions will rapidly accumulate in the Earth's atmosphere over the next century, and global average temperatures will almost certainly climb by 1.4–5.8°C.[8] Total global emissions stood at approximately 6 billion tons of carbon equivalent (GtC) per year in 1996, and by 2004 that number had risen to 7 billion GtC. Yet, to avoid dangerous anthropogenic interference with the climate system, scientists estimate that we need to cap atmo-spheric CO_2 concentrations at somewhere between 450 and 550 parts per million, or at roughly 9.4 billion GtC per year.[9] Given that by 2020 we will likely have already reached 9.8 billion GtC, stabilizing at 9.4 billion GtC will require an extraordinary effort that is without precedent in global environmental politics.

The fundamental political question is who will be responsible for the bulk of future global greenhouse gas emissions. As we saw in chapter 5, the current accumulated stock of carbon dioxide in the atmosphere is largely the responsibility of rich, industrialized countries. However, increases in future emissions will primarily take place in the developing world (owing to higher rates of population and economic growth). Developed countries are on track to register roughly 1 percent annual economic growth, yet developing countries are already pushing 3.5 per-cent and are expected to maintain a similar growth trajectory in the com-ing decades.[10] At the same time, the global population will continue to expand, from 6 billion to 8.4–12 billion people over the next hundred years, and the lion's share of this growth will take place in the develop-ing world. These two virtually unstoppable forces—economic development and population growth—are set to increase non-Annex I carbon emissions from 31 percent of the total in 1990 to 60 percent in 2030.[11] Stated differently, these trends will likely force us into a 9 or 10 billion GtC scenario by 2020, thereby pushing the climate perilously close to a tipping point.

We must therefore ask a number of important "what ifs": What if an exogenous shock, such as an abrupt climate change, occurs before late developers implement meaningful abatement measures? What if nations in the global South hold out for an environmental assistance program of Marshall Plan proportions? What if they demand a dramatic change in the development agenda before accepting a meaningful schedule for reducing carbon dioxide emissions? There is much uncertainty surrounding these questions, but we do know that a global climate accord that lacks the long-term participation of developing countries will not effect much change. Environmental treaty expert Scott Barrett puts it this way: "The countries for which the Kyoto constraints are binding account for just 19% of global emissions. And these countries are required to reduce their emissions by only a little over 5%. Such a small reduction in emissions by such a small piece of the climate problem over such a short period of time will barely have any effect on the climate."[12]

As awareness of Kyoto's complete inadequacy has increased, calls for greater participation by developing countries have grown louder and more frequent. One popular argument is that the marginal costs of abatement are lowest in the developing world; therefore scarce resources should be targeted in these regions. As we have seen, however, most low- and low-middle income nations are openly hostile to the idea of talking about post-2012 policy commitments.

What, then, are the long-term prospects for a meaningful post-2012 North-South global climate pact? Poor nations were not interested in the Montreal Protocol in the late 1980s, but they quickly changed their tune when rich nations agreed to include a significant financial transfer mechanism in the global treaty. Is this compensatory justice lesson transferable to the climate regime? Unfortunately, the answer is probably not. Unlike the ozone depletion issue, which required side payments of $1–2 billion, experts believe that stabilizing the climate could cost rich nations hundreds of billions of dollars.[13] The compensatory justice principle is important, and we will discuss it at greater length shortly, but a truly global consensus on climate change will most likely require a hybrid justice solution that accommodates the different circumstances and principled beliefs of many parties.

Theorists are deeply divided over the question of how fairness "focal points" (points of agreement) are identified and the likelihood that they can be agreed upon. Harvard economist Thomas Schelling argues that focal points will "endogenously and implicitly emerge out of a negotiation process and that therefore *no* explicit and rigorous allocation rule is really necessary."[14] Scott Barrett makes a similar suggestion about climate change negotiations—that states will have a natural tendency to arrive at a socially shared understanding of what is fair or ethical in order to lower the cost of bargaining.[15]

However, Oxford University professor Benito Müller finds the notion of tacit bargaining unpersuasive.[16] He points to a simple but indisputable empirical observation: despite bargaining inefficiencies, states continue to defend radically different understandings of what is "equitable."[17] In a relativistic world, he writes, where "different moral positions can be justifiably upheld, the chances of there being a solution which *all* the (relevant) parties consider to be *completely* fair are negligible."[18] For example, many poor nations are of the mind that human beings should be given equal rights to the atmosphere. Yet some rich nations argue that a per capita or historical responsibility approach would inflict insurmountable costs upon the world's most dynamic economies and hold the industrialized world accountable for a problem that they never knew existed until barely fifteen years ago.[19] Given these huge differences in perceptions of what is fair, bargaining will be most successful, according to Müller, when negotiators are explicit in identifying potential focal points. That is, when states begin to reconsider and negotiate their own beliefs about what is fair, a mutually acceptable definition will be more likely to emerge, coordinating the behavior of all players around a single equilibrium.[20]

Our research supports Müller's conclusions. In chapter 6, we empirically evaluated the ideational argument that poor nations will act upon their principled beliefs, and we found no evidence to support this claim. If anything, we found evidence to support the pure self-interest model. Anecdotally, we are also aware of numerous examples where countries fought hard to institutionalize particularistic conceptions of justice and where focal points failed to emerge spontaneously. At COP-8 and COP-9, for example, the United States formed an unusual coalition with some G-77 members (notably Saudi Arabia) in an attempt to undermine G-77 and EU efforts to move toward a per capita approach in the post-Kyoto period. Notions of fairness, in other words, can become political footballs, used in self-serving ways by shrewd negotiatiors.

Our findings also stand in contrast to a popular strand of social constructivism, which claims that "free-floating," socially shared understandings of "appropriate" behavior permeate the decision-making calculus of all rational decision makers.[21] As Michael Zürn puts it, "ceteris paribus in a communicative context social actors prefer just outcomes to unjust ones."[22] Proponents of legitimacy theory similarly argue that states will comply with international laws when they perceive them as "being in accordance with the *right* process."[23] The weight of the evidence in this book does not support such claims. The compensatory justice principle, for example, embedded in the Montreal Protocol and other institutions did not naturally emerge from a shared social understanding of fairness. Developing nations forcefully argued and bargained for the institutionalization of this principle.

Michael Zürn also suggests that students of international environmental relations should "carry out studies in which outcome observations are accompanied by process observations: did the negotiations include tough bargaining about the distribution of cooperative benefits or were they based on an early normative understanding that any agreement reached has to be a fair one?"[24] We have tried to do this in our research. We found, for example, that rich and poor nations did indeed share the social understanding that their behavior should be governed by common, but differentiated responsibilities at the outset of climate negotiations. However, in virtually every other process observation, we found that norms of fairness were the subject of acrimonious and protracted debate. We are therefore highly skeptical of the arguments that universally shared norms of justice exist and that tacit focal points will emerge spontaneously. In our judgment, for a solution to be possible, no one group can "win" their fairness argument. There needs to be an understanding that a consensus position, or "constructed" focal point, must accommodate the circumstances and principled beliefs of many parties. In the words of Frank Biermann, justice must be negotiated.[25]

Where to Begin? A Ready Stock of Fairness Principles

We believe that embedding strong principles of special and differential treatment in the climate regime would be a positive force for long-term North-South cooperation. However, this is not the same as specifying which principles are likely to be "consensus builders."

Fortunately, theory provides some indication of which fairness principles are best suited as useful points of reference in the consensus-building process. Rationalists hypothesize that institutional focal points, of which fairness principles are a large subset, help nations zero in on a more tightly circumscribed set of possible equilibria by reducing uncertainty and stabilizing expectations for future behavior. They also make agreements robust to exogenous shocks by forcing states to focus on their "shared beliefs about the spirit of agreements."[26] In addition, there is alleged causal significance in the "stickiness" of fairness principles because "international regimes are easier to maintain than to construct" (owing to the high transaction costs involved in identifying and negotiating new ones).[27] Time-honored principles therefore often represent the path of least resistance and a promising route to mutually beneficial cooperation.

Three brief examples illustrate this last point on "sticky" principles. The double majority voting rule, first applied to the Montreal Protocol Fund in 1990, gave poor nations a powerful voice for the first time in determining how environmental aid would flow from North to South. Without precedent fifteen years ago, this operational principle has quickly evolved into the gold standard in global environmental politics. It was introduced to the Global Environmental Facility in 1994, then the Kyoto Compliance Committee in 2001, and continues to emerge as *the* decision rule in multilateral environmental negotiations. Elizabeth DeSombre and Joanne Kaufmann have made a similar argument about the so-called compensatory justice principle: "Like it or not," they write, "the [Montreal Protocol] Fund *has* set a precedent for dealing with global environmental issues with North-South equity problems. It has created expectations that developing countries will be compensated for the foregone development opportunities or the added burdens required by environmental cooperation."[28] Finally, Susan Sell argues that Southern nations have done an exceptional job of taking Northern nations to task on deviations from a time-honored institutional focal point: the polluter pays principle. During ozone negotiations, for example, India's environment minister Ziuk Rahman Ansari reminded negotiating parties that "Lest someone in this conference think of this as charity, I would like to remind them of the excellent principle of polluter pays adopted in the developed world."[29]

Because of the "stickiness" of certain fairness principles, developed countries have also on occasion been drawn back into negotiations for fear of being perceived as a "rogue agent" operating outside the bounds of previously negotiated territory. It is also worth pointing out that the abrogation of a widely accepted principle in one regime can be exceedingly, even prohibitively, costly if that action makes a country look like an outlaw in other regimes that use that same principle as an institutional focal point.[30] In short, there is a strong theoretical rationale and empirical basis for building on the ready stock of strong principles already embedded in multiple global environmental regimes,[31] such as the polluter pays principle and the principle of common but differentiated responsibilities.[37]

Yet, we must not dismiss "weak principles" if they are necessary to ensure the environmental effectiveness of an agreement. Sustainable development may be one such principle. It is ill-defined, politically contentious, manipulable, and at times contradictory, but it is also essential for building civic and cooperative norms and eliciting the support of developing countries. The World Commission on Environment and Development (the Brundtland Commission) came up with the famous 1987 definition of sustainable development: "Development that meets the needs of the present without compromising the ability of future generations to meet their own needs."[33] There are many other interpretations of this principle, but, for better or for worse, this vague and unthreatening definition has become a global focal point.[34]

At Rio, roughly $110 billion a year was specifically promised for sustainable development projects in the South, in addition to $15 billion a year for global environmental problems.[35] According to our own estimates, based on the Project-Level Aid database covering more than 400,000 bilateral and multilateral projects between 1970 and 2002, Northern countries came up with a small fraction of what they promised on global environmental issues, and only a fraction of that promised for sustainable development. Roughly US$3 billion a year is being allocated for global environmental issues (20 percent of the Rio promise), while about $7 billion a year is being given for local environmental projects.[36]

Then at the UN General Assembly Special Session for Review and Appraisal of Agenda 21 (UNGASS) in 1997, developing countries sought to strengthen the sustainable development agenda by linking issues of climate change, forests, and biodiversity to issues of trade, investment, finance, and intellectual property rights. This was flatly rejected by rich nations.[37] By 2002, at the World Summit on Sustainable Development in Johannesburg, the failure of rich and poor nations to arrive at a consensus on the meaning and implementation of sustainable development had matured into deeper cynicism, distrust, and anger. Southern policy makers were outspoken, dismissing the event as a "three-ring circus," and nothing more than high-profile photo-ops and the pomp and circumstance of Western diplomats.[38]

Despite these failures to coalesce around a clearly defined principle of sustainable development, the dialogue on sustainable development is clearly more than semantics.[39] There are natural affinities between climate change and sustainable development that could expand "the zone of possible agreement" for developed and developing countries.[40] Our analysis in chapter 5 also suggests how important it is to integrate carbon reduction strategies into larger economic development strategies.[41]

A Long-Term Strategy for North-South Environmental Cooperation: Building Strategic Trust through Costly Signals

Trust is often singled out as one of the most important factors driving cooperation, but our understanding of it remains remarkably underdeveloped.[42] We believe the study of international environmental politics, in particular, stands to gain considerably from a closer focus on the costly signal, or strategic reassurance, literature developed elsewhere in the field of international relations.[43] Andrew Kydd's case study of U.S.–Soviet relations during the 1980s holds important lessons for students of North-South environmental politics. As Kydd argues, the more noticeable, irreversible, unconditional, and costly the signal from the sending state, the more trusting the receiving state will be and willing to engage in cooperative ventures. But importantly, this process of trust building is an incremental and long-term strategy that involves sending a series of costly signals, in some cases progressively more costly signals.

The conditions of mistrust plaguing North-South environmental relations can be understood as the product of a failed reassurance strategy. In the early 1990s, the North assured poorer nations that they would "take the lead" in stabilizing the climate.[44] However, subsequent efforts have been sluggish, litigious, uneven, and generally unimpressive. The lack of progress (and backsliding) by the United States in meeting its own target for carbon dioxide emissions by the end of the decade has provided developing nations with a ready excuse for not making reductions. As Brazil's leading newspaper put it, "Numbers like these [the U.S.'s emissions] reinforce the disposition of the Brazilian government to reject the idea of taking on additional costs to do its part in reducing the greenhouse effect."[45] Also contributing to the North's failed reassurance strategy have been the erosion of principles originally envisioned to govern the North-South climate regime, the unraveling of the Rio Bargain, strong resistance among industrialized nations toward placing any limits on their conspicuous consumption, and a general aversion toward helping developing countries address "brown" environmental problems and issues of sustainable development.

To be sure, trust-building efforts can be successful in global environmental politics. The Multilateral Ozone Fund and the reformed Global Environmental Facility enshrined the compensatory justice principle and gave developing countries a greater stake in the decision-making process governing the allocation of environmental aid.[46] The Montreal Protocol also gave developing countries a ten-year window to pursue "cheap" economic development before making serious reductions in chlorofluorocarbon emissions.

In the climate change arena, the way has begun to be paved with the three special funds set up at COP-6 in Bonn and COP-7 in Marrakech to help developing countries adapt to the adverse effects of climate change, facilitate technology transfer, and mitigate greenhouse gas emissions.[47] Developed countries have also served themselves well by inviting developing countries to participate in the compliance committee (without having to adopt scheduled commitments for emission reductions) and treating them as equal partners through the double-majority voting mechanism.

The past thirty years of negotiations, however, show very simply that "strategic trust" has its limits and that over the longer term conditions of diffuse reciprocity and generalized trust are absolutely essential for "deep" cooperation. Mark Twain once wrote that "the principle of diplomacy is to give one and take ten." That may have worked then, but climate change is different; real progress will require transcending this principle. Human psychology experts have confirmed that when people feel taken advantage of, marginalized, powerless, angry, envious, and spiteful, they are less likely to cooperate with those toward whom their emotions are directed. As international relations luminary Robert Keohane has argued, relations between sovereign states are not much different: "Egoists... have difficulty solving bargaining problems, *since they do not recognize norms of fairness that can provide focal points for agreement. Cool practitioners of self-interest, known to be such, may be less able to cooperate productively than individuals who are governed by emotions that send reliable signals, such as love or reliability.*"[48] These are critical and often overlooked points in the study of international environmental politics.

While the systematic relationship between environmental aid transfers and environmental treaty ratifications documented in chapter 6 lends some support to the idea that states are not like the "rational fools"[49] in our textbook models, our results do not allow us to discriminate between the hard-rationalist fairness argument that says Northern states must restructure the *incentives* facing developing countries in order to make participation economically rational, and the soft-rationalist fairness argument that says states must also send *signals of solidarity, empathy*, and *kindness* to would-be cooperators.

There are, however, a number of outstanding empirical anomalies that suggest the need for careful comparison of these two arguments. One particularly vexing question for hard rationalists is why environmental assistance for adaptation to climate change should exist at all. The orthodox view among rationalists is that rich states will use environmental aid to reward countries that demonstrate a credible commitment to reducing greenhouse gas emissions and to complying with international environmental agreements. Put differently, hard rationalists predict that scarce environmental aid resources will be spent on *mitigation*. We confirmed this expectation in chapter 6 in finding a robust relationship between the receipt of environmental aid and ratification of the Kyoto Protocol. Yet the fact remains that nontrivial amounts of adaptation assistance are materializing.[50]

Soft rationalists offer one plausible explanation for this social phenomenon. Environmental aid may be used as part of an effort to build conditions of generalized trust; signal confidence, solidarity, empathy, and kindness; and attract developing countries to a "new thinking" about global environmental issues. Critics might dismiss adaptation aid as a mere palliative or an irrational diversion of scarce resources needed to combat climate change, and in a world of scarce foreign aid resources, we agree that difficult decisions must be made between palliatives and remedies. At the same time, we would caution against making inflexible distinctions between these two types of environmental aid. While mitigation aid might have a direct impact on climate change, it does very little to address the longer-term corrosive effect of global inequality on North-South environmental relations. Adaptation assistance, by contrast, may foster civic and cooperative norms and thus increase the willingness of poor nations to participate in a global climate accord.

Another excellent example of the strain between soft rationalism and hard rationalism can be found in the ongoing reform of the Global Environmental Facility, the primary funding mechanism for the UNFCCC Convention and the Kyoto Protocol. In the summer of 2002, the U.S. government began to push for greater selectivity in GEF aid allocation. As part of a larger crusade to impose strict performance requirements on multilateral aid agencies, the U.S. Treasury offered the GEF $70 million in additional funding, over and above their $107.5 million contribution to the Third Replenishment of the GEF, if they could put in place a transparent performance-based allocation system. Under Secretary of the Treasury John Taylor said that "President Bush wants to ensure that the Global Environmental Facility has the funding it needs to meet its program priorities and the policies in place to use those funds effectively ... and the policy reforms and performance targets that have been agreed by donors, are vitally important steps forward in meeting these critical objectives."[51] As a relatively young institution thirsty for cash, this financial nudge from one of the largest GEF contributors sparked a heated (and continuing) discussion between donor and recipient nations on how scarce environmental aid resources should be allocated.

The U.S. government's proposal closely resembled the Millennium Challenge Account proposal being discussed in the U.S. Congress at the same time. U.S. negotiators argued that the GEF should reward political, economic, and environmental reformers with larger environmental aid allocations, and punish the worst offenders and countries that drag their feet on environmental reform by withholding funds. Many poor nations balked at this, arguing that aid would become a political issue and not reach the places where it was needed most. Some rich nations expressed serious reservations about this single-minded focus on countries' environmental policies and institutions, or in international relations parlance, the credibility of the recipient government's commitment. Germany's representative to the GEF said that his country would "not agree with an ex-ante system" of aid allocation "in which budgets will be fixed for each country according to their country performance." In his words, "To implement a GEF funded project according to *national* indicators would undermine the unique global character of the GEF. To forsake a project just because the host country is a bad economic or political performer could affect the whole [of] mankind in a negative manner."[52]

While Canada, France, and the United Kingdom sided with the United States in favor of an ex ante performance-based allocation system, Belgium, Germany, Denmark, and Switzerland argued that such changes would violate the earlier principle of "equal opportunity to access GEF resources." To be sure, no countries from this latter group explicitly argued that a fair distribution of GEF funds might have the effect of signaling solidarity, reliability, or sympathy to would-be cooperators; however, the tenor of their arguments strongly suggests an underlying belief that "cool practitioners of self-interest" finish last. In this regard, the United States may be hurting itself in the long term by insisting on unpopular criteria that were not developed in consultation with poorer nations.

Strategic Restraint on Development and Trade: The Second Prong of a Trust-Building Strategy

Trust building is not only about what you do, but also exercising strategic restraint. It is often what you don't do that matters most. Having argued in previous chapters that the current trade, aid, debt, investment, intellectual property rights, and finance regimes are a tremendous drag on Northern efforts to build conditions of diffuse reciprocity and generalized trust with the South, we believe another powerful way to demonstrate solidarity, empathy, kindness, friendship, and loyalty to would-be cooperators could be to show support for the concerns and priorities of developing countries in highly valued areas of international political economy. This may ultimately prove to be more important for the long-term success of global environmental accords than institutional reforms, carbon accounting schemes, or environmental aid.

First it is important for rich nations to take Swart's advice and acknowledge that "[i]n developing countries, the main concern is with *today's problems*...and the issue is to incorporate climate change mitigation in development policy in a way that does not [compromise their] primary objectives."[53] Western nations' track record on this score is not impressive: they have made heroic efforts to compartmentalize the climate change problem and dodge what are perceived to be issues of secondary concern (e.g., trade, aid, investment, debt, and intellectual property rights), even after thirty years of poorer nations trying to smuggle development issues back into the negotiations.[54] If anything, countries living under conditions of poverty, domestic unrest, and structural vulnerability to international economic and political conditions care even more about these issues today than they did when climate negotiations began in the early 1990s. They have also become keenly aware of their bargaining power and ability to walk away from negotiations, and have repeatedly shown their willingness to resort to zero-sum, retaliatory tactics.[55] According to seasoned analyst Herman Ott, at COP-8 in New Delhi, "it became clear that developing countries would not give up their 'right' for increasing emissions without serious concessions in other fields of the development agenda which satisfy the demand for global equity and poverty reduction."[56]

Scholars of environmental politics who are unfamiliar with the literature on the international political economy of development may view such demands as distracting and unconstructive, but the ongoing development crisis is at the very heart of the climate policy impasse. Developing countries want more "policy space"—that is, room to define and pursue their own development agendas—but today's international economic regimes present huge hurdles to export diversification, institutional experimentation, and upward mobility in the world economy.[57]

Robert Wade describes this pattern as "the shrinking of development space."[58] "The rules being written into multilateral and bilateral agreements," he writes, "actively prevent developing countries from pursuing the kinds of industrial and technology policies adopted by the newly developed countries of East Asia and by the older developed countries when they were developing, policies aimed at accelerating the 'internal' articulation of the economy."[59] This perception that the rich nations are promoting "do-as-I-say-not-as-I-do" policies is particularly damaging because successful transitions from carbon-intensive to climate-friendly development pathways will require "deep" cooperation between rich and poor nations, which must be underpinned by conditions of generalized trust and diffuse reciprocity.

This raises a more general point. There would almost certainly be an immediate and lasting payoff in terms of international environmental cooperation if Southern nations felt they were being dealt a fair and predictable hand in matters of international political economy. Western policy makers are no doubt aware that the only slightly non-Darwinian morality adopted in the international trade, debt, finance, investment, and intellectual property rights arenas is not costless;[60] however, these different policy domains are negotiated by delegations with specialized knowledge and values that are often inconsistent with those of other delegations from the same nations. This is in many ways the Achilles' heel of the rational, unitary actor model that we and many other IEP scholars have employed. Northern environmental delegations are often at the mercy of their home country's economic policies, which are many times drawn up in the absence of environmental policy makers.[61]

Working toward a "New Shared Thinking" about North-South Relations

Under circumstances of extreme mistrust, Andrew Kydd suggests that reluctant states may require more from demandants than strategic reassurance. In these situations it is more important for states to work toward establishing a "shared worldview." As Kydd explains, this is typically the result of one state (or group of states) trying to get another state (or group of states) to endorse a "new thinking."[62] During the Cold

War, for example, the U.S. and Soviet administrations used costly signals to demonstrate their interest in establishing new thinking about global security. When the Soviet Union withdrew from Afghanistan, an editorial appeared in the *New York Times* saying that its actions "begin to render credible Moscow's 'new thinking' about the Soviet role in the world."[63] Subsequently, when "asked if he still held to the idea that the Soviet Union was an evil empire,... [Reagan] responded, 'No, I was talking about another time, another era'."[64]

We have documented the existence of an enormous "worldview gap" between rich and poor nations in how they define the issue of climate change, in how they identify their environmental priorities, in how much agency they believe their governments possess to implement difficult environmental reforms, and so on. Readers unconvinced by this argument may find the words of one G-77 adviser more compelling: "It is tempting to dismiss the South's persistent distrust of the North as the paranoia of historical baggage. However, the South's anger is directed not at subjugation in the past, but what it sees as subjugation today. The frustration emerges not from what transpired in the past, but the South's inability to influence what might happen in the future."[65]

The fact that Southern worldviews are very much at odds with those of Western policy makers makes the task of establishing a shared "new thinking" about environment and development all the more difficult. Tom Athanasiou and Paul Baer rightly argue that the challenge is to ensure that the South "not [view] climate justice as the justice of following the North down the fossil-fuel path."[66] But to move away from "old North-South thinking," or what Edward Graham calls "residual 1970s thinking," an attractive alternative must be offered.[67] To do this, we believe that the North needs to form constructive, long-term partnerships with Southern nations and help tailor country-specific and sector-specific development strategies and climate policies to local conditions, culture, institutions, knowledge, and technologies.[68]

As important, rich nations must promote policies that explicitly signal concern for the structural obstacles facing developing countries. The practice of tariff escalation, for example, reinforces the structuralist perception that rich countries do not want poor countries to get rich the same way they did. The TRIPS agreement has a similar effect since rich nations historically had complete policy autonomy in this area, granting patents at their own discretion in order to encourage industrial transformation.[69] By contrast, investments in and dissemination of "win-win" technologies that address local environmental issues *and* reduce greenhouse gas emissions would send a strong signal that while solutions to climate change are urgently needed, the West also cares about the social and economic circumstances of developing countries. For example, a large-scale plan to distribute clean stove technologies would help the West demonstrate to developing countries that climate change can be addressed while also addressing urgent human health issues (approximately 2 million people continue to die every year from exposure to stove smoke inside their homes).[70] Investments in other "brown" environmental issues, such as clean water, sanitation, land degradation, and urban air pollution, would most likely also exert a positive perceptional impact.[71]

The remainder of our policy agenda is sweeping in its scope. Channeling longer-term, predictable budget support to reasonably well-governed countries would signal an understanding that onerous donor requirements increase the cost of aid and undermine the growth of strong, Weberian bureaucracies that are capable of delivering high-quality public services.[72] The creation of a commodity support fund to insulate countries reliant on natural resources from exogenous shocks (with grant funding rather than loans) might also render the proposed "new thinking" more credible in the minds of LDC policy makers.[73] Other possibilities include reining in the deep integration and anti-industrial policy crusade,[74] helping poor countries diversify their economies by setting up a special fund that compensates "political losers" generated by the diversification process; promoting greater stability and predictability in the trade, debt, aid, and investment regimes;[75] and redistributing voting power within the IFIs so that the institutions' main clients have a more meaningful voice in the programs targeting their populations.[76]

Decarbonization, Diversification, and the Politics of Upgrading Development Pathways

We now turn to what may be the most innovative policy ramifications of our research. There is a general consensus that stabilizing the climate requires delinking development and carbon use, particularly in the Third World where the greatest share of economic growth is projected to occur over the next century. Yet very few analysts, to our knowledge, have questioned the implementability of such a plan. The common assumption is that economic diversification, leapfrogging from high-to low-carbon technologies, and decarbonization are primarily a problem of revenue shortfall. If the West could only mobilize enough political will and taxpayer dollars, it is thought that a "renewables revolution" would be set in motion.[77] In this view, the process of leapfrogging from high- to low-carbon technologies will occur smoothly and spontaneously.[78] However, the process of industrial transformation, diversification, and by extension, decarbonization, is profoundly political.

To address these issues, we believe that new research on development paths should be funded and taken up as a starting point for building a North-South consensus on how different types of countries should go about reducing their current or future greenhouse gas emissions. Ideally, this would include a large-scale, multinational and multidisciplinary effort, including engineers, climate scientists, economists, political scientists, sociologists, economic and environmental planners, and policy makers, and it would require the integral participation and guidance of scholars and policy makers from the global South.[79] The IPCC's 2000 *Special Report on Emissions Scenarios* acknowledges that future emissions scenarios are highly contingent upon the "technological and socio-economic development pathway[s] chosen by developing countries,"[80] but the policy recommendations from this report are extremely abstract, apolitical, and unhelpful to policy makers.[81]

In chapter 5 we described how some development pathways—as indicated by a nation's main export products—insulate some countries from economic volatility more than others, cause less local environmental damage, and give more options to planners. Other pathways—especially those based on the extraction and production of raw materials, semiprocessed and low-value manufactured goods—are much less profitable, require huge amounts of raw materials and vast flows of fossil fuels for processing and transport, and produce very few social benefits. Manufacturing exports, for example, was long considered the ideal development path by many developing nations, but their carbon intensity and waning developmental significance require greater scrutiny.

Contrary to popular opinion, exporters of services are also not in the clear. Countries such as the United States, which increasingly specialize in areas like banking, tourism, advertising, sales, product design, procurement, and distribution, are in fact net importers of carbon-intensive goods coming primarily from developing countries. They therefore emit no less; they simply shift their emissions to other countries.

Exporters of primary products (except exporters of oil), who are largely producers of metals, minerals, and tropical agricultural commodities, also deserve special attention. At first glance, their economic development may not seem particularly relevant to the post-2012 climate regime. However, the problem of the transfer of polluting stages of production gives them greater strength in political negotiations. For countries with this type of commodity-reliant foreign exchange profile, we believe that climate policy makers stand to gain from a frank admission that while there are significant gains to be had from global integration, there are also important drawbacks. On the upside, trade can turn the growth engine. And growth, despite being highly disruptive, can create a steady stream of government revenue, something that redistributive programs cannot deliver.[82]

On the downside, the central governing principle of the integrationist agenda remains specialization based on comparative advantage. While a few sectors and products generate stable and high revenues and a great deal of dynamism in the domestic economy by promoting backward and forward linkages and internally articulated markets, others suffer from highly volatile prices and terms of trade deterioration, development limited to export enclaves, and corruption and authoritarianism at all levels of the state. Specialization in primary products is not only widely agreed to be a dead-end development path,[83] but it also strongly affects the ability of governments to implement meaningful environmental regulations.[84] Countries dependent on a small number of largely unprocessed or intermediate goods are typically faced with unstable government revenues, pressure by export elites to adopt weak environmental policies and suppress environmentalists and indigenous peoples, and escalation of tariffs when they export goods to rich nations.[85]

The globalization of economic production and trade is also causing many industrializing nations to become heavily reliant upon earnings from carbon-intensive export products. (These include oil and mineral extraction, petroleum-based input-intensive agriculture, and manufactures whose components require energy-intensive transport and processing.) These countries will find it much more difficult to diversify away from their current comparative advantage because of the "polluting elites" who have risen to economic and political power through the creation, growth, and dominance of those very sectors. Environmental reform and economic diversification do not take place in a political vacuum: There will inevitably be winners and losers, and for reforms to work, countries will need compensatory mechanisms that cushion their effects on losing firms and sectors.

As we mentioned earlier, the process of diversifying out of carbon-intensive products and sectors will most likely be intensely political. While in many poor nations there is a strong interest in economic diversification because of the desire for stronger and more predictable economic performance, diversification can dramatically change the balance of power within a nation, even leading to the ouster of political elites in some cases.[86] Thad Dunning points to the example of Indonesia, where "[t]e structural changes encouraged by Suharto's diversification efforts, over the long run, contributed to his eventual fall from power."[87] Michael Green, a former ambassador to Indonesia, writes, "In a way, Suharto was a victim of his own success. The growth of a significant middle class was a product of Indonesia's achievements in economic development under his leadership. Like middle classes elsewhere— Thailand's and South Korea's, for example—they were increasingly dissatisfied with political restrictions and, in particular, limits on their own participation in decision-making."[88]

For a state to successfully upgrade its comparative advantage, in both the economic and the environmental sense, it must have a plan for dealing with those who stand to lose economically and/or politically from such changes. This plan must include attention to both elites and workers. Here we take our theoretical cues from the conflict management literature developed in the study of domestic political economy. Acemoglu and Robinson argue that domestic elites who have built their fortunes and political power on the basis of old and inefficient technologies will vigorously oppose the introduction of new, more efficient technologies.[89] The important policy prescription associated with this literature is that domestic elites must not feel that their power is being undermined and must be compensated for losses they incur to ensure that reforms are politically viable. In the context of trade policy, Dani

Rodrik argues that governments must soften the fall for outgoing firms and sectors.[90]

Three brief examples may clarify this point. In the United States, a new movement is emerging that brings together labor unions and environmentalists to begin to create a "just transition" for workers in industries that will be affected most by the need to reduce or eliminate carbon dioxide emissions.[91] At the other end of the spectrum, the small African nation of Mauritius established an export processing zone (EPZ) during the 1970s as a way of encouraging diversification into textile production but continued to protect the import-substituting sugar industry to make trade reforms politically viable.[94] Botswana has also made efforts to diversify their economy, but importantly, they have delegated trade policy authority to a regional institution (Southern Africa Customs Union) and thus insulated the state from entrenched interests lobbying for protection.[92]

In terms of climate policy, it will be crucial to deal with the owners and managers of the coal, oil, mining, lumbering, and manufacturing (especially automobile) industries, as well as their many suppliers and dependents. Rich industrialized nations will essentially need to convince Southern governments that reducing carbon dioxide emissions is in their interest and that they genuinely want to assist them in their transition toward a decarbonized future. While the climate regime has not yet matured to the point where these discussions can take place, there are early indications that this will likely be a key point of contention in post-2012 negotiations. Summarizing the COP-9 negotiations in Milan, Dessai et al. write that "[t]he battle over economic diversification has been postponed but it will not go away easily."[93]

For diversification to be a realistic possibility, developing country governments probably need to begin "creating" new, more economically dynamic and climate-friendly comparative advantages, rather than taking the easy path of their natural comparative advantage. This creates an important and controversial window of opportunity for state intervention in the economy. Just as many of the most successful late developers strategically used artificial superprofits to jump-start local investment and encourage innovation, so too will LDC governments committed to climate policy reform need to nudge risk-averse entrepreneurs toward innovation.

Nevertheless, there are huge obstacles in the way of this kind of government intervention. Developing countries continue to face unfavorable trade, aid, debt, investment, and intellectual property rights rules that discipline governments choosing to intervene "unnecessarily" in their economies.[94] The so-called Washington Consensus closely adheres to the idea that if countries can "get the prices right"—that is, allow markets to freely express themselves by removing all "distortions"—economic growth and development will follow naturally and spontaneously.

The "neoclassical backlash" in development theory, which motivates much World Bank and IMF thinking about government intervention, finds its intellectual roots in the work of Douglass North and Anne Krueger—two economists who emphasized the need to eliminate rents and rent seeking from markets.[95] Rents are, of course, nothing more than superprofits: incomes larger than those that competitive markets offer. However, rents and rent seeking, North and Krueger argued, create and promote inefficiency and therefore should be kept to an absolute minimum.

Yet, it is extremely important to acknowledge that there are both innovation-enhancing and innovation-retarding rents, and effective government policy frequently produces and utilizes rents for long-term national goals.[97] In this regard, there are two reasons why waiting for the market to initiate a "renewables revolution" in developing countries is an exceedingly risky strategy: information externalities and coordination externalities. As Rodrik discusses in his paper, "Industrial Policy for the Twenty-First Century," countries that specialize in the export of raw materials are often caught in a "low-level equilibrium trap."[98] In the absence of government intervention, entrepreneurs many times view new technological investments as prohibitively risky. Rational, risk-averse entrepreneurs often lack adequate information about the true cost of new investments. Consequently, they may not experiment with new products, technologies, and sectors. In risk-laden developing countries, it is thought that governments can address this market failure by helping entrepreneurs discover the real cost structure of the economy. Hausmann and Rodrik refer to this as a process of "self-discovery."[99] Rodrik explains the underlying logic in layman's terms: "Entrepreneurs must experiment with new product lines. They must tinker with technologies from established producers abroad and adapt them to local conditions. When we put ourselves in the shoes of an entrepreneur engaged in cost discovery, we immediately see the key problem: this is an activity that has great social value and yet is very poorly remunerated. If the entrepreneur fails in his venture, he bears the full cost of his failure. If he is successful, he has to share the value of his discovery with other producers who can follow his example and flock into the new activity."[100]

How then can developing countries discover their marginal costs of abatement? The answer is simple: through experimentation. As Birdsall et al. point out, "[a]lmost all successful cases of development in the last 50 years have been based on creative—and often heterodox—policy innovations."[101] Climate-friendly development needn't be any different.

The Clean Development Mechanism, for example, allows poor nations who avoid or reduce emissions to sell those reductions to wealthier nations who need to buy some to meet the targets they agreed to in 1997. At Buenos Aires, Southern nations competed vigorously to attract the attention of potential CDM investors from the North. Latin American nations joined forces in advertising their efforts, holding a side event at COP-10 titled "Latinamerica: A Way Already Paved for Investments." Panama's assistant minister of finance introduced his team as ready to greet businesses who might buy current emission reductions and handed out a price list varying from $350 to $450 per ton of carbon dioxide. No one knows for sure, but some estimates have been made that the CDM might bring a flow of funds from North to South ten times the size of all current foreign aid. Since total development assistance adds up to about US$75 billion per year, of which environmental aid is about 10 percent, the CDM could have a huge impact on the way money flows to poor nations. Ideally, the CDM will solve one of the major dilemmas described in this book by helping poor nations to make investments in clean modern technology. Market-based solutions by themselves will most likely not be sufficient because states will still need to win over potential innovators. The CDM can be a key to upgrading nations from high-carbon to lower-carbon pathways of development that also create social development. However, major strategic planning is needed to guide the new market in tradable carbon permits from merely funding reclamation of landfill gases or endless miles of sterile pine or eucalyptus plantations.

Finally, coordination externalities may also suppress innovation and investment in late-developing economies. Rodrik offers the example of Taiwanese investors contemplating diversification into the highly profitable orchid industry: "An individual producer contemplating whether to invest in a greenhouse needs to know that there is an electrical grid he can access nearby, irrigation is available, the logistics and transport networks are in place, quarantine and other public health measures have been taken to protect his plants from his neighbors' pests, and his country has been marketed abroad as a dependable supplier of high quality orchids. All of these services have high fixed costs, and are unlikely to be provided by private entities unless they have an assurance that there will be enough greenhouses to demand their services in the first place."[102] Carefully planned interventions are therefore needed to anticipate and address these complex barriers to sustainable development as nations seek to upgrade their development paths.[103]

Final Thoughts: Change Happens

If we have accomplished anything in this book, we hope to have dissuaded readers from strict rationalist and institutionalist ideas that climate change can be addressed solely by designing better treaties, giving aid more strategically, or building capacity in poor nations. These are important measures, but climate change is a uniquely complex and global issue, one that will disrupt societies around the globe. The complex, layered nature of climate change forces us to dig deeper and look for the root causes of noncooperation. Because of the spillover of development issues like trade, debt, aid, and investment into negotiations about the global environment, changes will have to be profound.[104] However, every once in a while, windows of opportunity are opened because of an unusual confluence of events, a clever reform strategy, or an exogenous shock.

In the past, international aid agencies have played crucial roles in creating change. Armed with significant financial resources, these agencies have the ability to change the domestic balance of power in a country and increase the chances of meaningful (environmental) reform. Aid agencies and development banks may selectively withhold funds from corrupt local bureaucracies and bypass the government by backing ideationally motivated (environmental) NGOs.[105] Bilateral and multilateral agencies may also target individual politicians who are effectively blocking environmental reform.

In Zambia's one-party state, for example, the president was for a long time the most important source of influence and thus held the key to successful environmental reform. Clark Gibson's book *Politicians and Poachers: The Political Economy of Wildlife Policy in Africa* tells a compelling story about donors linking their desire for environmental reform with President Kaunda's ability to draw in other types of (more highly valued) aid and therefore increasing their chances of success.[106] In other countries, the key may be to target reform-minded bureaucracies or local environmental movements. The larger point is that the process of transferring environmental aid is a profoundly political intervention that requires knowledge of local institutions, power, knowledge, technologies, and culture. It must therefore be done with great care.

On a few occasions, "insider-outsider" networks have also achieved spectacular change. During the mid-1990s, for example, the NGO community formed a powerful coalition with the World Health Organization, the United Nations Development Programme, the World Bank, and a number of large developing countries, and effectively changed the nature of discussion on intellectual property rights and antiretroviral drug patents from a "piracy issue" to a "human rights issue." As "norm entrepreneurs," NGOs characterized pharmaceutical companies as greedy capitalists depriving HIV/AIDS victims of basic medical treatments. They also revealed inconsistencies in rich-country policies, which put greater domestic pressure on Western elected officials. As Sell and Prakash explain, "NGOs argued that if the United States was presumably willing to engage in compulsory licensing to address a national emergency, how could it possibly deny that same prerogative to developing countries daily facing thousands of preventable deaths (a national health emergency by any standard)? [And] if the U.S. had, by threatening compulsory licensing, achieved deep discounts in drug prices, why was it punishing Brazil for adopting the same strategy?"[107] NGOs have also achieved reforms in the international debt regime that were once inconceivable. By changing the discourse from an economic issue to a moral and religious issue and forging strategic partnerships with key insiders at the U.S. Treasury, the U.S. Congress, the White House, the

World Bank, and the IMF, a relatively small number of NGOs have significantly increased the size and scope of debt relief, changed the rules of the debt regime, redefined the purpose of debt relief, and ensured that the funds freed up by debt relief are spent on reducing poverty.[108]

There are some initial indications that insider-outsider networks are beginning to form around the issues of climate justice, ecological debt, and even contraction and convergence to a per capita accounting scheme for allocating greenhouse gas emissions. The G-77 and a coalition of more than thirty Western NGOs, policy institutes, and think tanks (many of whom were instrumental in changing the international debt regime) have begun the push for some remuneration of the ecological debt.[109] Key insiders, such as Britain's finance minister Gordon Brown and former World Bank President James Wolfensohn, have also signaled potential support for climate justice and payment of the ecological debt.[110] France, Switzerland, the EU, and some middle-income countries like Chile and Argentina have also begun arguing for a per capita framework, such as contraction and convergence. However, NGO coalitions and insider-outsider networks concerned with issues of fairness and justice face an obstacle in climate change that did not exist in the debt relief and intellectual property rights cases: Support for an equitable solution may cut deeply into Western taxpayers' pocketbooks.

Finally, a small literature on exogenous shocks suggests that minds are sometimes opened and new options considered under extraordinary circumstances. The atrocities of World War II are credited with driving a human rights revolution in Europe after the war finally ended.[111] The terrible Bhopal disaster in 1984 led to a series of progressive right-to-know laws being enacted in the United States during the Reagan administration. And the well-worn example of the discovery of the hole in the ozone layer motivated action before any serious human suffering had to occur. But does a natural disaster have to happen for society to address climate change at this level and with this broad an approach? Of course we believe that waiting for abrupt climate change to motivate people to act risks waiting too long. However, year after year our students seem to believe that a disaster is exactly what it will take, and sadly, they are beginning to win us over. The number and intensity of hurricanes hitting the United States in 2005, and the frightening and uncertain recovery from Katrina may be opening a new political window of opportunity for pro-climate action in the United States.

We will not speculate on what kind of disaster would be necessary for a dramatic shift in policy, but we doubt that a continuation of the trends in suffering from climate-related disasters documented in chapters 3 and 4 would motivate action from the world's most powerful. The waves will have to flow into Washington or New York (or at least Miami and New Orleans) and be irrefutably linked to climate change. One thing to hope for is that during the window of opportunity, national and global institutions will be open to serious proposals for long-term change. A key effort now is to have those proposals ready for that day.

Appendix A

Descriptions of Variables

Climate Disaster Indices (see chapter 3): Number killed: (lnkillmi): Number of people killed over the period 1980–2002 per million national population in 2000, natural log; (l0killmi): Number of people killed over the period 1980–2002 per million national population in 2000, natural log. Zeros excluded. Number made homeless: (lhomepo): Number of people made homeless over the period 1980–2002 as a proportion of national population in 2000, natural log; (l0homepo): Number of people made homeless over the period 1980–2002 as a proportion of national population in 2000, natural log. Zeros excluded. Number affected (lnaffpo): Number of people affected by climate disasters over the period 1980–2002 as a proportion of national population in 2000, natural log; (l0affpo): Number of people affected by climate disasters over the period 1980–2002 as a proportion of national population in 2000, natural log. Zeros excluded.[1]

Total Carbon Emissions by a Nation: Fossil fuel and cement manufacturing emissions of carbon by nations, 2000. Natural log.[2]

Carbon Intensity/GDP: Total fossil fuel carbon 2000[3] divided by national GDP, 2000, in current U.S. dollars. Natural log.[4]

Carbon Emissions per Capita: Fossil fuel carbon emissions per person in 1999 or 2000. Natural log.[5]

Cumulative Emissions 1950–1999: Sum of national fossil fuel carbon emissions reported by CDIAC for 1950–1999. Natural log.[6]

Environmental Treaty Ratification Index (TREFAC): Factor score of number of environmental treaties ratified for each nation. Data come from three sources. The first is the *Register of International Treaties and Other Agreements in the Field of the Environment, 1989* which is a presentation of data and information on all multilateral treaties deposited with the Secretary General of the United Nations as of December 13, 1988. Subsequent treaty information comes from the United Nations' on-line register of *Multilateral Treaties Deposited With the Secretary*

General, which contains the status of all treaties that came into force after 1988. The database used in this study was updated on April 6, 1999. The final source, *Participation in World Treaties on the Protection of the Environment: A Collection of Data* was used to verify the status of each treaty that came into force before 1990. The data include information on the response of 192 nations to twenty-two global conventions on the environment promulgated between 1946 and April 1999. We used factor analysis to create an index of participation by the countries to the treaties.[7]

Kyoto Ratification Status as of 2003 (kyotodum): 1 = countries that ratified Kyoto; 0 = countries that did not ratify Kyoto; (ratifyky): 2 = countries that ratified Kyoto; 1 = countries that signed Kyoto; 0 = countries that have neither signed nor ratified Kyoto; (kyo4pt): Countries that have neither signed nor ratified Kyoto received a 0; signatories were assigned a value of 1; ratifiers received a 4.

Total Green Aid Received (Lgreeaid): Green aid received by a given recipient country as a share of total green aid over the period 1990–2000. As part of a larger research project, we have coded more than 400,000 development projects on two dimensions: "environmental/neutral/dirty" and "green/brown." In our coding scheme, green projects deal with global environmental problems, such as climate change, deforestation, and biodiversity, while brown projects deal mostly with local environmental problems, such as sanitation, soil erosion, and sewerage. The criteria were extremely specific, so that coders did not have to make judgment calls about different projects. On the details of the project-level aid dataset and our specific coding criteria, see Parks et al.[8] All green aid receipts were logarithmically transformed.

Percent of Population Living Near Coasts (Coastper): Percent of the population living within 100 kilometers from the coast is derived from the Center for International Earth Science Information Network (CIESIN), World Resources Institute, and the International Food Policy Research Institute. Estimates based on 1995 population figures. "The Gridded Population of the World is a raster dataset that provides information on the spatial distribution of the world's human population. The grid cells are approximately 4.6 kilometer on each side. Populations are distributed according to administrative districts that vary in scale, level, and size from country to country. A 100-kilometer coastal buffer with a 10-kilometer 'safe area' falling into the sea was used in the geographic information system to calculate the number of people in the coastal zone for each country. The percentage of population in the coastal zone was calculated from 1995 United Nations population division totals for

each country." More information is available from http://www.wri.org/
wri/wri2000/coast_page.html.[9]

Percent Urban (urbanper):   Percent of the population living in an urban
area in 2001. Definitions vary by nation.[10]

Gini Index of Income Inequality: Measures inequality over the entire
distribution of income or consumption. A value of 0 represents perfect
equality and a value of 100 perfect inequality. Years of measurement
range from 1987 to 2001.[11]

Press Freedom (pressfr):   Press Freedom Index in 2000. "The degree to
which each country permits the free flow of information determines the
classification of its media as 'Free,' 'Partly Free,' or 'Not Free.' Countries
scoring 0–30 are regarded as having 'Free' media; 31–60, 'Partly Free'
media; and 61–100, 'Not Free' media. Scores are created by adding three
different measures: legal environment, political influences, and economic
pressures. The legal environment encompasses an examination of the
laws and regulations that could influence media content as well as the
government's inclination to use these laws to restrict the ability of media
to operate. We assess the positive impact of legal and constitutional
guarantees for freedom of expression, as well as the potentially negative
aspects of security legislation, the penal code and other criminal statutes,
penalties for libel and defamation, and registration requirements for both
media outlets and journalists. In considering political influences, we evaluate the degree of political control over the content of news media. Issues
examined in this category include access to information and sources,
editorial independence, official censorship and self-censorship, the ability
of the media to operate freely and without harassment, and the intimidation of journalists by the state or other actors. Finally, we examine economic pressures on the media, which include the structure of media
ownership, the costs of establishing media outlets as well as of production and distribution, the selective withholding of state advertising or
subsidies, official bias in licensing, and the impact of corruption and
bribery on content."[12]

Property Rights: "This factor scores the degree to which private property rights are protected and the degree to which the government
enforces laws that protect private property. It also accounts for the possibility that private property will be expropriated. In addition, it analyzes
the independence of the judiciary, the existence of corruption within the
judiciary, and the ability of individuals and businesses to enforce contracts. The less the legal protection of property, the higher the score; similarly, the greater the chances of government expropriation of property,
the higher the score."[13]   1 = Very high—Private property guaranteed by

the government; court system efficiently enforces contracts; justice system punishes those who unlawfully confiscate private property; corruption nearly nonexistent and expropriation unlikely. 5 = Very low—Private property outlawed or not protected; almost all property belongs to the state; country in such chaos (for example, because of ongoing war) that property protection is nonexistent; judiciary so corrupt that property is not effectively protected; expropriation frequent.[14]

Number of NGOs per Country in 2000:   Number of registered non-governmental organizations in a nation.[15]

Export Diversification Index (expdiv):   Measures the number of exported products worth more than $100,000 (or greater than 0.3 percent total national exports) in a country in 2000. The index itself is derived from the absolute deviation of the country share from world structure.[16] Higher scores reveal highly concentrated export structures. For more on the construction of this index, see Finger and Kreinin.[17]

Ecosystem Wellbeing Index (EWI):   Conceptualized as an indicator of national environmental vulnerability and overall condition of the environment. It includes fifty-one indicators, including indicators for land, water, air, species, and resource protection. Examples for land protection are how well a country conserves the diversity of its natural land ecosystems (four indicators) and maintains the quality of the ecosystems that it develops (one indicator). Note that this index is in a reverse direction, with high scores indicating poor ecosystem well-being.[18]

Voice and Accountability Index: "[C]aptures both the degree to which citizens choose those who govern them and the independent role that the media plays in keeping government accountable. This measure represents an aggregation of numerous political rights, civil liberties and political process indicators from various think tanks, NGOs and risk rating agencies."[19]

Government Effectiveness Index (effective):   "[C]ombine[s] the quality of public service provision, the quality of the bureaucracy, the competence of civil servants, the independence of the civil service from political pressures, and the credibility of the government's commitment to policies into a single grouping. The main focus of this index is on 'inputs' required for the government to be able to produce and implement good policies. The second cluster, which we refer to as 'regulatory burden,' is more focused on the policies themselves. It includes measures of the incidence of market-unfriendly policies such as price controls or inadequate bank supervision, as well as perceptions of the burdens imposed by excessive regulation in areas such as foreign trade and business development."[20]

Natural Capital Index (natcap): Nations scoring high have larger land areas, more valuable natural species diversity, and resources. We take a nation's natural capital as a proxy for its global environmental significance.[21]

Land Area: Total area of the country, including inland water bodies, in 2000.[22]

Total GDP 2000 (ln) (LnGDP00): GDP in current prices and exchange rates (expressed in millions of dollars) in 2000. We use the natural log in order to keep from seeing false trends that may come from the huge differences in population.[23]

Per Capita GDP in 2000 (ln) (LGDPPC00): Per capita GDP in current prices and exchange rates (expressed in millions of dollars) in 2000. We use the natural log in order to keep from seeing false trends that may come from the huge differences in population and national wealth.[24]

GDP per Capita Squared (GDPPC200): Given in current prices and current exchange rates (expressed in millions of dollars).[25]

Population: Total population in 2000 (expressed in thousands). We use the natural log in order to keep from seeing false trends that may come from the huge differences in population.[26]

ZBOREAL: Z-score of the percent of land area in boreal (cold) regions.[27]

Manufacturing Exporter (ExpManu): World Bank dummy variable for nations with over 50 percent of exports from the manufacturing sector (see chapter 5).

Service Exporter (Servexp2): World Bank dummy variable for nations with over 50 percent of exports from the service sector (see chapter 5).

Fuel Exporter (Fuelexps): World Bank dummy variable for nations with over 50 percent of exports from fuels (see chapter 5).

Trade/GDP: Trade as a percent of GDP, 2000.[28]

Trade × GDP (Interaction term): Trade as a percent of GDP times size of national economy.[29]

IUCN2001: IUCN is the oldest international environmental membership organization, currently with more than 900 members (governmental and NGO) worldwide, often including the most significant environmental NGOs in each country. This variable measures the number of IUCN member organizations in each country per million population.[30]

Appendix B
Why Narrowness of a Nation's Export Base?

As with any cross-national research design, the selection of variables that measure patterned differences across countries is critical. Here we seek to operationalize a fairly simple concept: national dependence on a narrow range of exports. Many cross-national variables are often plagued by idiosyncratic factors, outlying observations, and other types of "noise," and our measure is no exception. However, we believe it gets at a common causal mechanism that has systematic effects even across types of narrow export dependence.

Reliance on a small number of exports, we argue, promotes economic instability; concentrates power in the hands of a narrow group of elites; and creates disincentives to making long-term investments in the economy, health, education, and other public goods like environmental protection. Countries with all their eggs in one or two or even three baskets typically ride a rollercoaster of revenue instability as the prices of their exports—in many cases, low-priced commodities—rise and fall on the global market. Narrow reliance on such exports has been implicated as a causal agent of all kinds of dysfunctional national attributes: chronically unstable fiscal accounts,[1] diminished capacity to import essential goods and services,[2] reckless spending binges during resource "booms,"[3] "Dutch disease," civil conflict,[4] higher levels of income and asset inequality,[5] authoritarian rule,[6] weak public institutions,[7] lower levels of investment in and accumulation of human capital,[8] weaker environmental policies,[9] fewer backward and forward linkages and knowledge spillovers, less tacit accumulation of knowledge, and not surprisingly, lower economic growth.[10] And importantly, many of these variables feed off of each other and lead to vicious downward spirals and traps.[11]

Some countries exhibit more of these characteristics than others, but by and large, countries that are reliant on a small number of exports are those benefiting least from insertion into the global economy. Critics will charge that a nation can be extremely specialized in the production of one or two stable, high-valued exports, yet still score very poorly on the UNCTAD index we use. This is the case with Botswana (which specializes in the production of diamonds) and Mauritius (which specializes in the production of textiles), two of the only real shining examples of development in Africa. However, as an empirical matter, very few countries with concentrated export structures do not specialize in primary commodity production, and specialization in this particular area has been causally linked to many of the distorted policies and institutions listed earlier. Others might argue that the UNCTAD measure obscures much of the variation across narrow export reliance. That is to say, reliance on "point source" exports, "diffuse" exports, coffee and cocoa exports, or manufactures may set in motion different causal processes with different results.[12] We would not dispute the point; commodities matter, as do the social arrangements of their production and extraction. However, we maintain that narrow reliance on only a few exports may have systematic causal effects even across types of export dependence through the channels of social inequality, economic instability, and concentrated political power.

One final point is needed with a view toward the conclusions drawn in this book. While the countries we have described are highly dysfunctional, it is important to acknowledge that in many cases their policies and institutions are not of their own making. Rodrik makes a useful distinction between "purposeful policies and the exogenous component of policy," and we believe this kind of approach deserves greater attention in the study of international environmental politics.[13]

Notes

AOSIS Alliance of Small Island States

BBC British Broadcasting Corporation

CDIAC Carbon Dioxide Information and Analysis Center

CEC Commission for Environmental Cooperation

CRED-OFDA Centre for Research on the Epidemiology of Disasters

CSE Centre for Science and Environment

EIU Economist Intelligence Unit

ELAC Economic Commission for Latin America and the Caribbean

EO Economic Outlook Sources

EM-DAT Emergency Disasters Database

FAO Food and Agriculture Organization

IDNDR-ESCAP International Decade for Natural Disaster Reduction—United Nations Economic and Social Commission for Asia and the Pacific

IFRC International Federation of Red Cross and Red Crescent Societies

IISD International Institute for Sustainable Development

IPCC Intergovernmental Panel on Climate Change

OECD Organization for Economic Co-operation and Development

OPEC Organization of Petroleum-Exporting Countries

TERI Tata Energy Research Institute

UNCED United Nations Conference on Environment and Development

UNCTAD United Nations Conference on Trade and Development

UNDP United Nations Development Programme

UNEP United Nations Environment Programme

UNFCCC United Nations Framework Convention on Climate Change

USGS United States Geological Survey

WCED World Commission on Environment and Development

WHO World Health Organization

WMO World Meteorological Organization
WRI World Resources Institute
WTO World Trade Organization

Chapter 1

1. This scene, described by Athanasiou and Baer 2002: 23, was confirmed in a personal communication with Rahman in December 2004.

2. CRED-OFDA 2002.

3. Athanasiou and Baer 2002: 23.

4. As of May 24, 2004.

5. Baumert and Kete 2002: 8, emphasis added.

6. Najam 2002a, 2004a; Streck 2001; Sandbrook 1997; Clémençon 2004; Begley 1992; P. Lewis 1992; Weisskopf and Robinson 1992; Eilmer-Dewitt 1992; Baumert 2002.

7. Developing countries agreed to foot the rest of the bill (The Rio Declaration on Environment and Development, Section 4, Chapter 33).

8. To be fair, the alleged failure of the West's "green aid" promise may be attributable to the inability and/or unwillingness of recipient nations to implement their policy commitments. For a detailed examination of this topic, see Parks et al. 2006; Keohane and Levy 1996.

9. Agarwal et al. 1999.

10. United States Congress 1997.

11. The Byrd-Hagel Resolution is available online at http://www.nationalcenter .org/KyotoSenate.html, emphasis added.

12. Albright 1998; cited in Victor 2001.

13. Rossi 1997: A-15.

14. Office of the Press Secretary 2001, emphasis added.

15. Sprinz and Vaahoranta 1994; Rowlands 1995; Victor 2001.

16. Young 1994; Neumayer 2000; Sell 1996.

17. DeSombre 2000b. On bargaining power (who can credibly threaten to not participate or to defect), see Sell 1996; DeSombre 2000a. On coercive power (wealthy countries will institute sanctions of different types if you don't play along), see L. Martin 1992. On the ability to change the status quo unilaterally and gainfully, see Gruber 2000.

18. O. Young 1989; Vig and Axelrod 1999.

19. O. Young 2002.

20. Haas 1992.

21. Wapner 1995.

22. Inglehart 1995.

23. Haas 1990.

24. Keck and Sikkink 1998.

25. Levy and Kolk 2002; Levy and Newell 2002; Rowlands 2001; Levy and Egan 1998.

26. Meyer et al. 1997; Nielson and Tierney 2003.

27. O. Young 1994; Underdal 1994; Gupta and Grubb 2000.

28. Miller 1995; Müller 1999; Shue 1992; Agarwal et al. 1999, 2001. On the dangers of particularizing explanations, see King et al. 1994; Brady and Collier 2004; Sprinz and Wolinsky-Nahmias 2004.

29. Roberts and Thanos 2003; World Resources Institute 1995. The Global Environmental Facility (the GEF), founded to fund environmental projects in poorer nations, has in its mandate a focus on issues of global importance, but increasingly, the line between local benefits and global ones has grown impossible to pin down. The ongoing conflict over what can be defined as adaptation funding seen at the COP-10 in Buenos Aires shows how this is still is an area of deep dissent.

30. Connolly 1996: 330. On a number of key issues, rich nations have failed to honor their international policy commitments. Najam 2002a, 2004a,b; Bernstein and Bluesky 2000; Baumert 2002; Porter et al. 2000; Jokela 2002.

31. Moravcsik 2003b: 200.

32. It is also worth noting that many of our measures cannot capture the complexity of behavior in the real world. For this reason we have consciously integrated the statistical analysis with careful process tracing and theoretical conjecture.

33. Walt 1987; Snyder 1991; Van Evera 1990/1991.

34. Hawkins and Joachim 2004.

35. Sell and Prakash 2004; Sell 2003; Shadlen 2004.

36. Nielson et al. 2006.

37. Moravcsik 2003a: 133.

38. Lake 2002.

39. Tierney and Weaver 2004.

40. In chapter 2, we look at two additional types of global inequality: inequality in the global economic system and global environmental institutions.

41. IPCC 2001b. Certainly there is controversy about these points (Pielke 2002b).

42. Walter and Simms 2002; IFRC 2001.

43. Munich Reinsurance Company 2002.

44. IFRC 2001.

45. Blair 2000.

46. Houghton 2003.

47. The Economist 2002a.

48. Dow 1992; Liverman 2001.

49. IPCC 2001b.

50. Mathur and van Aalst 2004: 6.

51. By 2025, 90 percent of the increase in the world's urban population from 2.5 to 5.0 billion is expected to occur in the developing world (IPCC 2001b).

52. Their situation has indeed grown so severe that climatologists warn their homelands could vanish under the rising ocean waters.

53. Conisbee and Simms 2003.

54. Mendelsohn 2001.

55. McIntosh 1998.

56. Birdsall 2003.

57. David Dollar and Art Kraay, two World Bank economists, report in their much-celebrated article "Spreading the Wealth" that "The best evidence available shows...the current wave of globalization, which started around 1980, has actually promoted economic equality and reduced poverty" (Dollar and Kraay 2002a: 120; also see Wolf 2000, 2004b; Bhagwati 2004; Sala-i-Martin 2002; Firebaugh 1999, 2003; Firebaugh and Goesling 2004; Dollar and Kraay 2002a). However, they draw their conclusions from data on income inequality calculated between (rather than within) countries, weighted by national population, and measured in purchasing power parity (PPP) terms. This methodology represents only one of many highly defensible ways to measure global inequality. As one critic argues, "[T]he only valid short answer to the question, 'What is the trend of world income distribution?,' is: 'It depends.' It depends on the particular combination of measures, samples and data sets.... There is no single 'best' combination. At least 10 combinations are plausible, and they yield different conclusions about magnitudes and trends" (Wade 2004d: 575). Referring to the World Bank's household survey data, James K. Galbraith says "The result is just nonsense.... It's not consistent across countries, it's not consistent through time—it fails every reasonable standard of reliability" (quoted in Secor 2003: D1). It is interesting that when China and India are excluded from the World Bank's dataset, the trend showing convergence is reversed. Thus, "falling inequality is not a *generalized* feature of the world economy in the third (post-1980) wave of globalization, even using the most favorable [measure]" (Wade 2004d: 166, emphasis added).

58. World Bank 2000/01. This gap has doubled since 1960 (World Bank 2000/01).

59. UNDP 1999.

60. Milanovic 2002: 51–92. *Forbes* magazine finds that the 3 richest people in the world control assets greater than the income of all the least developed countries combined (49 nations), and the assets of the 200 richest people in the world roughly equal the income of 41 percent of the global population (*Forbes* magazine 1998).

61. Wade 2001b.

62. If national politics offer any exportable lessons to the study of international politics, a strong middle class lubricates the public policy-making process by reducing the heterogeneity of preferences associated with social polarization, rendering structuralist worldviews and causal beliefs less credible, fostering civic norms and strengthening conditions of trust, increasing the stability of policy coalitions, making it easier to coalesce around a socially shared understanding of what is fair, and making agreements more resilient to unforeseen, exogenous shocks. It is therefore not surprising that Easterly finds "a higher share of income for the middle class ... [is] associated with higher income and higher growth, as well as with more education, better health, better infrastructure, better economic policies, less political instability, less civil war and ethnic minorities at risk, more social modernization, and more democracy" (Easterly 2001: 317).

63. Najam 2004a: 226.

64. Birdsall et al. 2005a: 8. Wealthy nations have achieved this outcome by reducing and suspending special trade benefits as well as by threatening termination of IMF and World Bank funds (Shadlen 2004).

65. Birdsall et al. write that "[t]he WTO increasingly constrains the ability of developing countries to diversify and upgrade their economies. And countries that are negotiating entry into the WTO typically confront demands on their trade and industrial policies that go beyond WTO agreements" (Birdsall et al. 2005a: 10).

66. Collier 2004: 141, emphasis added.

67. Robert Wade argues that "We [should be] interested in income as a proxy for international purchasing power because this is more relevant than PPP for measuring relative impacts of one part of the world on others, including the ability of one set of people (for example, in a developing country) to import, to borrow, to repay loans, and also to participate in international rule-making fora" (Wade 2004d: 166–167).

68. Drahos 2003; Narlikar and Tussie 2004; Narlikar 2004; Gupta 2000b; Mitchell 1998; Mumma 2001; Egziabher 2003; Jawara and Kwa 2003; Kwa 2002; Wagner 1999; Richards 2001.

69. Wade 2004c: 575.

70. Richards 2001.

71. Gupta 2000b. The World Bank, the Climate Change Knowledge Network, the International Institute for Sustainable Development, Free University, the Center for Sustainable Development of the Americas, the United Nations for Training and Research (UNITAR), the UNEP Collaborating Centre on Energy and Environment, and ENDA-Tiers Monde have all offered training courses to enhance the negotiation skills of UNFCCC developing country delegates.

72. Richards 2001: 20.

73. Gupta 2000b: 65.

74. Chasek and Rajamani 2003: 251.

75. Woods 1999.

76. Moore 2003: 110.

77. Wade 2004b.

78. Chasek and Rajamani 2003.

79. Albin 2001, 2003; Mwandosya 2000.

80. In trade negotiations, a policy area arguably much more important to most developing countries than environmental protection, the situation has become so scandalous that one commentator has suggested that "[t]he criterion of 'agreement'...should be changed from the present rule—'you must be physically present in the negotiating room in order to record a disagreement, and if you are not there you are taken to agree'—to a rule of active agreement—'you are recorded as agreeing only if you signal your agreement'" (Wade 2003d).

81. Ashton and Wang 2003: 73.

82. In principle, all UNFCCC documents are required to be accessible in each of the "UN languages"; however, in practice many of the most important documents are not translated (from English) during "crunch time" (Gupta 2000b). Also see Grubb and Yamin 2001.

83. Gupta 2000b.

84. Wagner 1999.

85. Gupta 2000b.

86. Agarwal et al. 1999: 9.

87. Gupta 1997.

88. Kandlikar and Sagar 1999. Also see Agarwal 2002.

89. Working Groups II and III also showed wide inequalities in representation (Kandlikar and Sagar 1999). Much of this gap between developed and developing countries is no doubt a product of differences in absolute income, but a growing group of authors also point to the so-called brain-drain phenomenon, through which developing countries lose their best researchers and academics to Western universities (P. Evans and Finnemore 2001; Serageldin 1998).

90. Kandlikar and Sagar 1999; Haas 1990. UNEP argues that "scientists represent the *only* members of civil society to be consistently asked to advise government representatives" (UNEP 2000: 13, emphasis added).

91. Serageldin 1998.

92. UN System-Wide Earthwatch 2000: 20.

93. Richards 2001.

94. Chayes and Chayes 1993, 1995; Haas et al. 1993. As international agreements and organizations proliferate, the importance of international purchasing power has grown almost exponentially. The IFIs also make loan disbursements conditional on hiring foreign experts (Kapur and Webb 2000).

95. Lipson 1991: 511.

96. For example, the high levels of environmental vulnerability, weak civil society organizations, and underdeveloped institutions of many poor nations owe their origin in part to the influence of colonial governments. In many cases colonial occupiers actively suppressed civil society, enfeebled domestic institutions, and reinforced the host country's comparative advantage in primary products.

97. *Christian Science Monitor* 2004.

98. Birdsall et al. 2005a, 2005b.

99. There are two exceptions. The Special Report on Emissions Scenarios by the Intergovernmental Panel on Climate Change suggested that future greenhouse gas releases are highly contingent upon the "technological and socio-economic development pathway[s] chosen by developing countries" (Nakicenovic and Swart 2000; Swart et al. 2003: S27–S28). A group of four South Asian authors recently put it even more starkly: "Development pathways...societies choose today may be as important, possibly even more important, [than] the climate measures they take" (Najam et al. 2003a: S14).

Chapter 2

1. Brooke 1992: A6. The UNFCCC recognizes that "economic and social development and poverty eradication are the first and overriding priorities of the developing countries" (Article 4.7), and that "Parties have a right to and should promote sustainable development" (Article 3.4) (UNCED 1992a).

2. Brooke 1992: A6.

3. Sand 1993: 382.

4. UNCED 1992a,b. Also cited in Estrada-Oyuela 2002: 45, footnote 2.

5. Haas et al. 1993; Keohane and Levy 1996; Chayes and Chayes 1993; Weiss and Jacobson 1998; Mitchell 1998; Kandlikar and Sagar 1999.

6. Keohane and Levy 1996; Chayes and Chayes 1993; Weiss and Jacobson 1998; Mitchell 1998; Kandlikar and Sagar 1999.

7. Young 1999; Müller 2001a, 2001b; Hanensclever et al. 1999. Regime theorist Oran Young argues that "those who believe that they have been treated fairly and that their core demands have been addressed will voluntarily endeavour to make regimes work. Those who lack any sense of ownership regarding the arrangements because they have been pressured into pro forma participation, on the other hand, can be counted on to drag their feet in fulfilling the requirements of governance systems. It follows that even great powers have a stake in the development of international institutions that meet reasonable standards of equity" (1994: 134).

8. Vogler and Imber 1996: 16.

9. By their own admission, rational-choice institutionalists cannot account for "discrete trends" such as "unequal resource demands...and reliance on fossil fuel and chemical products" (Paterson 2000: 26). In a telling passage, Haas et

al. write in *Institutions for the Earth* that "[e]ach set of [environmental] issues has been considered separately,...independently of possible underlying causes such as population growth, patterns of consumer demand, and practices of modern industrial production" (1993: 423).

10. For example, Lange and Vogt 2003; Barrett 2003.

11. We seek throughout this book to differentiate between three types of causal explanations: grand theory, midrange theory, and issue-specific theory. Grand theory proposes clear, coherent, testable, and general causal explanations of empirical phenomena across a wide range of issue areas.

12. Krasner 1985.

13. E.g., A. Frank 1969; Wallerstein 1979; Cardoso and Faletto 1979; Chase-Dunn 1989.

14. Wade 2003c, 2004d; Rodrik 2001, 2004a, 2004b; Stiglitz 2002a; Stiglitz and Charlton 2004; Shadlen 2004, 2005; Bowles 2002, Birdsall et al. 2005a, 2005b.

15. Kenny 2005.

16. Najam 2004a, 2004b; Williams 1997; Porter et al. 2000.

17. Najam 2004a: 226.

18. Nations can move up or down the hierarchy, but the structure largely remains unchanged. In a relationship that has shifted but not reversed since colonial times, wealthy core nations import low-priced raw or intermediate materials from the poor, "periphery" nations. Wealthy nations also export higher-value industrial manufactures, and contain the headquarters of massive financial institutions and commodities markets. Unlike poorer nations who have accumulated oppressive burdens of debt to these institutions, wealthy states have the ability to impose monetary policies to stabilize their economies in times of crisis. And while manufacturing has shifted more to the periphery, these are often the low value-added phases of a product's life cycle. Further, with the imposition of environmental laws and greater enforcement in wealthier nations, increasingly poorer nations become the location of the most pollution-intensive parts of the commodity chain by which raw materials become finished products. What remains then in the core is increasingly only the research, development, design, marketing, and management phases of the cycle. Dispersed low-wage firms bid to contract the materials supply and assembly phases.

19. Cited in Timmerman 1995: 228.

20. Najam 2004a.

21. Hellman 2003; Kratochwil 2003. Katzenstein et al. 1999 refer to this as the rationalist-constructivist divide.

22. Goldstein and Keohane 1993; Fearon and Wendt 2002; Jupille et al. 2003; Sell and Prakash 2004; Tierney and Weaver 2004. Keohane explains: "Understanding beliefs is not opposed to understanding interests. On the contrary, interests are incomprehensible without an awareness of the beliefs that lie behind

them.... The values and beliefs that are dominant within a society provide the foundations for rational strategy" (2001: 8).

23. Goldstein and Keohane 1993.

24. Worldviews are conceptions of "the universe of possibilities for action" based on culture, modes of thought, discourse, cosmology, ontology, identity, emotions, and loyalty. Principled beliefs "[consist] of normative ideas that specify criteria for distinguishing right from wrong and just from unjust" (Goldstein and Keohane 1993: 9). Causal beliefs are "beliefs about cause-effect relationships which derive authority from the shared consensus of recognized elites" (Goldstein and Keohane 1993: 10).

25. Goldstein and Keohane 1993: 12.

26. Shadlen 2004; Gruber 2000; Abbott and Snidal 2000.

27. Najam 2004a, 2004b.

28. Ruggie 1983; Krasner 1985.

29. Barrett 2003.

30. Goldstein and Keohane 1993: 12.

31. For an alternative view, see Ott et al. 2004: 113.

32. Krasner 1985; Gore 2000; Najam 2004a. For an alternative perspective, see Owusu 2003.

33. Krasner 1985: 90. As to whether these beliefs affect public policy outcomes, Krasner concludes that "the development of a coherent intellectual position has provided a basis for Third World meta-political demands, enhanced Third World cooperation, and weakened the unity of the North" (Krasner 1985: 86). Hence, the beliefs of Southern policy makers do seem to have a nontrivial effect on international outcomes.

34. Kay 1999; Gore 2000; Najam 2004a.

35. Roberts and Hite 2000 review some of this discussion.

36. We describe some of these differences in Roberts and Hite 2000. Perhaps most famously, Brazilian sociologist Fernando Henrique Cardoso, who was elected that nation's president in the 1990s, was among the former group. Frank and Baran and Sweezy were among the latter.

37. E.g., Chase-Dunn 1989.

38. Najam 1995: 258.

39. Mwandosya 2000; Agarwal and Narain 1991; Shue 1992; Baumert et al. 2002.

40. Baumert 2002; Williams 1997; Miller 1995; Von Moltke and Rahman 1996; Parikh and Parikh 2002.

41. Kristof 1997.

42. Cited in Sell 1996: 108. The Brazilian ambassador's comments were actually made with respect to the consumption of ozone-depleting substances. However, this has been a recurring theme throughout the climate negotiations as well.

43. Porter and Brown 1991: 124. Also see Kufour 1991.

44. Mohamed 1995: 288. Also see DeSombre and Kauffman 1996.

45. Porter and Brown 1991: 124, emphasis added. They argue (1991: 124) that "[these] perceptions are based on the reality of the industrialized countries' dominance of world trade and financial systems and the continued evolution of those systems to the disadvantage of developing countries."

46. Najam 1995: 254.

47. Former Jamaican Prime Minister Michael Manley (1991: 9) argues that "there is an underlying and binding cement to be found in [developing countries'] common experience of imperialism and colonialism together with the common disadvantage they suffer under the present world economic order."

48. Najam 1995: 249.

49. Najam 1995: 258.

50. Birdsall et al. 2005a, 2005b; Wade 2003c; Shadlen 2004; Bhagwati 2004.

51. Rodrik 2001: 27.

52. Ricupero 1998: 17.

53. Deep integration is a costly and somewhat intrusive process of harmonizing behind-the-border regulatory policies and institutions (Birdsall and Lawrence 1999).

54. Cited in Kwa 2002: 7, emphasis added. It is certainly not the case that developing countries see all matters of international political economy through a dependency or structuralist lens. Rodrik (1999a: 37), for example, argues that "the attitude of many developing country policymakers toward [foreign direct investment] has undergone a remarkable turn-around in the last couple of decades.... Multinational enterprises used to be seen as the emblem of dependency; they have now become the saviors of development."

55. Summers 2000.

56. Wade 2000; Pettis 2001; Bowles 2002; Stiglitz 2000; Gowan 1999.

57. Sridharan 1998; *The Economist* 1997; Bowles 2002.

58. Gowan 1999.

59. Kissinger 1998: A19. On this topic, also see Bowles 2002.

60. Putnam 1993, 2000; Ostrom 1990; Keohane 1984, 1988; Stein 1990; Knack and Keefer 1997; Keohane 2001; Ostrom 1998; Kydd 2000a, 2000b.

61. Knight 1998.

62. Durkheim 1933 [1893].

63. Putnam 1993, 173–174.

64. Cited in Putnam 1993: 172.

65. North 1990.

66. Putnam 1993: 165.

67. As Russell Hardin (1992: 161) puts it, "In a Hobbesian view . . . trust is underwritten by a strong government to enforce contracts and to punish theft. Without such a government, cooperation would be nearly impossible and trust would be irrational."

68. Waltz 1979; Keohane 1984; Oye 1986a.

69. Keohane 1984: 105. The absence of a centralized coercive authority makes a good reputation incredibly valuable. Guzman 2002 uses the metaphor of a bond rating: "The value of a good reputation for states can be compared to the value of a high bond rating. Just as a good rating increases investor confidence and, therefore, allows the firm to raise money more cheaply, a strong reputation increases the confidence of counter-parties to an international agreement, allowing a state to extract more in exchange for its own promises" (2001: fn 123).

70. Keohane 1984; Hoel 1992; Carraro and Siniscalco 1993; Barrett 1994, 2003.

71. Mearsheimer 1994/95: 11.

72. Stein 1990: 39.

73. Intergovernmental agreements grew from 15,000 in 1960 to a staggering 55,000 in 1997, and multilateral treaty ratifications have grown at almost the same rate (Zürn 2004).

74. Keohane 1986: 4.

75. Cited in Hovi et al. 2003: 7.

76. Keohane 1986: 4.

77. Putnam 2000: 20.

78. Keohane argues that most manifestations of long-term cooperation are rooted in diffuse, not specific, reciprocity (1984: 127–131).

79. Knight 1998.

80. Sari 2003.

81. Kydd (2000a: 326) defines costly signals as "signals designed to persuade the other side that one is trustworthy by virtue of the fact that they are so costly that one would hesitate to send them if one were untrustworthy."

82. Kydd 2000a: 326. Keohane (2001: 6) suggests that "[e]goists have a hard time overcoming problems of mistrust, because they know that everyone has an incentive to disguise his or her preferences. Only costly signals will be credible; but the cost of signaling reduces the prospective value of cooperation and limits the agreements that can be reached."

83. Beyond ensuring that recalcitrant actors reap absolute gains, powerful nations may need to reassure weaker nations that the distribution of future gains will not disproportionately accrue to a few countries or widen existing North-South inequalities (Koremenos et al. 2001). In game theory, when one factors distributional preferences—that is, a concern for relative gains—into the cost-benefit calculation, actors in a prisoners' dilemma no longer prefer mutual cooperation to mutual defection. When one state prefers deadlock, mutual defection becomes the preferred strategy.

84. Kydd 2000a. For example, rich nations may devise compensation schemes or promote issue linkage to account for LDCs' competing policy priorities and high discount rates. In the case of the Montreal Protocol, developing countries refused to participate in the ozone regime until the threat to trade sanctions was offset by positive incentives (Benedick 1998; Barrett 2003; Mitchell and Keilbach 2001).

85. Tollison and Willett 1979; Sebenius 1983; Viguier 2004; Carraro and Siniscalco 1993, 1998; Martin 1994; Raiffa 1982. Issue linkage allows states to move toward the Pareto frontier as well as resolve thorny distributional issues.

86. Benedick 1998; Barrett 2003; Mitchell and Keilbach 2001.

87. Since preferences are a product of expectations, and expectations are a product of beliefs, we must be careful not to conflate a wide dispersion of fixed, well-defined, and exogenous interests with preference heterogeneity. Heterogeneous preferences may just as well be the result of different views about how the world works or how it should work.

88. Knack and Keefer 1997: 1278. Uslaner (2003) also offers evidence in support of the claim that income inequality is the strongest predictor of trust cross-nationally. Global inequality may also affect trust negatively if conditions of institutionalized suspicion exist; that is, if some countries seem to always reap a disproportionate amount of the joint gains. In domestic political economy, Bardhan (2000) has shown that a priori income and asset inequality may keep certain social groups from making individual sacrifices for the collective good. East Asia, he argues, has been far more successful than India in establishing an efficient property rights regime because their initial income distribution was far less skewed before such efforts began. In countries like India, he describes a social phenomenon of "institutionalized suspicion," where highly fragmented and polarized societies impose strict systems of checks and balances on their leaders to prevent any one ethnicity or religious groups from reaping disproportionate gains.

89. Baumert et al. 2002: 40; Ott 2001, 2003; Huq 2002; Barnett and Desai 2002: 236.

90. Gupta 2000b: 58.

91. Downs et al. 1996.

92. Uslaner 2003: 2, emphasis added. Uslaner (2001: 9) defines generalized trust as "the perception that *most* people are part of your moral community."

93. E.g., Parks and Roberts 2005.

94. Haas et al. 1993.

95. Sebenius 1991: 128.

96. Ruggie (1983) argues that much of the original Bretton Woods architecture was steeped in "developmentalist" norms.

97. Najam 1995: 249.

98. Albin 2001; Barrett 2003; Paterson 2001.

99. Sell 1996; DeSombre 2000a.

100. Cited in Sell 1996: 101.

101. Cited in Sell 1996: 103.

102. Cited in Sell 1996: 104.

103. Sell 1996: 103.

104. *Hartford Courant* 1992.

105. DeSombre 2000a; Sell 1996; Raustiala 1997.

106. Keohane and Levy 1996; Porter et al. 2000.

107. Raustiala 1997.

108. Robinson 1992; UNCED 1992.

109. Agarwal et al. 1999; Porter et al. 2000: 178; Najam 2002a; Baumert 2002.

110. Najam 1995.

111. Dessai 2001.

112. Jeter 2002.

113. Najam 2003: 370. On this issue, also see Raustiala 1997: 491; Bernstein and Bluesky 2000; Baumert 2002; Ott 2001; Mwandosya 2001; Najam and Robins 2001; Porter et al. 2000: 179; Grubb et al. 2001: 49; Athanasiou and Baer 2002; O. Young 1994; Jacoby and Reiner 2001; DeSombre and Kaufmann 1996: 94; Agarwal et al. 1999: 372.

114. Gupta 2000b: 58.

115. Murshed 2003.

116. McMichael 2000.

117. Wade 2003.

118. Rodrik 2001.

119. Conversely, positive spillovers may advance the cause of generalized trust and diffuse reciprocity and promote long-term cooperative ventures.

120. Murshed 2003; Bowles 2002.

121. Ruggie 1982: 396.

122. Ruggie 1982; Ikenberry 1992. The idea of embedded liberalism is that international economic relations should remain capitalist but tightly bound to the needs of society. Trying to live in the balance between these two objectives opened an important window of opportunity for state intervention in the market.

123. Evans 1992; Babb 2003; Shadlen 2004; Wade 2003b.

124. Easterly 2001: 135.

125. This is the textbook explanation for Wall Street's loose lending. A more convincing explanation is that large commercial banks began to pool their risk by including many smaller banks in loan deals to developing countries (Shadlen 2003). This process was called loan syndication.

126. This pattern has not changed. Under the "dollar standard" (the past thirty years), global liquidity has grown by 2000 percent (Duncan 2003). Nixon's decision was the result of structural changes in the U.S. economy as it became a net importer and incurred large trade deficits. Large, volatile capital inflows into developing countries are in many ways a product of the United States' unique ability to sustain large current account deficits, with surplus countries accumulating dollars around the world (*The Economist* 2002, 2004; Wolf 2004a; Pettis 1996, 1998, 2001; Wade 2000).

127. Shadlen 2003.

128. Shadlen 2003 provides one of the best summaries of the 1980s debt crisis and subsequent debt crises.

129. Williamson 1990.

130. Stiglitz 2002a, 2002b.

131. Generally, the poorer a country is, the less leverage it will possess vis-à-vis IFIs and thus the more intrusive its loan conditions will be. This is because poor countries are often strapped for cash and the Bank and the Fund are usually not as worried about getting repaid by smaller shareholders. As former chairman of the Federal Reserve Paul Volcker has stated quite bluntly, "When the Fund consults with a poor and weak country, the country gets in line. When it consults with a big and strong country, the Fund gets in line" (Volcker and Gyoten 1992: 143).

132. Kapur and Webb 2000; Rodrik 2004a. Between the years of 1980 and 2001, sub-Saharan African GNP per capita (excluding South Africa) fell by 44 percent (Kapur and Webb 2000). Three important econometric studies, Przeworski and Vreeland (2000), Barro and Lee (2002), and Dreher (2004), identify a causal link between IMF structural adjustment programs and economic stagnation.

133. Stiglitz 2002a.

134. Easterly 2001: 135.

135. Rodrik 2004a; Easterly 2001; Arrighi et al. 2003; Stiglitz 2002a. Dani Rodrik offers a useful thought experiment, which is worth quoting at some length: "Imagine that we gave [a list of first- and second-generation Washington Consensus policy reforms] to an intelligent Martian and asked him to match the [real] growth record . . . with the expectations that the list generates. How successful would he be in identifying which of the regions adopted the standard policy agenda and which did not? Consider first the high performing East Asian countries. Since this region is the only one that has done consistently well since the early 1960s, the Martian would reasonably guess that there is a high degree of correspondence between its policies and the list [of first-generation reforms]. But he would be at best half-right. South Korea's and Taiwan's growth policies, to take two important illustrations, exhibit significant departures from the Washington Consensus. Neither country undertook significant deregulation or liberalization of their trade and financial systems well into the 1980s. Far from

privatizing, they both relied heavily on public enterprises. South Korea did not even welcome direct foreign investment. And both countries deployed an extensive set of industrial policies that took the form of directed credit, trade protection, export subsidization, tax incentives, and other non-uniform interventions. Using the minimal scorecard of the original Washington Consensus, the Martian would award South Korea a grade of 5 (out of 10) and Taiwan perhaps a 6.... The Martian would also be led astray by China's boom since the late 1970s and by India's less phenomenal, but still significant growth pickup since the early 1980s. While both of these countries have transformed their attitudes towards markets and private enterprise during this period, their policy frameworks bear very little resemblance to what is described in [the Washington Consensus Plus]. India deregulated its policy regime slowly and undertook very little privatization. Its trade regime remained heavily restricted late into the 1990s. China did not even adopt a private property rights regime and it merely appended a market system to the scaffolding of a planned economy.... The Martian would [also] be puzzled that the region that made the most determined attempt at remaking itself in the image of [the Washington Consensus Plus] namely Latin America, has reaped so little growth benefit out of it. Countries such as Mexico, Argentina, Brazil, Colombia, Bolivia, and Peru did more liberalization, deregulation and privatization in the course of a few years than East Asian countries have done in four decades" (Rodrik 2004: 6).

136. Stiglitz 1998.

137. Stiglitz 2002b: A20.

138. Krasner 1978: 52.

139. In 1996, during a North-South debate over the WTO's dispute settlement mechanism (DSM), Jamaican Ambassador Celso Lafer stated that the DSM's recognized procedures "contributed to security and predictability in the rule-based multilateral trading system," explaining that such principles are especially important to developing countries (WTO 1996: 6).

140. Shadlen 2004: 2.

141. Shadlen 2004: 6.

142. Gruber 2000: 8. Also see Braithwaite and Drahos 2000; Drahos 2003.

143. Ostry 1999; Narlikar 2004; Narlikar and Tussie 2004; Drahos 2003; *The Economist* 2003; Wade 2004b; Stiglitz and Charlton 2004.

144. Cited in Bowles and Gintis 1993: 88. There is evidence that the "Single Undertaking" had a significant impact on Southern worldviews and causal beliefs. After the disastrous Cancun negotiations in 2003, the president of Tanzania and a champion of G-77 interests in trade negotiations, Benjamin Mkapa, wrote that "there are times when a bad deal is worse than no deal at all" (Mkapa 2004: 133).

145. UNDP 2003; Ostry 1999. TRIMS is the Agreement on Trade-Related Investment Measures. TRIPs is the Agreement on Trade-Related Aspects of Intellectual Property Rights. GATs is the General Agreement on Trade in Services.

146. Stiglitz and Charlton 2004. At first blush, this would seem to come as a surprise. Why would developing countries yield sovereignty to an international organization on issues where they presumably cherish their national autonomy? There are several plausible explanations. Rodrik (2003a) suggests that many LDCs simply did not understand the full ramifications of their actions, and this is supported anecdotally in statements made by Southern policymakers (Ricupero 1998: 17). Stiglitz (2002a) argues that the threat of bilateral reprisals and more subtle, behind-the-scenes pressure played a role. An equally plausible argument is that more than a decade of Washington Consensus conditionality had already opened up these economies and thus for many countries what was being demanded by the West was not viewed as a particularly intrusive. Amsden and Hikino (2000) advance an different argument. They suggest that even with TRIMS, TRIPS, and GATS, the WTO provides plenty of policy space for LDCs to pursue their developmental objectives. Still others propose that the incentive of market access—that is, the prospect of liberalization of Northern agricultural markets—was irresistible for many LDCs because of the sheer size, or "gravitational pull," of Northern internal markets (Shadlen 2005).

147. Wade 2003; UNDP 2003. Throughout the 1990s, the United States and other Western countries pushed for an even stronger multilateral investment agreement, which many wanted to model upon the United States' bilateral investment treaty (BIT) template (Walter 2001). The U.S. BIT grants unrestricted rights of repatriation of investment capital, payments, profits, and royalties; it grants preestablishment rights to investors; it eliminate all forms of "national treatment"; it pushes tariff rates toward 0 percent; it abolishes export subsidies and restricts subsidylike duty drawbacks; it makes license requirements illegal and limits tax incentives; it defines expropriation in broad terms (e.g., ex post labor and foreign direct investment environmental standards) and investment in broad terms [e.g., (FDI) *and* portfolio investment]. It provides for investor-state arbitration; it makes compulsory licensing the exception rather than the rule; it extends the scope of patentability; and it eliminates all performance requirements, compelled joint ventures and technology transfer (Shadlen 2005). In short, investors, not sovereign governments, are given most "rights." In Andrew Guzman's provocatively titled article, "Why LDCs sign treaties that hurt them," he concludes that "The rise of BITs has reduced the market power held by developing countries which, in turn, reduces the benefit they capture from any particular investment. For this reason, the BIT regime is likely to have the effect of reducing the overall welfare of developing countries and should not be cheered by those who seek the interests of LDCs" (Guzman 1998). Shadlen comes to an even stronger conclusion: "The greatest source of concern for development analysts should not be the WTO, but rather the initiative towards regional [integration] agreements that threaten to mothball industrial strategies and simply freeze an international division of labor based on static comparative advantages" (Shadlen 2004: 3).

148. Chang and Green 2003.

149. Unlike portfolio investment, which often takes the form of highly volatile speculative capital, when harnessed carefully by the state, FDI can generate

employment, promote complementary domestic industries, introduce cutting-edge technologies, provide an important source of foreign exchange, and boost international productivity and competition (J. H. Dunning 1993, 1997; Lall 1995).

150. UNDP 2003.

151. Shadlen 2004; UNDP 2003.

152. Harvard economist Dani Rodrik has been particularly outspoken about adding TRIPS to the WTO agenda. He summarized his position in a recent interview: "I think TRIPS was a terrible idea. I think developing countries knew it was a terrible idea, but two things happened: one is that they did not appreciate how terrible an idea it was; and, second, that they thought by agreeing to TRIPS they would be getting substantial amounts of liberalization and market access in return, which, by and large, I think has not happened.... I think this was largely driven by the interest of pharmaceutical companies in the United States, and I wish we had never come down that path.... [A] lot of transfer of new technology to developing countries, historically, has happened through a process of reverse engineering. Taiwan and South Korea benefited tremendous amounts from reverse engineering, things that they would not have been able to do if WTO rules applied to them at the time.... I think that this is again an area where developing countries gave way too much and now they're trying to negotiate a retreat with the United States which has been very adamant" (Rodrik 2003a: 4–5). Also see Bichsel 1994.

153. UNDP 2003, especially chapter 11. As Cambridge economist H. J. Chang notes, "when they were developing countries themselves the developed countries used virtually none of the policies that they are recommending to developing countries. Nowhere is this discrepancy between historical facts and today's conventional wisdom bigger than in the area of industrial, trade and technology policies" (2003b: 22).

154. Rodrik 2001: 55.

155. Finger and Schuler 2000: 523, emphasis added.

156. See Stiglitz 2002a: 61.

157. Busch and Reinhardt 2003: 721–2.

158. *The Economist* 2002; Wolf 2004a; Wade 2003a, 2004a.

159. The United States today spends far more abroad than it earns abroad and remains cushioned from the harsh effects of readjustment that other countries experience when they overspend: cutting imports, devaluing currencies, increasing interest rates, and curbing government spending (Gowan 1999; Duncan 2003). In short, the United States no longer needs to choose between guns and butter; it can have both. If it wants to reduce its debt, all it needs to do is devalue the dollar. If it wants to finance expensive wars overseas without accumulating huge sums of debt, that too can be easily achieved with a simple dollar devaluation (Wade 2004a). As one commentator puts it, it is "the largest free lunch in history" (Hudson 2003).

160. Peter Gowan's account of the "securitization" of financial flows is an excellent introductory text on this topic. "When the American central bank, the Federal Reserve Board, intervened in late September 1998 to save the Long Term Capital Management Fund (LTCM)," he writes, "it threw a beam of light into the black hole at the heart of what has come to be called [economic] globalization. Federal Reserve Board Chairman Alan Greenspan was issuing a simple, clear set of messages: that, since the Fed steps in only to tackle 'systemic risk,' the safety of the entire American credit system was apparently threatened by the behavior of a single, speculative Hedge Fund; that the international constellations of financial markets revolving around their American centre were in fact subordinated to a center of speculators; that the welfare of literally billions of people, whose livelihoods depend in one way or the other on the functioning of credit systems, was potentially jeopardized by a couple of Nobel Prize winners and a former deputy chairman of the Fed who had been engaged in an orgy of reckless speculation; that the macro-economic policies of the rest of the world should be shifted by lowering interest rates to help bail out a Cayman Islands company" (1999: 120).

161. One of the key features of mutual fund, hedge fund, and pension fund operators is that they often base their decisions on other investors' behavior, rather than on the economic fundamentals. They face a collective action problem in that information gathering and processing is expensive. Every investor therefore has an incentive to free ride by following the lead of other investors.

162. Gowan 1999: 104.

163. Gowan 1999; Stiglitz 2002a. IMF managing director Camdessus announced in 1999, "I believe it is now time for momentum to be reestablished. . . . Full liberalization of capital movements should be promoted in a prudent and well-sequenced fashion. . . . the liberalization of capital movements [should be made] one of the purposes of the Fund" (cited in Wade 2003b: xlvi).

164. Stiglitz 2002a: 62. Former U.S. Treasury Secretary Lawrence Summers explained at a World Bank country directors' retreat in 2001 that "[t]imes of financial emergency are often moments when [our] leverage is greatest, when there is the greatest malleability with respect to structural change" (Summers 2001).

165. Murshed 2003; McMichael 2000.

166. Jeter 2002. Also see Mendoza 2003.

167. BBC 2002.

168. Benedick 2001: 73. On the Kyoto Protocol's "compliance committee," see Ott 2001.

169. Stavins voices similar reservations about treating LDCs differentially: "A frequently voiced response to this assertion, is that . . . industrialized countries should—on their own—take the initial steps of making serious emissions reductions. But the simple reality is that developing countries provide the greatest opportunities now for relatively low cost emissions reductions. Hence, it would be excessively and unnecessarily costly to focus emissions-reductions activities

exclusively in the developed world" (2004: 8). Also see Kallbekken and West-skog 2005.

170. In particular, Benedick overlooks the point made recently by the World Resources Institute that "[f]or some developing countries, wealthier nations' promises on climate protection seem empty and faithless" (Baumert and Kete 2002: 9–10).

171. Wade 2003c: 629. Also see Zoellick 2003; Najam 2004a; Group of 77 2000a, 2000b; Sandbrook 1997.

172. Shadlen (2004) makes a similar argument about the North-South dynamic in intellectual property rights negotiations.

173. Abbott and Snidal (2000) explain this aversion with the idea of "sover-eignty costs."

174. Abbott and Snidal 2000.

175. Lipson 1991.

176. Abbott and Snidal 2000.

177. Rothstein 2002: 28.

178. Keohane 2001. There is, of course, no Leviathan in international politics, but states have the option of pursuing both formal and informal institutions. They may choose more "shallow" cooperation through informal pacts and exec-utive agreements, or "deeper" cooperation through treaty ratification or the cre-ation of dispute resolution mechanisms (Lipson 1991; Guzman 2002; Martin 2003). Participating in formal institutions may impose sovereignty costs, but the long-term costs of pursuing an informal approach may also prove greater.

179. Baumert and Kete have written that "despite North-South differences in emissions, wealth, and priorities, these disparities are not the largest barrier to cooperation....[A] more potent obstacle is the enduring and *growing lack of trust*....For some developing countries, wealthier nations' promises on climate protection seem empty and faithless. Furthermore, some developing countries are concerned that repeated bids on the part of the industrialized countries...to include emission limitation commitments for developing countries on the negoti-ating agenda for the Kyoto Protocol are but thinly veiled attempts to impede poorer countries' economic development prospects" (2002: 9–10).

180. Estrada-Oyuela 2002; Athanasiou and Baer 2002; Shue 1992, 1993; Rose 1998; Rose et al. 1998; H. P. Young 1994; Najam 1995, 2003, 2004a.

181. H. P. Young 1994: xi.

182. Victor 2001: 3

183. These nations have begun to argue loudly that they are "among the most vulnerable to impacts of climate and sea-level changes...the inhabitable land tends to be on the coastal fringe....climate change could mean changes in storm frequencies and intensity and lead to increased risk of flooding. It could upset sediment balances on the islands, leading to beach erosion and displacement of settlements and infrastructure" (AOSIS 1999).

184. These countries include most of Central America and Ecuador and are being led by Costa Rica (Dunn 1998).

185. Sprinz and Vaahtoranta 1994: 78; M. A. Levy 1993; Andersen and Agrawala 2002.

186. Dunn 1998; Roberts 2001.

187. Victor 1999. The case of Europe's eagerness to accept binding limits on its CO_2 emissions requires more explanation than we address here. Often cited are Holland's coastal vulnerability, widespread postmaterialist values, Europe's long experience with the ability of transboundary solutions to address environmental problems, and the European Union's desire to distinguish and separate itself from the United States. Finally, some authors cite the "green technology" industry, which Europe currently dominates and for which regulatory imperatives would create a huge market.

188. Victor 2001.

189. Victor 1999, 2001.

190. Hardin 1968; Olson 1965; Axelrod 1984.

191. Barrett 2003. Although self-enforcing agreements are remarkably difficult to create and enforce, there are a few empirical examples. The Montreal Protocol's innovative use of carrots and sticks probably most closely resembles the ideal typical self-enforcing agreement (Barrett 2003; Mitchell and Kreiback 2001; DeSombre and Kauffman 1996).

192. Barrett 2003; Downs et al. 1998. This is the classic tradeoff between depth and breadth of international cooperation. See Kahler 1992; Oye 1986a; Koremenos et al. 2001; Drezner 2000; Putnam 1993; Ostrom 1990).

193. The likelihood that parties will trust each other decreases as the number of players increases because each player requires more information (Axelrod and Keohane 1986: 237).

194. Hasenclever et al. 1999: Oran Young writes that "If an actor does not know or cannot predict how the operation of the regime will affect its interests over the course of time, it will experience an unmistakable incentive to favour the creation of arrangements that can be counted on to generate outcomes *that are fair to everyone* regardless of where they stand on specific issues" (1999: 254, emphasis added).

195. Since those who voluntarily participate in international treaties cannot be forced to disclose information about their actions or be kept from backsliding or defecting, those who possess such preferences must have their interests meaningfully addressed to ensure that the agreement is self-enforcing.

196. A similar argument concerning the amount of environmental space being used by rich and poor nations could be made. Wuppertal Institute scholar Wolfgang Sachs (1999: 167) has calculated that if every person on earth was allowed to emit as much carbon as the average German citizen, "mankind would be in need of five planets to have sufficient sinks for CO_2."

197. United Nations 1948.

198. Shadlen 2004; Abbott and Snidal 2000.

199. Each of these factors affecting bargaining, monitoring, and enforcement outcomes draws attention to the Achilles heel of game theory: its inability to explain beliefs and preferences (Jervis 1988).

200. Cecilia Albin, who has conducted extensive interviews with senior international negotiators, concludes in her book *Justice and Fairness in International Negotiation* that principled beliefs "[are] not the primary driving force or objective behind...deliberation or decisions....Yet in structuring negotiations and formulating broadly acceptable agreements..., it has almost always been necessary to take justice and fairness into account" (2001: 269).

201. Realists and neo-Marxian scholars both consider international law to be irrelevant, but as Louis Henkin (1979: 47) has pointed out, this perspective is difficult to reconcile with the empirical fact that "almost all nations observe almost all principles of international law and almost all of their obligations almost all of the time." Nor can realists and neo-Marxians offer a satisfactory answer for why nations spend tremendous time, energy, and resources negotiating, renegotiating, implementing, monitoring, and enforcing international treaties. The rational functionalist interpretation of such uniform compliance with international law is that states seek to maintain their reputations, avoid international sanctions, and minimize domestic audience costs (Henkin 1979).

202. Keohane 1984; Abbott and Snidal 2000; Martin 2000. North (1981: 201–202) defines institutions as "a set of rules, compliance procedures, and moral and ethical behavior norms designed to constrain the behavior of individuals in the interest of maximizing the wealth or utility of principals."

203. Krasner (1991) argues that state power is the primary determinant of which cooperative equilibrium states end up at.

204. Snidal 2002: 85; Keohane 2001: 6; Mitchell 2002b; Schelling 1960; Müller 1999; Garrett and Weingast 1993; O. Young 1999.

205. Müller 1999. Since no single actor's fairness principle will be mutually acceptable to all parties, Müller believes that hybrid proposals accounting for conflicting national positions hold the greatest promise for future negotiations. As he (1999: 3) puts it, "we merely need a solution which is commonly regarded as sufficiently fair to remain acceptable." On negotiated focal points, also see Garrett and Weingast 1993 and Biermann 1999.

206. In simple coordination games, states have no incentive to defect from the established focal point since everyone benefits from a shared standard. In the classic case, once all actors agree to drive on the right side of the road, no one is tempted to defect and drive on the left side of the road. Likewise, if all states can agree on a single equity principle to guide climate negotiations, no state will have an incentive to defect. Compliance is achieved in equilibrium. However, coordination dilemmas are only one type of cooperation problem. In the real world, actors must address issues of monitoring and enforcement. Game theorists use

the (iterated) prisoner's dilemma metaphor to explain these so-called problems of international collaboration. By forcing governments to "specify strict patterns of behavior and ensure no one cheats," collaboration ensures that agreements have teeth (Stein 1990: 39). For example, meaningful participation by developing countries requires some kind of punishment technology through which errant behavior can be penalized. Sometimes collaboration also requires positive incentives. Financial compensation schemes and issue linkage are two ways that rich nations can make compliance economically rational for poor nations (O. Young 1994). But when demandeurs negotiate with short-term mentalities (i.e., high discount rates) and must balance competing policy priorities, bargaining costs are typically higher and the probability of a stalemate is greater. This is because actors with a shorter "shadow of the future" are less concerned with future reputational costs (Fearon 1998). Such governments are also more likely to renege at the monitoring and enforcement stage of cooperation because of their relative indifference to loss of reputation.

207. Oran Young summarizes why collaboration dilemmas often require addressing issues of fairness: "[I]t is virtually impossible to achieve high levels of implementation and compliance over time through coercion. Those who believe that they have been treated fairly and that their core demands have been addressed will voluntarily endeavour to make regimes work. Those who lack any sense of ownership regarding the arrangements because they have been pressured into pro forma participation, on the other hand, can be counted on to drag their feet in fulfilling the requirements of governance systems" (1994: 134).

208. Estrada-Oyuela 2002: 37.

209. Müller 1999: 12–13, emphasis added.

210. Cited in Fredriksson and Gaston 2000: 345.

211. Krasner 1991; Koremenos et al. 2001.

212. Krasner 1985; Abbott and Snidal 2000.

213. Najam 2004b: 128.

214. Gruber 2000; Abbott and Snidal 2000; Shadlen 2004.

215. Fearon 1998; Koremenos et al. 2001; Najam 1995. When distributional issues threaten cooperation, Koremenos et al (2001: 784, emphasis added) argue that "one remedy is to rearrange the terms of cooperation so *that the benefits are more equally balanced*, but this may be difficult or costly."

216. Rabin 1993; Barrett 1994; Jeppesen and Andersen 1998; Fehr and Schmidt 1999; Falk et al. 2000, 2003b, 2005.

217. Rabin 1993.

218. Fehr and Gachter 2000. Interestingly, the 2002 Nobel Prize winner in economics, Daniel Kahneman, was praised for his work on behavioral deviations from rational egoism.

219. Barrett 2003.

220. Barrett 2003: 299. Jon Elster (1989: 100) has similarly suggested that social norms "have a grip on the mind…due to the strong emotions they can trigger." And these "social norms [are] irreducible to rationality or indeed to any other form of optimizing mechanism" (Elster 1989: 15).

221. O. Young 1994; Barrett 2003; Najam 1995; Porter and Brown 1991.

222. O. Young 1994: 50, emphasis added.

223. On what motivates envious and spiteful behavior, see Falk et al. 2000, 2003a,b, 2005; Kirchsteiger 1994.

224. On the role of emotion in international relations, see Najam 1995: 262; Stiglitz 2002a: 61; Wade 2004a: 584; Sjöstedt 2001; Jokela 2002; Kydd 2000a.

Chapter 3

1. Bracken 2004a.

2. Bracken 2004b.

3. Bracken 2004a.

4. Bracken 2004a.

5. Bohle and Downing 1994; Chambers 1989; Adger 1999; Dow 1992; Dow and Downing 1995; Clark et al. 2000; Handmer et al. 1999; Watts and Bohle 1993; Kasperson and Kasperson 2001; Wisner and Luce 1993; Leichenko and O'Brien 2002; O'Brien and Leichenko 2000, 2003; Stephen and Downing 2001; Cutter 1996; Kates 2000; Ribot 1995; Ribot et al. 1996; O'Brien et al. 2004; Alexander 2000; Comfort et al. 1999.

6. Blaikie et al. 1994.

7. In recent years, a growing number of studies have relied on CRED data as a proxy for natural disaster impacts. See Crespo et al. 2004; Skidmore and Toya 2002; Kahn 2005; Yohe and Tol 2001; Brooks and Adger 2003a, 2003b; Brooks et al. 2005.

8. Rich people and rich countries, by definition, have more to lose than poor people and poor countries. This systematically skews income-dependent measures such that wealthy people appear to be more vulnerable. Yet many of the most vital assets drawn upon by poor people during times of crisis are non-income assets; for example, public goods like education, information, health care, clean water, sanitation, and social capital, and private goods like a buffer stock of grain, livestock, or one's local natural resources base (Adger and Brooks 2003). "Considering insured damage claims for the 1999 floods in Austria, Germany and Switzerland, at least 42.5 percent of damage was covered by disaster insurance. But in Venezuela the same year, only 4 percent of flood damage was covered" (UNEP 2002: 271).

9. The CRED-OFDA definition of "killed" is "[p]ersons confirmed as dead and persons missing and presumed dead (official figures when available)." "Homeless" refers to "[p]eople needing immediate assistance for shelter." And

"affected" includes people who are displaced, evacuated, homeless, injured, and those "requiring immediate assistance during a period of emergency" (CRED-OFDA 2004).

10. For example, climate risk and vulnerability can be exacerbated by either shocks, such as hurricanes, droughts, and winter storms, or stresses, like seasonality (Chambers 1989). While shocks are much more visible, extended stress can be equally devastating (Wisner et al. 2004). For reasons of data availability, we have limited our analysis to climatic shocks. Future work on climatic stress would be extremely useful.

11. "For a disaster to be entered into the database, at least one of the following criteria must be fulfilled: 10 or more people reported killed, 100 people reported affected, declaration of a state of emergency, or a call for international assistance" (CRED-OFDA 2004).

12. Forest and brush fires are typically the result of arson, careless human behavior, volcanic eruptions, or lightning. Famines are usually the result of poverty, war, deliberate government policies, earthquakes, pestilence, and rainfall shortages. Epidemics are often influenced by the climate, but in many cases—example, rabies, anthrax, and smallpox—climatic factors are completely irrelevant.

13. IPCC 2001b. Many leading climate scientists argue that we have witnessed a sharp increase in the frequency, intensity, and magnitude of extreme weather events over the past two and a half decades. The best science suggests that these changes may be the by-product of human-induced warming. Left unaddressed, experts warn that climate change will lead to higher maximum and minimum temperatures over most land areas, more frequent precipitation events, a generalized increase in heat index, increased drought in dryland areas, and higher tropical cyclone wind and precipitation intensities (IPCC 2001a). Our analysis does not rely on there being an increase in climate-related disasters; rather, it provides a picture of what will almost certainly continue to happen and what increasingly will occur if the Earth's climate becomes more unstable.

14. One recent econometric study has analyzed natural disasters using each event as an observation (Kahn 2005).

15. Wisher et al. 2004.

16. Blaikie et al. 1994; Cross 2001.

17. CRED-OFDA 2004.

18. CRED-OFDA 2004. Hurricane Katrina's U.S. impact, after this chapter went to press, was highly unusual.

19. USGS 2000.

20. All are reported in the CRED database.

21. National Institute of Health 2004.

22. Klinenberg 2003.

23. The French heat wave of 2003 was outside the time period for our analysis, which only included disasters from 1980 to 2002.

24. CRED-OFDA 2004.

25. CRED-OFDA 2004.

26. Both scales were logarithmically transformed to show the pattern.

27. Cutter 1996; Rodgers 1999; Wisner 2001b.

28. McGuire et al. 2002; Blaikie et al. 1994.

29. Roberts and Thanos 2003; Paige 1997.

30. Stonich 1993; Paige 1997.

31. EIU 2004a: 6; Acker 1988.

32. Comfort et al. 1999; Diaz and Pulwarty 1997.

33. Kay 2002.

34. Christian Aid n.d.

35. The so-called "scissors effect"—when large-scale capital pushes peasants to the social and geographical margins—is widely believed to be a main cause of the huge loss in land cover (50 percent) that has occurred since 1950 (Stonich 1993).

36. UNDP 2004.

37. EIU 2004a: 21.

38. EIU 2004a.

39. UNDP 2004.

40. Lopez-Claros 2004–2005.

41. Gold-Biss 2005: 284.

42. Carlos Medina, the former environment minister of Honduras, estimates that deforestation intensified the effects of Hurricane Mitch by at least 30 percent (Christian Aid n.d.).

43. Comfort et al. 1999; Blaikie et al. 1994; Morris et al. 2002.

44. Rodgers 1999.

45. FAO 1999. The Economist Intelligence Unit (2004a) estimates that damage was closer to 95 percent of Honduras' GDP.

46. Rohter 1998.

47. ECLAC 1999; Ranganath 2000; Rodgers 1999.

48. EIU 2004a.

49. CRED-OFDA 2004; EIU 2004a.

50. Best estimates suggest that 60 percent of the population lives within 50 kilometers of the coast.

51. B. Martin et al. 2001.

52. B. Martin et al. 2001; CRED-OFDA 2004; EIU 2004b.

53. EIU 2004b: 27.

54. Biggs et al. 1999: 8.

55. Biggs et al. 1999: 8.

56. UNDP 2004. Despite a reasonably wide export structure consisting of primary commodities like cashews, copra, prawns, cotton, coconut, sugarcane, cassava, rice, sorghum, vegetables, and nuts, Mozambique continues to struggle with unreliable transportation networks, dilapidated communications, few marketing opportunities, and chronically poor access to credit—all products of a brutal colonial legacy (Cramer 1999).

57. UNDP 2004. This reliance on weather-dependent products not only dramatically increases Mozambique's economic vulnerability, but makes it particularly susceptible to hydrometeorological shocks and stresses. The agriculture, fishing, and forestry sectors employ roughly 80 percent of the population (EIU 2004b).

58. UNDP 2004.

59. Tarp et al. 2002: 20. Even after independence, there was extraordinarily little accumulation of technical and management expertise among Mozambicans. Civil war, extended drought during the 1980s, central planning policies, and the mass exodus of skilled workers also created serious obstacles to sustained economic growth (United Nations 1995; Biggs et al. 1999).

60. Stasavage 1999.

61. EIU 2004b.

62. Stasavage 1999.

63. Kaufmann et al. 2004.

64. Lopez-Claros 2004–2005; Stasavage 1999.

65. The murder of investigative journalist Carlos Cardoso, a scandal in which President Chissano's son was deeply implicated, was a powerful reminder of the fragility of press freedom in Mozambique.

66. Stasavage 1999: 10.

67. In Mozambique, the problem is not only the number of regulations but also their vagueness, which confers even more discretionary power on bureaucrats (Stasavage 1999).

68. World Bank 2004: 19; Stasavage 1999.

69. Acemoglu et al. 2001.

70. Bowren 2000.

71. Cramer 1998; Tanner 2002; Norfolk et al. 2003. Abolition of private land ownership is a legacy of the postcolonial backlash seen in many newly independent African states.

72. Lopez-Claros 2004–2005.

73. O'Laughlin 1996; Tanner 2002.

74. Jenkins 2000; Sidaway and Power 1995.

75. Sidaway and Power 1995: 1471.

76. UN-HABITAT.

77. UN-HABITAT 1998.

78. Sidaway and Power 1995: 1469.

79. This description draws heavily on Christie and Hanlon 2001 and personal communication with the USAID director of natural resource management, David Hess.

80. Christie and Hanlon 2001: 106–108.

81. Christie and Hanlon 2001: 117.

82. Christie and Hanlon 2001: 1.

83. Christie and Hanlon 2001. See also B. Martin et al. 2001.

84. Christie and Hanlon 2001: 2.

85. Christie and Hanlon 2001: 4.

86. Barkham 2002.

87. On colonialism in the South Pacific, see Mackensen and Hinrichsen 1984.

88. United Nations 2003: 21.

89. Briguglio 1995; Atkins et al. 2000.

90. Briguglio 1995: 1619.

91. Atkins et al. 2000.

92. UNDP 2002b.

93. Adger 2001: 925.

94. WMO 2001.

95. Bigio 2002: 4.

96. Nicholls et al. 1999.

97. During the 1990s, Tuvalu was hit by seven cyclones.

98. CRED-OFDA 2004.

99. CIA Factbook 2004. Neighboring Tonga watched 3,000 of its citizens become homeless after Cyclone Hina in 1997 (CRED-OFDA 2004).

100. Conisbee and Simms 2003. Barkham (2002) ties the response of many locals to sea level rise to its religiosity: "Tuvalu is one of the most Christian countries in the world ... more than 97 percent of the islanders are Christians." Paani Laupepa, assistant secretary of Tuvalu's environment department, reports that because of the belief in God's covenant after Noah's flood that he would not flood the earth again, "We are trying to explain the scientific facts to Christian people. It is coming through slowly."

101. J. Lewis 1990; Cutter 1996; Pelling and Uitto 2002.

102. Wisner et al. 2004.

103. Atkins et al. 2000.

104. Hydrometeorological instability has also affected local health conditions. The IPCC reports that tropical islands have experienced a higher incidence of vector- and waterborne diseases because of changes in temperature and rainfall (IPCC 2001b). Of particular concern is the spread of dengue and malaria (IPCC 2001b). Given higher temperatures, increased precipitation, and lack of access to clean water, these projections seem almost certain.

105. WHO 2004.

106. Associated Press 2004.

107. Gauthier 1986.

108. Louisiana Department of Health and Hospitals 2005. *Vital Statistics of All Bodies at St. Gabriel Morgue 11/18/2005.* http://www.dhh.louisiana.gov/offices/publications/pubs-145/DECEASED%20Victims%20released_11-18-2005_publication.pdf

109. Roberts and Toffolon-Weiss 2001, chapter 2.

110. Roberts and Toffolon-Weiss 2001: 26.

111. Roberts and Toffolon-Weiss 2001: 15.

Chapter 4

1. Achenbach 2004.

2. Kaul et al. 2003: 175; UNEP 2002.

3. IFRC 2000; Mathur et al. 2004: 6; Pelling 2004.

4. We focus on climate disasters, not stresses like malaria, and more erratic rainfall because the latter are not so certainly tied to climate change.

5. Again, we can be agnostic about whether these past events are the result of past climate change; rather, they reflect precisely the types of disasters predicted in IPCC and many other scientific analyses to increase as the climate warms.

6. Clark et al. 2000.

7. Watts and Bohle 1993: 45.

8. Clark et al. 2000: 3.

9. Moravscik (2003b) sharply criticizes the so-called everything matters approach.

10. Wisner et al. 2004: 10.

11. Clark et al. 2000; Hewitt 1995.

12. McLaughlin and Dietz forthcoming: 4.

13. Adger and Kelly 1999; Bohle et al. 1994; Downing et al. 2001; Handmer et al. 1999; Leichenko and O'Brien 2002; Wisner et al. 2004.

14. Wisner et al. 2004: 5.

15. In Central America, deforestation is a structural problem. Large numbers of poor people, who are forced onto more marginal lands because of government favoritism toward large landowners and multinational corporations, must deforest steep slopes to eke out an existence on subsistence and cash crops. In the process, they remove the very tree roots and topsoil that stabilize the ground beneath their feet. Even as early as 1975, flooding in deforested areas had resulted in large-scale human disaster (2,500 deaths) in Honduras (Blaikie et al. 1994: 149).

16. Blaikie et al. 1994; Susman et al. 1983; Boyce 2000.

17. Sen 1999: 8.

18. Keen 1994.

19. Mitra 2002; Drury and Olson 1998; Olson and Drury 1997; Olson 2000.

20. Chambers 1989; Bates and Pelanda 1994; Buttel 1996; Kates 1971; Corbett 1988.

21. McLaughlin and Dietz forthcoming: 10. Also see Adger 1999.

22. Acemoglu et al. 2001, 2002; Engerman and Sokoloff 2002; Bunker 1985; Roberts et al. 2004.

23. Adger 1999: 250.

24. O'Keefe et al. 1976: 566.

25. Schiller et al. 2001; Kasperson and Kasperson 2001.

26. Other authors emphasize insured economic losses, uninsured losses, biodiversity loss, or temporary disruptions in livelihood; for example, a flooded basement or a tree on one's roof.

27. Alexander 2000: 13.

28. Systematic collection of data on the strength of climate-related natural hazards would be extremely valuable for future modeling. Kahn (2005) has attempted to do this for geophysical disasters.

29. Because of space limitations, further justification for each causal link is available from the authors.

30. Kahn 2005; Bigio 2002; World Bank 2003; Wisner et al. 2004.

31. UNCTAD 2003.

32. Bunker 1985; Shafer 1994; Karl 1997; Ross 1999; Roberts and Grimes 1999.

33. Rodrik et al. 2004; Acemoglu et al. 2001, 2002.

34. Some of the other types of export dependence are "point source" economies, "diffuse" economies, coffee and cocoa economies, and dependence on a narrow range of manufactures (Isham et al. 2005). Our UNCTAD index does not allow us to test which of these narrow export bases lead to worse vulnerability to climate disasters; that would be an excellent follow-up to this research.

35. UNCTAD 2001. For more on the construction of this index, see Finger and Kreinin 1979.

36. Kahn 2005; Yohe and Tol 2001.

37. One public health study in the United States found that states with higher inequality experienced higher death rates, which the authors conjectured was because when the gap is wider, the wealthy—who have private schools, health care facilities, and even security forces—can ignore the plight of the poor (Kaplan et al. 1996; Kennedy et al. 1996; Kawachi and Kennedy 2002).

38. Adger 2001.

39. Cross 2001; Wisner et al. 2004.

40. Knack and Keefer 1997.

41. Rothstein 2002.

42. Alesina et al. 1999.

43. Adger 1999: 255.

44. Ben Wisner (2001c) suggests that the top-down approach of Cuba's socialist government has been equally, if not more, effective than that of many democratic governments. In the run-up to Hurricane Michelle, the government evacuated 700,000 people from the least storm-resistant homes, cut the electricity and water supply to avoid electrocution and water contamination, educated the public, and mobilized neighborhood clean-up groups. The result: only five reported deaths. A similar effort was made in preparation for Hurricane Ivan in 2003—when 1.9 million people were evacuated from the island's western end—with even more impressive results: no reported deaths.

45. World Bank 2003. The index we use measures income inequality, not accumulated wealth. The latter might be a better proxy for ability to cope with disasters, but is far less available for cross-national analysis.

46. Acemoglu et al. 2004; Acemoglu 2003; Acemoglu and Robinson 2006.

47. E.g., Wolf and Hansen 1972; Roberts and Thanos 2003.

48. Institutions are of course slow moving, often taking hundreds of years to develop.

49. de Janvry 1981; Wolf and Hansen 1972.

50. Mitchell 1999.

51. Maskrey (1993: 463) argues that emergency response systems in Latin America demonstrate strong urban bias and "are totally inadequate for dealing with the very different characteristics of disasters in peripheral regions."

52. UNDP 2003.

53. Acemoglu et al. 2001, 2002.

54. Bunker makes similar points about extractive colonies (1985). Earlier discussion over Latin American cities and colonial control included Portes and Walton 1976; Hay 1977; Morse 1974.

55. IPCC 2001; Pelling 2004.

56. De Soto (2000, emphasis added) explains that "those in the informal sector cannot go to a court of justice to enforce their contracts; *they cannot insure themselves against risk*; and they cannot acquire secure property rights."

57. Wisner et al. 2004.

58. O'Driscoll et al. 2003: 72.

59. Acemoglu et al. 2001: 1370.

60. Prescott-Allen 2001.

61. Lappé et al. 1998: 42–43.

62. Calvert and Calvert 1999: 9.

63. Nicholls 1995; Timmerman and White 1997; Pelling and Uitto 2002.

64. Nicholls et al. 1999; Solomon and Forbes 1999; Kasperson and Kasperson 2001a, 2001b; Schiller et al. 2001.

65. WRI 2004.

66. See e.g., Sassen 2000.

67. Turner et al. 1996; Hausmann 2001.

68. Wisner et al. 2004: 247.

69. Acemoglu et al. 2001, 2002.

70. Besley and Burgess 2002; Kahn 2005.

71. Mitra 2002: 48. Also see Olson and Drury 1997; Drury and Olson 1998; Olson 2000; Platt 1999.

72. Wisner et al. 2004.

73. Kartlekar 2003.

74. A. Frank 1969; Shafer 1994; Karl 1997; Bunker 1985; Acemoglu et al. 2001, 2002; Engerman and Sokoloff 2000, 2002; Ross 1999, for example.

75. Engerman and Sokoloff 2002.

76. Acemoglu et al. 2001. Also see Acemoglu and Robinson 2000; Engerman and Sokoloff 2002.

77. Reuschemeyer et al. 1992: 6.

78. Paul 1992.

79. UNDP 2003.

80. Dunning 2005.

81. Ross 1999; Karl 1997.

82. Dunning 2005.

83. Ross 1999; North 1990; Karl 1997; Shafer 1994; Roberts et al. 2003, 2004.

84. Viola 1992; Roberts and Thanos 2003.

85. See Karl 1997; Shafer 1994; and Roberts and Grimes 1999.

86. However, removing zeros actually reduced the explanatory power of our models for percentage of the population affected by climate-related disasters. Doing so has some justification, but also means we are explaining the extent of death by disaster, not whether these disasters were recorded. Our solution is to report both. We discuss this issue shortly.

87. Because of the close correlation between per capita GDP and the number of NGOs and our index of property rights, we had to run separate models for these variables.

88. CRED-OFDA 2004, emphasis added.

89. Notice that this does not appear to be picking up the effect of the highly correlated per capita GDP. Model 10 shows per capita GDP registering a negative but statistically insignificant effect. In other estimations, per capita GDP similarly showed up as negative and statistically significant.

90. For models 9–17, in order, the total indirect effects of a narrow export base on these dependent variables were 0.33, 0.29, 0.34, 0.15, 0.21, 0.30, 0.41, 0.37, and 0.38.

Chapter 5

1. Khastagir 2002.

2. Khastagir 2002.

3. Ott 2003.

4. UNFCCC 2002.

5. UNFCCC 2002.

6. Friends of the Earth, UK 2002.

7. Shah 2002.

8. Ott 2002: 3.

9. Ott 2002: 9.

10. R. E. Kasperson et al. 2001.

11. To be more precise, here we are investigating only carbon dioxide emissions from fossil fuels and from cement manufacturing and flaring waste gas (CDIAC 1999). The latter two categories account for only about 3 percent of industrial CO_2 emissions, and carbon dioxide is currently estimated to cause over 70 percent of greenhouse warming. Commercial and residential sources are included, but emissions from changes in land use (mostly deforestation, which accounts for about an additional 25 percent of carbon releases, are not included.

12. While much of this is the result of the normal process of an emerging field of science, some of this debate about the validity of different measures and estimates has been fueled by those concerned about their nations or industries being forced to meet stringent requirements under any particular system of measurement. After the science is fed into the agreement-making system, the real political implications of who would win and who would lose create more controversy (Gelbspan 2004; Levy and Egan 1998, 2003; Levy and Kolk 2002).

13. In other cases, notions of fairness are also used strategically to achieve political aims.

14. One AOSIS delegate from Samoa puts it this way: "We're motivated by survival. We're motivated by the threat of extinction."

15. "Given the array of differentiation rules, coupled with the lack of consensus on any one of them, it is easy to understand why the literature depicts the application of principles of justice in international relations as hotly debated, disputed, and often unattempted solution" (Blanchard et al. 2003: 285).

16. Blanchard et al. 2003.

17. Biermann 1999; Blanchard et al. 2003; Müeller 1999; Zartman et al. 1996; Rose et al. 1998. Blanchard et al. (2003: 286), for example, argue that

"any future burden-sharing agreement involving developing countries will probably be based on a complex differentiation scheme combining different basic rules."

18. Roberts 1996a,b; Roberts and Grimes 1999; Roberts et al. 2004.

19. The year 1990 was chosen because climate science became well known then, with the first assessment report of the Intergovernmental Panel on Climate Change.

20. Because national emissions can vary greatly, depending on economic conditions in any year, the target date of 2010 was expanded into a five-year average of 2008–2012.

21. Goldstein and Keohane 1993.

22. Aslam 2002: 176.

23. Figure 5.2 shows how of the more than 189 billion tons of carbon dioxide currently being released into the atmosphere from fossil fuel use, 120 billion tons come from the 24 high-income nations at the top of the world's class structure. The 115 low-middle and low-income nations only emit a total of 45 billion tons. Fifty-three middle- and high-middle income nations emit only about 24 billion tons.

24. Müller 2001a, 2001b; Albin 2003.

25. Albin 2001, 2003; Gauthier 1986.

26. Albin 2003: 373.

27. White House, 2002a.

28. White House, 2002b.

29. Gauthier 1986.

30. Stavins 2004: 8.

31. Kim and Baumert 2002. Southern nations view pressure for scheduled emission reduction commitments as part of a larger Northern crusade to rein in their economic development. Former UNFCCC Secretariat staff member Joanna Depledge (2002: 56) writes that "[a]bsolute caps on emissions are generally viewed, especially by developing countries themselves, as caps on development."

32. See Roberts and Grimes 1997; Roberts et al. 2003. Figure 5.2 shows how the most carbon-intense nations in terms of CO_2/GDP are the poorest, and the most efficient are the most wealthy. This suggestive pattern allows many scholars to project that efficiency improvements will sweep around the world with prosperity, a point we will return to shortly.

33. Baumert et al. 2003: 6.

34. Harlan L. Watson, senior climate negotiator and special representative and head of the U.S. delegation, remarks to the Eighth Session of the Conference of Parties (COP-8) to the UN Framework Convention on Climate Change, New Delhi, India, October 25, 2002.

35. Dobriansky 2003.

36. Two groups have been promoting the idea of a per capita framework for years. The Global Commons Institute, led by Aubrey Meyer, has been promoting a contraction-and-convergence approach that makes stringent demands for reductions on the global North, but allows a transition period and a lot of tradable permits to emit greenhouse gases in the short-term transition period. The other group, with perhaps more leverage because of their location in New Delhi, India, is the Centre for Science and the Environment, led by Anil Agarwal and Sunita Narain. More recently, a third group called EcoEquity has been forcefully arguing for a per capita climate accord, saying it would be efficient, fast, equitable, and global. They argue that nations such as China will never agree to unequal limits on emissions, and so "climate equity, far from being a 'preference,' is essential to ecological sustainability" (Athanasiou and Baer 2002: 74–75). To be sure, it is difficult to imagine any rapid convergence of nations where one nation is consuming twice the fuel and emitting twice the carbon dioxide of another. This is why table 5.1 and figures 5.1 and 5.2 reveal such a desperate picture; so many of the world's people emit so little, while a very few emit so much.

37. Other rich countries (e.g., Japan, Norway, Iceland, Poland) would reportedly accept the per capita principle if it were integrated into a larger approach (i.e., a multisectoral, menu approach) (Baumert 2002).

38. Grubb et al. 1999: 270. The European Parliament has advocated a "progressive convergence towards an equitable distribution of emission rights on a per capita basis by an agreed date in the next century" (cited in Baumert et al. 2003: 182).

39. Baumert 2002.

40. Grubb et al. 1999.

41. Population Action International 1998.

42. Data for the current analysis come from the World Bank and from the Carbon Dioxide Information and Analysis Center (CDIAC 2000, and updated in 2003). CDIAC's estimates of CO_2 emissions from industrial activities by country were converted to kilos of carbon and are based largely on energy consumption figures.

43. This book and nearly all the analysis and discussion of emissions inequality focuses on inequality among nations. However, it is important to acknowledge and suggest future research on inequality of emissions within nations. We currently lack much data on intracountry variation in carbon dioxide emissions, especially in the poor nations, but Loren Lutzenheizer's 1996 analysis shows how U.S. citizens with incomes over $75,000 emitted nearly 4 times the amount of carbon dioxide as those whose income is under $10,000. We lack analysis on this inequality within other nations, but if the average American emits 540 times more than the average residents of Chad, Ethiopia, Afghanistan, Burundi, Cambodia, Mali, and Zaire (table 5.1), 10,000–100,000 or more poor residents of these nations most likely emit as much as one millionaire in the United States. In most poor nations there are wealthy elites who emit at levels near or exceeding

those of the average citizen of wealthy nations like the United States, so it can be said with confidence that the world's richest people cause emissions thousands of times greater than those of the world's poorest.

44. The "polluter pays" principle was endorsed by all OECD countries in 1974 (OECD 1974).

45. La Rovere et al. 2002: 158. Since the late 1990s, the Brazilian proposal has been significantly revised with improved understanding of how carbon dioxide is absorbed and released by the oceans, land, and plants.

46. CDIAC 1999.

47. Neumayer 2000.

48. CDIAC 1999.

49. La Rovere et al. 2002.

50. Group of 77 2000a, emphasis added. On the South's perception of responsibility for anthropogenic climate change, see Williams 1997; Najam 1995; Agarwal and Narain 1991; Parikh 1992a,b; O. Young 1994; Grubb et al. 1999; Paterson 2001; Grubb 1995; Miller 1995; Porter and Brown 1991; Von Moltke and Rahman 1996; Tangen et al. 2001; Gupta 2001.

51. Baumert et al. 2002.

52. Rovere et al. 2002: 168.

53. Readers should note that more nations are missing from this analysis; we have 150 cases instead of the 170–190 for the other measures.

54. Sagar and Najam 1998; Müller 2001a,b; Blanchard et al. 2003; Biermann 1999; Wiegandt 2001; Zartman et al. 1996; Rose et al. 1998; Albin 2001, 2003.

55. Stavins 2004; Aldy et al. 2003; Baumert et al. 2002, 2003. "[A]ny future burden-sharing agreement involving developing countries will probably be based on a complex differentiation scheme combining different basic rules," write Blanchard et al. (2003: 286).

56. Barrett and Stavins 2003. Take for instance the precarious position in which small island states find themselves.

57. Bartsch and Müller 2000. Critics charge that even this approach freezes North-South inequalities and is therefore unlikely to build consensus (A. Evans 2002).

58. S. Gupta and Bhandari 1999; TERI 1997; Blanchard et al. 2003; Baumert et al. 2003: 190; Agarwal et al. 1999; Ybema et al. 2000; Ringus et al. 2002; Torvanger and Ringius 2002; Torvanger and Godal 2004.

59. Claussen and McNeilly 1998.

60. Not surprisingly, developed countries tend to fall under the former category and developing countries under the latter.

61. Groenenberg et al. 2001: 1008.

62. Groenenberg et al. 2001; A. Evans 2002.

63. Sijm et al. 2000; Ybema et al. 2000.

64. Biermann 1999; Wiegandt 2001; Blanchard et al. 2003; Müller 1999; Zartman et al. 1996; Rose et al. 1998. Blanchard et al. (2003: 286), as we noted, argue that "any future burden-sharing agreement involving developing countries will probably be based on a complex differentiation scheme combining different basic rules."

65. Neumayer 2000: 191. It is estimated that the developing world holds 91 percent of the world's natural capital, while the developed world holds just 9 percent (Kunte et al. 1998).

66. Selden and Song 1994; Grossman and Krueger 1995; World Bank 1992; Holtz-Eakin and Selden 1995; Roberts and Grimes 1997; Heil and Selden 2001; Neumayer 2004.

67. As we have discussed elsewhere: Roberts et al. 2004; Roberts and Grimes 1997.

68. We remind readers that our measures of carbon dioxide emissions are based on industrial sources from the burning of fossil fuels, and exclude emissions from deforestation and other land use changes.

69. We are of course aware of the extensive efforts to create better indicators of economic prosperity or development, but here we are examining only the raw size of national economies.

70. Inglehart 1995.

71. Neumayer 2004.

72. He argues that people in hot areas are able to manage without the kind of space heating that is required in severely cold areas to merely survive (Neumayer 2004).

73. World Bank 1992; Bhagwati 2004; Neumayer 2002b; de Soysa and Neumayer 2005. For a contrary view, see Botcheva-Andonova et al. 2004; Roberts and Grimes 1997; Muradian and Martinez-Alier 2001a.

74. Heil and Selden 2001.

75. Kaufmann et al. 2004.

76. Roberts et al. 2003.

77. Roberts et al. 2004.

78. Roberts and Grimes 1997.

79. Heil and Selden 2001.

80. Neumayer 2004.

81. Adriaanse et al. 1997; Ruth 1998; Inglehart 1995.

82. Rich nations indeed continue to consume more natural resources than ever before by almost any measure. In 1998, the richest 20 percent of the world's population consumed 46 percent of all meat and fish, 65 percent of all electricity, 58 percent of all energy, 74 percent of all telephones, 84 percent of all paper, and 87 percent of all cars. The poorest 20 percent, by contrast, consumed less than 10 percent of all these products (UNDP 1998). Also see Parikh 1992a; Rahman et al. 1992; Princen et al. 2002. There is a strong body of evidence that suggests

that many of these resources originate in poor and middle-income nations. Arden-Clarke (1992) reports that two-thirds of all primary commodity exports come from the Third World. However, dollar-dependent export measures mask even deeper inequalities. Measuring national export-import ratios in terms of physical weight, the developed world becomes a much greater net importer of environmentally intensive products (Andersson and Lindroth 2001; Fischer-Kowalski and Amman 2001).

83. Giljum and Eisenmenger 2004.

84. World Bank 1992; Neumayer 2002b; de Soysa and Neumayer 2005; Bhagwati 2004.

85. Cabeza-Gutés and Martinez-Alier 2001; Hornborg 1998a,b, 2001; Muradian et al. 2002; Simms 2002; Muradian and O'Connor 2001; Russi and Muradian 2003; Martinez-Alier 2003; Muradian and Martinez-Alier 2001a, 2001b, 2001c; Sachs 1999; Heil and Selden 2001; Bunker 1985, 1996a,b; Parks and Roberts 2005; Giljum and Eisenmenger 2004; Giljum and Hubacek 2001, 2004a,b; Giljum 2003, 2004; Bringezu 2002, 2003; Bringezu and Schütz 2001a,b,c; Hubacek and Giljum 2003; Andersson and Lindroth 2001; Damian and Graz 2001.

86. According to Røpke (1999: 45), "prices are distorted not only because of the present [environmental] externalities, but also because such externalities have existed for nearly two centuries and have been built into the social and physical structures of society as accumulated externalities." Also see Cabeza-Gutés and Martinez-Alier 2001.

87. Fischer-Kowalski and Amann 2001; Giljum and Eisenmenger 2004.

88. Smith 1991; Parikh 1992a, 1995; Martinez-Alier 1995; Sachs 1999; Agarwal and Narain 1991, 1999, 2001; Athanasiou and Baer 2002; J. Clapp 2002; Princen et al. 2002; Borrero Navia 1994; Robleto and Marcelo 1992; Guha and Martinez Alier 1997; Agyeman 2003; Carpintero 2002, 2004; McLaren 2003; Parks and Roberts 2005; Russi et al. 2003; Alcántara and Roca 1999; Opschoor 1995; Munasinghe 1999; Bermann 1999.

89. Martinez-Alier 2003. Acción Ecológica 2003.

90. Simms et al. 2004; Sachs 2002.

91. Braudel 1981; Wallerstein 1972; A. Frank 1969. More recently, see Hornborg 1998a,b; Giljum and Eisenmenger 2004.

92. Roberts and Thanos 2003.

93. Giljum 2003: 17.

94. Roberts et al. 2004. Also see chapter 6.

95. Bunker 1985: 24

96. Bunker 1985: 33.

97. Bunker (1985) tried to extend thermodynamic law to global political economy. He argued that energy and matter are "withdrawn from the natural environment of the extractive economies and flow toward and are concentrated in

the social and physical environments of the productive economies, where they fuel the linked and mutually accelerating processes of production and consumption." His argument, then, could be characterized as one of social entropy. Industrial capitalism, with all of its high-quality energy outputs (i.e., material wealth) requires a constant flow of low-entropy inputs from other areas, in particular the periphery and semiperiphery, which house the majority of low-entropy stocks.

98. Some would argue that this is nowhere more evident than in the climate change arena, where core nations undercompensate peripheral nations for their critical energy sources and at the same time insist that they sequester their "luxury emissions" by reforestation projects, potentially creating green deserts that provide limited job opportunities and economic progress in the short term.

99. Muradian et al. 2002; Giljum 2004.

100. Giljum 2004. Amann et al. 2002; Chen and Qiao 2001; Hammer and Hubacek 2002. Rayen Quiroga of El Instituto de Ecología Política in Santiago likens Chile's rapid economic ascendance to that of the Asian Tigers. However, their natural resource-intensive development path has left them with the infamous title "El Tigre sin Selva," or "the Tiger without a Jungle" (Quiroga 1994).

101. Giljum 2004.

102. Muradian and Martinez-Alier 2001a,b.

103. Muradian and Martinez-Alier 2001a.

104. Bringezu and Schütz 2001a,b,c.

105. Giljum and Eisenmenger 2004: 84, emphasis added. The United States is different, they say, because it exports more raw materials than most developed nations.

106. Andersson and Lindroth 2001.

107. Ruth 1998.

108. Fisher-Kowalski and Amman 2001; Muradian et al. 2002. In a recently published article, Giljum and Eisenmenger suggest that the North's ecological debt is accumulating at an accelerating rate. They also point out that "[t]he implementation of a strategy of *absolute dematerialization* would lead to radical changes of economic structures in both North and South and to price changes on international commodity markets" (2004: 92).

109. One might take a look at a social and physical quality of life index per unit of pollution; see Rosa and Krebill-Prather 1995 for some examples of such analysis for higher-income nations.

110. Shafer's argument provides an excellent response to critics on the one side who maintain that dependency theory was wrong to say development is impossible and those on the other, who challenge neoliberal arguments that with the correct policy choices by planners, development is possible everywhere. While still quite preliminary, Shafer's leading-sector approach provides a good starting point from which to build a new comparative political economy that acknowledges both structural constraints on states and the agency of national actors (an evolving goal of world-systems theorists).

111. Shafer 1994: 2. Shafer distinguishes between sectors that are high in capital intensity and economies of scale, or low in these and therefore more flexible. Taking case studies of mining in Zambia, coffee production by peasants in Costa Rica, plantation crops in Sri Lanka, and light manufacturing in South Korea, Shafer discovers that countries forced into operations requiring a large amount of capital will be highly vulnerable to world prices, transnational corporations, paralyzing foreign debt, and a boom-and-bust cycle. This explains disastrous experiences in Sri Lanka and Zambia, while the governments of South Korea and Costa Rica have much more flexibility and control over their destinies.

112. Data are from CDIAC 2003 and Boden, personal communication; World Bank 2002a.

113. E.g., Lipietz 1986; Harvey 1989; Mandel 1980; see Roberts and Hite 2000.

114. Covello and Frey 1990; Reed 1992; Kazis and Grossman 1991; CEC 1996; Roberts and Thanos 2003.

115. E.g., Dewar 1997; CSE 1996; Stevens 1997. One branch of world-systems theory—the commodity chain approach—has examined some economic and social implications of how incremental but revolutionary improvements in communications and transportation have allowed the global sourcing and offshoring of polluting portions of the productive chain (see e.g., Gereffi and Korziniewitz 1994). The findings of the commodity chains researchers might assuage some fears of industry and government planners, since most earnings remain in the core nations in spite of their productive facilities being relocated to the noncore. On the one hand, there is some mostly anecdotal evidence that some firms have moved for environmental reasons and that some national governments in Latin America and elsewhere in the periphery explicitly sought to cultivate lax environmental enforcement as a comparative advantage (see e.g., Roberts 1996a,b). However as a whole, environmental protection measures do not represent a major portion of firms' expenses. Low and Yeats (1992) of the World Bank, for example, estimated that for even the most polluting types of industries, meeting environmental standards of even the strictest nations represents less than 3 percent of operating costs and is usually much less. Furthermore, overall patterns of firm movements by sector have not shown en masse shifts of the polluters to haven nations (Leonard 1988; also, a series of articles have appeared in the Journal of Environment and Development). An important critique of this view is that such broad sectoral averages cloud what is essentially a phenomenon of the margins (David Barkin, personal communication). However, it does in fact appear that many other factors outweigh environmental concerns in most relocations. These include cheap, compliant, and hardworking labor; cheap resources; access to internal markets; and government incentive programs (see e.g., CEC 1996: 123–124).

116. World Bank 1995: 251, emphasis added.

117. World Bank 1995: 251.

118. EO Sources 2004.

119. Finally, twenty-one nations (10 percent) were not classified in export profile in the World Bank report. These nations include several ex-USSR states for which

data were not yet available and several small islands in the Pacific. Where there was information, these nations were included in global totals and analyses for income levels and for levels of debt. They were by necessity excluded from analyses by export sector and path.

120. There is evidence that this may be changing with greater competition between low-wage nations. (Arrighi et al. 2003).

121. The efficiency of the Chinese manufacturing sector, as well as the sheer quantity of Chinese manufacturing exports, has made it increasingly difficult for other developing countries to compete.

122. Arrighi et al. 2003.

123. Wade 2004d: 171.

124. Roberts and Grimes 1997.

125. Gupta 2001.

126. Cited in Tangen et al. 2001: 243.

127. J. Gupta 2001.

128. UNCTAD 1994.

129. Baumert et al. 2003.

130. Stavins (2004: 5, emphasis added). Aldy et al. also underscore the need for a truly global agreement: "If an international (but not fully global) climate policy results in differences in marginal compliance costs among countries, then emissions may "leak" from participating high-cost countries to non-participating low- or zero-cost countries through one of two economic channels. First, a policy may foster comparative advantage for low-cost countries (for example, countries without emissions commitments) in the production of greenhouse-gas-intensive goods and services. There may be a shift in production of greenhouse-gas-intensive output. Some firms may relocate manufacturing plants from countries with emissions commitments (and higher energy costs) to countries without emissions commitments. In this case, countries with commitments may comply with their obligations, but some of their emissions reductions would be offset by increases in emissions in countries without commitments. Second, the higher energy costs associated with compliance would reduce world energy demand, depressing oil and coal prices. Countries without emissions commitments would consume more fossil fuels, offsetting some of the emissions reductions by countries with commitments. Therefore, a 'narrow-but-deep' agreement may not significantly reduce net emissions, but largely redistribute emissions" (2003: 375).

131. Giljum and Eisenmenger 2004.

132. The huge amount of international air travel is a significant issue, however, and deciding who has to count the carbon against their national allowances is still under debate.

133. Imbs and Wacziarg 2003; Wade 2004b.

134. Recent studies of commodity chains trace the source of products back to their component raw materials and follow their transformation and assembly to the point of sale. As noted earlier, this exercise illuminates inequalities in the sys-

tem by documenting at which links in the chains the most benefits accrue (Gereffi and Korzeniewitz 1994). Most poor nations are stuck in very low-value links of supplying cheap labor and cheap resources, while wealthy nations continue to do the high-wage and high-profit stages of research, product development, and marketing.

135. Machado et al. 2001; Muradian et al. 2002.

136. Machado et al. 2001.

137. According to the authors, "[t]he nonmonotonicity holds above and beyond the well-known shift of factors of production from agriculture to manufacturing and on to services.... It is valid whether a sector's size is measured by its share in total employment or whether it is measured by shares in value added. It holds within countries through time as well as in a pure cross section, for a variety of levels of disaggregation and data sources" (Imbs and Wacziarg 2003: 64).

138. Imbs and Wacziarg 2003: 64, emphasis added.

139. Imbs and Wacziarg 2003. It is possible that India will be an enduring exception to this observation, having both made huge investments in high-tech and education and containing enormous supplies of low-wage labor.

140. But see Shadlen 2003.

141. Cited in Barnett et al. 2004.

142. OPEC 1998: 2. Statement by Dr. Rilwanu Lukman, secretary general of OPEC, available at http://www.opec.org. Cited in Barnett et al. 2004.

143. Barnett and Desai 2002.

144. As we said earlier, since there are thirty nations where it would take more than a hundred citizens to match the emissions of one American, and because there are tremendous inequalities within nations on both sides of the comparison, we can say with confidence that one wealthy American contributes thousands, or tens of thousands, more emissions than one poor citizen in these nations.

145. Najam et al. 2003a, 2003b.

146. Najam et al. 2003a.

147. Interestingly, many are dependent upon the import of these products, which suggests another type of future analysis.

148. E.g., Selden and Song 1994; Grossman and Krueger 1995; World Bank 1992; Holtz-Eakin and Selden 1995; Roberts and Grimes 1997; Heil and Selden 2001; Neumayer 2004.

149. Roberts and Grimes 1997.

Chapter 6

1. B-SPAN 2001.

2. B-SPAN 2001.

3. Weiss and Jacobson 1998; Mitchell 1994; Hurrell and Kingsbury 1992.

4. Hurrell and Kingsbury 1992: 1. Critics rightly point out that many nations sign environmental treaties to gain a positive international image, and that the treaties lack viable enforcement mechanisms (Hurrell and Kingsbury 1992; O. Young 1994; Congleton 2002/2003). However, in spite of their many limitations, other scholars argue that international environmental agreements can function as important tools to help foster equitable and efficient strategies to ameliorate the effects of ecological damage (e.g., Mitchell 1994; Weiss and Jacobson 1998; Athanasiou and Baer 2002; Barrett 2003). Because resolving global environmental problems will require international cooperation, we believe there is value in understanding state behavior on environmental treaties regardless of their current effectiveness.

5. Victor and Skolnikoff 1999; Meyer et al. 1997; and Roberts 1996b, 2001.

6. Benedick 1991; Sprinz and Vaahtoranta 1994; O. Young 1994; Susskind 1994; Weiss and Jacobson 1998; Schelling 2002.

7. Mitchell 2002a,b; Sprinz 2004. A few scholars have addressed the puzzle of environmental treaty ratification in a large-N empirical context. However, these studies have either focused on particular treaties, single theories, or subsets of potential signatories (Roberts 1996b; Meyer et al. 1997; Recchia 2001; Neumayer 2002a).

8. We have excluded all bilateral and regional agreements to isolate those cases where all states had the opportunity to participate.

9. Theories are, of course, limited ontologically and epistemologically in the questions that they can address, but international relations commentators observe that even when complementarities are self-evident, opportunities for synthesis are routinely overlooked (and often for highly dubious reasons). See Lake 2002; Moravscik 2003a; Jupille et al. 2003; Tierney and Weaver 2004.

10. For example, Vaillancourt n.d.; and Guimaraes n.d.

11. Keohane 1982, 1984; Axelrod 1984; Oye 1986a,b; Yarborough and Yarborough 1990.

12. O. Young 1994.

13. Keohane 1997; Abbott and Snidal 2000; Simmons 2000.

14. Lipson 1991: 508; Also see Martin 2005.

15. Oye 1986a, 1986b; Keohane 1988; L. Martin 2000. We define a credible commitment as the belief by one party to an international agreement that a potential cooperator will live up to their end of the bargain. Credibility, then, requires that the receiving state make a positive assessment of the sending state's willingness and ability to carry out its promises (Schelling 1960).

16. Following Simmons (2000: 819), we assume that "the acceptance of treaty obligations [represents] . . . a bid to make a credible commitment to a particular policy stance . . . . that, once made [is] reputationally costly for governments to violate." However, some treaties also impose *economic* costs on defectors. The Montreal Protocol is said to contain a credible punishment technology by issuing

both trade sanctions and providing environmental assistance, thus "ensur[ing] that no developing country or transition economy will lose by being party to the agreement...[and] any country will lose by not signing" (Barrett 1999: 216). For a large-N quantitative look at the relationship between environmental aid and environmental treaties, see Parks et al. n.d.

17. Axelrod and Keohane 1986.

18. New institutionalists have studied the relationship between state credibility and electoral structure (Cowhey 1993), regime type (Lake 1991; Fearon 1994; L. Martin 2000; Schultz and Weingast 2003), ideological orientation (Simmons 1994), transparency and government effectiveness (Tierney 2003).

19. Note that many of these unit-level characteristics are ascriptive rather than behavioral. As our argument unfolds, it will become increasingly clear why this is such an important distinction.

20. Sprinz and Vaahtoranta 1994: 79. Also see Fredriksson and Gaston 2000.

21. Dalton 1994, 1.

22. The underlying assumption is that receiving states strategically assess their potential cooperator's environmental vulnerability and civil society strength to determine credibility.

23. Lake 1991.

24. Fearon 1994.

25. Gaubatz 1996.

26. Leeds 1999.

27. L. Martin 2000.

28. Mansfield et al. 2002.

29. Schultz and Weingast 2003.

30. Jensen 2003.

31. Tierney 2003.

32. Lisa Martin's book *Democratic Commitments: Legislatures and International Cooperation* is perhaps the most thorough treatment of this popular hypothesis (Martin 2000).

33. Fearon 1994.

34. Tierney 2003: 50. Implicit in the logic of this argument is that democratic leaders who take on treaty obligations are willing and able to implement their commitments. If this is indeed true and the empirical evidence matches up with theoretical expectations, there would be greater reason to celebrate the current push for democratization in the developing world.

35. Neumayer 2002a.

36. Neumayer 2002a: 140. This alternative argument suggests that democracies will implement better domestic and international environmental policies. The author thus ignores a large body of evidence in the international relations literature on why democracies are better able to make international policy commitments

(of all types). For Neumayer, the defining characteristic of democracies is that they enable environmentalists to influence policy makers, not that they increase the credibility of state commitments.

37. Lake 1991; Fearon 1994; Gaubatz 1996; Leeds 1999; L. Martin 2000; Mansfield et al. 2002; Schultz and Weingast 2003; Jensen 2003; Tierney 2003. A further problem exists with Neumayer's methodology. While the results of his large-*N* empirical study appear robust, the left side of his equation raises serious cause for concern. Participation is measured for only four environmental agreements—the Kyoto Protocol, the Montreal Protocol, the Rotterdam Convention, and the Cartagena Protocol—and the type of cases to which the argument applies is not made clear.

38. For two excellent reviews of the literature, see Mitchell 2002b and Zürn 1998. Notable institutionalist contributions include Haas 1990; Hurrell and Kingsbury 1992; Haas et al. 1993; Keohane and Levy 1996; Mitchell 1994; Schreurs and Economy 1997; Weiss and Jacobson 1998; O. Young 1989, 1994; Sprinz and Vaahtoranta 1994; Victor et al. 1998; Wettestad 1999.

39. Like the drunk who searches for his keys beneath the lampost "because that's where the light is," the inability of rational-choice institutionalism to explain the deeper social determinants of environmental degradation is more a reflection of its epistemological and ontological limitations than some egregious oversight on the part of its proponents. As Snidal (2004: 227) puts it, "[models] are descriptively incomplete and even inaccurate, yet they are tremendously valuable." Indeed, a "good model is a radically simplified description that isolates the most important considerations for the purpose at hand" (2002: 231).

40. Keohane 1984.

41. For example, O. Young 1989; Hurrell and Kingsbury 1992; Haas et al. 1993.

42. Parks and Roberts 2005; Roberts et al. 2004.

43. Most social scientists, we suspect, would agree (at least in principle) that an understanding of agency and structure is necessary for any meaningful representation of our socially complex world (Dessler 1989; Granovetter 1985 and Wendt 1987). Yet the international relations and IEP literatures are awash with rational-choice theorization, which denies by omission the structural positions in which choices are made.

44. Roberts and Thanos 2003.

45. Some useful sources are the review by Shannon 1996; Wallerstein 1974, 1979; Chase-Dunn 1989 and pieces in Roberts and Hite 2000. The world-systems literature has not addressed environmental treaties, and some authors may believe, with realists, that such treaties are mere epiphenomena, corporate and national obfuscations of power relationships. Again, we take an agnostic approach, attempting here to explain participation without judging value.

46. Snidal (2002: 73) provides excellent commentary on this point. In a discipline increasingly dominated by regression equations, one commentator jokes, "History is irrelevant, ... except when it provides a longitudinal data set" (Halliday 1995: 738).

47. Bunker 1985; Shafer 1994; Chew 2001; Roberts and Grimes 1999.

48. Arden-Clarke 1992.

49. P. Evans 1995; Karl 1997. Without recognizing these constraints, our collective understanding of the causes and consequences of environmental degradation and retrogressive environmental policy will remain theoretically lopsided and empirically frail. On the rare occasions when institutionalists have discussed social structure, they have done so only in vague terms. Haas et al. (1993: 7), for instance, make mention of "population pressures, unequal resource demands, and reliance on fossil fuel and chemical products," but these factors are presented as unrelated, free floating, and theoretically ungrounded. They do acknowledge that "while environmental degradation is ultimately the result of aggregated individual decisions and choices, individual choices are responses to incentives and other forms of guidance from governments and other national institutions via laws, taxes, and even normative pronouncements" (1993: 7). Yet notably, there is no discussion of the international structures that guide and constrain behavior.

50. Ross 1999; Leite and Weidmann 1999; Karl 1997; Auty 2000; Acemoglu et al. 2001; Bunker 1985.

51. Ross 1999: 332.

52. Acemoglu et al. 2002: 19.

53. Putnam 1993: 182.

54. Engerman and Sokoloff 2000; Acemoglu et al. 2001.

55. History is a therefore a theoretical starting point, not just evidence to be marshaled in support of extant theories.

56. Acemoglu et al. 2001.

57. D. Frank 1997; Meyer et al. 1997; Boli and Thomas 1999; Yearly 1996.

58. What is not made clear is why countries participate to different extents in this global scientific and diplomatic culture. To say that participation in global culture and institutions causes countries to ratify environmental treaties is to risk offering a spurious explanation; underlying causes may be driving both processes.

59. Congleton (2002/2003: 6) explains that "treaty language is often vague in both environmental and nonenvironmental sections of treaty documents and little provision is made to enforce the environmental commitments of signatory nations. For example, there are no explicit penalties for failure to make contributions to the Rio trust funds, nor a clear statement of the methods by which those funds would be used."

60. Waltz 1979.

61. Grieco 1988; Waltz 1979.

62. To be fair, realist theorization is now much less dismissive of voluntary international cooperation and more focused on developing nuanced power-based explanations (Gruber 2000; DeSombre 2000a,b; Drezner 1999).

63. DeSombre 2000a,b. For a contrasting view, see Zürn 1998.

64. O. Young 1989.

65. DeSombre 2000b.

66. Mitchell 2002b.

67. There appears to be virtually no disagreement among IEP analysts that the revealed environmental policy preferences of wealthy OECD countries have coalesced around issues of global concern (Keohane and Levy 1996; Nielson and Tierney 2003; Parks et al. n.d.).

68. Koremenos et al. 2001.

69. Koremenos et al. 2001.

70. Najam 1995: 262; Kydd 2000a.

71. Barrett 2003.

72. It is no coincidence that Article 4.7 of the UNFCCC makes developing country participation contingent upon *"the receipt of assistance from the industrialized countries"* (Depledge 2002: 38, emphasis added).

73. Sikkink 1993.

74. Jackson 1993.

75. Sprinz and Vaahtoranta 1994: 79. Also see Fredriksson and Gaston 2000.

76. Roberts et al. 2003; Roberts and Grimes 1999; see also Sklair 2002.

77. See Karl 1997; Shafer 1994; Roberts and Grimes 1999.

78. Raymond Vernon's work (1993) also suggests that to understand a country's willingness or hesitance to participate in global environmental agreements, one needs to pay attention to the structure of the state and its dependence on the "polluting elites" that are tied to these export sectors. Vernon's analysis points out the complexities of the internal political structures that affect approaches taken by states, especially whether the division of powers among its branches influences the country's negotiating flexibility.

79. Krasner 1985; Katzenstein 1985.

80. Kaufmann et al. 2004. The list of possible indicators of that internal climate is potentially endless, but here we have chosen Kaufmann et al.'s carefully constructed measure, which captures both the degree to which citizens choose those who govern them and the independent role that the media plays in keeping government accountable. This measure represents an aggregation of numerous political rights, civil liberties, and political process indicators from various think tanks, NGOs, and risk rating agencies.

81. David Frank (1999) uses the number of international scientific and environmental organizations to which a nation belongs. We consider this an inadequate proxy of environmental activism by civil society groups since it excludes domestic environmental NGOs.

82. Haas et al. 1993. At the same time, it is plausible that without an open and accountable government, the voice of civil society will be ignored or marginalized.

83. Meyer et al. 1997; D. Frank 1999.

84. Esty 2001.

85. Rodenburg et al. 1995.

86. Roberts and Grimes 1999.

87. Prescott-Allen 2001.

88. Data for a few variables were lacking in nonrandom ways for different sets of countries. In this less than ideal situation we believe pairwise deletion of missing data creates less bias in the sample. By this method all cases that have data for any two of the variables are used to determine the relationship between these two, and that information is used to estimate the overall model.

89. Dietz and Kalof 1992. These authors also developed a factor score as a second index.

90. Roberts et al. 2004. A significant amount of detail on the construction of the indices is contained in two appendices to that article.

91. See Parks et al. 2006. Significant detail on the construction of this index is also available from the authors.

92. Certainly there are other ways to do so, including when nations signed, how much reduction in greenhouse gases they committed to, or how much they have actually reduced their emissions. We developed an indicator of reductions in emissions from the baseline 1990 to 1999 and found that almost no variables predicted it. Economic growth is an obvious reason to begin with, but this analysis requires further exploration.

93. In this analysis we follow the approach of Boswell and Dixon 1990.

94. These findings are consistent with our earlier models reported in Roberts et al. 2004.

95. New institutionalist critics may suggest that the more relevant domestic institutional variable is the ability of governments to effectively and dependably deliver public goods. Environmental protection is, after all, the archetypal public good and requires strong state capacity. We shared the same suspicion, and Kaufmann et al.'s (2004) measure of government effectiveness seemed ideal for testing this alternative hypothesis. Combining measures of "the quality of public service provision, the quality of the bureaucracy, the competence of civil servants, the independence of the civil service from political pressures, and the credibility of the government's commitment to policies" (Kaufmann et al. 2004: 255), their index captured many of the characteristics that we would expect a "willing and able" government to possess. When we substituted voice and accountability with government effectiveness, and held all else constant in models 1, 3, and 4, we obtained remarkably similar results. In the first model, our "insertion into the world economy" measure had a statistically and substantively significant effect (-0.565) on government effectiveness, accounting for 31 percent of the total variance in our treaty ratification measure. In model 3, government effectiveness and insertion in the world economy were both statistically and substantively significant and explained 74 percent of the variance (adjusted $r^2 = 0.745$). Both of these models performed in a way similar to the original models 1 and 3. Yet it is

interesting that in model 4 only export diversification and civil society strength were statistically and substantively significant, accounting for 74 percent of the variance (adjusted $r^2 = 0.749$). Government effectiveness did, however, exhibit a 0.622 bivariate correlation with the environmental treaty ratification index (adjusted $r^2 = 0.383$).

96. Hurrell and Kingsbury 1992: 10.

97. Koremenos et al. 2001: 1052.

98. Voice and accountability, government effectiveness, and environmental vulnerability also correlated in the expected direction with our environmental treaty ratification index.

99. Meyer et al. 1997.

100. Parks and Roberts 2005.

101. This was also the case with the causal pathway from a world-systems position to environmental vulnerability.

102. Dietz and Kalof 1992.

103. Barrett 2003; Parks et al. n.d.

Chapter 7

1. The Least Developed Countries (LDC) Fund is designated to receive 2 percent of the profits gained through the Kyoto Protocol's mechanism for North-South trading in carbon permits, the Clean Development Mechanism.

2. However, less than half of the OECD countries have even contributed to the LDC Fund.

3. A similar argument could be made concerning the willingness of rich nations to support the Clean Development Mechanism. The chronically underfunded executive board of the CDM has faced some serious difficulties in streamlining their administrative processes. With a few million dollars, it is thought that these problems could be resolved.

4. Connolly 1996; Najam 2002a; Baumert 2002; Parks et al. n.d.

5. Callaghy (2004) coined this phrase.

6. No single policy in this package can be expected to have an unambiguously positive effect on North-South climate negotiations by itself, but we believe the package as a whole would breathe new life into North-South efforts to cooperate on behalf of the global environment.

7. The need to address the broad crisis of global inequality is becoming clear even to the World Bank: "the (often implicit) cost-benefit calculus that policymakers use to assess the merits of various policies too often ignores the long-term, hard-to-measure but real benefits of greater equity. Greater equity implies more efficient economic functioning, reduced conflict, greater trust, and better institutions" (World Bank 2006: 3).

8. IPCC 2001a. There is, of course, much debate on this point, especially in the United States.

9. Baumert et al. 2003. This is the IPCC position. Climate scientists argue that 60–80 percent reductions will be necessary to realize this goal. Others have suggested that 90 percent reductions are necessary (Evans 2002). Considering other greenhouse gases, research suggests that in 2006 we have passed the 420 ppm mark (McCarthy 2006).

10. Of course, some developed countries pose a greater risk than others. Since 1990, U.S. greenhouse gas emissions have risen by more than 14 percent.

11. Blanchard et al. 2003; Viguier 2004.

12. Barrett 2002: 38.

13. Victor 1999; Schelling 2002. Grubb estimates that the South will require financial transfers amounting to $100 billion a year (Grubb 1990: 287).

14. Wiegandt 2001: 114. Also see Barrett 1992. Schelling (1960) offers the example of two individuals who are unable to communicate with each other but are asked to identify a time and a place to meet in New York. Although an almost infinite number of times and locations could be chosen, Schelling finds from experimental evidence that more than half of all respondents choose the same time and place—Grand Central Station's information booth at noon.

15. Barrett 1992.

16. Müller 1999: 3.

17. Empirically, Müller's position does seem to enjoy much support, such as during the acrimonious Kyoto ratification process.

18. Müller 1999, emphasis added. An example of different nations staking out different climate justice positions are the small island states, India/China, United States, Russia, and Brazil.

19. Recent comments from Atiq Rahman reflect this moral ambiguity: "Why should developing countries commit to binding limits on emissions when those who have polluted the most historically are not reducing emissions?...The whole fairness question has been turned upside down."

20. Müller 1999. Since no single actor's fairness principle will be mutually acceptable to all parties, Müller believes that hybrid proposals accounting for conflicting national positions hold the greatest promise for future negotiations. As he (1999: 3, emphasis added) puts it, "we merely need a solution which is commonly regarded as *sufficiently fair* to remain acceptable." On negotiated focal points, also see Garrett and Weingast 1993; Biermann 1999.

21. Kratochwil and Ruggie 1986; Finnemore 1996; Katzenstein 1996; Legro 1997.

22. Zürn 1998: 630.

23. Franck 1995: 706, emphasis added. Constructivists and scholars of international law also argue that because (legitimate) social norms ought to be followed, they will be (Chayes and Chayes 1995: 113; see also Florini 1996: 364).

24. Zürn 1998: 630.

25. Biermann 1999.

26. Najam et al. 2004.

27. Keohane 1984: 102. Also see Albin 2001: 29.

28. DeSombre and Kaufmann 1996: 126.

29. Cited in Sell 1996: 103.

30. Abbott and Snidal 2000.

31. Najam et al. 2004; Goldstein and Keohane 1993; Garrett and Weingast 1993; Schelling 1966.

32. Adil Najam and his colleagues argue that three of the strongest fairness principles available are additionality, polluter pays, and common but differentiated responsibilities. Their research suggests that negotiating efforts are probably best directed toward these principles, not outliers like the right to development and intergenerational equity.

33. WCED 1987: 43. The commission was made up of Six Westerners, three East Europeans, and twelve representatives of poor nations.

34. See Humphry et al. 2002 for some interesting discussion on this definition.

35. Robinson 1992.

36. Parks et al. n.d. Of course what was meant by sustainable development projects may include many other types of funding.

37. Sandbrook 1997; Clémençon 2004; Najam 2002b; Wagner 1999.

38. Clémençon 2004; Najam 2002a.

39. One commentator summarizes the upsides and downsides of sustainable development this way: "The good news is that the South has now totally internalized the concept of sustainable development and has become a persistent advocate for its operationalization.... The bad news is that the concept—at least within the intergovernmental debates—has become more, rather than less, murky over time. Sustainable development was originally deemed powerful— and even threatening—because it suggested the possibility of change in the status quo. Today, it is on the verge of becoming ineffectual because in searching either for definitional precision or for fuzzy sloganeering the concept has become increasingly divorced from its initial action orientation" (Najam 2002a: 47). Almost fifteen years ago, Sharachandram Lele warned policy makers that this was already happening. The author criticized the sustainable development concept as having a far too large a "tent" and becoming a "'metafix' that ... unite[d] everybody from the profit-minded industrialist and risk minimising subsistence farmer to the equity seeking social worker, the pollution-concerned or wildlife-loving First Worlder, the growth-maximising policy maker, the goal-oriented bureaucrat, and therefore, the vote-counting politician" (1991: 613). For more on the sustainable development debate, see Redclift 1987.

40. Sebenius 1983: 314. On the relationship of climate change and sustainable development, see Najam et al. 2003a: Najam and Sagar 1998; Swart et al. 2003; Rayner and Malone 2000; Beg et al. 2002.

41. A final principle that is not yet strongly institutionalized in the existing climate regime deserves greater attention: equality of opportunity. Very simply, if less developed countries feel as though they are not being afforded the same development possibilities as rich countries, we believe civic and cooperative norms will quickly erode. Inequality of opportunity at the national level has been shown to lead to higher crime, lower trust, and more socially destructive behavior, and there are early signs that this is indeed already happening at the global level (World Bank 2005; Zak and Knack 2001; Birdsall 2004; Easterly 2001; Saegert et al. 2002; Putnam 1993, 2000).

42. Arrow 1972; Ostrom 1998.

43. Kydd 2000a: 350. "[I]n looking at the end of the Cold War," he writes, "[we] can observe a series of costly signals leading to mutual trust between former adversaries. The attitudes of Western leaders, press, and publics toward the Soviet Union all underwent a substantial transformation. Soviet military and geopolitical concessions, particularly the [Intermediate-range Nuclear Forces] treaty, the withdrawal from Afghanistan, the December 1988 conventional arms initiative, and the withdrawal from Eastern Europe were decisive in changing overall Western opinion about the Soviet Union. By 1990 most observers viewed the Soviet Union as a state that had abandoned its hegemonic ambitions and could be trusted to abide by reasonably verified arms control agreements and play a constructive role in world politics" (2000: 350). See also Checkel 1997.

44. UNFCCC 1992, Article 3.1.

45. Rossi 1997. Grubb et al. (2001: 49) suggest that by taking early action, rich nations "would effectively lay to rest the myth that [their] climate commitments are mere lip-service."

46. Woods 1999; Streck 1996.

47. These funds are an important start, but require much more stable and substantial funding.

48. Keohane 2001: 6, emphasis added.

49. Sen 1977.

50. Barnett and Dessai 2002; Dessai 2003; Ott 2001, 2003. While there is little adaptation funding available through the Least Developed Countries Fund, a significant financing is coming through the Special Climate Change Fund, the Global Environment Facility, bilateral donors, and especially the CDM.

51. United States Department of the Treasury, Office of Public Affairs 2002.

52. A group of NGOs took a similar position: "The GEF, based on its mandate, should be primarily focused on global environmental priorities, rather than country performance for its resource allocation" (Global Environment Facility 2004).

53. Swart et al. 2003: S32, emphasis added.

54. On the North's desire to compartmentalize environmental issues, see Porter et al. 2000: 132–133. On the inevitability of issue spillover, see J. Gupta 2000a, 2000b; Raustiala 1997; Tangen et al. 2001; Agarwal 2002; Mitchell and Keilbach 2001.

55. Najam (2004a: 231) argues that "although the jury is still out on whether and how the global environment might become a win-win issue, all indications suggest that it can very easily be transformed into a lose-lose proposition."

56. Ott et al. 2004.

57. One must remember that for decades development was about getting a foothold in dynamic niche markets, finding economic areas that offered increasing returns to scale, socializing investment risk, learning by doing, creating new ideas with useful industrial applications, institutional development and experimentation, conflict management, resource mobilization, investment coordination, and creating new productive capacities through industrial policy and export diversification (Hirschman 1958; Gerschenkron 1962; Amsden 1989; Dasgupta and Stiglitz 1985; Wade 1990, 2003b; Imbs and Wacziarg 2003; Chang 2003a, 2003b; Evans 1992; Shadlen 2004). However, during the 1980s and 1990s, an epistemic development consensus began to coalesce around the notion that countries needed to get their policies and institutions right, which was essentially code for securing private property rights, belt tightening, liberalization, deregulation, privatization, and later, good governance. This new development orthodoxy was best summarized by the former chief economist of the World Bank and U.S. Treasury Secretary Lawrence Summers: "The laws of economics . . . are like the laws of engineering. There's only one set of laws and they work everywhere" (cited in George and Sabelli 1994: 106). Albert Hirschman once called this monoeconomics. According to this line of reasoning, there is nothing uniquely difficult about late development, nor is there much context specificity to the process of development. The structural impediments faced by poor nations, such as volatile commodity prices, deterioration in terms of trade, internally unarticulated economies, decreasing returns to scale, and feeble postcolonial institutions are all considered artifacts of an outdated development era.

58. Wade 2003c: 629. H. J. Chang calls this kicking away the development ladder.

59. Wade 2003: 627. Also see UNDP 2003; Rodrik 2001; Stiglitz and Charlton 2004; Shadlen 2004, 2005. Nancy Birdsall, Dani Rodrik, and Arvind Subramanian argue that "if we want to assist LDCs, the way to move forward is not through more onerous conditionality. It's through greater policy space" (earlier iteration of Birdsall et al. 2005a: 11). University of Pennsylvania professor Thomas Callaghy characterizes conditionality this way: "One of the most dramatic, systematic, and intrusive forms of external intervention in developing, especially very poor, countries over the last two decades has been what is usually referred to as 'structural adjustment'" (Callaghy 2004: 4).

60. Wade 2003c: 629.

61. It is of course possible that some rich nations sometimes pursue coordinated strategies with poor nations. However, the rationalist expectation that countries with intense preferences for global environmental protection will adopt integrated approaches is strongly disconfirmed by the empirical evidence in this book.

62. Kydd 2000a. Sebenius (1991) argues for new thinking about climate change and North-South relations.

63. Cited in Kydd 2000a: 346.

64. Kydd 2000a: 346. Another example of new thinking in international relations is post-World War II Keynesianism. Despite having different international economic preferences after the war (the United States favored free trade; Britain favored a more interventionist state), both the Americans and the British eventually adopted John Maynard Keynes's causal beliefs about the world economy (and Harry Dexter White's, to a lesser extent) (Ikenberry 1992).

65. Najam 1995: fn 79.

66. Athanasiou and Baer 2002: 83.

67. Graham 1996: 216.

68. Besley and Burgess (2003: 1452) strongly disagree: "Responsibility for achieving the goal of cutting global poverty rates in half lies firmly at the door of domestic governments. The possibility of concerted international action playing a major role is remote."

69. Shadlen 2004.

70. Household use of solid fuels is a leading cause of mortality and morbidity in the developing world. Yet, with modest investments, such diseases are preventable. Ezzati and Kammen (2002) estimate that a person can be saved from life-threatening indoor air pollution for a few dollars. Widespread dissemination of clean stove technologies would also have a significant impact on global greenhouse gas emissions. As Jorgenson (2006: 1781) points out, "methane emissions are the second largest overall human generated contributor to global warming, and ... [w]hile atmospheric carbon dioxide is two hundred times more plentiful than atmospheric methane, molecule-for-molecule methane is ten times more effective at absorbing and reradiating infrared energy and heat back to the earth's surface, which impacts global warming."

71. For example, roughly 3 million people die every year from exposure to waterborne diseases. Here again, relatively inexpensive donor interventions can have a tremendous impact on human health and productivity.

72. Jamison and Radelet 2005; Birdsall 2004.

73. Collier (2004) provides an interesting commodity support fund proposal.

74. Wade 2003b, 2003c; Birdsall et al. 2005; Rodrik 2004b.

75. Shadlen 2004, 2005.

76. Rustomjee 2004.

77. E.g., Athanasiou and Baer 2002.

78. The IPCC has taken a similar technocratic approach to the topic.

79. In the early 1990s, IPCC chair Bert Bolin lamented that "right now, many countries, especially developing countries, simply do not trust assessments in which their scientists and policymakers have not participated. Don't you think global credibility demands global representation?" (cited in Schneider 1991).

80. Swart et al. 2003: S27–S28.

81. The authors write that "[c]hoices made in the key energy sector are particularly important. While reserves of conventional oil and gas resources are expected to decrease in the course of the century, they can either be replaced or supplemented by coal or unconventional oil and gas resources with higher GHG emissions, or by alternative non-fossil energy resources. These developments will determine if, and at what level, CO_2 concentrations can be stabilized. But also other sectors play a role that should not be forgotten" (Swart et al. 2003: S26–S28).

82. Imports provide countries with access to essential consumer goods as well as equipment and technologies that are too expensive to produce at home, and exports help generate foreign exchange, pay for imports, attract investment, and increase firm efficiency (as exposure to the rigors of the global market increases). That said, "a free trade regime and a rule-based multilateral regime are not one and the same thing" (Rodrik 1998: 18).

83. Ross 1999, 2001; Sachs and Warner 2001; Auty 2001.

84. Ascher 1999; Roberts et al. 2004; Roberts and Grimes 1999.

85. Muradian et al. 2002.

86. Dunning 2005. According to Dunning (2005: 452), "while diversification may be economically rewarding, it can also be politically costly."

87. Dunning 2005: 471.

88. Green 2002: 7.

89. Acemoglu and Robinson (2000, 2003, 2006).

90. Rodrik 2000. Also see R. Mendoza 2003. Nonetheless, this is no quick solution. Khan and Jomo point out that the usefulness of an artificially created rent depends critically upon the political context: "[t]he recipient of the rent has to accept that the state will use its best judgement if things go wrong to decide whether to keep subsidizing, to restructure, or terminate the project" (Khan and Jomo 2000).

91. Gould et al. 2004.

92. Subramanian and Roy 2003; Rodrik 1999a.

93. Acemoglu et al. 2003a.

94. Dessai et al. 2005: 109.

95. UNDP 2003; Shadlen 2005, 2004; Wade 2003c; Rodrik 2001.

96. North 1990; Krueger 1974.

97. In virtually all cases, the rents that neoclassical economists refer to are "monopoly rents," which tend to be growth-retarding. However, many other types of rents, including Schumpterian rents, innovation rents, and monitoring rents can be growth-enhancing (Khan and Jomo 2000).

98. Rodrik 2004b.

99. Hausmann and Rodrik 2003.

100. Rodrik 2004b: 9.

101. Birdsall et al. 2005: 145.

102. See Roger Clapp 1995 for an example of an industrial policy that worked economically but had devastating environmental effects (Giljum 2004).

103. Nations will need to think about complementary investments that would encourage climate-friendly technologies.

104. Similar lessons are being learned by environmentalists within the United States, as they are confronted by the broad agenda of environmental justice communities (see e.g., Roberts and Toffolon-Weiss 2001).

105. Ross 1996: 179.

106. Gibson 1999a,b.

107. Sell and Prakash 2004: 34.

108. Callaghy 2004; Fogarty 2003; Traub 2005.

109. Simms et al. 2004. This coalition includes the New Economics Foundation, Jubilee Research, Oxfam, the World Wildlife Fund, World Vision, Friends of the Earth, Greenpeace, Christian Aid, Action Aid, the Heinrich Böll Foundation, the International Institute for Environment and Development, Corporate Watch, the Centre for Science and the Environment, and EcoEquity.

110. At a recent G-8 Energy and Environment Ministerial Roundtable in London, Gordon Brown emphasized that *"climate change is an issue of justice as much as of economic development.* It is a problem caused by the industrialized countries, whose effects will disproportionately fall on developing countries" (G. Brown 2005, emphasis added). At a Greenpeace Business Lecture in the spring of 2004, James Wolfensohn was asked whether he thought the South should together a financial program for the North to pay back their ecological debt. He responded, "It is a painful issue, and I believe it will come up in the next few years. Can the developing world hold the developed world accountable for their profligate use of fossil fuels? ... Equity is an inevitable issue" (Wolfensohn 2004).

111. Sikkink 1993.

Appendix A

1. OFDA-CRED 2004.

2. CDIAC 2003: T. Boden, personal communication.

3. CDIAC 2003.

4. World Bank 2003.

5. CDIAC 2003; T. Boden, personal communication.

6. Calculated from CDIAC 2003.

7. See Roberts et al. 2004 and Dietz and Kalof 1992.

8. Parks et al. 2006.

9. WRI 2004.

10. United Nations 2004.

11. World Bank 2004.

12. Karlekar 2003.

13. O'Driscoll et al. 2003: 72.

14. O'Driscoll et al. 2003: 72.

15. UNDP 2002c, table A1.2.

16. UNCTAD 2003.

17. Finger and Kreinin 1979.

18. Prescott-Allen 2001.

19. Kaufmann et al. 2004: 254.

20. Kaufmann et al. 2004: 255.

21. Rodenberg et al. 1995.

22. UNCTAD 2003.

23. UNCTAD 2003.

24. UNCTAD 2003.

25. UNCTAD 2003.

26. UNCTAD 2003.

27. Gallup et al. 1999.

28. Calculated from World Bank 2003.

29. See Heil and Selden 2001.

30. Esty 2001.

Appendix B

1. Dunning 2005; Collier 2004.

2. Birdsall and Hamondi 2002.

3. Atkinson and Hamilton 2003.

4. Ross 2004.

5. Engerman and Sokoloff 2002. High levels of income and asset inequality are correlated with lower levels of social trust, provision of public goods, and economic performance (Knack and Keefer 1997).

6. Ross 1999, 2001; Acemoglu et al. 2001; Isham et al. 2005.

7. Isham et al. 2005.

8. Gylfason 2001.

9. Bulte et al. 2005; Atkinson and Hamilton 2003; Roberts et al. 2004.

10. Sachs and Warner 2001.

11. For example, narrow export profiles create inequality, and higher levels of inequality are associated with lower levels of growth, weaker democratic institutions, and higher levels of corruption. Narrow reliance on a small number of

low-value, highly volatile export commodities also consolidates power in a small group of elites, thereby weakening democracy, while democracy leads to higher levels of political stability, rule of law, investor protection, social trust, public good provision, income equality, and greater resilience to exogenous shocks.

12. Isham et al. 2005. For example, Engermann and Sokoloff (2002) argue that specialization in large plantation crops leads to asset inequality. Others have argued that point source resources are the worst types of commodity exports in terms of their impact on institutions and instability (Dunning 2005; Isham et al. 2005).

13. Rodrik 2005.

References

Abbott, Kenneth, and Duncan Snidal. 2000. Hard and soft law in international governance. *International Organization* 54(3): 421–456.

Accion Ecologica. 2003. Que es la deuda ecológica? Available at http://www.accionecologica.org. Accessed July 14, 2003.

Acemoglu, Daron. 2003. Why not a political Coase theorem? Social conflict, commitment, and politics. *Journal of Comparative Economics* 31: 620–652.

Acemoglu, Daron, and James A. Robinson. 2000. Why did the West extend the franchise? Democracy, inequality and growth in historical perspective. *Quarterly Journal of Economics* 115: 1167–1199.

Acemoglu, Daron, and James A. Robinson. 2001. A theory of political transitions. *American Economic Review* 91: 938–963.

Acemoglu, Daron, and James A. Robinson. 2006. *Economic Origins of Dictatorship and Democracy*. Cambridge: Cambridge University Press.

Acemoglu, D., S. Johnson, and J. Robinson. 2001. The colonial origins of comparative development: An empirical investigation. *American Economic Review* 91(5): 1369–1401.

Acemoglu, Daron, Simon Johnson, and James A. Robinson. 2002. Reversal of fortune: Geography and institutions in the making of the modern world income distribution. *Quarterly Journal of Economics* 117: 1231–1294.

Acemoglu, Daron, Scott Johnson, and James A. Robinson. 2003a. An African success story: Botswana. In *In Search of Prosperity: Analytic Narratives on Economic Growth*, edited by D. Rodrik. Princeton, NJ: Princeton University Press.

Acemoglu, Daron, Simon Johnson, James A. Robinson, and Yunyong Thaicharoen. 2003b. Institutional causes, macroeconomic symptoms: Volatility, crises and growth. *Journal of Monetary Economics* 50: 49–123.

Acemoglu, Daron, Simon Johnson, and James Robinson. 2004. Institutions as the fundamental cause of long-run growth. In *Handbook of Economic Growth*, edited by Philippe Aghion and Steven Durlauf. Amsterdam: North-Holland.

Achenbach, Joel. 2004. Quaking in our boots: Can humans weather the growing wave of calamity? *Washington Post* October 6, p. C1.

Acker, Alison. 1988. *The Making of a Banana Republic*. Boston: South End Press.

Adger, W. N. 1999. Social vulnerability to climate change and extremes in coastal Vietnam. *World Development* 27(2): 249–269.

Adger, W. N. 2001. Scales of governance and environmental justice for adaptation and mitigation of climate change. *Journal of International Development* 13: 921–931.

Adger, W. N. 2004. Social capital, collective action and adaptation to climate change. *Economic Geography* 79(4): 387–404.

Adger, W. N., and N. Brooks. 2003. Does global environmental change cause vulnerability to disaster? In *Natural Disasters and Development in a Globalising World*, edited by M. Pelling. Routledge: London, pp. 19–42.

Adger, W. N., and M. Kelly. 1999. Social vulnerability to climate change and the architecture of entitlement. *Mitigation and Adaptation Strategies for Global Change* 4: 253–266.

Adger, W. N., P. M. Kelly, and N. H. Ninh (eds.). 2001b. *Living with Environmental Change: Social Resilience, Adaptation and Vulnerability in Vietnam*. Routledge: London.

Adriaanse, A., S. Bringezu, A. Hamond, Y. Moriguchi, E. Rodenburg, D. Rogich, et al. 1997. *Resource Flows: The Material Base of Industrial Economies*. Washington, DC: World Resources Institute.

Agarwal, Anil. 2002. A Southern perspective on curbing global climate change. In *Climate Change Policy: A Survey*, edited by Stephen H. Schneider, John O. Niles, and Armin Rosencranz. Washington, DC: Island Press, pp. 375–419.

Agarwal, A., and S. Narain. 1991. *Global Warming: A Case of Environmental Colonialism*. New Delhi: Centre for Science and Environment.

Agarwal, A., and S. Narain. 2002. The atmospheric rights of all people on earth. Available at http://www.cseindia.org/html/cmp/cmp335.htm.

Agarwal, A., S. Narain, and A. Sharma (eds.). 1999. *Green Politics: Global Environmental Negotiation-1: Green Politics*. New Delhi: Centre for Science and Environment.

Agarwal, A., S. Narain, A. Sharma, and A. Imchen (eds.). 2001. *Green Politics: Global Environmental Negotiation-2 (Poles Apart)*. New Delhi: Centre for Science and Environment.

Agyeman, Julian (ed.). 2003. *Just Sustainabilities: Development in an Unequal World*. Cambridge, MA: MIT Press.

Alesina, Alberto, and Dani Rodrik. 1994. Distributive politics and economic growth. *Quarterly Journal of Economics* 109: 465–490.

Albin, Cecilia. 2001. *Justice and Fairness in International Negotiation*. Cambridge: Cambridge University Press.

Albin, Cecilia. 2003. Negotiating international cooperation: Global public goods and fairness. *Review of International Studies* 29(3): 365–385.

Albright, Madeleine. 1998. Earth Day 1998. Global problems and global solutions. Speech at the National Museum of Natural History, Washington, DC, April 21, 1998.

Alcántara, V., and J. Roca. 1999. CO_2 emissions and the occupation of the "environmental space." An empirical exercise. *Energy Policy* 27(9): 505–508.

Aldy, Joseph E., Scott Barrett, and Robert N. Stavins. 2003. Thirteen plus one: A comparison of global climate policy architectures. *Climate Policy* 3: 373–397.

Alesina, Alberto, and Dani Rodrik. 1994. Distributive politics and economic growth. *Quarterly Journal of Economics* 109: 465–490.

Alesina, Alberto, and Eliana La Ferrara. 2000. Participation in heterogeneous communities. *Quarterly Journal of Economics* 115(3): 847–904.

Alesina, Alberto, Reza Baqir, and William Easterly. 1999. Public goods and ethnic divisions. *Quarterly Journal of Economics* 114(4): 1243–1284.

Alexander, D. E. 2000. *Confronting Catastrophe: New Perspectives on Natural Disasters*. New York: Oxford University Press.

Amann, C., W. Bruckner, M. Fischer-Kowalski, and C. Grünbühel. 2002. Material Flow Accounting in Amazonia. A Tool for Sustainable Development. Working Paper No. 63. Vienna: Institute for Interdisciplinary Studies of Austrian Universities.

Amsden, Alice H. 1989. *Asia's Next Giant: South Korea and Late Industrialization*. New York: Oxford University Press.

Amsden, Alice, and Takashi Hikino. 2000. The bark is worse than the bite: New WTO law and late industrialization. *Annals of the American Academy of Political and Social Sciences* 570: 104–114.

Andersen, Steinar, and Shardul Agrawala. 2002. Leaders, pushers and laggards in the making of the climate regime. *Global Environmental Change* 12: 41–51.

Andersson, J. O., and M. Lindroth. 2001. Ecologically unsustainable trade. *Ecological Economics* 37: 113–122.

AOSIS (Alliance of Small Island States). 1999. AOSIS homepage. The Impacts of Climate Change on Pacific Island Countries. http://chacmool.sdnp.org/sidsdocs/cc.htm.

Arden-Clarke, C. 1992. South-North terms of trade: Environmental protection and sustainable development. *International Environmental Affairs* 4(2): 122–139.

Arrighi, G., B. Silver, and B. Brewer. 2003. Industrial convergence, globalization and the persistence of the North-South divide. *Studies in Comparative International Development* 38(1): 3–31.

Arrow, K. J. 1972. Gifts and exchanges. *Philosophy and Public Affairs* 1: 343–362.

Ascher, William. 1999. *Why Governments Waste Natural Resources: Policy Failures in Developing Countries*. Baltimore, MD: Johns Hopkins University Press.

Ashton, John, and Xueman Wang. 2003. Equity and climate: In principle and practice. In *Beyond Kyoto: Advancing the International Effort Against Climate Change*. Arlington, VA: Pew Center on Global Climate Change, pp. 61–84.

Aslam, Malik Amin. 2002. Equal per capita entitlements: A key to global participation on climate change? In *Building on the Kyoto Protocol: Options for Protecting the Climate*, edited by Kevin A. Baumert. Washington, DC: World Resources Institute, pp. 175–202.

Associated Press. 2004. Island nation seeks to import residents: Cyclone sent many packing, so Niue looks to neighbor. Available at http://www.msnbc.msn .com/id/3977999/. Accessed January 16, 2004.

Associated Press. 1998. December 5.

Athanasiou, Tom, and Paul Baer. 2002. *Dead Heat: Global Justice and Climate Change*. New York: Seven Stories Press.

Atkins, J., S. Mazzi, and C. D. Easter. 2000. *A Commonwealth Vulnerability Index for Developing Countries: The Position of Small States*. Economic Paper No. 40. London: Commonwealth Secretariat.

Atkinson, G., and K. Hamilton. 2003. Savings, growth, and the resource curse hypothesis. *World Development* 31: 1793–1807.

Auty, R. 2000. How natural resources affect economic development. *Development Policy Review* 18: 347–364.

Auty, Richard M. 2001. *Resource Abundance and Economic Development*. Oxford: Oxford University Press.

Axelrod, Robert. 1984. *The Evolution of Cooperation*. New York: Basic Books.

Axelrod, Robert, and Robert Keohane. 1986. Achieving cooperation under anarchy: Strategies and institutions. In *Cooperation Under Anarchy*, edited by Kenneth Oye. Princeton, NJ: Princeton University Press, pp. 226–254.

Babb, Sarah. 2003. The IMF in sociological perspective: A tale of organisational slippage. *Studies in Comparative International Development* 38(2): 3–27.

Baer, P., J. Harte, B. Haya, A. V. Herzog, J. Holdren, N. E. Hultman, D. M. Kammen, R. B. Norgaard, and L. Raymond. 2000. Climate change: Equity and greenhouse gas responsibility. *Science* 289(5488): 2287.

Bardhan, P. 1989. The new institutional economics and development theory. *World Development* 17(9): 1389–1395.

Bardhan, P. 2000. Institutional impediments to development. In *A Not-So-Dismal Science: A Broader View of Economies and Societies*, edited by M. Olson and S. Kähkönen. Oxford: Oxford University Press, pp. 245–267.

Barham, B., S. G. Bunker, and D. O'Hearn. 1994. *States, Firms and Raw Materials. The World Economy and Ecology of Aluminum*. Madison: University of Wisconsin Press.

Barkham, Patrick. 2002. Tuvalu: going down. *Guardian*, 2/16/2002. Online at http://www.tuvaluislands.com/news/archives/2002/2002-02-16.htm.

Barnett, J., and W. N. Adger. 2003. Climate dangers and atoll countries. *Climatic Change* 61(3): 321–337.

Barnett, J., and S. Dessai. 2002. Articles 4.8 and 4.9 of the UNFCCC: Adverse effects and the impacts of response measures. *Climate Policy* 2(2–3): 231–239.

Barrett, Scott. 1992. "Acceptable" allocation of tradable carbon emission entitlements in a global warming treaty. In *Tradable Entitlements for Carbon Emission Abatement*. Geneva: UNCTAD, pp. 85–113.

Barrett, Scott. 1994. Self-enforcing international environmental agreements. *Oxford Economic Papers* 46: 878–894.

Barrett, Scott. 1999. Montreal v. Kyoto: International cooperation and the global environment. In *Global Public Goods: International Cooperation in the 21st Century*, edited by I. Kaul, I. Grunberg, and M. A. Stern. New York: Oxford University Press.

Barrett, Scott. 2002. Towards a better climate treaty. *World Economics* 3(2): 35–45.

Barrett, Scott. 2003. *Environment and Statecraft: The Strategy of Environmental Treaty-Making.* Oxford: Oxford University Press.

Barrett, Scott, and Robert Stavins. 2003. Increasing participation and compliance in international climate change agreements. *International Environmental Agreements: Politics, Law, and Economics* 3(4): 349–376.

Barro, Robert J., and Jong-Wha Lee. 2002. IMF Programs: Who is chosen and what are the effects? National Bureau of Economic Research Working Paper 8951.

Bartsch, U., and B. Müller. 2000. *Fossil Fuels in a Changing Climate: Impacts of the Kyoto Protocol and Developing Country Participation.* Oxford: Oxford University Press.

Bates, Frederick L., and Pelanda, Carlo. 1994. An ecological approach to disasters. In *Disasters, Collective Behavior, and Social Organization*, edited by R. Dynes and K. Tierney. Newark: University of Delaware Press, pp. 145–162.

Baumert, Kevin A., and Nancy Kete. 2002. Introduction: An architecture for climate protection. In *Building on the Kyoto Protocol: Options for Protecting the Climate*, edited by Kevin A. Baumert. Washington, DC: World Resources Institute, pp. 1–30.

Baumert, Kevin A. (ed.). 2002. *Building on the Kyoto Protocol: Options for Protecting the Climate.* Washington, DC: World Resources Institute.

Baumert, K. A., J. F. Perkaus, and N. Kete. 2003. Great expectations: Can international emissions trading deliver an equitable climate regime? *Climate Policy* 3(2): 137–148.

Beg, Noreen, Jan Corfee Morlot, Ogunlade Davidson, Yaw Afrane-Okese, Tyani Lwazikazi, Fatma Denton, Youba Sokona, Jean Philippe Thomas, Emilio Lèbre La Rovere, Jyoti Parikh, Kirit Parikh and Atiq Rahman. 2002. Linkages between climate change and sustainable development. *Climate Policy* 2(2–3): 129–144.

Bigio, Anthony M. 2002. Cities and climate change. Paper presented at *The Future of Disaster Risk: Building Safer Cities* World Bank Conference. December 2002.

Begley, Sharon. 1992. The grinch of Rio. *Newsweek* June 15, pp. 30–33.

Benedick, Richard E. 1991. *Ozone Diplomacy*. Cambridge, MA: Harvard University Press.

Benedick, Richard. 1998. *Ozone Diplomacy: New Directions in Safeguarding the Planet* (enlarged ed.). Cambridge, MA: Harvard University Press.

Benedick, R. E. 2001. Striking a new deal on climate change. *Issues in Science and Technology Online* (Fall): 71–76.

Berk, Marcel M., and Michel G. J. den Elzen. 2001. Options for differentiation of future commitments in climate policy: How to realise timely participation to meet stringent climate goals? *Climate Policy* 1(4): 465–480.

Bermann, Célio. 1999. *Perspectivas Norte-Sul de Sustentabilidade: Uma Redistribuição Global do Espaço Ambiental/Política Energética e Emissões de CO_2 no Brasil*. Rio de Janeiro: Federação de Órgãos para Assistêcia Social e Educacional.

Bernstein, Johannah, and Melissa Bluesky. 2000. *Highlighting Southern Priorities for Earth Summit 2002*. Workshop Final Report. June 16–18, 2000. Brussels: Heinrich Böll Foundation and Stockholm Environment Institute.

Besley, Timothy, and Robin Burgess. 2002. The political eçonomy of government responsiveness. Theory and evidence from India. *Quarterly Journal of Economics* 117(4): 1415–1452.

Besley, Timothy, and Robin Burgess. 2003. Halving global poverty. *Journal of Economic Perspectives* 17(3): 3–22.

Bhagwati, Jagdish. 2004. *In Defense of Globalization*. New York: Oxford University Press.

Bichsel, Anne. 1994. The World Bank and the International Monetary Fund from the perspective of the executive directors of developing countries. *Journal of World Trade* 28(6): 141–167.

Biermann, Frank. 1999. Justice in the greenhouse: Perspectives from international law. In *Fair Weather?: Equity Concerns in Climate Change*, edited by F. Toth. London: Earthscan, pp. 160–172.

Biggs, Tyler, John Nasir, and Ray Fisman. 1999. Structure and Performance of Manufacturing in Mozambique. RPED Paper No. 107. Washington, DC: World Bank.

Bigio, Anthony M. 2002. Cities and climate change. Paper presented at The Future of Disaster Risk: Building Safer Cities, World Bank Conference. December 2002.

Birdsall, Nancy. 2003. Asymmetric globalization. *Brookings Review* 21(2): 22–27.

Birdsall, Nancy. 2004. Seven Deadly sins: Reflections on Donor Failings. Working Paper No. 50. Washington, DC: Center for Global Development.

Birdsall, Nancy, and Amar Hamoudi. 2002. Commodity dependence, trade, and growth: When "openness" is not enough. Working Paper 7. Washington DC: Center for Global Development.

Birdsall, Nancy, and Robert Z. Lawrence. 1999. Deep integration and trade agreements: Good for developing countries? In *Global Public Goods: International Cooperation in the 21st Century*. Oxford: Oxford University Press, pp. 128–151.

Birdsall, Nancy, Dani Rodrik, and Arvind Subramanian. 2005a. If Rich Governments Really Cared About Development. Working Paper.

Birdsall, Nancy, Dani Rodrik, and Arvind Subramanian. 2005b. How to help poor countries. *Foreign Affairs* 84(4): 136–152.

Blaikie, Piers, Terry Cannon, Ian Davis, and Ben Wisner. 1994. *At Risk: Natural Hazards, People's Vulnerability, and Disasters*. London: Routledge.

Blair, Tony. 2000. Speech delivered to the Green Alliance/CBI Conference on the Environment on 24 October 2000.

Blanchard, O., P. Criqui, A. Kitous, and L. Viguier. 2003. Combining efficiency with equity: A pragmatic approach. In *Providing Global Public Goods: Managing Globalization*, edited by I. Kaul, P. Conceicao, K. Le Goulven and R. U. Mendoza. New York: Oxford University Press, pp. 280–303.

Bohle, Hans-Georg. 2001. Vulnerability and criticality. Perspectives from social geography. *IHDP Update* 2: 1, 3–5.

Bohle, H. G., T. E. Downing, et al. 1994. Climate change and social vulnerability: Towards a sociology and geography of food insecurity. *Global Environmental Change* 4(1): 37–48.

Bohle, H. G., T. E. Downing, and M. J. Watts. 1994. Climate change and social vulnerability: Towards a sociology and geography of food insecurity. *Global Environmental Change* 4(1): 37–48.

Boli, John, and George M. Thomas (eds.). 1999. *Constructing World Culture: International Nongovernmental Organizations since 1875*. Stanford, CA: Stanford University Press.

Borrero Navia, Jose Maria. 1994. *La Deuda Ecológica: Testimonio de una Reflexión*. Cali: Fipma y Cela.

Boswell, Terry, and William J. Dixon. 1990. Dependency and rebellion: A Cross-national analysis. *American Sociological Review* 55(4): 540–559.

Botcheva-Andonova, Liliana, Edward D. Mansfield, and Helen V. Milner. 2004. Racing to the bottom in the post-communist world: Domestic politics, international trade, and environment governance. Paper prepared for APSA 2004 Annual Meeting, Chicago.

Bowen, M. L. 2000. *The State against the Peasantry: Rural Struggles in Colonial and Post-colonial Mozambique*. Charlottesville, VA: University Press of Virginia.

Bowles, Paul. 2002. Asia's post-crisis regionalism: Bringing the state back in, keeping the (United) States out. *Review of International Political Economy* 9(2): 244–270.

Bowles, S., and H. Gintis. 1993. The revenge of Homo oeconomicus. Contested exchange and the revival of political economy. *Journal of Economic Perspectives* 7(1): 83–102.

Boyce, James K. 2000. Let them eat risk? Wealth, rights and disaster vulnerability. *Disasters* 24(3): 254–261.

Bracken, Amy. 2004a. Deadly floods in Haiti blamed on deforestation, poverty. Associated Press. September 22.

Bracken, Amy. 2004b. Ravaged Haiti suffers amid slow pace of relief. Associated Press. September 24.

Brady, H., and D. Collier. 2004. *Rethinking Social Inquiry: Diverse Tools, Shared Standards*. Lanham, MD: Rowman & Littlefield.

Braithwaite, John, and Peter Drahos. 2000. *Global Business Regulation*. Cambridge: Cambridge University Press.

Braudel, Fernand. 1981. *The Structures of Everyday Life*. Vol. 1 of *Civilization and Capitalism, 15th–18th Century*. New York: Harper & Row.

Briguglio, L. 1995. Small island states and their economic vulnerabilities. *World Development* 23: 1615–1632.

Bringezu, Stefan. 2002. Material flow analysis: Unveiling the physical basis of economies. In *Unveiling Wealth: On Money, Quality of Life and Sustainability*, edited by Peter Bartelmus. Dordrecht, Netherlands: Kluwer, pp. 109–134.

Bringezu, S., and H. Schütz. 2001a. Material Use Indicators for the European Union, 1980–1997. Economy-wide Material Flow Accounts and Balances and Derived Indicators of Resource Use. EUROSTAT Working Paper No. 2/2001/B/2. Wuppertal, Germany: Wuppertal Institute.

Bringezu, S., and H. Schütz. 2001b. Total Material Requirement of the European Union. Technical Report No. 55. Copenhagen: European Environmental Agency.

Bringezu, S., and H. Schütz. 2001c. Total Material Requirement of the European Union. Technical Part. Technical Report. No. 56. Copenhagen: European Environmental Agency.

Bringezu, S., and H. Schütz. 2001d. Total Material Resource Flows of the United Kingdom. Final Report. EPG 1/8/62. Wuppertal, Germany: Wuppertal Institute.

Bringezu, Stefan, Helmut Schütz, and Stephan Moll. 2003. Rationale for and interpretation of economy-wide materials flow analysis and derived indicators. *Journal of Industrial Ecology* 7(2): 43–64.

Brooks, N., and W. N. Adger. 2003a. Country-Level Risk Measures of Climate-Related Natural Disasters and Implications for Adaptation to Climate Change. Working Paper No. 26. Tyndall Centre Norwich, UK.

Brooks, N., and W. N. Adger. 2003b. Country-level risk indicators from outcome data on climate-related disasters: An exploration of the EM-DAT database. Tyndall Centre Working Paper. Norwich, UK.

Brooks, N., W. N. Adger, and M. Kelly. 2005. The determinants of vulnerability and adaptive capacity at the national level and the implications for adaptation. *Global Environmental Change* Part A 15: 151–162.

Brown, Gordon. 2005. Keynote address delivered at the G-8 Energy and Environment Ministerial Roundtable in London, on March 16, 2005.

British Broadcasting Corporation (BBC). 2002. BBC Interview with Margot Wallstrom. September 2, 2002. Available online at http://news.bbc.co.uk/2/low/talking_point/forum/2222808.stm#1.

B-SPAN. 2001. Climate change: A challenge for the 21st century. Available at http://www.worldbank.org/wbi/B-SPAN/sub_EM5.htm. Accessed January 5, 2005.

Bulte, Erwin H., Richard Damania, and Robert T. Deacon. 2005. Resource intensity, institutions, and development. *World Development* 33(7): 1029–1044.

Bunker, Stephen. 1985. *Underdeveloping the Amazon: Extraction, Unequal Exchange and the Failure of the Modern State.* Urbana: University of Illinois Press.

Bunker, Stephen. 1996a. Materias primas y la economía global: Olvidos y distorsiones de la ecología industrial. *Ecología Política* 12: 81–89.

Bunker, Stephen G. 1996b. Raw material and the global economy: Oversights and distortions in industrial ecology. *Society and Natural Resources* 9: 419–429.

Busch, M. L., and E. Reinhardt. 2003. Developing countries and General Agreement on Tariffs and Trade/World Trade Organization dispute settlement. *Journal of World Trade* 37(4): 719–735.

Buttel, Frederick H. 1996. Environmental and resource sociology: Theoretical issues and opportunities for synthesis. *Rural Sociology* 61(1): 56–76.

Cabeza-Gutés, M., and J. Martinez-Alier. 2001. L'échange écologiquement inégal. In *Commerce International et Développement Soutenable*, edited by M. Damian and J. C. Graz. Paris: Economica.

Callaghy, Thomas. 2004. Innovation in the Sovereign Debt Regime: From the Paris Club to Enhanced HIPC and Beyond. Washington DC: World Bank Operation Evaluations Department.

Calvert, P., and S. Calvert. 1999. *The South, the North, and the Environment.* London: Pinter.

Cannon, T. 2000: Vulnerability analysis and disasters. In *Floods*, edited by D. J. Parker. London: Routledge, pp. 45–55.

Carbon Dioxide Information and Analysis Center (CDIAC). G. Marland, T. A. Boden, and R. J. Andres. 1999, 2000, and 2003. Global, regional, and national fossil fuel CO_2 emissions. In *Trends: A Compendium of Data on Global Change.* Oak Ridge, TN: Carbon Dioxide Information Analysis Center, Oak Ridge National Laboratory.

Cardoso, Fernando Henrique, and Enzo Faletto. 1979. *Dependency and Development in Latin America.* Berkeley: University of California Press.

Carpintero, Óscar. 2002. La economía española: el 'dragón europeo' en flujos de energía, materiales y huella ecológica, 1955–1995. *Ecología Política* 23: 85–125.

Carpintero, Óscar. 2004. *El Metabolismo Económico de España: Flujos de Energía, Materials y Huella Ecológica (1955–2000)*. Lanzarote: Colección Economía versus Naturaleza, Fundación César Manrique.

Carraro, Carlo, and Domenico Siniscalco. 1993. Strategies for the international protection of the environment. *Journal of Public Economics* 52: 309–328.

Centre for Research on the Epidemiology of Disasters and Office of U.S. Foreign Disaster Assistance (CRED-OFDA). 2004. EM-DAT: The OFDA/CRED International Disaster Database. Available at http://www.cred.be/emdat.

Chambers, Robert. 1989. Vulnerability, coping and policy. *IDS Bulletin* 20(2): 1–7.

Chang, H.-J. 2003a. Institutional development in historical perspective. In *Rethinking Development Economics*, edited by H.-J. Chang. London: Anthem Press, pp. 499–521.

Chang, H.-J. 2003b. Kicking away the ladder—Infant industry promotion in historical perspective. *Oxford Development Studies* 31(1): 21–32.

Chang, H.-J., and D. Green. 2003. *The Northern WTO Agenda on Investment—Do as We Say, Not as We Did*. Geneva: South Centre and Catholic Agency for Overscas Development.

Chase-Dunn, Christopher. 1989. *Global Formation: Structures of the World-Economy*. New York: Basil Blackwell.

Chasek, Pamela, and Lavanya Rajamani. 2003. Steps toward enhanced parity: Negotiating capacities and strategies of developing countries. In *Providing Global Public Goods: Managing Globalization*, edited by Inge Kaul, Pedro Conceição, Katell Le Goulven, and Ronald U. Mendoza. New York: Oxford University Press, pp. 245–262.

Chaudhry, Kiren Aziz. 1994. Economic liberalization and the lineages of the rentier state. *Comparative Politics* 27(1): 1–25.

Chayes, Abram, and Antonia Handler Chayes. 1993. On compliance. *International Organization* 47(2): 175–205.

Chayes, Abram, and Antonia Chayes Handler. 1995. *The New Sovereignty. Compliance with International Regulatory Agreements*. Cambridge, MA: Harvard University Press.

Checkel, Jeffrey T. 1997. *Ideas and International Political Change: Soviet/Russian Behavior and the End of the Cold War*. New Haven, CT: Yale University Press.

Chen, X., and L. Qiao. 2001. A preliminary material input analysis of China. *Population and Environment* 23(1): 117–126.

Chew, Sing. 2001. *World Ecological Degradation: Accumulation, Urbanization, and Deforestation 3000 B.C.–A.D. 2000*. Walnut Creek, CA: AltaMira Press.

Christian Aid. n.d. Honduras: Background information. Available at http://www.christian-aid.org.uk/caweek02/infopacks/honduras.htm#top.

Christian Science Monitor. 2004. Is Kyoto kaput? December 20. Available at http://www.csmonitor.com/2004/1220/p08s01-comv.html.

Christie, Frances, and Joseph Hanlon. 2001. *Mozambique and the Great Flood of 2000.* Bloomington: James Currey/Indiana University Press.

CIA Factbook. 2004. Tuvalu Country Information. Available at http://www.cia.gov/cia/publications/factbook/geos/tv.html.

Clapp, Jennifer. 2002. Distancing of waste: Overconsumption in a global economy. In *Confronting Consumption*, edited by Thomas Princen, Michael Maniates, and Ken Conca. Cambridge, MA: MIT Press, pp. 155–176.

Clapp, Roger Alex. 1995. Creating competitive advantage: Forest policy as industrial policy in Chile. *Economic Geography* 71(3): 273–296.

Clark, William C., et al. (30 authors). 2000. Assessing Vulnerability to Global Environmental Risks: Report of the Workshop on Vulnerability to Global Environmental Change: Challenges for Research, Assessment and Decision Making, May 22–25, Airlie House, Warrenton, VA. Research and Assessment Systems for Sustainability Program Discussion Paper 2000-12.

Claussen, E., and L. McNeilly. 1998. *Equity and Global Climate Change: The Complex Elements of Fairness.* Arlington, VA: Pew Center on Climate Change.

Clémençon, Raymond. 2004. On the back burner again: Environment and development politics since the 1992 Rio Conference. *Journal of Environment and Development* 13(2): 111–118.

Collier, Paul. 2004. Primary commodity dependence and Africa's future. In *The New Reform Agenda*, edited by Boris Pleskovic and Nicholas Stern. New York: Oxford University Press, pp. 139–162.

Collier, P., and A. Hoeffler. 1998. On economic causes of civil war. *Oxford Economic Papers* 50(4): 563–573.

Comfort, L., B. Wisner, S. Cutter, R. Pulwarty, K. Hewitt, A. Oliver-Smith, J. Weiner, M. Fordham, W. Peacock, and F. Krimgold. 1999. Reframing disaster policy: The global evolution of vulnerable communities. *Environmental Hazards* 1(1): 39–44.

Commission for Environmental Cooperation (CEC). 1996. *State of the Environment Report for North America.* Montreal, Quebec: Commission for Environmental Cooperation.

Congleton, Roger. 2002/2003. Agency Problems and the Allocation of International Environmental Grants: The Return to Rio. *Economia Delle Scelte Pubbliche* 20: 125–146.

Connolly, Barbara. 1996. Increments for the Earth: The politics of environmental aid. In *Institutions for Environmental Aid*, edited by Robert O. Keohane and Marc A. Levy. Cambridge, MA: MIT Press, pp. 327–365.

Corbett, Jane. 1988. Famine and household coping strategies. *World Development* 16(9): 1099–1112.

Covello, Vincent T., and R. Scott Frey. 1990. Technology-based environmental health risks in developing nations. *Technological Forecasting and Social Change* 37: 159–179.

Cowhey, Peter F. 1993. Domestic institutions and the credibility of international commitments: Japan and the United States. *International Organization* 47(2): 299–326.

Cramer, Christopher. 1998. Rural poverty and poverty alleviation in Mozambique: What's missing from the debate? *Journal of Modern African Studies* 36(1): 101–138.

Cramer, Christopher. 1999. Can Africa industrialize by processing primary commodities? The Case of Mozambican cashew nuts. *World Development* 27(7): 1247–1266.

Crawley, Richard. 1993. Translation of Thucydides' *History of the Peloponnesian War*. London: Everyman.

Crespo Cuaresmay, Jesus, Jaroslava Hlouskovaz, and Michael Obersteiner. 2004. Natural disasters as creative destruction: Evidence from developing countries. Vienna: University of Vienna Working Paper.

Cross, John A. 2001. Megacities and small towns: Different perspectives on hazard vulnerability. *Environmental Hazards* 3: 63–80.

Cutter, Susan L. 1996. Vulnerability to environmental hazards. *Progress in Human Geography* 20(4): 529–539.

Dalton, Russell. 1994. *The Green Rainbow: Environmental Interest Groups in Western Europe*. New Haven, CT: Yale University Press.

Damian, M., and J. C. Graz (eds.). 2001. *Commerce International et Développement Soutenable*. Paris: Economica.

Dasgupta, P. 1993. *An Inquiry into Well-Being and Destitution*. Oxford: Clarendon Press.

De Janvry, Alain. 1981. *The Agrarian Question and Reformism in Latin America*. Baltimore: Johns Hopkins University Press.

de Soysa, Indra, and Eric Neumayer. 2005. False prophet, or genuine savior? Assessing the effects of economic openness on sustainable development, 1980–1999. *International Organization* 59 (Summer): 731–772.

Deaton, Angus. 2001. Counting the world's poor: Problems and possible solutions. *World Bank Research Observer* 16(2): 125–147.

Deaton, Angus. 2002. Is world poverty falling? *Finance and Development* 39(2): 4–7.

Denoon, Donald. 1983. *Settler Capitalism: The Dynamics of Dependent Development in the Southern Hemisphere*. Oxford: Clarendon Press.

Depledge, Joanna. 2002. Continuing Kyoto: Extending absolute emission caps to developing countries. In *Building on the Kyoto Protocol: Options for Protecting the Climate*, edited by Kevin A. Baumert. Washington, DC: World Resources Institute, pp. 31–60.

DeSombre, Elizabeth R. 2000a. Developing country influence in global environmental negotiations. *Environmental Politics* 9: 23–42.

DeSombre, Elizabeth R. 2000b. *Domestic Sources of International Environmental Policy: Industry, Environmentalists, and U.S. Power*. Cambridge, MA: MIT Press.

DeSombre, Elizabeth R., and Joanne Kauffman. 1996. The Montreal Protocol multilateral fund: Partial success story. In *Institutions for Environmental Aid: Pitfalls and Promise*, edited by Robert O. Keohane and Marc A. Levy. Cambridge, MA: MIT Press.

De Soto, Hernando. 2000. *The Mystery of Capital: Why Capitalism Triumphs in the West and Fails Everywhere Else*. New York: Basic Books.

Dessai, S. 2001. Why did The Hague climate conference fail? *Environmental Politics* 10(3): 139–144.

Dessai, S. 2003. The special climate change fund: Origins and prioritisation assessment. *Climate Policy* 3: 295–302.

Dessai, Suraje, Lisa F. Schipper, Esteve Corbera, Bo Kjellén, María Gutiérrez, and Alex Haxeltine. 2005. Challenges and outcomes at the ninth session of the conference of the parties to the united nations framework convention on climate change. *International Environmental Agreements: Politics, Law and Economics* 5(2): 105–124.

Dessler, David. 1989. What's at stake in the agent structure debate? *International Organization* 43(3): 441–473.

Dewar, Helen. 1997. Senate advises against emissions treaty that lets developing nations pollute. *Washington Post* July 26, p. A11.

Diaz, H., and Pulwarty, R. (eds.). 1997. *Hurricanes: Climate and Socio-Economic Impacts*. Berlin: Springer-Verlag.

Dietz, Thomas, and Linda Kalof. 1992. Environmentalism among nation-states. *Social Indicators Research* 26: 353–366.

Dobriansky, Paula. 2003. Only new technology can halt climate change. *Financial Times* December 1.

Dollar, David, and Aart Kraay. 2002a. Spreading the wealth. *Foreign Affairs* 81(1): 120–133.

Dollar, David, and Aart Kraay. 2002b. Growth is good for the poor. *Journal of Economic Growth* 7(3): 195–225.

Dow, Kirstin. 1992. Exploring differences in our common future(s): The meaning of vulnerability to global environmental change. *Geoforum* 23(3): 417–436.

Dow, K., and T. E. Downing. 1995. Vulnerability research: Where things stand. *Human Dimensions Quarterly* 1(3): 3–5.

Downing, Thomas E., Ruth Butterfield, Stewart Cohen, Saleemul Huq, Richard Moss, Atiq Rahman, Youba Sokona, and Linda Stephen. 2001. *Climate Change Vulnerability: Linking Impacts and Adaptation*. Report to the Governing

Council of the United Nations Environment Programme. Nairobi: United Nations Environment Programme.

Downs, George W., David M. Rocke, and Peter N. Barsoom. 1996. Is the good news about compliance good news about cooperation? *International Organization* 50(3): 379–406.

Downs, George W., David M. Rocke, and Peter N. Barsoom. 1998. Managing the evolution of multilateralism. *International Organization* 52: 397–419.

Drahos, Peter. 2003. When the weak bargain with the strong: Negotiations in the World Trade Organization. *International Negotiation* 8(1): 79–109.

Dreher, Alex. 2006. IMF and economic growth: The effects of programs, loans, and compliance with conditionality. *World Development* 34(5).

Dreher, Axel. 2004. IMF and Economic Growth: The Effects of Programs, Loans, and Compliance with Conditionality. *World Development* 34(5).

Drezner, Daniel W. 1999. *The Sanctions Paradox: Economic Statecraft and International Relations.* Cambridge: Cambridge University Press.

Drezner, Daniel W. 2000. Bargaining, enforcement, and sanctions: When is cooperation counterproductive? *International Organization* 54: 73–102.

Drury, A. Cooper, and Richard Stuart Olson. 1998. Disasters and political unrest: An empirical investigation. *Journal of Contingencies and Crisis Management* 6(3): 153–161.

Duncan, Richard. 2003. *The Dollar Crisis: Causes, Consequences, Cures.* Chichester, UK: John Wiley & Sons.

Dunn, Seth. 1998. Dancing around the climate issue. Can the North and South get in step? *WorldWatch* (November/December) 11: 19–27.

Dunning, J. H. 1993. *Multinational Enterprises and the Global Economy.* Wokingham, UK: Addison Wesley.

Dunning, J. H. 1997. *Alliance Capitalism and Global Business.* London: Routledge.

Dunning, Thad. 2005. Resource dependence, economic performance, and political stability. *Journal of Conflict Resolution* 49(4): 451–482.

Durkheim Emile. 1933. [1893]. *On the Division of Labor in Society.* Translated by G. Simpson. New York: Macmillan.

Easterly, William. 2001. *The Elusive Quest for Growth: Economists' Adventures and Misadventures in the Tropics.* Cambridge, MA: MIT Press.

Easterly, William, and Ross Levine. 2003. Tropics, germs and crops: How endowments influence economic development. *Journal of Monetary Economics* 50: 3–39.

Economic Commission for Latin America and the Caribbean (ECLAC). 1999. Evaluación de los Daños Ocasionados del Huracán Mitch 1998: Sus Implicaciones para el Desarrollo Económico, Social y el Medio Ambiente. Tegucigalpa, Honduras: ECLAC.

Economist Intelligence Unit (EIU). 2004a. Country profile: Honduras. London: Economist Intelligence Unit.

Economist Intelligence Unit (EIU). 2004b. Country profile: Mozambique. London: Economist Intelligence Unit.

Egziabher, Tewolde Berhan Gebre. 2003. When Northern elephants fight over GMOs. *Review of African Political Economy* 98: 650–653.

Eilmer-Dewitt, Philip. 1992. Summit to save the Earth: Rich vs. poor. *Time* magazine, June 1, pp. 42–48.

Elster, Jon. 1989. Social norms and economic theory. *Journal of Economic Perspectives* 3(4): 99–117.

Elster, Jon. 1989. *The Cement of Society: A Survey of Social Order*. Cambridge, UK: Cambridge University Press.

Engerman, Stanley L., and Kenneth L. Sokoloff. 1997. Factor endowments, institutions, and differential growth paths among New World economies. In *How Latin America Fell Behind*, edited by Stephen Haber. Stanford, CA: Stanford University Press, pp. 260–304.

Engerman, Stanley L., and Kenneth L. Sokoloff. 2000. Institutions, factor endowments, and paths of development in the New World. *Journal of Economic Perspectives* 3: 217–232.

Engerman, Stanley, and Kenneth Sokoloff. 2002. Factor endowments, inequality, and paths of development among New World economies. *Economia* 3(1): 41–88.

Estrada-Oyuela, Raúl A. 2002. Equity and climate change. In *Ethics, Equity and International Negotiations on Climate Change*, edited by Luiz Pinguelli-Rosa and Mohan Munasinghe. Cheltenham, UK: Edward Elgar, pp. 36–46.

Esty, Daniel C. 2001. Environmental Sustainability Index. New Haven, CT: Yale Center for Environmental Law and Policy. Available online at http://www.ciesin.columbia.edu/indicators/ESI/.

Etkin, D. 1999. Risk transference and related trends: Driving forces towards more mega-disasters. *Environmental Hazards* 1: 69–75.

Evans, Alex. 2002. *Fresh Air? Options for the Future Architecture of International Climate Change Policy*. London: New Economics Foundation.

Evans, Peter. 1992. The state as problem and solution: Predation, embedded autonomy, and structural change. In *The Politics of Economic Adjustment: International Constraints, Distributive Conflicts, and the State*, edited by Stephan Haggard and Robert Kaufman. Princeton, NJ: Princeton University Press, pp. 139–181.

Evans, Peter. 1995. *Embedded Autonomy: States and Industrial Transformation*. Princeton, NJ: Princeton University Press.

Evans, Peter, and Martha Finnemore. 2001. Organizational reform and the expansion of the South's voice at the fund. Paper presented at G-24 Technical Group Meeting, April 17–18, Washington, DC.

Ezzati, Majid, and Daniel M. Kammen. 2002. Evaluating the health benefits of transitions in household energy technologies in Kenya. *Energy Policy* 30(10): 815–826.

Falk, Armin, Ernst Fehr, and Urs Fischbacher. 2000. Testing Theories of Fairness—Intentions Matter. Working Paper. Institute for Empirical Research in Economics, University of Zürich.

Falk, Armin, Ernst Fehr, and Urs Fischbacher. 2003a. Reasons for conflict: Lessons from bargaining experiments. *Journal of Institutional and Theoretical Economics* 59: 171–187.

Falk, Armin, Ernst Fehr, and Urs Fischbacher. 2003b. On the nature of fair behavior. *Economic Inquiry* 41(1): 20–26.

Falk, Armin, Ernst Fehr, and Urs Fischbacher. 2005. Driving forces behind informal sanctions. *Econometrica* 73(6): 2017–2030.

Fearon, James. 1994. Domestic political audiences and the escalation of international disputes. *American Political Science Review* 88(3): 577–592.

Fearon, James D. 1998. Bargaining, enforcement, and international cooperation. *International Organization* 52(2): 269–305.

Fearon, James, and Alexander Wendt. 2002. "Rationalism versus constructivism: A skeptical view. In *Handbook of International Relations*, edited by Walter Carlsnaes, Thomas Risse, and Beth Simmons. New York: Sage, pp. 52–72.

Fehr, Ernst, and Simon Gachter. 2000. Cooperation and punishment in public goods experiments. *American Economic Review* 90: 980–994.

Fehr, Ernst, and Klaus Schmidt. 1999. A theory of fairness, competition, and cooperation. *Quarterly Journal of Economics* 114: 817–868.

Finger, J. M., and M. E. Kreinin. 1979. A measure of "export similarity" and its possible uses. *Economic Journal* 89: 905–912.

Finger, Michael, and Philip Schuler. 2000. Implementation of Uruguay Round commitment: The development challenge. *World Economy* 23(3): 511–525.

Finnemore, Martha. 1996. Norms, culture and world politics: Insights from sociology's institutionalism. *International Organization* 50 (Spring): 325–348.

Firebaugh, Glen. 1999. Empirics of world income inequality. *American Journal of Sociology* 104(6): 1597–1630.

Firebaugh, Glen. 2003. *The New Geography of Global Income Inequality*. Cambridge, MA: Harvard University Press.

Firebaugh, Glen, and B. Goesling. 2004. Accounting for the recent decline in global income inequality. *American Journal of Sociology* 110(2): 283–312.

Fischer-Kowalski, Marina, and Christof Amman. 2001. Beyond IPAT and Kuznets Curves: Globalization as a vital factor in analyzing the environmental impact of socio-economic metabolism. *Population and Environment* 23(1): 7–47.

Fischer-Kowalski, M., and W. Hüttler. 1999. Society's metabolism. The intellectual history of materials flow analysis. Part II, 1970–1998. *Journal of Industrial Ecology* 2(4): 107–136.

Florini, Ann M. 1996. The evolution of international norms. *International Studies Quarterly* 40: 363–389.

Fogarty, E. 2003. Moving mountains (of debt). In *Sovereign Debt: Origins, Crises and Restructuring*, edited by V. Aggarwal and B. Granville. London: Royal Institute of International Affairs, pp. 229–254.

Food and Agriculture Organization (FAO). 1999. *The State of Food Insecurity in the World*. Rome: FAO.

Forbes magazine. 1998. The world's richest people. July 6.

Franck, Thomas M. 1995. *Fairness in International Law and Institutions*. Oxford: Oxford University Press.

Frank, Andre Gunder. 1969. *Latin America: Underdevelopment or Revolution?* New York: Monthly Review Press.

Frank, David John. 1997. Science, nature, and the globalization of the environment, 1870–1990. *Social Forces* 76(2): 409–435.

Frank, David John. 1999. The social bases of environmental treaty ratification, 1900–1990. *Sociological Inquiry* 69 (Fall): 523–550.

Fredriksson, Per G., and Noel Gaston. 2000. Ratification of the 1992 climate change convention: What determines legislative delay? *Public Choice* 104: 345–368.

Friends of the Earth, UK. 2002. Delhi climate talks—update, October 31, press release. Available at http://www.foe.co.uk/resource/press_releases/20021031152914.html.

Friends of the Earth. 2003. Bush administration facing storm of global warming criticism. August 28, news release. Also see http://www.climatelawsuit.org.

Galbraith, James K. 2002. A perfect crime: Inequality in the age of globalization. *Daedalus* 131: 11–25.

Gallup, John Luke, and Jeffrey D. Sachs, with Andrew D. Mellinger. 1999. Geography and economic development. In *World Bank Annual Conference on Development Economics 1998*, edited by Boris Pleskovic and Joseph E. Stiglitz, pp. 127–178. Washington, DC: World Bank.

Garrett, Geoffrey, and Barry Weingast. 1993. Ideas, interests and institutions: Constructing the European Community's internal market. In *Ideas and Foreign Policy: Beliefs, Institutions and Political Change*, edited by Judith Goldstein and Robert Keohane. Ithaca, NY: Cornell University Press, pp. 173–206.

Gaubatz, Kurt Taylor. 1996. Democratic states and commitment in international relations. *International Organization* 50(1): 109–139.

Gauthier, D. 1986. *Morals by Agreement*. Oxford: Clarendon Press.

Gelbspan, Ross. 2004. *Boiling Point: How Politicians, Big Oil and Coal, Journalists, and Activists Have Fueled a Climate Crisis—And What We Can Do to Avert Disaster*. New York: Basic Books.

George, Susan, and Fabrizio Sabelli. 1994. *Faith and Credit: the World Bank's Secular Empire*. Boulder, CO: Westview Press.

Gereffi, Gary, and Miguel Korzeniewicz (eds.). 1994. *Commodity Chains and Global Capitalism.* Westport, CT: Praeger.

Gerschenkron, A. 1962. *Economic Backwardness in Historical Perspective.* Cambridge, MA: Harvard University Press.

Gibson, Clark. 1999a. Bureaucracies and environmental politics in Africa: A structural choice approach. *Comparative Politics* 31: 273–294.

Gibson, Clark C. 1999b. *Politicians and Poachers: The Political Economy of Wildlife Policy in Africa.* New York: Cambridge University Press.

Giljum, Stefan. 2003. Biophysical Dimensions of North-South Trade: Material Flows and Land Use. Ph.D. Thesis, University of Vienna.

Giljum, Stefan. 2004. Trade, material flows and economic development in the South: The example of Chile. *Journal of Industrial Ecology* 8(1–2): 241–261.

Giljum, Stefan, and N. Eisenmenger. 2004. North-South trade and the distribution of environmental goods and burdens. A biophysical perspective. *Journal of Environment and Development* 13(1): 73–100.

Giljum, Stefan, and Klaus Hubacek. 2001. International Trade, Material Flows and Land Use: Developing a Physical Trade Balance for the European Union. Interim Report. Laxenburg, Austria: International Institute for Applied Systems Analysis (IIASA).

Giljum, Stefan, and Klaus Hubacek. 2004a. International trade and material flows: A physical trade balance for the European Union. Interim Report. Laxenburg, Austria: International Institute for Applied Systems Analysis (IIASA).

Giljum Stefan, and Klaus Hubacek. 2004b. Alternative approaches of physical input-output analysis to estimate primary material inputs of production and consumption activities. *Economic Systems Research* 16(3): 301–310.

Global Environment Facility. 2004. Compilation of NGO interventions. GEF Council Meetings. May 2004. Available at www.gefweb.org.

Goering, L. 2000. Honduras still mired in misery of '98 hurricane. *Chicago Tribune* August 27, pp. 1, 14.

Gold-Biss, Michael. 2005. Country Report: Honduras. In *Countries at the Crossroads: A Survey of Democratic Governance*, pp. 271–292. New York: Rowman and Littlefield.

Goldstein, J., and R. Keohane (eds.). 1993. *Ideas and Foreign Policy. Beliefs, Institutions, and Political Change.* Ithaca, NY: Cornell University Press.

Gore, Charles. 2000. The rise and fall of the Washington Consensus as a paradigm for developing countries. *World Development* 28(5): 789–804.

Gould, Kenneth, Tammy Lewis, and J. Timmons Roberts. 2004. Blue-green coalitions: Constraints and possibilities in the post 9–11 political environment. *Journal of World-System Research* X(1): 90–116.

Gowan, Peter. 1999. *The Global Gamble: Washington's Faustian Bid for World Domination.* London: Verso.

Graham, Edward M. 1996. Direct investment and the future agenda of the World Trade Organization. In *The World Trading System: Challenges Ahead*, edited by Jeffrey J. Schott. Washington, DC: Institute for International Economics, pp. 205–217.

Granovetter, Mark. 1985. Economic action and social structure: The problem of embeddedness. *American Journal of Sociology* 91: 481–510.

Green, Michael. 2002. Reflections on Indonesia's transition. *New Zealand International Review* 27(4): 6–10.

Grieco, Joseph. 1988. Anarchy and the limits of cooperation: A realist critique of the newest liberal institutionalism. *International Organisation* 43(3): 485–507.

Groenenberg, Heleen, Dian Phylipsen, and Kornelis Blok. 2001. Differentiating commitments world wide: Global differentiation of GHG emissions reductions based on the triptych approach—a preliminary assessment. *Energy Policy* 29: 1007–1030.

Grossman, G. M., and A. B. Kreuger. 1995. Economic growth and the environment. *Quarterly Journal of Economics* 110(2): 353–377.

Group of 77. 2000a. Declaration of the South Summit. Held in Havana, Cuba. April 10–14, 2000.

Group of 77. 2000b. Havana Program of Action. Group of 77 South Summit. Havana, Cuba, April 10–14, 2000.

Grubb, Michael J. 1990. *Energy Policies and the Greenhouse Effect*. Vol. 1. London: Dartmouth/Royal Institute of International Affairs.

Grubb, M. 1995. Seeking fair weather: Ethics and the international debate on climate change. *International Affairs* 71(3): 463–495.

Grubb, Michael, and Farhana Yamin. 2001. Climate collapse at The Hague: What happened, why, and where do we go from here? *International Affairs* 77(2): 261–276.

Grubb, M., C. Vrolijk, and D. Brack. 1999. *The Kyoto Protocol: A Guide and Assessment*. London: Royal Institute of International Affairs.

Grubb, Michael, Jean-Charles Hourcade, and Sebastian Oberthür. 2001. Keeping Kyoto. A study of approaches to maintaining the Kyoto Protocol on climate change. Climate Strategies Report. Available at http://www.climate-strategies .org/projects&reports.htm.

Gruber, Lloyd. 2000. *Ruling the World: Power Politics and the Rise of Supranational Institutions*. Princeton, NJ: Princeton University Press.

Guha, Ramachandra, and J. Martinez Alier. 1997. *Varieties of Environmentalism: Essays North and South*. London: Earthscan.

Guimaraes, Roberto. 2000. Sociological reflections on sustainability. Paper presented at International Sociological Association Miniconference. Rio de Janeiro, Brazil. August 1–5, 2000.

Guimaraes, Roberto. n.d. Brazil and global environmental politics: Same wine in new bottles? In *Sustainability and Unsustainability on the Road from Rio*, edited by J. Timmons Roberts, Eduardo Viola, Frederick Buttel, and Amy Hite. Book manuscript in revision.

Gupta, Joyeeta. 1997. *The Climate Change Convention and Developing Countries: From Conflict to Consensus?* Dordrecht, Netherlands: Kluwer Academic Publishers.

Gupta, Joyeeta. 2000a. North-South aspects of the climate change issue: Towards a negotiating theory and strategy for developing countries. *International Journal of Sustainable Development* 3(2): 115–135.

Gupta, Joyeeta. 2000b. *"On Behalf of My Delegation, ..." A Survival Guide for Developing Country Climate Negotiators.* Washington, DC: Center for Sustainable Development in the Americas.

Gupta, Joyeeta. 2001. India and climate change policy: Between diplomatic defensiveness and industrial transformation. *Energy and Environment* 12(2/3): 217–236.

Gupta, Joyeeta, and Michael Grubb (eds.). 2000. *Climate Change and European Leadership: A Sustainable Role for Europe?* Dordrecht: Kluwer Academic Publishers.

Gupta, S., and P. Bhandari. 1999. An effective allocation criterion for CO_2 emissions. *Energy Policy* 27: 727–736.

Gylfason, T. 2001. Natural resources education and economic development. *European Economic Review* 45(4–6): 847–859.

Guzman, Andrew. 1998. Why LDCs sign treaties that hurt them: Explaining the popularity of bilateral investment treaties. *Virginia Journal of International Law* 38: 639–645, 666–688.

Guzman, Andrew T. 2002. The cost of credibility: Explaining resistance to interstate dispute resolution mechanisms. *Journal of Legal Studies* 31: 303–326.

Haas, Peter M. 1990. *Saving the Mediterranean: The Politics of International Environmental Cooperation.* New York: Columbia University Press.

Haas, Peter M. 1992. Banning chlorofluorocarbons. *International Organization* 46(1): 187–224.

Haas, P. M., R. O. Keohane, and M. A. Levy (eds.). 1993. *Institutions for the Earth: Sources of Effective International Environmental Protection.* Cambridge, MA: MIT Press.

Halliday, Fred. 1995. International relations and its discontents. *International Affairs* 71(4): 733–746.

Hammer, M., and K. Hubacek. 2002. Material Flows and Economic Development. Material Flow Analysis of the Hungarian Economy. Interim Report. No. 02-057. Laxenburg, Austria: International Institute for Applied Systems Analysis (IIASA).

Handmer, J. W., D. Dovers, and T. E. Downing. 1999. Social vulnerability to climate change and variability. *Mitigation and Adaptation Strategies for Global Change* 4: 267–281.

Hardin, Garrett. 1968. The tragedy of the commons. *Science* 162: 1243–1248.

Hardin, Russell. 1992. The street-level epistemology of trust. *Analyse & Kritik* 14: 152–176.

Hartford Courant. 1992. June 8, p. A2.

Harvey, D. 1989. *The Condition of Postmodernity. An Enquiry into the Origins of Cultural Change.* Oxford: Basil Blackwell.

Hasenclever, Andreas, Peter Mayer, and Volker Rittberger. 1999. Distributive Justice and the Robustness of International Regimes: A Preliminary Project Report. Paper prepared for the Workshop on the Study of Regime Consequences, Oslo, Norway.

Hausmann, Ricardo. 2001. Prisoners of geography. *Foreign Policy* 122: 44–53.

Hausmann, Ricardo, and Dani Rodrik. 2003. Economic development as self-discovery. *Journal of Development Economics* 72(2): 603–633.

Hawkins, Darren, and Jutta Joachim. 2004. Legalizing human rights and democracy: Comparing the EU and the OAS. Paper presented at the conference on Theoretical Synthesis in the Study of International Organization, Washington, DC, February 6–7, 2004.

Hay, Richard. 1977. Patterns of urbanization and socio-economic development in the third world: An overview. In *Third World Urbanization*, edited by Janet Abu-Lughod and Richard Hay, Jr. New York: Methuen, pp. 71–101.

Heil, M. T., and T. M. Selden. 2001. International trade intensity and carbon emissions: A cross-country econometric analysis. *Journal of Environment and Development* 10: 35–49.

Hellman, G. 2003. Forum: Are dialogue and synthesis possible in international relations? *International Studies Review* 5: 123–153.

Henisz, Witold J. 2000. The institutional environment for economic growth. *Economics and Politics* 12(1): 1–31.

Henkin, Louis. 1979. *How Nations Behave.* New York: Columbia University Press.

Hewitt, K. 1995. Sustainable disasters? Perspectives and powers in the discourse of calamity. In *Power of Development*, edited by J. Crush. London: Routledge, pp. 115–128.

Hirschman, A. O. 1958. *The Strategy of Economic Development.* New Haven, CT: Yale University Press.

Hoel, M. 1992. International environmental conventions: The case of uniform reductions of emissions. *Environmental and Resource Economics* 2: 141–159.

Holtz-Eakin, D., and T. Selden. 1995. Stoking the fires? CO_2 emissions and economic growth. *Journal of Public Economics* 57(1): 85–101.

Hornborg, Alf. 1998a. Towards an ecological theory of unequal exchange: Articulating world system theory and ecological economics. *Ecological Economics* 25: 127–136.

Hornborg, Alf. 1998b. Ecosystems and world systems: Accumulation as an ecological process. *Journal of World-Systems Research* 4: 169–177.

Hornborg, Alf. 2001. *The Power of the Machine: Global Inequalities of Economy, Technology, and Environment*. Walnut Creek, CA: AltaMira Press.

Houghton, John. 2003. Global warming is now a weapon of mass destruction. *The Guardian* July 28.

Hovi, Jon, Tora Skodvin, and Steinar Andresen. 2003. The persistence of the Kyoto Protocol: Why other Annex I countries move on without the United States. *Global Environmental Politics* 3(4): 1–23.

Hubacek, K., and S. Giljum. 2003. Applying physical input-output analysis to estimate land appropriation of international trade activities. *Ecological Economics* 44 (1): 137–151.

Hudson, Michael. 2003. *Super Imperialism: The Economic Strategy of American Empire*, 2nd ed. London: Pluto Press.

Humphrey, Craig R., Tammy L. Lewis, and Frederick H. Buttel. 2002. *Environment, Energy, and Society: A New Synthesis*. Belmont, CA: Wadsworth.

Huq, S. 1999. Environmental hazards in Dhaka. In *Crucibles of Hazard: Mega-Cities and Disasters in Transition*, edited by J. K. Mitchell. Tokyo: United Nations University Press, pp. 119–137.

Huq, S. 2002. The Bonn-Marrakech agreements on funding. *Climate Policy* 2: 243–246.

Huq, S., Z. Karim, M. Asaduzzaman, and F. Mahtab (eds.). 1999. *Vulnerability and Adaptation to Climate Change in Bangladesh*. Dordrecht, Netherlands: Kluwer.

Hurrell, Andrew, and Benedict Kingsbury (eds.). 1992. *The International Politics of the Environment*. Oxford: Oxford University Press.

Ikenberry, G. John. 1992. A world economy restored: Expert consensus and the Anglo-American postwar settlement. *International Organization* 46(1): 289–321.

Ikenberry, G. John. 1993. Creating yesterday's new world order: Keynesian "new thinking" and the Anglo-American postwar settlement. In *Ideas and Foreign Policy: Beliefs, Institutions and Political Change*, edited by Judith Goldstein and Robert O. Keohane. Ithaca, NY: Cornell University Press, pp. 57–86.

Imbs, Jean, and Romain Wacziarg. 2003. Stages of diversification. *American Economic Review* 93(1): 63–86.

Inglehart, Ronald. 1995. Public support for environmental protection: objective problems and subjective values in 43 societies. *PS: Political Science and Politics* 28(1): 57–72.

Intergovernmental Panel on Climate Change (IPCC). 2001a. *Climate Change 2001: The Scientific Basis*. Contribution of Working Group I to the Third Assessment Report of the IPCC. Cambridge: Cambridge University Press.

Intergovernmental Panel on Climate Change (IPCC). 2001b. *Climate Change 2001: Third Assessment Report of the Intergovernmental Panel on Climate Change.* Including reports of all three working groups. Cambridge: Cambridge University Press.

International Decade for Natural Disaster Reduction—United Nations Economic and Social Commission for Asia and the Pacific (IDNDR-ESCAP). 1999. Water hazards, resources and management for disaster prevention: A review of the Asian conditions. Paper presented at the IDNDR-ESCAP Regional Meeting for Asia: Risk Reduction & Society in the 21st Century, February 23–26, 1999, Bangkok.

International Federation of Red Cross and Red Crescent Societies (IFRC). 2000. *World Disasters Report 2000.* Geneva: IFRC.

International Federation of Red Cross and Red Crescent Societies (IFRC). 2001. *World Disasters Report 2001.* Geneva: IFRC.

International Federation of Red Cross and Red Crescent Societies (IFRC). 2002. *World Disasters Report 2002.* Geneva: IFRC.

Isham, Jonathan, Michael Woolcock, Lant Pritchett, and Gwen Busby. 2005. The varieties of resource experience: Natural resource export structures and the political economy of economic growth. *World Bank Economic Review* 19(2): 141–174.

Jackson, Robert H. 1993. The weight of ideas in decolonization: Normative change in international relations. In *Ideas and Foreign Policy: Beliefs, Institutions, and Political Change,* edited by Judith Goldstein and Robert O. Keohane. Ithaca, NY: Cornell University Press, pp. 111–138.

Jacoby, H. D., and D. M. Reiner. 2001. Getting climate policy on track after The Hague. *International Affairs* 7: 297–312.

Jamison, Dean T., and Steven Radelet. 2005. Making aid smarter. *Finance & Development* 42(2).

Jawara, Fatoumata, and Aileen Kwa. 2003. *Behind the Scenes at the WTO: The Real World of International Trade Negotiations.* London: Zed Books.

Jenkins, P. 2000. Urban management, urban poverty and urban governance: planning and land management in Maputo. *Environment & Urbanization* 12(1): 137–152.

Jensen, Nathan. 2003. Democratic governance and multinational corporations: Political regimes and inflows of foreign direct investment. *International Organization* 57(3): 587–616.

Jeppesen, T., and P. Andersen. 1998. Commitment and fairness in environmental games. In *Game Theory and the Environment,* edited by Nick Hanley and Henk Folmer. Cheltenham, UK: Edward Elgar, pp. 65–83.

Jervis, Robert. 1988. Realism, game theory, and cooperation. *World Politics* 40: 317–349.

Jeter, Jon. 2002. Mistrust reigns as second Earth Summit commences. *Washington Post,* August 26.

Jokela, Minna. 2002. European Union as a global policy actor: The case of desertification. In *Proceedings of the 2001 Berlin Conference on the Human Dimensions of Global Environmental Change*, edited by Frank Biermann, Rainer Brohm, and Klaus Dingwerth. Potsdam: Potsdam Institute for Climate Impact Research, pp. 308–316.

Jorgenson, Andrew K. 2006. Global warming and the neglected greenhouse gas: A cross-national study of methane emissions intensity, 1995. *Social Forces* 84: 1779–1796.

Jupille, Joseph, James Caporaso, and Jeffrey Checkel. 2003. Integrating institutions: Rationalism, constructivism, and the study of the European Union. *Comparative Political Studies* 36(1): 7–40.

Kahler, Miles. 1992. Multilateralism with large and small numbers. *International Organization* 46 (Summer): 681–708.

Kahn, Matthew. 2005. The death toll from natural disasters: The role of income, geography, and institutions. *Review of Economics and Statistics* 87(2): 271–284.

Kahn, Robert S., Paul H. Wise, Bruce P. Kennedy, and Ichiro Kawachi. 2000. State income inequality, household income, and maternal mental and physical health: Cross-sectional national survey. *British Medical Journal* 321: 1311–1315.

Kallbekken, Steffen, and Hege Westskog. 2005. Should developing countries take on binding commitments in a climate agreement? An assessment of gains and uncertainty. *Energy Journal* 26(3): 41–92.

Kandlikar, Milind, and Ambuj Sagar. 1999. Climate change research and analysis in India: An integrated assessment of a South-North divide. *Global Environmental Change* 9(2): 119–138.

Kaplan, George A., Elsie R. Pamuk, John W. Lynch, Richard D. Cohen, and Jennifer L. Balfour. 1996. Inequality in income and mortality in the United States: Analysis of mortality and potential pathways. *British Medical Journal* 312: 999–1003.

Kapur, Devesh, and Richard Webb. 2000. Governance-related conditionalities of the international financial institutions. G-24 Discussion Paper No. 6.

Karl, T. L. 1997. *The Paradox of Plenty: Oil Booms and Petro-States*. Berkeley: University of California Press.

Karlekar, Karin Deutsh. 2003. *Freedom of the Press: a Global Survey of Media Independence*. New York: Freedom House.

Kasperson, J. X., and R. E. Kasperson (eds.). 2001. *Global Environmental Risk*. Tokyo: United Nations University Press.

Kasperson, R. E., and J. X. Kasperson. 2001. *Climate Change, Vulnerability and Social Justice*. Stockholm: Stockholm Environment Institute.

Kasperson, R. E., J. X. Kasperson, and Kirsten Dow. 2001. Equity, vulnerability, and global environmental change. In *Global Environmental Risk*, edited by J. X. Kasperson and R. E. Kasperson. Tokyo: United Nations University Press, pp. 247–272.

Kates, Robert. 1971. Natural hazard in human ecological perspective: Hypotheses and models. *Economic Geography* 47: 438–451.

Kates, Robert W. 2000. Cautionary tales: Adaptation and the global poor. *Climatic Change* 45(1): 5–17.

Katzenstein, Peter. 1985. *Small States in World Markets: Industrial Policy in Europe*. Ithaca, NY: Cornell University Press.

Katzenstein, Peter J. 1996. *Cultural Norms and National Security: Police and Military in Postwar Japan*. Ithaca, NY: Cornell University Press.

Katzenstein, Peter J., Robert O. Keohane, and Stephen D. Krasner (eds.). 1999. *Exploration and Contestation in the Study of World Politics*. Cambridge, MA: MIT Press.

Kaufmann, Daniel, Aart Kraay, and Massimo Mastruzzi. 2004. Governance matters III: Governance indicators for 1996, 1998, 2000, and 2002. *World Bank Economic Review* 18(2): 253–287.

Kaul, Inge, Isabelle Grunberg, and Marc A. Stern (eds.). 1999. *Global Public Goods: International Cooperation in the 21st Century*. New York: Oxford University Press.

Kaul, Inge, Pedro Conceicao, Katell Le Goulven, and Ronald U. Mendoza. 2003. *Providing Global Public Goods: Managing Globalization*. New York: Oxford University Press.

Kawachi, Ichiro, and Bruce P. Kennedy. 2002. *The Health of Nations: Why Inequality Is Harmful to Your Health*. New York: New Press.

Kay, Cristóbal. 1998. Relevance of Structuralist and Dependency Theories in the Neoliberal Period: A Latin American Perspective. Working Paper Series No. 281. The Hague: Institute of Social Sciences.

Kay, Cristóbal. 2002. Why East Asia overtook Latin America: Agrarian reform, industrialization and development. *Third World Quarterly* 23: 1073–1102.

Kazis, Richard, and Richard L. Grossman. 1991. *Fear at Work: Job Blackmail, Labor and the Environment*. Philadelphia: New Society Publishers.

Keck, Margaret, and Kathryn Sikkink. 1998. *Activists Beyond Borders: Advocacy Networks in International Politics*. Ithaca, NY: Cornell University Press.

Keefer, Philip, and Stephen Knack. 1997. Why don't poor countries catch up? A cross-national test of an institutional explanation. *Economic Inquiry* 35: 590–602.

Keen, David. 1994. *The Benefits of Famine: A Political Economy of Famine and Relief in Southwestern Sudan, 1983–89*. Princeton, NJ: Princeton University Press.

Kennedy, Bruce P., Ichiro Kawachi, and Deborah Prothrow-Stith. 1996. Income distribution and mortality: Cross-sectional ecological study of the Robin Hood index in the United States. *British Medical Journal* 312: 1004–1007.

Kenny, Charles. 2005. Why are we worried about income? Nearly everything that matters is converging. *World Development* 33(1): 1–19.

Keohane, Robert O. 1982. The demand for international regimes. *International Organization* 36(2): 325–355.

Keohane, Robert O. 1984. *After Hegemony: Cooperation and Discord in the World Political Economy*. Princeton, NJ: Princeton University Press.

Keohane, Robert O. 1986. Reciprocity in international relations. *International Organization* 40(1): 1–27.

Keohane, Robert. 1988. Reputation, reciprocity and international cooperation. Paper presented at the American Political Science Association meeting, Washington, D.C.

Keohane, Robert. O. 1997. International relations and international law: Two optics. *Havard International Law Journal* 38: 487–502.

Keohane, Robert O. 2001. Governance in a partially globalized world [2000 APSA presidential address]. *American Political Science Review* 95(1): 1–13.

Keohane, Robert O., and Marc A. Levy (eds.). 1996. *Institutions for Environmental Aid: Pitfalls and Promise*. Cambridge, MA: MIT Press.

Keohane, Robert O., and Joseph S. Nye. 2000. Globalization: What's new? What's not? (and so what?) *Foreign Policy* 118: 104–119.

Khan, Mushtaq, and K. S. Jomo. 2000. *Rents, Rent Seeking and Economic Development*. Cambridge: Cambrige University Press.

Khastagir, Nadia. 2002. The human face of climate change: Thousands gather in India to demand climate justice. November 4, 2002. CorporateWatch website. Available at http://www.corpwatch.org/campaigns/PCD.jsp?articleid=4728.

Kim, Yong-Gun, and Kevin A. Baumert. 2002. Reducing uncertainty through dual-intensity targets. In *Building on the Kyoto Protocol: Options for Protecting the Climate*, edited by Kevin A. Baumert. Washington, DC: World Resources Institute, pp. 109–135.

King, G., R. Keohane, and S. Verba. 1994. *Designing Social Inquiry: Scientific Inference in Qualitative Research*. Princeton, NJ: Princeton University Press.

Kirchsteiger, G. 1994. The role of envy in ultimatum games. *Journal of Economic Behavior and Organization* 25(3): 373–390.

Kissinger, Henry. 1998. The Asian collapse: One size does not fit all economies. *Washington Post*, February 9, p. A19.

Klein, R. J. T., R. J. Nicholls, and F. Thomalla. 2002. The Resilience of Coastal Megacities to Weather-Related Hazards: A Review. Workshop on Building Safer Cities: The Future of Disaster Risk. ProVention Consortium and the Disaster Management Facility, World Bank, Washington, DC, December 4–6, 2002.

Klinenberg, Eric. 2003. *Heat Wave: A Social Autopsy of Disaster in Chicago*. Chicago: University of Chicago Press.

Knack, Stephen. 2002. Social capital and the quality of government: Evidence from the states. *American Journal of Political Science* 46(4): 772–785.

Knack, Stephen, and Philip Keefer. 1995. Institutions and economic performance: Cross-country tests using alternative institutional measures. *Economics and Politics* 7(3): 207–227.

Knack, Stephen, and Philip Keefer. 1997. Does social capital have an economic payoff? A cross-country investigation. *Quarterly Journal of Economics* 112(4): 1251–1288.

Knight, Danielle. 1998. Environment: In defence of developing nations. Inter-Press Service, October 25.

Koremenos, Barbara, Charles Lipson, and Duncan Snidal. 2001. The rational design of international institutions. *International Organization* 55(4): 761–799.

Korzeniewicz, Roberto, and Timothy Moran. 1997. World-economic trends in the distribution of income, 1965–1992. *American Journal of Sociology* 102(4): 1000–1039.

Korzeniewicz, Roberto, and Timothy Moran. 2000. Measuring world income inequalities. *American Journal of Sociology* 106(1): 209–214.

Krasner, Stephen. 1978. United States commercial and monetary policy: Unraveling the paradox of external strength and internal weakness. In *Between Power and Plenty: Foreign Economic Policies of Advanced Industrial States*, edited by Peter J. Katzenstein. Madison: University of Wisconsin Press, p. 52.

Krasner, Stephen D. 1985. *Structural Conflict: The Third World Against Global Liberalism*. Berkeley: University of California Press.

Krasner, Stephen. 1991. Global communications and national power: Life on the Pareto frontier. *World Politics* 43 (April): 336–366.

Kratochwil, Friedrich. 2003. The monologue of "science." *International Studies Review* 5(1): 124–128.

Kratochwil, Friedrich V., and John G. Ruggie. 1986. International organization: A state of the art on the art of the state. *International Organization* 40: 753–775.

Krebill-Prather, Rose, and Eugene A. Rosa. 1994. Societal consequences of carbon-dioxide: Impacts to well-being. Paper presented at the Annual Meetings of the American Sociological Association, Los Angeles, CA.

Kristof, Nicholas. 1997. Island nations fear sea could swamp them. *New York Times*. November 28.

Krueger, Anne. 1974. The political economy of the rent-seeking society. *American Economic Review* 64: 291–303.

Kufour, Edward. 1991. G77: We won't negotiate away our sovereignty. *Third World Resurgence* 14–15: 17.

Kunte, Arundhati, Kirk Hamilton, John Dixon, and Michael Clemens. 1998. Estimating National Wealth: Methodology and Results. Environmental Economics Series No. 57. Washington, DC: World Bank.

Kunte, Arundhati, Kirk Hamilton, John Dixon, and Michael Clemens. 1998. Estimating national wealth: Methodology and results. Environmental Economics Series no. 57. Washington, DC: World Bank.

Kwa, Aileen. 2002. *Power Politics in the WTO*. Bangkok: Focus on the Global South.

Kydd, Andrew. 2000a. Trust, reassurance, and cooperation. *International Organization* 54(2): 325–357.

Kydd, Andrew. 2000b. Overcoming mistrust. *Rationality and Society* 12(4): 397–424.

La Porta, Rafael, Florencio Lopez-de-Silanes, Andrei Shleifer, and Robert Vishny. 1999. The quality of governance. *Journal of Law, Economics and Organization* 15: 222–279.

La Prensa. 1999. San Pedro Sula, Honduras, January 5.

La Rovere, Emilio L., Laura Valente de Macedo, and Kevin A. Baumert. 2002. The Brazilian proposal on relative responsibility for global warming. In *Building on the Kyoto Protocol: Options for Protecting the Climate*, edited by K. Baumert. Washington, DC: World Resources Institute, pp. 157–173.

Lake, David A. 1991. Powerful pacifists: Democratic states and war. *American Political Science Review* 86(1): 24–37.

Lake, David A. 2002. Beyond paradigms in the study of institutions. In *Realism and Institutionalism in International Studies*, edited by Michael Brecher and Frank Harvey. Ann Arbor: University of Michigan Press, pp. 135–152.

Lake, David, and Mattthew Baum 2001. The invisible hand of democracy: Political control and the provision of public services. *Comparative Political Studies* 34: 587–621.

Lall, S. 1995. Industrial strategy and policies on foreign direct investment in East Asia. *Transnational Corporations* 4: 1–26.

Lange, A., and C. Vogt. 2003. Cooperation in international environmental negotiations due to a preference for equity. *Journal of Public Economics* 87, 2049–2067.

Lappé, Frances Moore, Joseph Collins, and Peter Rosset with Luis Esparza. 1998. *World Hunger: Twelve Myths*, 2nd edition. London: Earthscan.

Leeds, Brett Ashley. 1999. Domestic political institutions, credible commitments, and international cooperation. *American Journal of Political Science* 43(4): 979–1002.

Legro, Jeffrey. 1997. Which norms matter? Revisiting the failure of internationalism. *International Organization* 51: 31–63.

Leichenko, R. M., and K. L. O'Brien. 2002. The dynamics of rural vulnerability to global change: The case of Southern Africa. *Mitigation and Adaptation Strategies for Global Change* 7: 1–18.

Leite, Carlos, and Jens Weidmann. 1999. Does Mother Nature Corrupt? Natural Resources, Corruption, and Economic Growth. Working Paper WP/99/85. Washington, DC: International Monetary Fund.

Lele, Sharachandram M. 1991. Sustainable development: A critical review. *World Development* 19(6): 607–621.

Leonard, J. H. 1998. *Pollution and the Struggle for the World Product: Multinational Corporations, Environment, and International Comparative Advantage.* New York: Cambridge University Press.

Levy, David L., and Daniel Egan. 1998. Capital contests: National and transnational channels of corporate influence on the climate change negotiations. *Politics and Society* 26(3): 337–361.

Levy, David L., and Daniel Egan. 2003. A neo-Gramscian approach to corporate political strategy: Conflict and accommodation in the climate change negotiations. *Journal of Management Studies* 40(4): 803–830.

Levy, David L., and Ans Kolk. 2002. Strategic responses to global climate change: Conflicting pressures on multinationals in the oil industry. *Business and Politics* 4(3): 275–300.

Levy, David L., and Peter Newell. 2002. Business strategy and international environmental governance: Toward a neo-Gramscian synthesis. *Global Environmental Politics* 2(4): 84–101.

Levy, M. A. 1993. European acid rain: The power of tote-board diplomacy. In *Institutions for the Earth: Sources of Effective International Environmental Protection*, edited by P. Haas, R. O. Keohane, and M. Levy. Cambridge, MA: MIT Press, pp. 75–132.

Lewis, J. 1990. The vulnerability of small island-states to sea level rise: The need for holistic strategies. *Disasters* 14(3): 241–248.

Lewis, J. 1999. *Development in Disaster-Prone Places: Studies of Vulnerability.* London: Intermediate Technology Publications.

Lewis, Paul. 1992. Pact on environment near, but hurdles on aid remain. *New York Times*, June 12, p. A6.

Lipietz, A. 1986. New tendencies in the international division of labor: Regimes of accumulation and modes of regulation. In *Production, Work, Territory: The Geographical Anatomy of Industrial Capitalism*, edited by A. J. Scott and M. Storper. Boston: Allen and Unwin, pp. 16–40.

Lipson, Charles. 1991. Why are some international agreements informal? *International Organization* 45(4): 495–538.

Liverman, Diana M. 2001. Vulnerability to global environmental change. In *Global Environmental Risk*, edited by J. X. Kasperson and R. E. Kasperson. Tokyo: United Nations University Press.

Lopez-Claros, Augusto (ed.). 2004. *The Global Competitiveness Report 2004–2005.* New York: Palgrave.

Low, Patrick, and Alexander Yeats. 1992. Do "dirty" industries migrate? In *International Trade and the Environment*, edited by Patrick Low. Washington, DC: World Bank, pp. 89–104.

Lutzenheiser, Loren. 1996. Riding in style. Presentation at the American Sociological Association Annual Meeting. 16 August. New York.

Lutzenhiser, Loren. 2001. The contours of U.S. climate non-policy. *Society and Natural Resources* 14(6): 511–523.

Machado, G., R. Schaeffer, and E. Worrell. 2001. Energy and carbon embodied in the international trade of Brazil: An input-output approach. *Ecological Economics* 39(3): 409–424.

Mackensen, G., and D. Hinrichsen. 1984. A "new" South Pacific. *Ambio* 13: 291–293.

Maffei, Pineschi, Laura Pineschi, Tullio Scovazzi, and Tullio Treves (eds.). 1996. *Participation in World Treaties on the Protection of the Environment: A Collection of Data.* London: Kluwer Law International.

Mandel, Ernest. 1980. *Long Waves of Capitalist Development: The Marxist Interpretation.* Cambridge: Cambridge University Press.

Manley, Michael. 1991. *The Poverty of Nations.* London: Pluto Press.

Mansfield, Edward D., Helen V. Milner, and B. Peter Rosendorff. 2002. Why democracies cooperate more: Electoral control and international trade agreements. *International Organization* 56(3): 477–513.

Martin, Lisa. 1992. *Coercive Cooperation: Explaining Multilateral Economic Sanctions.* Princeton, NJ: Princeton University Press.

Martin, Lisa. 1994. Heterogeneity, linkage and commons problems. *Journal of Theoretical Politics* 6(4): 473–493.

Martin, Lisa. 2000. *Democratic Commitments: Legislatures and International Cooperation.* Princeton, NJ: Princeton University Press.

Martin, Lisa. 2005. The United States and International Commitments: Treaties as Signaling Devices. Presidential Studies Quarterly 35(3): 440–465.

Martin, B., M. Capra, G. van der Heide, M. Stoneham, and M. Lucas. 2001. Are disaster management concepts relevant in developing countries? The case of the 1999–2000 Mozambican floods. *Australian Journal of Emergency Management* 16(4): 25–33.

Martinez-Alier, J. 1995. The environment as a luxury good, or "too poor to be green"? *Ecological Economics* 13: 1–10.

Martinez-Alier, J. 2003. *The Environmentalism of the Poor: A Study of Ecological Conflicts and Valuation.* Cheltenham, UK: Edward Elgar.

Maskrey, A. 1993. Vulnerability accumulation in peripheral regions of Latin America: The challenge for disaster prevention and management. In *Natural Disasters: Protecting Vulnerable Communities,* edited by P. A. Merriman and C. W. A. Browitt. London: Thomas Telford, pp. 461–472.

Mathur, Ajay, Ian Burton, and Maarten van Aalst (eds.). 2004. *An Adaptation Mosaic: A Sample of the Emerging World Bank Work in Climate Change Adaptation.* Washington, DC: World Bank.

McCarthy, Michael. 2006. Global Warming: Passing the "Tipping Point." *Independent,* February 11.

McGuire, B., I. Mason, and C. Kilburn. 2002. *Natural Hazards and Environmental Change.* London: Arnold.

McIntosh, David M. 1998. Statement to the US House of Representatives Subcommittee on National Economic Growth, Natural Resources, and Regulatory Affairs. May 20.

McLaren, D. 2003. Environmental space, equity and the ecological debt. In *Just Sustainabilities: Development in an Unequal World*, edited by Julian Agyeman, Robert Bullard, and Bob Evans. Cambridge, MA: MIT Press.

McLaughlin, Paul, and Thomas Dietz. Forthcoming. Vulnerability to global environmental change. In *The Human Dimensions of Global Environmental Change*, edited by E. Rosa, A. Diekmann, T. Dietz, and C. Jaeger. Cambridge, MA: MIT Press.

McMichael, Philip. 2000. *Development and Social Change: A Global Perspective*, 2nd ed. Thousand Oaks, CA: Sage.

Mearsheimer, John J. 1994/95. The false promise of international institutions. *International Security* 19(3): 5–49.

Mendelsohn, Robert. 2001. *Global Warming and the American Economy: A Regional Assessment of Climate Change Impacts*. Northampton, MA: Edward Elgar.

Mendoza, Enrique G. 1997. Terms-of-trade uncertainty and economic growth. *Journal of Development Economics* 54: 323–356.

Mendoza, Ronald U. 2003. The multilateral trade regime: A global public good for all? In *Providing Global Public Goods: Managing Globalization*, edited by Inge Kaul, Pedro Conceicao, Katell Le Goulven, and Ronald U. Mendoza. New York: Oxford University Press.

Meyer, John W., David John Frank, Ann Hironaka, Evan Schofer, and Nancy Brandon Tuma. 1997. The structuring of a world environmental regime, 1870–1990. *International Organization* 51(4): 623–629.

Milanovic, Branko. 2002. True world income distribution, 1988 and 1993: First calculations based on household surveys alone. *Economic Journal* 112(476): 51–92.

Milanovic, Branko. 2005a. Can we discern the effect of globalization on income distribution? Evidence from household budget surveys. *World Bank Economic Review* 19(1): 21–24.

Milanovic, Branko. 2005b. *Worlds Apart: Measuring International and Global Inequality*. Princeton, NJ: Princeton University Press.

Miller, Marian. 1995. *The Third World in Global Environmental Politics*. Boulder, CO: Lynne Reinner.

Mitchell, J. K. 1999. *Crucibles of Hazard: Mega-Cities and Disasters in Transition*. Tokyo: UNU Press.

Mitchell, Ronald B. 1994. *Intentional Oil Pollution at Sea: Environmental Policy and Treaty Compliance*. Cambridge, MA: MIT Press.

Mitchell, R. 1998. Sources of transparency: Information systems in international regimes. *International Studies Quarterly* 42: 109–130.

Mitchell, Ronald B. 2002a. A quantitative approach to evaluating international environmental regimes. *Global Environmental Politics* 2(4): 58–83.

Mitchell, Ronald B. 2002b. International environment. In *Handbook of International Relations*, edited by Thomas Risse, Beth Simmons, and Walter Carlsnaes. Thousand Oaks, CA: Sage, pp. 500–516.

Mitchell, Ronald B., and Patricia Keilbach. 2001. Reciprocity, coercion, or exchange: Symmetry, asymmetry and power in institutional design. *International Organization* 55(4): 893–919.

Mitra, Barun S. 2002. Dealing with natural disaster: Role of the market. In *Liberty and Hard Cases*, edited by Tibor R. Machan. Stanford, CA: Hoover Institution, pp. 35–58.

Mkapa, Benjamin. 2004. Cancún's false promise: A view from the south. *Foreign Affairs* 83(3): 133–135.

Mohamed, Mahathir. 1995. Statement to the U.N. Conference on Environment and Development. In *Green Planet Blues: Environmental Politics from Stockholm to Rio*, edited by Ken Conca, Michael Alberty, and Geoffry D. Dabelko. Boulder, CO: Westview Press, pp. 33.

Moore, Mike. 2003. *A World Without Walls: Freedom, Development, Free Trade and Global Governance*. Cambridge: Cambridge University Press.

Moravcsik, Andrew. 2003a. Theory synthesis in international relations: Real not metaphysical. *International Studies Review* 5(1): 131–136.

Moravcsik, Andrew. 2003b. Liberal international relations theory: A scientific assessment. In *Progress in International Relations Theory: Appraising the Field*, edited by Colin Elman and Miriam Fendius Elman. Cambridge, MA: MIT Press, pp. 159–204.

Morris, Saul S., Oscar Neidecker-Gonzales, Calogero Carletto, Marcial Munguia, Juan Manuel Medina, and Quentin Wondon. 2002. Hurricane Mitch and the livelihoods of the rural poor in Honduras. *World Development* 30(1): 49–60.

Morse, Richard M. 1974. Trends and patterns of Latin American urbanization, 1750–1920. *Comparative Studies in Society and History* 6(4): 416–447.

Müller, B. 1999. *Justice in Global Warming Negotiations: How to Obtain a Procedurally Fair Compromise*. Oxford: Oxford Institute for Energy Studies.

Müller, B. 2001a. Fair compromise in a morally complex world. Paper presented at Pew Equity Conference, Washington, DC, April 17–18, 2001.

Müller, B. 2001b. Varieties of distributive justice in climate change: An editorial comment. *Climatic Change* 48: 273–288.

Mumma, Albert. 2001. The poverty of Africa's position at the climate change negotiations. *UCLA Journal of Environmental Law and Policy* 19(2): 181–208.

Munasinghe, M. 1999. Development, equity and sustainability (DES) in the context of climate change. Paper prepared for the IPCC Expert Meeting on Development, Equity and Sustainability, Colombo, Sri Lanka, April 27–29, 1999.

Munich Reinsurance Company. 2002. *Annual Review of Natural Catastrophes*. Munich: Munich Reinsurance Group.

Muradian, R., and J. Martinez-Alier. 2001a. Trade and the environment: From a "Southern" perspective. *Ecological Economics* 36: 281–297.

Muradian, R., and J. Martinez-Alier. 2001b. South-North materials flow: History and environmental repercussions. *Innovation: The European Journal of Social Science Research* 14(2): 171–187.

Muradian, R., and J. Martinez-Alier. 2001c. *Globalization and Poverty: An Ecological Perspective*. Berlin: Heinrich Böll Foundation.

Muradian, Roldan, and Martin O'Connor. 2001. Inter-country environmental load displacement and adjusted national sustainability indicators: Concepts and their policy applications. *International Journal of Sustainable Development* 4(3): 321–347.

Muradian, Roldan, Martin O'Connor, and Joan Martinez-Alier. 2002. Embodied pollution in trade: Estimating the "environmental load displacement" of industrialized countries. *Ecological Economics* 41: 51–67.

Murshed, S. Mansoob. 2003. The decline of the development contract and the development of violent internal conflict. Inaugural address as the Prince Claus Chair in Development and Equity, Utrecht University, May 12, 2003.

Mwandosya, M. J. 2000. *Survival Emissions: A Perspective from the South on Global Climate Change Negotiations*. Dar es Salaam: Dar es Salaam University Press and the Centre for Energy, Environment, Science and Technology.

Najam, Adil. 1995. International environmental negotiations: A strategy for the South. *International Environmental Affairs* 7(2): 249–287.

Najam, Adil. 2002a. The unraveling of the Rio bargain. *Politics and the Life Sciences* 21(2): 46–50.

Najam, Adil. 2002b. Financing sustainable development: Crises of legitimacy. *Progress in Development Studies* 2(2): 153–160.

Najam, Adil. 2003. The case against a new international environmental organization. *Global Governance* 9: 367–384.

Najam, Adil. 2004a. The view from the South: Developing countries in global environmental politics. In *The Global Environment: Institutions, Law, and Policy*, 2nd ed., edited by Regina Axelrod, David Downie, and Norman Vig. Washington, DC: CQ Press, pp. 225–243.

Najam, Adil. 2004b. Dynamics of the Southern collective: Developing countries in desertification negotiations. *Global Environmental Politics* 4(3): 128–154.

Najam, A., and A. Sagar. 1998. Avoiding a COP-out: Moving towards systematic decision-making under the climate convention. *Climatic Change* 39(4): iii–ix.

Najam, Adil, Atiq A. Rahman, Saleemul Huq, and Youba Sokona. 2003a. Integrating sustainable development into the Fourth Assessment Report of the Intergovernmental Panel on Climate Change. *Climate Policy* 3(1) (Suppl.): S9–S17.

Najam, Adil, Saleemul Huq, and Youba Sokona. 2003b. Climate negotiations beyond Kyoto: Developing countries concerns and interests. *Climate Policy* 3(3): 221–231.

Najam, Adil, Ioli Christopoulou, and William R. Moomaw. 2004. The emergent "system" of global environmental governance. *Global Environmental Politics* 4(4): 23–35.

Nakicenovic, N., and R. Swart (eds.). 2000. *Special Report on Emissions Scenarios: A Special Report of Working Group III of the Intergovernmental Panel on Climate Change.* Cambridge, UK: Cambridge University Press.

Narlikar, Amrita. 2004. The ministerial process and power dynamics in the WTO: Understanding failure from Seattle to Cancun. *New Political Economy* 9(3): 413–428.

Narlikar, Amrita, and Diana Tussie. 2004. The G20 at the Cancun Ministerial: Developing countries and their evolving coalitions in the WTO. *World Economy* 27(7): 947–966.

Neumayer, Eric. 2000. In defence of historical accountability for greenhouse gas emissions. *Ecological Economics* 33: 185–192.

Neumayer, Eric. 2002a. Do democracies exhibit stronger international environmental commitment? *Journal of Peace Research* 39(2): 139–164.

Neumayer, Eric. 2002b. Trade openness and environmental cooperation. *World Economy* 25(6): 815–832.

Neumayer, Eric. 2004. National carbon dioxide emissions: Geography matters. *Area* 36(1): 33–40.

New York Times. 1997. For Pacific Islanders, global warming is no idle threat. December 1, p. K9.

Nicholls, R. 1995. Coastal megacities and climate change. *GeoJournal* 37(3): 369–379.

Nicholls, R. J., and C. Small. 2002. Improved estimates of coastal populations and exposure to hazards released. *EOS* 83(28): 301–305.

Nicholls, R., F. Hoozemans, and M. Marchand. 1999. Increasing flood risk and wetland losses due to global sea-level rise: Regional and global analyses. *Global Environmental Change* 9: 69–87.

Nielson, D., and M. Tierney. 2003. Delegation to international organizations: Agency theory and World Bank environmental reform. *International Organization* 57(2): 241–276.

Nielson, Daniel, Catherine Weaver, and Michael Tierney. 2006. Bridging the Rationalist-Constructivist Divide: Re-engineering the Culture of the World Bank. Journal of International Relations and Development.

Norfolk, S., I. Nhantumbo, and J. Pereira. 2003. "Só para o Inglese ver"—The policy and practice of tenure reform in Mozambique. Sustainable Livelihoods in Southern Africa Research Paper 11. Brighton, UK: Institute of Development Studies.

North, Douglass C. 1981. *Structure and Change in Economic History*. New York: W.W. Norton.

North, Douglass C. 1990. *Institutions, Institutional Change and Economic Performance*. Cambridge: Cambridge University Press.

North, Douglass, and Barry Weingast. 1989. Constitutions and commitment: The evolution of institutions governing public choice in seventeenth-century England. *Journal of Economic History* 49(4): 803–832.

O'Brien, K., and R. Leichenko. 2000. Double exposure: Assessing the impacts of climate change within the context of globalization. *Global Environmental Change* 10: 221–232.

O'Brien, K. L., and R. Leichenko. 2003. Winners and losers in the context of global change. *Annals of the Association of American Geographers* 93(1): 89–103.

O'Brien, K., R. Leichenko, U. Kelkar, H. Venema, G. Aandahl, H. Tompkins, A. Javed, S. Bhadwal, S. Barg, L. Nygaard, and J. West. 2004. Mapping vulnerability to multiple stressors: Climate change and economic globalization in India. *Global Environmental Change* 14: 303–313.

O'Driscoll, Gerald P. 2003. *2003 Index of Economic Freedom*. Washington, DC: Heritage Foundation.

Office of the Press Secretary. Text of a Letter from the President to Senators Hagel, Helms, Craig, and Roberts. March 13, 2001. Available at http://www.whitehouse.gov/news/releases/2001/03/20010314.html.

O'Keefe, P., K. Westgate, and B. Wisner. 1976. Taking the naturalness out of natural disasters. *Nature* 260: 566–567.

O'Laughlin, B. 1996. Through a divided glass: dualism, class and the agrarian question in Mozambique. *Journal of Peasant Studies* 23(4): 1–39.

Olson, Mancur. 1965. *The Logic of Collective Action*. Cambridge: Harvard University Press.

Olson, Richard S. 2000. Toward a politics of disaster: Losses, values, agendas, and blame. *International Journal of Mass Emergencies and Disasters* 18(2): 265–287.

Olson, Richard, and A. Cooper Drury. 1997. Un-therapeutic communities: A cross-national analysis of post-disaster political unrest. *International Journal of Mass Emergencies and Disasters* 15(2): 221–238.

Opschoor, J. B. 1995. Ecospace and the fall and rise of throughput intensity. *Ecological Economics* 15(2): 137–141.

Organization for Economic Co-operation and Development (OECD) 1974. Recommendation on the Implementation of the Polluter-Pays Principle. C(74)223. Paris: OECD.

Organization of Petroleum-Exporting Countries (OPEC) 1998. OPEC Statement by Dr. Rilwanu Lukman, Secretary General of OPEC. Available at http://www.opec.org.

Ostrom, Elinor. 1990. *Governing the Commons: The Evolution of Institutions for Collective Action*. Cambridge: Cambridge University Press.

Ostrom, Elinor. 1998. A behavioral approach to the rational choice theory of collective action. *American Political Science Review* 92(1): 1–23.

Ostry, Sylvia. 1999. The Uruguay Round North-South grand bargain: Implications for future negotiations. In *The Political Economy of International Trade Law*, edited by Daniel L. M. Kennedy and James D. Southwick. Cambridge: Cambridge University Press.

Ott, Hermann E. 2001. The Bonn Agreement to the Kyoto Protocol—Paving the way for ratification. *International Environmental Agreements: Politics, Law and Economics* 1(4): 469–476.

Ott, Herman, E. 2003. Warning signs from Delhi: Troubled waters ahead for global climate policy. In *Yearbook of International Environmental Law*, Vol. 13. Oxford: Oxford University Press.

Ott, Hermann E., and Wolfgang Sachs. 2002. The ethics of international emissions trading. In *Ethics. Equity and International Negotiations on Climate Change*, edited by Luiz Pinguelli-Rosa and Mohan Munasinghe. Cheltenham, UK: Edward Elgar, pp. 158–178.

Ott, Konrad, Gernot Klepper, Stephan Lingner, Achim Schäfer, Jürgen Scheffran, and Detlef Sprinz. 2004. *Reasoning Goals of Climate Protection. Specification of Article 2 UNFCCC*. Berlin: German Federal Environmental Agency.

Owusu, Francis. 2003. Pragmatism and the gradual shift from dependency to neoliberalism: The World Bank, African leaders and development policy in Africa. *World Development* 31(10): 1655–1672.

Oye, Kenneth A. (ed.). 1986a. *Cooperation Under Anarchy*. Princeton, NJ: Princeton University Press.

Oye, Kenneth A. 1986b. Explaining cooperation under anarchy: Hypotheses and strategies. In *Cooperation Under Anarchy*, edited by Kenneth Oye. Princeton, NJ: Princeton University Press.

Paige, Jeffrey M. 1997. *Coffee and Power: Revolution and the Rise of Democracy in Central America*. Cambridge, MA: Harvard University Press.

Parikh, Jyoti. 1992a. *Consumption Patterns: the Driving Force of Environmental Stress*. New Delhi: Indira Ghandi Institute of Development Research.

Parikh, Jyoti. 1992b. IPCC strategies unfair to the South. *Nature* 360: 507–508.

Parikh, Jyoti K., and Kirit Parikh. 2002. *Climate Change: India's Perceptions, Positions, Policies and Possibilities*. Paris: OECD.

Parks, Bradley C., and J. Timmons Roberts. 2005. Environmental and ecological justice. In *Palgrave Advances in International Environmental Politics*. Basingstoke, UK: Palgrave Macmillan, pp. 329–360.

Parks, Bradley C., and J. Timmons Roberts. 2006. Globalization, vulnerability to climate change and perceived injustice. *Society and Natural Resources* 19(4): 337–355.

Parks, Bradley C., and Michael J. Tierney. 2004. Cooperation or collusion: Explaining bilateral and multilateral environmental aid to developing countries.

Paper presented at the American Political Science Association Annual Meeting, September 2–5, 2004, Chicago, Illinois.

Parks, Bradley C., Michael J. Tierney, Robert Hicks, and J. Timmons Roberts. 2006. Greening Aid? Understanding Environmental Assistance to Developing Countries. Book manuscript. College of William and Mary, VA.

Paterson, Matthew. 2000. *Understanding Global Environmental Politics: Domination, Accumulation and Resistance*. London: Macmillan.

Paterson, Matthew. 2001. Principles of justice in the context of global climate change. In *International Relations and Global Climate Change*, edited by Urs Luterbacher and Detlef Sprinz. Cambridge, MA: MIT Press, pp. 119–126.

Paul, S. 1992. Accountability in public services: exit, voice and control. *World Development* 20(7): 1047–1060.

Pelling, M. 1998. Participation, social capital and vulnerability to urban flooding in Guyana. *Journal of International Development* 10: 469–486.

Pelling, M. 2004. Social capital and justice in adaptation to climate change. In *Justice and Adaptation to Climate Change*, edited by W. N. Adger, S. Huq, M. J. Mace, and J. Paavola. Cambridge, MA: MIT Press.

Pelling, M., and J. Uitto. 2002. Small island developing states: Natural disaster vulnerability and global change. *Environmental Hazards* 3: 49–62.

Pettis, M. 1996. The liquidity trap: Latin America's free market past. *Foreign Affairs* 75(6): 2–7.

Pettis, M. 1998. The new dance of the millions: Liability management and the next debt crisis. *Challenge* 41(4): 90–100.

Pettis, Michael. 2001. *The Volatility Machine: Emerging Economies and the Threat of Their Financial Collapse*. Oxford: Oxford University Press.

Pielke, Roger A. Sr., 2002a. The U.S. National Climate Change Assessment: Do the Climate Models Project a Useful Picture of Regional Climate? House Subcommittee on Oversight and Investigations. July 25, 2002. Available at http://energycommerce.house.gov/107/hearings/07252002Hearing676/Pielke,Sr.1144.htm.

Pielke, Roger A. Jr. 2002b. Statement of Dr. Roger A. Pielke, Jr., to the Committee on Environment and Public Works of the United States Senate. March 13, 2002. Available at http://sciencepolicy.colorado.edu/about_us/meet_us/roger_pielke/rp_senate/13_2002/testimony.pdf.

Platt, Rutherford H. 1999. *Disasters and Democracy: The Politics of Extreme Natural Events*. Washington, DC: Island Press.

Population Action International. 1998. Appendix—Carbon profiles: Countries' annual per capita carbon dioxide emissions from fossil fuel combustion and dement production, 1950–1995. Available at http://www.populationaction.org/why_pop/carbon/carbon_pdf.htm. Accessed July 30, 1999.

Porter Gareth, and Janet W. Brown. 1991. *Global Environmental Politics*. Boulder, CO: Westview Press.

Porter, Gareth, Janet Welsh Brown, and Pamela Chasek. 2000. *Global Environmental Politics*, 3rd edition. Boulder, CO: Westview Press.

Portes, Alejandro. 1990. Latin American urbanization during the years of the crisis. *Latin American Research Review* 25: 7–44.

Portes, Alejandro. 1997. Neoliberalism and the sociology of development: Emerging trends and unanticipated facts. *Population and Development Review* 23 (June): 229–259.

Portes, Alejandro, and John Walton. 1976. *Urban Latin America: The Political Condition from Above and Below*. Austin: University of Texas Press.

Prebisch, Raul. 1950. *The Economic Development of Latin America and Its Principal Problems*. New York: United Nations.

Prescott-Allen, Robert. 2001. *The Wellbeing of Nations: A Country-by-Country Index of Quality of Life and the Environment*. Washington, DC: Island Press and International Development Research Centre, Ottawa.

Princen, Thomas, Michael Maniates, and Ken Conca (eds.). 2002. *Confronting Consumption*. Cambridge, MA: MIT Press.

Przeworski, Adam, and James Raymond Vreeland. 2000. The effects of IMF programs on economic growth. *Journal of Development Economics* 62: 385–421.

Putnam, Robert D. 1993. *Making Democracy Work: Civic Traditions in Modern Italy*. Princeton, NJ: Princeton University Press.

Putnam, Robert D. 2000. *Bowling Alone: The Collapse and Revival of American Community*. New York: Simon and Schuster.

Quiroga, Rayen (ed.). 1994. *El Tigre sin Selva. Consecuencias Ambientales de la Transformación Económica de Chile: 1974–93*. Santiago: Instituto de Ecología Política.

Rabin, Matthew. 1993. Incorporating fairness into game theory and economics. *American Economic Review* 83: 1281–1302.

Rahman, A., N. Robbins, and A. Roncerel (eds.). 1992. *Consumption vs. Population: Which Is the Climate Bomb?* Brussels: Climate Network Europe.

Raiffa, Howard. 1982. *The Art and Science of Negotiation*. Cambridge, MA: Harvard University Press.

Rajan, M. K. 1997. *Global Environmental Politics*. Delhi: Oxford University Press.

Ramo, Joshua C. 1999. The three marketers. *Time* magazine February 15, pp. 34–42.

Ranganath, P. 2000. *Mitigation and the Consequences of International Aid in Postdisaster Reconstruction*. Boulder, CO: University of Colorado, Institute of Behavioral Science, Natural Hazards Research and Applications Information Center.

Raustiala, Kal. 1997. Domestic institutions and regulatory cooperation: Comparative responses to the global biodiversity regime. *World Politics* 49(4): 482–509.

Recchia, Steven. 2001. Explaining the International Environmental Cooperation of Democratic Countries. Paper 01-02. Center for the Study of Democracy. University of California, Irvine.

Redclift, Michael. 1987. *Sustainable Development: Exploring the Contradictions*. London and New York: Methuen.

Reed, David. 1992. *Structural Adjustment and the Environment*. London: Earthscan.

Reuschemeyer, Dietrich, Evelyne Stephens, and John Stephens. 1992. *Capitalist Development and Democracy*. Cambridge, UK: Polity Press.

Reuters News Service. 2002. Lawsuits may be next weapon in climate change fight. March 6.

Ribot, J. C. 1995. The causal structure of vulnerability: Its application to climate impact analysis. *GeoJournal* 35: 119–122.

Ribot, J. C. 1996. Climate variability, climate change and vulnerability: Moving forward by looking back. In *Climate Variability, Climate Change and Social Vulnerability in the Semi-Arid Tropics*, edited by J. C. Ribot, A. R. Magalhaes, and S. Panagides. Cambridge: Cambridge University Press, pp. 1–10.

Ribot, J. C., A. R. Magalhaes, and S. S. Panagides (eds.). 1996. *Climate Variability, Climate Change and Social Vulnerability in the Semi-Arid Tropics*. Cambridge: Cambridge University Press.

Richards, M. 2001. *A Review of the Effectiveness of Developing Country Participation in the Climate Change Convention Negotiations*. London: Overseas Development Institute. Available at www.odi.org.uk/iedg/wps_intro.html.

Ricupero, Rubens. 1998. Integration of developing countries into the multilateral trading system. In *The Uruguay Round and Beyond. Essays in Honour of Arthur Dunkel*, edited by J. Bhagwati and M. Hirsch. Berlin: Springer-Verlag, p. 17.

Ringius, Lasse, Asbjorn Torvanger, and Arild Underdal. 2002. Burden sharing and fairness principles in international climate policy. *International Environmental Agreements: Politics, Law and Economics* 2: 1–22.

Roberts, J. Timmons. 1996a. Global restructuring and the environment in Latin America. In *Latin America in the World Economy*, edited by Roberto P. Korzeniewicz and William C. Smith. Westport, CT: Greenwood Press, pp. 187–210.

Roberts, J. Timmons. 1996b. Predicting participation in environmental treaties: A world system analysis. *Sociological Inquiry* 66(1): 38–57.

Roberts, J. Timmons. 2001. Global inequality and climate change. *Society and Natural Resources* 14(6): 501–509.

Roberts, J. Timmons, and Peter E. Grimes. 1997. Carbon intensity and economic development 1962–1991: A brief exploration of the environmental Kuznets curve. *World Development* 25(2): 181–187.

Roberts, J. Timmons, and Peter E. Grimes. 1999. Extending the world-system to the whole system: Toward a political economy of the biosphere. In *Ecology and the World System*, edited by Walter L. Goldfrank, David Goodman and, Andrew Szasz. Westport, CT: Greenwood Press, pp. 59–83.

Roberts, J. Timmons, and Amy Hite. 2000. *From Modernization to Globalization: Perspectives on Development and Social Change*. London: Blackwell.

Roberts, J. Timmons, and Melissa Toffolon-Weiss. 2001. *Chronicles from the Environmental Justice Frontline*. Cambridge, UK: Cambridge University Press.

Roberts, J. Timmons, and Nikki D. Thanos. 2003. *Trouble in Paradise: Globalization and Environmental Crises in Latin America*. New York: Routledge.

Roberts, J. Timmons, Peter E. Grimes, and Jodie L. Manale. 2003. Social roots of global environmental change: A world-systems analysis of carbon dioxide emissions. *Journal of World-Systems Research* 9(2): 277–315.

Roberts, J. Timmons, Bradley C. Parks, and Alexis Vásquez. 2004. Who ratifies environmental treaties and why? Institutionalism, structuralism and participation by 192 nations in 22 treaties. *Global Environmental Politics* 4(3): 22–64.

Robinson, N. A. (ed.). 1992. *Agenda 21 and UNCED Proceedings*, Vols. 1 and 2. New York: Oceana Publications.

Robleto, M., and W. Marcelo. 1992. *La Deuda Ecológica. Una Perspectiva Sociopolítica*. Santiago: Instituto Ecología Política.

Rodenburg, Eric, Dan Tunstall, and Frederik van Bolhuis. 1995. Environmental Indicators for Global Cooperation. Working Paper 11. Global Environmental Facility. Washington, DC: World Bank.

Rodgers, Malcolm. 1999. *In Debt to Disaster: What Happened to Honduras after Hurricane Mitch*. London: Christian Aid. Available online at http://www.christian-aid.org.uk/indepth/9910inde/indebt2.htm.

Rodney, Walter. 1972. *How Europe Underdeveloped Africa*. Washington, DC: Harvard University Press.

Rodrik, Dani. 1998. The global fix. *New Republic* 2 (November): 17–19.

Rodrik, Dani. 1999a. *The New Global Economy and Developing Countries: Making Openness Work*. Baltimore, MD: Johns Hopkins University Press.

Rodrik, Dani. 1999b. Where did all the growth go? External shocks, social conflicts, and growth collapses. *Journal of Economic Growth* 4(4): 385–412.

Rodrik, Dani. 2000. Institutions for high-quality growth: What they are and how to acquire them. *Studies in Comparative International Development* 35(3): 3–31.

Rodrik, Dani. 2001. Trading in illusions. *Foreign Policy* 123 (March–April): 54–62.

Rodrik, Dani. 2003a. Interview at La Universidad de los Andes, Colombia. March 2003. Available online at http://www.webpondo.org/.

Rodrik, D. (ed.). 2003b. *In Search of Prosperity: Analytic Narratives on Economic Growth*. Princeton, NJ: Princeton University Press.

Rodrik, Dani. 2004a. Growth strategies. In *Handbook of Economic Growth*, edited by Philippe Aghion and Steven Durlauf. New York: Elsevier.

Rodrik, Dani. 2004b. Industrial Policy for the Twenty-First Century. Cambridge, MA: Harvard University. Working Paper.

Rodrik, Dani. 2005. Why we learn nothing from regressing economic growth on policies. Harvard University Working Paper. Cambridge, MA.

Rodrik, Dani, Arvind Subramanian, and Francesco Trebbi. 2004. Institutions rule: The primacy of institutions over geography and integration in economic development. *Journal of Economic Growth* 9(2): 131–165.

Rohter, Larry. 1998. Now ruined economies afflict Central America. *New York Times* November 13, p. A12.

Røpke. 1999. Prices are not worth that much. *Ecological Economics* 29: 45–46.

Rose, Adam. 1998. Global warming policy: Who decides what is fair? *Energy Policy* 26(1): 1–3.

Rose, A., B. Stevens, J. Edmonds, and M. Wise. 1998. International equity and differentiation in global warming policy. *Environmental and Resource Economics* 12: 25–51.

Ross, Michael. 1996. Conditionality and logging reform in the tropics. In *Institutions for Environmental Aid*, eds. Robert O. Keohane and Marc A. Levy. Cambridge, MA: MIT Press, pp. 167–197.

Ross, Michael L. 1999. The political economy of the resource curse. *World Politics* 51: 296–322.

Ross, Michael L. 2001. Does oil hinder democracy? *World Politics* 53: 325–361.

Ross, Michael. 2004. How does natural resource wealth influence civil wars? Evidence from thirteen cases. *International Organization* 58: 35–67.

Rossi, Clóvis. 1997. Controle da emissão de gases divide FHC e Clinton. *Folha de Sao Paulo*, October 10, p. A-15.

Rothstein, Bo. 2002. Social capital and quality of government: The causal mechanism. Paper read at The Honesty and Trust Project: Theory and Experience in the Light of Post-Socialist Transformation. Collegium Budapest, November 22–23, 2002.

Rowlands, I. H. 1995. *The Politics of Global Atmospheric Change.* Manchester, UK: Manchester University Press.

Rowlands, Ian. 2001. Transnational corporations and global environmental politics. In *Non-State Actors in World Politics*, edited by Daphné Josselin and William Wallace. Basingstoke, UK: Palgrave.

Ruggie, John Gerard. 1982. International regimes, transactions, and change: Embedded liberalism in the postwar economic order. *International Organization* 36(2): 379–415.

Ruggie, John Gerard. 1983. Political structure and change in the international economic order: The North-South dimension. In *The Antinomies of Interdependence*, edited by John Gerard Ruggie. New York: Columbia University Press, pp. 423–487.

Russi, D., and R. Muradian. 2003. Gobernanza global y responsabilidad ambiental. *Ecologia Política* 24: 95–105.

Russi, Daniela, Ignasi Puig Ventosa, Jesús Ramos Martín, Miquel Ortega Cerdà, and Paula Ungar. 2003. *Deuda Ecológica ¿Quién Debe a Quién?* Barcelona: el Observatorio de la deuda en la Globalización.

Rustomjee, Cyrus. 2004. Why developing countries need a stronger voice. Running faster at the IMF, but where's the progress? *Finance & Development* 41(3): 21–23.

Ruth, M. 1998. Dematerialization in five US metals sectors: Implications for energy use and CO_2 emissions. *Resources Policy* 24(1): 1–18.

Sachs, Jeffrey D., and Andrew Warner. 1995. *Natural Resource Abundance and Economic Growth*. Cambridge, MA: National Bureau of Economic Research.

Sachs, Jeffrey, and Andrew M. Warner. 1999. The big push, natural resource booms and growth. *Journal of Development Economics* 59: 43–76.

Sachs, Jeffrey D., and Andrew M. Warner. 2001. The curse of natural resources *European Economic Review* 45: 827–838.

Sachs, Wolfgang. 1999. *Planet Dialectics: Explorations in Environment and Development*. London: Zed Books.

Sachs, Wolfgang (ed.). 2002. *The Jo'burg Memo: Fairness in a Fragile World*. Berlin: Heinrich Böll Foundation.

Saegert, Susan, Gary Winkel, and Charles Swartz. 2002. Social capital and crime in New York city's low-income housing. *Housing Policy Debate* 13(1): 189–226.

Sagar, A. D., and Najam, A. 1998. The human development index: A critical review. *Ecological Economics* 25: 249–264.

Sala-i-Martin, Xavier. 2002. The Disturbing "Rise" in Global Income Inequality. Working Paper 8904. Cambridge, MA: National Bureau of Economic Research. Available online at http://papers.nber.org/papers/w8904.

Sand, Peter. 1993. International environmental law after Rio. *European Journal of International Law* 4(3): 377–389.

Sandbrook, Richard. 1997. UNGASS has run out of steam. *International Affairs* 73: 641–654.

Sari, Agus. 2003. COP-9 in Milan: A fashionable trend for climate agreements. Centre for Science and Environment. Available online at http://www.cseindia .org/campaign/ew/agreements.htm.

Sassen, Saskia. 2000. *The Global City*, Rev. ed. Princeton, NJ: Princeton University Press.

Schelling, Thomas. 1960. *The Strategy of Conflict*. Cambridge, MA: Harvard University Press.

Schelling, Thomas. 2002. What makes greenhouse sense? Time to rethink the Kyoto Protocol. *Foreign Affairs* 81(3): 2–9.

Schiller, Andrew, and Alex de Sherbinin, Wen-hua Hsieh, and Alex Pulsipher 2001. The vulnerability of global cities to climate hazards. Paper presented at the 2001 Open Meeting of the Human Dimensions of Global Environmental Change Research Community October, 6–8, 2001, Rio de Janeiro, Brazil.

Schneider, S. 1991. Three reports of the Intergovernmental Panel on Climate Change. *Environment* 33(1): 25–30.

Schreurs, Miranda A., and Elizabeth Economy (eds.). 1997. *The Internationalization of Environmental Protection*. Oxford: Oxford University Press.

Schultz, Kenneth A., and Barry R. Weingast. 2003. The democratic advantage: Institutional foundations of financial power in international competition. *International Organization* 57(1): 3–42.

Scott, J. C. 1976. *The Moral Economy of the Peasant: Rebellion and Subsistence in Southeast Asia*. New Haven, CT: Yale University Press.

Sebenius, J. K. 1983. Negotiation arithmetic: Adding and subtracting issues and parties. *International Organization* 32: 281–316.

Sebenius, James K. 1991. Designing negotiations towards a new regime: The case of global warming. *International Security* 15(4): 110–148.

Secor, Laura. 2003. The debate over global inequality heats up. *Boston Globe*, January 5, p. D1.

Seelye, K. Q. 2001. Global warming may bring new variety of class action. *New York Times*, September 6, p. A14.

Selden, T. M., and D. Song. 1994. Environmental quality and development: Is there a Kuznets curve for air pollution emissions? *Journal of Environmental Economics and Management* 27: 147–162.

Sell, Susan. 1996. North-South environmental bargaining: Ozone, climate change, and biodiversity. *Global Governance* 2(1): 97–118.

Sell, Susan. 2003. *Private Power, Public Law: The Globalization of Intellectual Property Rights*. Cambridge: Cambridge University Press.

Sell, Susan, and Aseem Prakash. 2004. Using ideas strategically: The contest between business and NGO networks in intellectual property rights. *International Studies Quarterly* 48(1): 143–175.

Sen, Amartya. 1977. Rational fools: A critique of the behavioural foundations of economic theory. *Philosophy and Public Affairs* 6(4): 317–344.

Sen, Amartya. 1982. *Poverty and Famines : An Essay on Entitlements and Deprivation*. Oxford: Clarendon Press.

Sen, Amartya. 1999. Democracy as a universal value. *Journal of Democracy* 10(3): 3–17.

Serageldin, T. H. Ismail. 1998. The social-natural science gap in educating for sustainable development. In *Organizing Knowledge for Environmentally Sustainable Development*, edited by T. H. Ismail Serageldin, Joan Martin-Brown, Gustavo Lopez Ospina, Jeann Damlamian, and Tariq Husain. Washington, DC: World Bank.

Shadlen, Ken. 2003. Debt, finance, and the IMF: Three decades of debt crises in Latin America. In *South America, Central America and the Caribbean 2004*. London: Europa Publications, pp. 8–12.

Shadlen, Ken. 2004. Patents and pills, power and procedure: The North-South politics of public health in the WTO. *Studies in Comparative International Development* 39(3): 76–108.

Shadlen, Ken. 2004. Regional vs. multilateral strategies for economic integration: Exchanging market access for development? Working Paper. London School of Economics and Political Science.

Shadlen, Ken. 2005. Exchanging development for market access? Deep integration and industrial policy under multilateral and regional-bilateral trade agreements. *Review of International Political Economy* 12(5): 750–775.

Shafer, Michael D. 1994. *Winners and Losers: How Sectors Shape the Developmental Prospects of States.* Ithaca, NY: Cornell University Press.

Shah, Anup. 2002. COP8-Delhi Conference. Climate Change and Global Warming Website. http://www.globalissues.org/EnvIssues/GlobalWarming/Delhi.asp. Last updated Nov. 2, 2002.

Shannon, Thomas. 1996. *An Introduction to the World System Perspective.* Boulder, CO: Westview Press.

Shue, Henry. 1992. The unavoidability of justice. In *The International Politics of the Environment*, edited by A. Hurrell and B. Kingsbury. Oxford: Clarendon Press, pp. 373–397.

Shue, Henry. 1993. Subsistence emissions and luxury emissions. *Law and Policy* 15(1): 39–53.

Sidaway, J. D., and M. Power. 1995. Socio-spatial transformations in the "postsocialist" periphery: The case of Maputo, Mozambique. *Environment and Planning A* 27(2): 1463–1491.

Sijm, J. P. M. et al. 2000. *The Multi-Sector Convergence Approach of Burden Sharing: An Analysis of its Cost Implications.* Oslo: Center for International Climate and Environmental Research (CICERO).

Sikkink, Kathryn. 1993. The power of principled ideas: Human rights policies in the United States and Western Europe. In *Ideas and Foreign Policy: Beliefs, Institutions and Political Change*, edited by Judith Goldstein and Robert Keohane. Ithaca, NY: Cornell University Press, pp. 139–170.

Simmons, Beth. 1994. *Who Adjusts: Domestic Sources of Foreign Economic Policy.* Princeton, NJ: Princeton University Press.

Simmons, Beth. 2000. International law and state behavior: Commitment and compliance in international monetary affairs. *American Political Science Review* 94(4): 819–836.

Simms, Andrew, Aubrey Meyer, and Nick Robins. 1999. *Who Owes Who: Climate Change, Debt, Equity and Survival.* London: Christian Aid.

Simms, Andrew, John Magrath, and Hannah Reid. 2004. *Up in Smoke? Threats From, and Response To, the Impact of Global Warming on Human Development.* London: New Economics Foundation.

Sjöstedt, Gunnar. 2001. International negotiation and the management of transboundary risks. In *Transboundary Risk Management*, edited by J. Linnerooth-Bayer, R. E. Löfstedt, and G. Sjöstedt. London: Earthscan.

Skidmore, Mark, and Hideki Toya. 2002. Do natural disasters promote long-run growth? *Economic Inquiry* 40(4): 664–687.

Sklair, Leslie. 2002. *Globalization: Capitalism and Its Alternatives*. Oxford: Oxford University Press.

Smith, K. R. 1991. Allocating responsibility for global warming: The natural debt index. *Ambio* 20(2): 95–96.

Snidal, Duncan. 2002. Rational choice and international relations. In *Handbook of International Relations*, edited by Walter Carlsnael, Thomas Risse, and Beth Simmons. New York: Sage, pp. 73–94.

Snidal, Duncan. 2004. Formal models of international politics. In *Models, Numbers, and Cases: Methods for Studying International Relations*, edited by D. Sprinz and Y. Wolinsky-Nahmias. Ann Arbor: University of Michigan Press, pp. 227–260.

Snyder, Jack. 1991. *Myths of Empire: Domestic Politics and International Ambition*. Ithaca, NY: Cornell University Press.

Solomon, S. M., and Forbes, D. L. 1999. Coastal hazards and associated management issues on South Pacific islands. *Ocean and Coastal Management* 42: 523–554.

Sprinz, D. 2004. Environment meets statistics: Quantitative analysis of international environmental policy. In *Models, Numbers, and Cases: Methods for Studying International Relations*, edited by D. Sprinz and Y. Wolinsky-Nahmias. Ann Arbor: University of Michigan Press, pp. 177–192.

Sprinz, D., and T. Vaahtoranta. 1994. The Interest-based explanation of international environmental policy. *International Organization* 48(1): 77–105.

Sprinz, Detlef F., and Yael Wolinsky-Nahmias (eds.). 2004. *Models, Numbers and Cases: Methods for Studying International Relations*. Ann Arbor: University of Michigan Press.

Sridharan, K. 1998. G-15 and South-South cooperation: Promise and performance. *Third World Quarterly* 19(3): 357–373.

Stasavage, David. 1999. Causes and consequences of corruption: Mozambique in transition. *Commonwealth and Comparative Politics* 37(3): 65–97.

Stavins, Robert. 2004. Can an Effective Global Climate Treaty be Based Upon Sound Science, Rational Economics, and Pragmatic Politics? Discussion Paper. Washington, DC: Resources for the Future.

Stein, Arthur. 1990. *Why Nations Cooperate: Circumstance and Choice in International Relations*. Ithaca: Cornell University Press.

Stephen, L., and T. E. Downing. 2001. Getting the scale right: A comparison of analytical methods for vulnerability assessment and household-level targeting. *Disasters* 25(2): 113–135.

Stevens, William K. 1997. U.S. and Japan key to outcome in climate talks. *New York Times* August 12, p. C1.

Stiglitz, Joseph E. 1998. More Instruments and Broader Goals: Moving Toward the Post-Washington Consensus. WIDER Annual Lectures 2. Helsinki, January 1998.

Stiglitz, Joseph E. 2000. Capital market liberalization, economic growth, and instability. *World Development* 28(6): 1075–1086.

Stiglitz, Joseph E. 2002a. *Globalization and Its Discontents.* New York: Penguin Books.

Stiglitz, Joseph E. 2002b. Globalism's discontents. *American Prospect* (Winter 2002): A16–A21.

Stiglitz, Joseph E., and Andrew Charlton. 2004. A development round of trade negotiations? Paper presented at the Annual Bank Conference on Development Economics, Europe, May 11, 2004.

Stonich, Susan. 1993. *I am Destroying the Land: The Political Ecology of Poverty and Environmental Destruction in Honduras.* Boulder, CO: Westview Press.

Streck, C. 2001. The Global Environment Facility—A role model for international governance? *Global Environmental Politics* 1(2):71–94.

Subramanian, A., and D. Roy. 2003. Who can explain the Mauritian miracle: Meade, Romer, Sachs, or Rodrik? In *In Search of Prosperity: Analytic Narratives on Economic Growth*, edited by D. Rodrik. Princeton, NJ: Princeton University Press, pp. 205–243.

Summers, Lawrence. 2000. Cited in D. Mishra, A. Mody, and A. P. Murshid, Private capital flows and growth. *Finance and Development* 38(2).

Summers, Larry. 2001. Remarks at the World Bank Country Directors' Retreat. May 2, 2001.

Susman, P., P. O'Keefe, and B. Wisner. 1983. Global disasters, a radical interpretation. In *Interpretations of Calamity*, edited by K. Hewitt. London: Allen & Unwin, pp. 263–283.

Susskind, Lawrence E. 1994. *Environmental Diplomacy.* New York: Oxford University Press.

Sutcliffe, Bob. 2004. World inequality and globalization. *Oxford Review of Economic Policy* 20(1): 15–37.

Swart, Rob, John Robinson, and Stewart Cohen. 2003. Climate change and sustainable development: Expanding the options. *Climate Policy* 3S1: S19–S40.

Tangen, Kristian, Gørild Heggelund, and Jørund Buen. 2001. China's climate change positions: At a turning point? *Energy and Environment* 12(2–3): 237–252.

Tannner, Christopher. 1997. The land question in Mozambique (Part 2): Donor assistance and present status of the problem. Available at http://www.fao.org/sd/ltdirect/LTan0011.htm. Accessed February 22, 2004.

Tanner, Christopher. 2002. Law-making in an African Context: The 1997 Mozambican Land Law. Online Legal Papers 26. Rome: Food and Agricultural Organization.

Tarp, Finn, Channing Arndt, Henning Tarp Jensen, Sherman Robinson, and Rasmus Heltberg. 2002. *Facing the Development Challenge in Mozambique: An Economywide Perspective*. Washington, DC: International Food Policy Research Institute.

Tata Energy Research Institute (TERI). 1997. *Long Term Carbon Emission Targets Aiming Towards Convergence*. New Delhi: TERI.

The Economist. 1997. Mahathir, Soros and the currency markets. September 27.

The Economist. 2002a. Blowing hot and cold. July 6, p. 9.

The Economist. 2002b. The dollar and the deficit. September 12.

The Economist. 2003. The WTO under fire: Why did the world trade talks in Mexico fall apart? And who is to blame? September 20, pp. 26–28.

The Economist. 2004. The disappearing dollar: How long can it remain the world's most important reserve currency? December 2.

The Guardian. 2003. Global warming is now a weapon of mass destruction. July 28.

Tierney, Michael J. 2003. Commitments, Credibility and International Cooperation: The Integration of Soviet Successor States into Western Multilateral Regimes. Ph.D. Dissertation, University of California, San Diego.

Tierney, Michael J., and Catherine Weaver. 2004. Principles and principals? The possibilities for theoretical synthesis and scientific progress in the study of international organizations. Paper presented at Conference on Theoretical Synthesis in the Study of International Organizations. February 6–7, 2004, Washington, DC.

Timmerman, P. 1996. Breathing room: Negotiations on climate change. *Earthly Goods: Environmental Change and Social Justice*, edited by F. O. Hampson and J. Reppy. Ithaca, NY: Cornell University Press.

Timmerman, P., and R. White. 1997. Magahydropolic: Coastal cities in the context of global environmental change. *Global Environmental Change* 7(3): 205–234.

Tol, R. S. J. 1995. The damage cost of climate change: Towards more comprehensive calculations. *Environmental and Resource Economics* 5: 353–374.

Tollison, R. D., and T. D. Willett. 1979. On economic theory of mutually advantageous issue linkages in international negotiations. *International Organization* 33: 425–449.

Torvanger, Asbjorn, and Odd Godal. 2004. An evaluation of Pre-Kyoto differentiation proposals for national greenhouse gas abatement targets. *International Environmental Agreements: Politics, Law and Economics* 4: 65–91.

Torvanger, Asbjorn, and Lasse Ringius. 2002. Criteria for evaluation of burden-sharing rules in international climate policy. *International Environmental Agreements: Politics, Law and Economics* 2: 221–235.

Toye, J. 1995. The NIE and its implications for development theory. In *New Institutional Economics and Third World Development*, edited by J. Harriss, J. Hunter, and C. Lewis. London: Routledge, pp. 49–68, 323–353.

Traub, James. 2005. The statesman. *New York Times*, September 18.

Turner, R. K., S. Subak, and N. Adger. 1996. Pressures, trends and impacts in coastal zones: Interactions between socio-economic and natural systems. *Environmental Management* 20: 159–173.

Tuvalu Online. 2003. Tuvalu statement by the Honorable Saufatu Sopoanga OBE. Prime Minister and Minister of Foreign Affairs at the 58th Session of the United Nations General Assembly, New York, 24th September 2003. Available at http://www.tuvaluislands.com/news/archived/2003/2003_un_speech.htm.

Tuvalu Online. 2004a. French film company to release Tuvalu documentary. March 21, 2004. Available at http://www.tuvaluislands.com/news/archives/2004/2004-03-etcfrance1.htm.

Tuvalu Online. 2004b. Tuvalu statement delivered by the Honourable Maatia Toafa, Acting Prime Minister at the General Debate of the 59th Session of the United Nations General Assembly New York, 24th September 2004. Available at http://www.tuvaluislands.com/news/archived/2004/2004-09-24.htm.

Underdal A. 1994. Leadership theory: Rediscovering the arts of management. In *International Multilateral Negotiation: Approaches to the Management of Complexity*, edited by I. W. Zartman. San Francisco: Jossey-Bass, pp. 178–197.

United Nations. 1948. The Universal Declaration of Human Rights. 10 December.

United Nations. 1995. *The United Nations and Mozambique, 1992–1995*. New York: UN Department of Public Information.

United Nations. 1999. *Multilateral Treaties Deposited with the Secretary General, in the Field of the Environment*. Nairobi: United Nations Environment Programme.

United Nations. 2000. *World Economic and Social Survey 2000*. New York: United Nations.

United Nations. 2003. Committee for Development Policy: Report on the Fifth Session. 7–11 April 2003. United Nations Economic and Social Council. Supplement No. 13. Accessed online at http://www.un.org/esa/policy/devplan/cdp2003report.pdf.

United Nations Conference on Environment and Development (UNCED). 1992a. *Annex I: Rio Declaration on Environment and Development*. A/Conf.151/26 (Vol. I).

United Nations Conference on Environment and Development (UNCED). 1992b. Report of the United Nations Conference on Environment and Development (Rio de Janeiro, June 3–14, 1992). Available at http://www.un.org/documents/ga/conf151/aconf15126-4.htm.

United Nations Conference on Trade and Development (UNCTAD). 2003. *UNCTAD Handbook of Statistics*. New York and Geneva: United Nations. Available online at http://www.unctad.org/Templates/Page.asp?intItemID=1890.

United Nations Development Programme (UNDP). 1998. *Human Development Report 1998*. New York: United Nations.

United Nations Development Programme (UNDP). 1999. *Human Development Report 1999*. New York: Oxford University Press.

United Nations Development Programme (UNDP). 2002. *Human Development Report 2002*. New York: Oxford University Press.

United Nations Development Programme (UNDP). 2002a. A Climate Risk Management Approach to Disaster Reduction and Adaptation to Climate Change. UNDP Expert Group Meeting Integrating Disaster Reduction with Adaptation to Climate Change, Havana, June 19–21, 2002.

United Nations Development Programme (UNDP). 2002b. *The Growing Vulnerability of Small Island Developing States*. Prepared by the United Nations Development Programme Capacity 21 Project and the West Indies Centre for Environment and Development. Kingston, Jamaica: UNDP.

United Nations Development Programme (UNDP). 2003. *Making Global Trade Work for People*. London: Earthscan.

United Nations Development Programme (UNDP). 2004. *Human Development Report*. New York: Oxford University Press.

United Nations Environment Programme (UNEP). 2000. *The Second Report on International Scientific Advisory Processes on the Environment and Sustainable Development*. UNEP/DEWA/TR.01-1, Nairobi: United Nations Environment Programme.

United Nations Environment Programme (UNEP). 2002. *Global Environmental Outlook 3*. London: Earthscan.

United Nations Framework Convention on Climate Change (UNFCCC). 1998. Group of 77 and China position paper on preparations for COP-4 (proposed provisional agenda). Submission by the Group of 77 and China. Document number FCCC/SBI/1998/MISC.3.

United Nations Framework Convention on Climate Change (UNFCCC). 2002. Delhi Ministerial Declaration on Climate Change and Sustainable Development. October 31.

United Nations Human Settlements Program (UN-HABITAT). 1998. Global Urban Indicators Database 2. Accessed online at http://www.unhabitat.org/programmes/guo/urban_indicators.asp.

United Nations System-Wide Earthwatch. 2000. *International Expert Meeting on Information for Decision-Making and Participation. Ottawa, Canada 25–28 September 2000. Background Paper.*

United States Congress. 1997. *Congressional Record Daily Edition*. July 27, pp. S8113–8138.

United States Department of the Treasury, Office of Public Affairs. 2002. U.S. Pledges $500 million for fund to combat global environmental threats. August 7. Washington, DC: U.S. Department of the Treasury.

United States Geological Survey (USGS). 2000. Fact Sheet 024-00 March 2000. Significant Floods of the 20th Century (USA). Reston, VA: USGS.

Uslaner, Eric. 2001. Trust as a moral value. Prepared for the Conference "Social Capital: Interdisciplinary Perspectives," University of Exeter, United Kingdom, 15–20 September, 2001.

Uslaner. Eric. 2003. *The Moral Foundations of Trust*. Cambridge: Cambridge University Press.

Vaillancourt, J. G. 2000. Sociological Reflections on Sustainability. Paper presented at International Sociological Association Miniconference. Rio de Janeiro, Brazil. August 1–5, 2000.

Vaillancourt, Jean G. n.d. Sustainability and Agenda 21. In Sustainability and Unsustainability on the Road from Rio, edited by J. Timmons Roberts, Eduardo Viola, Frederick Buttel, and Amy Hite. Book manuscript in revision.

Van Evera, Stephen. 1990/1991. Primed for peace: Europe after the Cold War. *International Security* 61(3): 7–57.

Vernon, Raymond. 1993. Behind the scenes: How policymaking in the European Community, Japan and the United States affects global negotiations. *Environment* 35(5): 12–20, 35–42.

Victor, David. 1999. Enforcing international law: Implications for an effective global warming regime. *Duke Environmental Law and Policy Forum* 10(1): 147–184.

Victor, David. 2001. *The Collapse of the Kyoto Protocol and the Struggle to Slow Global Warming*. Princeton, NJ: Princeton University Press.

Victor, David G., and Eugene B. Skolnikoff. 1999. Translating intent into action: Implementing environmental commitments. *Environment* 41(2): 16–20, 39–43.

Victor, David G., Kal Raustiala, and Eugene B. Skolnikoff (eds.). 1998. *The Implementation and Effectiveness of International Environmental Commitments*. Cambridge, MA: MIT Press.

Vig, Norman J., and Regina S. Axelrod (eds.). 1999. *The Global Environment: Institutions, Law and Policy*. Washington, DC: Congressional Quarterly Press.

Viguier, L. 2004. Proposal to increase developing country participation in international climate policy. *Environmental Science and Policy* 7(3): 195–204.

Viola, Eduardo J. 1992. O movimento ambientalista no Brasil (1979–1991): Da denúncia e conscientização pública para a institucionalização e o desenvolvimento sustentável. In *Ecologia, Ciência e Política*, edited by Mirian Goldenberg. Rio de Janeiro: Editora Revan, pp. 49–75.

Vogler, John, and Mark F. Imber (eds.). 1996. *The Environment and International Relations*. New York: Routledge.

Volcker, Paul, and Toyoo Gyoten. 1992. *Changing Fortunes*. New York: Times Books.

Von Moltke, Konrad, and Atiq Rahman. 1996. External perspectives on climate change: A View from the United States and the Third World. In *Politics of Cli-*

mate Change: A European Perspective, edited by in Tim O'Riordan and Jill Jager. London: Routledge.

Wade, Robert. 1990. *Governing the Market*. Princeton, NJ: Princeton University Press.

Wade, Robert. 1996. Japan, the World Bank, and the art of paradigm maintenance: "The East Asian Miracle" in political perspective. *New Left Review* 217: 3–36.

Wade, Robert. 2000. Wheels within wheels: Rethinking the Asian crisis and the Asian model. *Annual Review of Political Science* 3: 85–115.

Wade, Robert. 2001a. The rising inequality of world income distribution. *Finance and Development* 38(4): 37–39.

Wade, Robert. 2001b. Winners and losers. *The Economist*, April 26, pp. 79–82.

Wade, Robert. 2003a. The invisible hand of the American empire. *Ethics and International Affairs* 17(2): 77–88.

Wade, Robert. 2003b. *Governing the Market: Economic Theory and the Role of Government in East Asia's Industrialization*, 2nd ed. Princeton, NJ: Princeton University Press.

Wade, Robert. 2003c. What strategies are viable for developing countries today? The World Trade Organization and the shrinking of development space. *Review of International Political Economy* 10(4): 627–644.

Wade, Robert. 2003d. Book review of Michael Moore's "World Without Walls." Unpublished manuscript.

Wade, Robert. 2004a. Bringing the economics back in. *Security Dialogue* 35(2): 243–249.

Wade, Robert. 2004b. The ringmaster of Doha. *New Left Review* 25: 146–152.

Wade, Robert. 2004c. Is globalization reducing poverty and inequality? *World Development* 32(4): 567–589.

Wade, Robert. 2004d. On the causes of increasing world poverty and inequality, or why the Matthew effect prevails. *New Political Economy* 9(2): 163–188.

Wagner, L. 1999. Negotiations in the UN Commission on Sustainable Development: Coalitions, processes, and outcomes. *International Negotiation* 4(2): 107–131.

Wallerstein, Immanuel. 1972. Three paths to national development in 16th century Europe. *Studies in Comparative International Development* 8: 95–101.

Wallerstein, Immanuel. 1974. *The Modern World-System I: Capitalist Agriculture and the Origins of the European World Economy in the Sixteenth Century*, Vol. 1. New York: Academic Press.

Wallerstein, Immanuel. 1979. *The Capitalist World-Economy*. New York: Cambridge University Press.

Walt, Stephen. 1987. *The Origins of Alliances*. Ithaca, NY: Cornell University Press.

Walter, Andrew. 2001. NGOs, business, and international investment rules: MAI, Seattle and beyond. *Global Governance* 7(1): 51–73.

Walter, J., and A. Simms. 2002. *The End of Development? Global Warming, Disasters and the Great Reversal of Human Progress.* London: New Economics Foundation.

Waltz, Kenneth. 1979. *Theory of International Politics.* New York: Random House.

Wapner, Paul. 1995. Politics beyond the state: Environmental activism and world civic politics. *World Politics* 47 (April): 311–340.

Watts, M. J., and H. G. Bohle. 1993. The space of vulnerability: The causal structure of hunger and famine. *Progress in Human Geography* 17(1): 43–67.

Weaver, Catherine E., and Ralf J. Leiteritz. 2002. "Our poverty is a world full of dreams": The World Bank's strategic compact and the tenacity of organizational culture. Paper presented at the International Studies Association Annual Conference, New Orleans, March 2002.

Weiss, Edith Brown, and Harold K. Jacobson (eds.). 1998. *Engaging Countries: Strengthening Compliance with International Environmental Accords.* Cambridge, MA: MIT Press.

Weisskopf, Michael, and Eugene Robinson. 1992. Rio Summit highlights North-South schism. *Washington Post* June 3, pp. A21, 23.

Wendt, A. 1987. The agent-structure problem in international relations theory. *International Organization* 41(3): 335–370.

Wettestad, Jorgen. 1999. *Designing Effective Environmental Regimes: The Key Conditions.* Cheltenham, UK: Edward Elgar.

White House. 2002a. Fact Sheet: President Bush announces clear skies & global climate change initiative. Retrieved February 14, 2002.

White House. 2002b. Global climate change policy book. Retrieved February 14, 2002.

Wiegandt, E. 2001. Climate change, equity, and international negotiations. In *International Relations and Global Climate Change*, edited by Urs Luterbacher Detlef Sprinz. Cambridge: MIT Press, pp. 127–150.

Wiegandt, E. 2001. Climate change, equity, and international negotiations. In *International Relations and Global Climate Change*, edited by Urs Luterbacher and Detlef Sprinz. Cambridge, MA: MIT Press, pp. 127–150.

Williams, M. 1997. The Group of 77 and global environmental politics. *Global Environmental Change* 7: 295–298.

Williamson, J. 1990. What Washington Means by Policy Reform. In *Latin American Adjustment: How Much Has Happened?*, edited by John Williamson. Washington, DC: Institute for International Economics.

Wisner, Ben. 2000. "Acts of God" to "Water Wars": The urgent analytical and policy role of political ecology in mitigating losses from flood: A view from South Africa and Central America. In *Floods*, edited by D. J. Parker, Vol. 1. London: Routledge, pp. 89–99.

Wisner, B. 2001a. Disasters: What the United Nations and its world can do. *Environmental Hazards* 3: 125–127.

Wisner, B. 2001b. Risk and the neoliberal state: Why Post-Mitch lessons didn't reduce El Salvador's earthquake loss. *Disasters* 25(3): 251–268.

Wisner, B. 2001c. Socialism and storms. *The Guardian* November 14.

Wisner, B., and H. R. Luce. 1993. Disaster vulnerability: Scale, power and daily life. *GeoJournal* 30(2): 1878-A.

Wisner, B., P. Blaikie, T. Cannon, and I. Davis. 2004. *At Risk: Natural Hazards, People's Vulnerability, and Disasters*. London: Routledge.

Wolf, Eric R., and Edward C. Hansen. 1972. *The Human Condition in Latin America*. London: Oxford University Press.

Wolf, Martin. 2000. The big lie of global inequality. *Financial Times* February 8, p. 13.

Wolfensohn, James. 2004. The World Bank Challenge: Tackle Poverty and Protect the Environment. Annual Greenpeace Business Lecture at The Royal Society of Arts in London, May 13, 2004.

Woods, Ngaire. 1999. Good governance in international organizations. *Global Governance* 5(1): 36–61.

World Bank. 1992. *World Development Report 1992: Development and the Environment*. Washington, DC: World Bank.

World Bank. 1995. *World Development Report 1995. Workers in an Integrating World*. Oxford University Press. 1995.

World Bank. 2000/2001. *World Development Report 2000/2001: Attacking Poverty*. New York: World Bank and Oxford University Press.

World Bank. 2001a. *Global Economic Prospects and Developing Countries 2002*. Washington, DC: World Bank.

World Bank. 2001b. *Global Economic Prospects and the Developing Countries 2001*. Washington, DC: World Bank.

World Bank. 2004a. *World Development Indicators*. Washington, DC: World Bank.

World Bank. 2002b. *Global Economic Prospects and the Developing Countries 2002: Making Trade Work for the World's Poor*. Washington, DC: World Bank.

World Bank. 2002c. *Globalization, Growth, and Poverty: Building an Inclusive World Economy*. New York: World Bank and Oxford University Press.

World Bank. 2003. *Poverty and Climate Change: Reducing the Vulnerability of the Poor through Adaptation*. Washington, DC: World Bank.

World Bank. 2004. *Doing Business in 2004: Understanding Regulation*. Oxford: Oxford University Press.

World Bank. 2005. *World Development Report 2006: Equity and Development*. Washington, DC: World Bank.

World Commission on Environment and Development (WCED) 1987.

World Health Organization (WHO). 2004. CHIPS: Country Health Information Profiles. 2004 Revision, Western Pacific: Tuvalu. WHO: Geneva. Available at http://www.wpro.who.int/chips/chip04/tuv.htm.

World Meteorological Organization (WMO). 2001. *Statement on the Status of the Global Climate in 2001*. Geneva: WMO.

World Resources Institute (WRI). 1995. *World Resources 1995–96*. Oxford: Oxford University Press.

World Resources Institute (WRI). 1998. *World Resources 1998–99*. Oxford: Oxford University Press.

World Resources Institute (WRI). 2004. WRI Earthtrends: The environmental information portal. Available online at http://earthtrends.wri.org/.

World Trade Organization (WTO). 1996. Document WT/DSB/M/22, Representative of Jamaica, Minutes of the meeting of the dispute settlement body (September 27, 1996), p. 6.

Yarborough, Beth V., and Robert M. Yarborough. 1990. International institutions and the new economics of organization. *International Organization* 44: 235–259.

Ybema, J. R., J. J. Battjes, J. C. Jansen, and F. Ormel. 2000. *Burden Differentiation: GHG Emissions, Undercurrents and Mitigation Costs*. Oslo, Norway: CICERO.

Yearly, Stephen. 1996. *Sociology, Environmentalism, Globalization*. London: Sage.

Yohe, G., and R. S. J. Tol. 2001. Indicators for social and economic coping capacity—moving toward a working definition of adaptive capacity. *Global Environmental Change* 12(1): 25–40.F

Young, Crawford. 1994. *The African Colonial State in Comparative Perspective*. New Haven, CT: Yale University Press.

Young, H. P. 1994. *Equity in Theory and Practice*. Princeton, NJ: Princeton University Press.

Young, Oran R. 1989. *International Cooperation: Building Regimes for Natural Resources and the Environment*. Ithaca, NY: Cornell University Press.

Young, Oran R. 1992. The effectiveness of international institutions: Hard cases and critical variables. In *Governance without Government: Order and Change in World Politics*, edited by J. Rosenau and E. O. Czempiel. Cambridge: Cambridge University Press.

Young, Oran R. 1994. *International Governance: Protecting the Environment in a Stateless Society*. Ithaca, NY: Cornell University Press.

Young, Oran R. 1999. Fairness matters: The role of equity in international regime formation. In *Global Ethics and the Environment*, edited by Nicholas Low. London: Routledge, pp. 247–263.

Zak, P., and S. Knack. 2001. Trust and growth. *The Economic Journal* 111: 295–321.

Zartman, I. W., D. Druckman, L. Jensen, D. Pruitt, and P. Young. 1996. Negotiation as a search for Justice. *International Negotiation* 1(1): 79–98.

Zoellick, Robert B. 2003. America will not wait for the won't-do countries. *Financial Times* September 22, p. 23.

Zürn, Michael. 1998. The rise of international environmental politics: A review of current research. *World Politics* 50(4): 617–649.

Zürn, Michael. 2004. Global governance and legitimacy problems. Paper presented at IDRC meeting 'The G20 at Leaders' Level?' on February 29, 2004, Ottawa, Canada.

Index

Global Environmental Accord: Strategies for Sustainability and Institutional Innovation
Nazli Choucri, series editor

Nazli Choucri, ed., *Global Accord: Environmental Challenges and International Responses*

Peter M. Haas, Robert O. Keohane, and Marc A. Levy, eds., *Institutions for the Earth: Sources of Effective International Environmental Protection*

Ronald B. Mitchell, *Intentional Oil Pollution at Sea: Environmental Policy and Treaty Compliance*

Robert O. Keohane and Marc A. Levy, eds., *Institutions for Environmental Aid: Pitfalls and Promise*

Oran R. Young, ed., *Global Governance: Drawing Insights from the Environmental Experience*

Jonathan A. Fox and L. David Brown, editors, *The Struggle for Accountability: The World Bank, NGOS, and Grassroots Movements*

David G. Victor, Kal Raustiala, and Eugene B. Skolnikoff, eds., *The Implementation and Effectiveness of International Environmental Commitments: Theory and Practice*

Mostafa K. Tolba, with Iwona Rummel-Bulska, *Global Environmental Diplomacy: Negotiating Environmental Agreements for the World, 1973–1992*

Karen T. Litfin, ed., *The Greening of Sovereignty in World Politics*

Edith Brown Weiss and Harold K. Jacobson, eds., *Engaging Countries: Strengthening Compliance with International Environmental Accords*

Oran R. Young, ed., *The Effectiveness of International Environmental Regimes: Causal Connections and Behavioral Mechanisms*

Ronie Garcia-Johnson, *Exporting Environmentalism: U.S. Multinational Chemical Corporations in Brazil and Mexico*

Lasse Ringius, *Radioactive Waste Disposal at Sea: Public Ideas, Transnational Policy Entrepreneurs, and Environmental Regimes*

Robert G. Darst, *Smokestack Diplomacy: Cooperation and Conflict in East-West Environmental Politics*